ONE WEEK LOAN

1 2 APR

GENDER AND RURAL MODERNITY

Gender and Rural Modernity
Farm Women and the Politics of Labor in Germany, 1871–1933

ELIZABETH B. JONES
Department of History, Colorado State University, USA

ASHGATE

Published by
Ashgate Publishing Limited
Wey Court East
Union Road
Farnham
Surrey, GU9 7PT
England

Ashgate Publishing Company
Suite 420
101 Cherry Street
Burlington
VT 05401-4405
USA

www.ashgate.com

British Library Cataloguing in Publication Data
Jones, Elizabeth Bright
   Gender and rural modernity: farm women and the politics of labor in Germany, 1871–1933. – (Studies in labour history)
   1. Rural women – Germany – Social conditions 2. Germany – Rural conditions 3. Germany – Politics and government – 1871–1933
   I. Title
   305.4'363'0943'09041

Library of Congress Cataloging-in-Publication Data
Jones, Elizabeth B. (Elizabeth Bright)
   Gender and rural modernity: farm women and the politics of labor in Germany, 1871–1933 / Elizabeth B. Jones.
    p. cm. – (Studies in labour history)
   Includes bibliographical references.
   ISBN 978-0-7546-6499-4 (alk. paper)
   1. Women agricultural laborers – Germany – History. 2. Agricultural laborers – Political activity – Germany. I. Title.
   HD6077.2.G3J66 2009
   331.4'83094309041–dc22

2008048280

ISBN 978-0-7546-6499-4

Mixed Sources
Product group from well-managed
forests and other controlled sources
www.fsc.org Cert no. SA-COC-1565
© 1996 Forest Stewardship Council
FSC

Printed and bound in Great Britain by
MPG Books Ltd, Bodmin, Cornwall.

Contents

List of Figures

List of Tables

List of Terms

Amtshauptmannschaft (AH)	Sub-district
Aussenwirtschaft	Field work
Deutschnationale Volkspartei (DNVP)	German National People's Party
Dienstbuch	Reference book
Dienstherr	"Master" or employer
Gemeindevorstand (GV)	Village, local magistrate
Gesinde	Hired hands (agricultural)
Gesindevermittler	Labor broker for hired hands
Gesindeordnungen (GesO)	Laws regulating hired hands during Empire
Innenwirtschaft	Stall, garden work
Kaiserreich	German Empire, 1871–1918
Kreishauptmannschaft (KH)	District
Knecht	Male hired hand
Magd	Female hired hand
Mietgeld	Small bonus paid to *Gesinde* when hired
Reichsverband landwirtschaftlicher Hausfrauenvereine (RLHV)	National Rural Housewives' Association
Sächsisches Landvolk (SLV)	Saxon Rural People's Party
Vaterländisches Hilfsdienstgesetz	Patriotic Auxiliary Service Law (1916)

Studies in Labour History
General Editor's Preface

This series of books provides reassessments of broad themes in labour history, along with more detailed studies arising from the latest research in the field. Most books are single-authored but there are also volumes of essays, centred on key themes and issues, usually emerging from major conferences organized by the British Society for the Study of Labour History. Every author approaches their task with the needs of both specialist and non-specialist readerships in mind, for labour history is a fertile area of historical scholarship, stimulating wide-ranging interest, debate and further research, within both social and political history and beyond.

When this series was first launched (with Chris Wrigley as its general editor) in 1998, labour history was emerging, reinvigorated, from a period of considerable introspection and external criticism. The assumptions and ideologies underpinning much labour history had been challenged by postmodernist, anti-Marxist and, especially, feminist thinking. There was also a strong feeling that often it had emphasized institutional histories of organized labour, at the expense of histories of work generally, and of workers' social relations beyond their workplaces - especially gender and wider familial relationships. The Society for the Study of Labour History was concerned to consolidate and build upon this process of review and renewal through the publication of more substantial works than its journal Labour History Review could accommodate, and also to emphasize that though it was a British body, its focus and remit extended to international, transnational and comparative perspectives.

Arguably, the extent to which labour history was narrowly institutionalized has been exaggerated. This series therefore includes studies of labour organizations, including international ones, where there is a need for modern reassessment. However, it is also its objective to maintain the breadth of labour history's gaze beyond conventionally organized workers, sometimes to workplace experiences in general, sometimes to industrial relations, and naturally to workers' lives beyond the immediate realm of work.

Malcolm Chase
Society for the Study of Labour History
University of Leeds

Acknowledgments

This book was a long time in the making and it gives me great pleasure to acknowledge the many people and institutions that offered support along the way.

First, I would like to thank the Council of European Studies, the Fulbright Program, the University of Minnesota Graduate School, the College of Liberal Arts at Colorado State University, the history departments at Mount Holyoke College and Colorado State, and the German Academic Exchange Service for funding numerous research trips to the German archives. While there, I would not have found so many rich primary sources without help from the archivists at the Bundesarchiv Berlin, the Sächsisches Staatsarchiv Leipzig, and especially the Sächsisches Hauptstaatsarchiv in Dresden. The librarians at the Staatsbibliothek and Humboldt Universitätsbibliothek in Berlin, the Sächsische Landesbibliothek and Deutsche Fotothek in Dresden, and the Deutsche Nationalbibliothek in Leipzig and Frankfurt/Main also assisted me in tracking down vital materials and images. Special thanks also to the librarians at the Technische Universität in Berlin, who made numerous contemporary periodicals available to me so quickly and easily. Closer to home, I am grateful to Morgan Library at Colorado State University, especially Inter-Library Loan, for filling a steady stream of requests for books and articles.

A great number of people have supported this endeavor, offering fruitful advice and constructive criticism over many years. All of them, in different ways, have made me a better historian. Thanks go first to Jonathan Lipman for sparking my interest in rural and social history and to Atina Grossmann for introducing me to the women of Weimar. At the University of Minnesota, David F. Good was an inspiring teacher during my first years of graduate school and our lively discussions persuaded me that I was in the right place. Hanna Schissler and Allen Isaacman also provided support in the early stages of the project. Eric Weitz gave extensive and insightful comments on several drafts of this manuscript, and I always appreciated both his unreserved candor and sense of humor. Above all I am grateful to my advisor, Mary Jo Maynes, for providing crucial guidance throughout graduate school and beyond, and for pushing me to think in new ways as well as to follow my instincts. I am extremely fortunate to have her as a mentor and friend. Thanks also to Marynel Ryan for her friendship and for her helpful comments on various pieces of the project. In addition, I thank my present and former colleagues in the history department at Colorado State University, including Margaret Paton Walsh, Alison Smith, Frank Towers, and especially Prachi Deshpande. Caitlin Murdock became a much-needed sounding board and travel companion during my first trip to the Saxon archives, and Michael Blümel was an invaluable source on Saxon geography and local history. Filmmaker and photographer Ernst Hirsch in Dresden generously gave me permission to use some of the images by August Kotzsch. Thanks finally to Celia Applegate, Moritz Foellmer, Buddy Gray, and Richard Wall for their backing at key moments.

In addition to the anonymous reviewers of the manuscript, I would like to thank commissioning editor Emily Yates at Ashgate for her willingness to consider the project and for her help in answering all my practical questions. Lianne Sherlock was a patient and careful editor. In particular, I would like to thank series editor Malcolm Chase at Leeds University for his enthusiastic support and for his comments. It has been a pleasure to work with all of them.

Finally, I thank my family, especially my mother, for their understanding and encouragement over the years. Mary Baremore, Bobbi Cordano, and Sandra Singer are the best of friends. Most of all, I would like to thank my husband, Thaddeus Sunseri. His contributions to this work are immeasurable, and his passion for history inspires me daily. This book is dedicated to him.

Introduction

Gender and Politics in the German Countryside, 1871–1933

It is easier to find a capable chancellor than a capable *Magd*.[1]

This complaint about female farm hands, or *Mägde*, speaks volumes about the importance of women's agricultural labor in late Imperial Germany. Attributed to an anonymous rural politician, it appeared in a multi-volume study of women's agricultural work completed just before the First World War by the Standing Committee on Improving the Interests of Women Workers.[2] The project's organizer, social scientist Gertrud Dyhrenfurth, agreed that the younger generation of German rural women seemed less willing than their mothers and grandmothers to remain on the farm. However, she blamed the long hours and intolerable working conditions for the shortage of *Mägde*, and urged farmers and state authorities to work together to remedy the problem. Dyhrenfurth condemned the plight of farm wives and daughters with equal vehemence, adding "all one has to do is look at the mother's fate to see why the daughter rejects it."[3]

Dyhrenfurth's concerns were not isolated ones, and signaled a major shift in the contemporary debate over the importance of family farms in the nation's political economy and the nature of Germany's agricultural labor shortage. Certainly generalized worries about rural flight had existed since the mid-nineteenth century and intensified considerably after the Empire's unification in 1871. But by the eve of the First World War, repeated warnings that national ruin was inevitable if the new generation of farm women rejected their productive and reproductive duties had swept away any hint of irony in the observation that

---

[1]   Cited in Gertrud Dyhrenfurth, *Ergebnisse einer Untersuchung über die Arbeits- und Lebensverhältnisse der Frauen in der Landwirtschaft*, vol. 7 of *Schriften des ständigen Ausschusses zur Förderung der Arbeiterinnen-Interessen* (Jena: Gustav Fischer, 1916), p. 25. Translation mine and all those hereafter.

[2]   Ten major organizations supported the study and belonged to the Standing Committee, including the *Bund Deutscher Frauenvereine*, Catholic and Protestant social welfare groups, and *Verband der Deutschen Gewerkvereine*, see Dyhrenfurth, *Ergebnisse*, p. 8, fn. 1.

[3]   Dyhrenfurth, *Ergebnisse*, p. 50.

it was easier to find an effective national leader than a young woman to clean out the barn.[4]

Gender and Rural Modernity traces how and why women's productive and reproductive roles on German family farms assumed ever larger significance in the eyes of contemporary observers and how farm women themselves shaped debates over their labor and the nation's future before, during, and after the First World War. These years witnessed Germany's rapid transition from an agrarian to an industrial state, when industry decisively outpaced agriculture in terms of overall output and employed more and more workers, while the rural population declined.[5] In particular, as Ute Daniel has shown, it was during the last two prewar decades that large numbers of women entered the Empire's industrial workforce.[6] At the same time, an unmistakable feminization of agricultural work also took place, due in large part to the intensification and diversification of family farms during the Great Depression of the 1870s and 1880s. Therefore despite the fact that female industrial employment rose steadily, more women still worked full-time in German agriculture than in any other economic sector during the Kaiserreich, and the only category of agricultural worker that increased between 1882 and 1907 was female farm dependents.[7] Moreover, the first postwar census in 1925 reported that agriculture was still the largest employer of German women.[8]

---

[4]   This was a distinct departure from the nineteenth century. See Barbara Krug-Richter, 'Agrargeschichte der frühen Neuzeit in geschlechtergeschichtlicher Perspektive: Anmerkungen zu einem Forschungsdesiderat', in Werner Troßbach and Clemens Zimmermann (eds), *Agrargeschichte: Positionen und Perspektiven* (Stuttgart: Lucius & Lucius, 1998), pp. 33–55, esp. p. 43; Marion Gray, *Productive Men, Reproductive Women: The Agrarian Household and the Emergence of Separate Spheres during the German Enlightenment* (New York: Berghahn Books, 2000); Christina Vanja, 'Zwischen Verdrängung und Expansion, Kontrolle und Befreiung: Frauenarbeit im 18. Jahrhundert im deutschsprachigen Raum', *Vierteljahresheft für Sozial- und Wirtschaftsgeschichte* 79 (1992): 457–82.

[5]   Volker Berghahn, *Imperial Germany, 1871–1914: Economy, Society, Culture, and Politics*, (New York: Berghahn Books, 1994), pp. 3–5.

[6]   Ute Daniel, 'Fiktionen, Friktionen und Fakten – Frauenlohnarbeit im Ersten Weltkrieg', in Günther Mai (ed.), *Arbeiterschaft in Deutschland 1914–1918. Studien zu Arbeitskampf und Arbeitsmarkt im Ersten Weltkrieg* (Düsseldorf: Droste Verlag, 1985), pp. 277–323; see also Daniel, 'Der Krieg der Frauen 1914–1918: Zur Innenansicht des Ersten Weltkriegs in Deutschland', in Gerhard Hirschfeld, Gerd Krumeich, and Irina Renz (eds), *Keiner fühlt sich hier als Mensch ... Erlebnis und Wirkung des Ersten Weltkriegs* (Essen: Klartext Verlag, 1993), pp. 131–49, esp. 134; Kathleen Canning, *Languages of Labor and Gender: Female Factory Work in Germany, 1850–1914* (Ithaca: Cornell University Press, 1996).

[7]   Elisabeth Baldauf, *Die Frauenarbeit in der Landwirtschaft* (Borna-Leipzig: Universitätsverlag Robert Noske, 1932), p. 7.

[8]   Baldauf, *Frauenarbeit*, p. 4.

Of course, women had always worked on family farms and the intensification of German agriculture was a long-term process that had begun in the early nineteenth century or earlier. As David Sabean has observed for the southeastern state of Württemberg, "Perhaps it is an exaggeration to speak of the 'feminization' of the village in the second and third quarters of the nineteenth century, but the changing sexual division of labor appears to have rooted women more in the village and agricultural labor, while dispersing some of the men into the surrounding countryside and cities."[9] Still, by 1900 numerous observers noted that female dependents on family farms were working harder than ever, putting in longer hours and responsible for more tasks than their husbands, fathers, or brothers. Besides helping men in the fields during planting and harvest time, women's duties included caring for small livestock and milking cows; planting, hoeing, weeding, and harvesting root crops; tending fruits and vegetables; and processing milk, meat, eggs, and cheese for sale. In addition to their productive tasks, women prepared meals, cleaned, washed, and mended clothing, and looked after children and other household members.

Figure 0.1 **"Farm Daughter from the Erz Mountain Region (Saxony) Turning Hay, *c.* 1930" [Source: Beck R 44/1, Deutsche Fotothek Dresden].**

---

[9]   David W. Sabean, *Property, Production, and Family in Neckarhausen, 1700–1870* (Cambridge: Cambridge University Press, 1990), pp. 29, 147–62; see also J. A. Perkins, 'The Agricultural Revolution in Germany, 1850–1914', *Journal of European Economic History* 10 (1981): 71–118, esp. p. 107; Merry Wiesner, *Women and Gender in Early Modern Europe*, 2nd edn (Cambridge: Cambridge University Press, 2000), p. 107.

The feminization of agricultural work was reinforced by conventional and expert wisdom that designated many of the most labor-intensive tasks on family farms as women's work, for example weeding or milking. By the same token, prewar agricultural experts frequently observed that such chores were utterly unsuitable for men. Yet they did not wonder how women managed the extra burdens or about its impact on farm households. That changed abruptly with the outbreak of the First World War, when the departure of many men for the front and the need to increase domestic food supplies meant that farm women came under new and intense scrutiny. But the recognition of their contributions to the war effort reinforced existing expectations rather than raising doubts about whether or not such work was appropriate. Furthermore, although agricultural experts frequently conceded that their prescriptions regarding gender divisions of labor often did not match reality, especially during the war, these notions remained remarkably durable throughout the Weimar period. As agricultural economist Georg Stieger commented dispassionately in 1922, "Many experts ... have reached the conclusion independently of one another that the agricultural labor question is, in many cases, purely a woman question."[10] Likewise farmers continued to complain vociferously and incessantly about the shortage of female agricultural workers, especially of *Mägde*, and insisted that the fate of family enterprises depended on the availability of their labor.

In addition to the rising expectations of farm women as agricultural producers, Weimar experts also expressed new concerns about their biological and cultural duties. By the mid-1920s, newly-trained rural social welfare reformers and farm women's organizations enthusiastically promoted the rationalization of their productive and household work, asserting that this would allow farm wives to become better mothers and more active promoters of German rural culture. They also sought to transform girls' negative perceptions of farm life at rural continuation schools, where curriculums included lessons in home economics, caring for small livestock, gardening, and proper infant care. Although these measures appeared to have little impact on young women's flight from the Weimar countryside, their messages about the urgent need to professionalize farm women's work further underscored its perceived importance for the survival of family farms, and by extension for the survival of the nation itself.

Yet farm women were not merely objects of concern for those anxious about the prosperity of Germany's agricultural sector, the burgeoning demands of urban consumers, or the health of the next generation. Farm women themselves shaped perceptions of their roles in the nation's economy and society, often by resisting these new demands. Despite prewar experts' idealization of German family farms as exemplars of the "unity between property, family, and work," there is rich evidence that both farm daughters and especially *Mägde* had begun

---

[10] Georg Stieger, *Der Mensch in der Landwirtschaft. Grundlagen der Landarbeitslehre* (Berlin: Paul Parey, 1922), pp. 347–8.

to chafe under their heavy workloads by the end of the nineteenth century.[11] In addition to grievance petitions lodged by *Mägde* against their employers, contemporary sociologists like Dyhrenfurth also documented growing gender and generational tensions in individual farm households. Furthermore, while most young women left few traces about the decision to leave agriculture before the war, strict bans on farm labor's freedom of movement led to very public confrontations between young women and state authorities between 1915 and 1922. Indeed, the growing resistance of some young women to agricultural work undermined longstanding assumptions about farm women and their duties to family, community, and nation. Expressions of discontent by farm wives are harder to find, even during and after the war. However, there is plentiful evidence that they took part in the rising tide of anti-government protests in the countryside after 1925 and cast their votes for parties who pledged to restore citizens' respect for German agriculture. Significantly, among the long list of grievances that fueled rural discontent was the relentless overburdening of farm dependents, especially wives.

This book also traces the efforts of state authorities to meet the demand for women's agricultural labor in both prosperous and desperately uncertain times, in particular the demand for young hired women. Before the war local and provincial officials, like agricultural experts, ignored the growing pressures on women that resulted from intensive farming and relied on the laws regulating hired hands, or *Gesindeordnungen*, to manage the incipient "unruliness" of *Mägde*. At the national level, they were far more concerned about regulating the flow of migrant Slavic workers to and from large agricultural estates, mostly in Germany's northeastern provinces, than with farmers' gripes about young hired women.[12] However, official complacence toward the labor problems plaguing family farms ended abruptly with the war's outbreak. In collaboration with agricultural experts and women's organizations, state authorities launched a multi-faceted mobilization campaign that made farm women responsible for maintaining the food supply and framed their sacrifices in terms of national survival. After mid-1915 officials also were charged with enforcing military decrees that banned all agricultural workers' freedom-of-

---

[11]   Clemens Zimmermann, 'Ländliche Gesellschaft und Agrarwirtschaft im 19. und 20. Jahrhundert: Transformationsprozeße als Thema der Agrargeschichte', in Troßbach and Zimmermann, *Agrargeschichte*, pp. 137–63, esp. pp. 144–5. In contrast, Ulbrich argues that this unity was always a myth, even during the early modern period. Claudia Ulbrich, 'Überlegungen zur Erforschung von Geschlechterrollen in der ländlichen Gesellschaft', in Jan Peters (ed.), *Gutsherrschaft als soziales Modell: Vergleichende Betrachtungen zur Funktionsweise frühneuzeitlicher Agrargesellschaften* (München: R. Oldenbourg, 1995), pp. 359–64, esp. p. 360.

[12]   Ulrich Herbert, *A History of Foreign Labor in Germany: Seasonal Workers, Forced Laborers, Guestworkers*, trans. William Templer (Ann Arbor: University of Michigan Press, 1990); Simon Constantine, *Social Relations in the Estate Villages of Mecklenburg ca. 1880–1924* (Aldershot: Ashgate Publishing, 2007).

movement. Yet as the outraged complaints from local agricultural associations
and individual farmers attested, the new laws had little impact. Moreover, while
national officials endlessly debated the merits and drawbacks of coercion to stem
the crisis, their district and village counterparts were left to wrestle with the details
of the ban's enforcement and spent countless hours negotiating the mass of red
tape they generated.

After the war, Weimar officials across the political spectrum searched
unsuccessfully for legal means to control young women's continued migration
from farm to factory.[13] After suspending the *Gesindeordnungen* in late 1918, a
national ban on farm workers' freedom of movement was reintroduced in March
1919 as part of a broad demobilization effort. It was lifted in 1922 accompanied by
admissions of defeat, but the various private and state-sponsored educational efforts
that replaced them were too little, too late. This time, however, policymakers' failure
to remedy the shortage had broad consequences for rural politics, above all for the
battles between established conservative parties and the insurgent agrarian splinter
parties that sprang up in the late 1920s. What had been a longstanding irritation for
Wilhelmine farmers became emblematic of the Weimar state's profound betrayal
of agricultural interests. Although the new right-wing splinter parties offered no
solutions either to the shortage of *Mägde* or to farm wives' overburdening, their
relentless politicization of farm women's sacrifices laid the groundwork for the
National Socialist campaign to mobilize the German countryside after 1930.
Right-wing youth organizations used similar rhetoric to recruit rural girls into the
anti-Weimar fold, exemplified by the slogans of the young women's branch of the
Rural League's youth group, the *Junglandbund,* after 1925.[14]

The Case of Saxony

Gender and Rural Modernity is set mostly in the Saxon countryside where, as
elsewhere in Germany, the vast majority of women in agriculture worked on family
farms as wives, daughters, or hired hands. The Kingdom (and after 1918, the
Freestate) of Saxony might seem like a surprising choice for exploring the history
of the modern German countryside. Its dense urban population, early renown as
a manufacturing center, and the strength of the Saxon Socialist and Communist
Parties meant that it was often dubbed "the Red Kingdom" by contemporaries.[15]

---

[13]   Elizabeth Bright Jones, 'The Gendering of the Postwar Agricultural Labor Shortage
in Saxony, 1918–1925', *Central European History* 32/3 (Fall 1999): 311–29.

[14]   Ludger Elsbroek, *Vom Junglandbund zur Landjugend: Ländliche Jugendverbandsarbeit zwischen Berufsstand und Jugendkultur* (Frankfurt/Main: Peter Lang, 1996), pp.
85–94.

[15]   See for example William Carl Mathews, 'The Rise and Fall of Red Saxony', in David
E. Barclay and Eric D. Weitz (eds), *Between Reform and Revolution: German Socialism
and Communism from 1840 to 1990* (New York: Berghahn Books, 1998), pp. 293–313. See

But Saxony's reputation as an industrial powerhouse dominated by prosperous Burghers or as a hotbed of left-wing urban radicalism did not mean that rural inhabitants disappeared. Beginning in the 1870s, small and medium-sized family farms that comprised the majority of Saxon agricultural enterprises intensified their production of foodstuffs in response both to new markets created by an expanding industrial labor force and to sharply declining grain prices caused by the Great Depression.[16] As the primary producers of meat, dairy products, fruits, and vegetables, Saxon farm women supplied growing numbers of consumers in the large cities of Leipzig, Dresden, and Chemnitz, and in the numerous district towns that dotted the landscape.[17]

GERMAN
EMPIRE

Kingdom
of
Saxony

Figure 0.2   "Map: Kingdom of Saxony and the German Empire."

---

especially the contributions by Karsten Rudolph, James Retallack, and Christoph Nonn in Simone Lässig and Karl Heinrich Pohl (eds), *Sachsen im Kaiserreich: Politik, Wirtschaft und Gesellschaft in Umbruch* (Weimar: Böhlau Verlag, 1997).

[16]   Christoph Nonn, *Verbraucherprotest und Parteiensystem im wilhelminischen Deutschland* (Düsseldorf: Droste Verlag, 1996), p. xxx.

[17]   Gerald Feldman, *Army, Industry and Labor in Germany, 1914–1918*, 2nd edn (Providence, RI: Berg Publishers, 1992), pp. 127–8, 287–90.

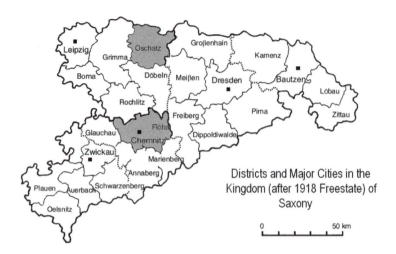

Figure 0.3   "Map: Administrative Districts in Saxony."

In addition to its importance on family farms, women's labor also was essential for Saxony's network of textile and clothing industries. Just before the war, approximately two-thirds of the Kingdom's 380,000 textile and clothing workers were women.[18] The dispersion of textile factories in the Saxon countryside as well as opportunities for home work like sewing gloves or making artificial flowers meant that young farm women did not have to look far for alternatives to agricultural work.[19] In 1908, Bruno Moll gloomily underscored the worsening shortage of *Mägde* in Saxony since the 1870s and noted that industry was largely to blame.[20] At the same time, numerous scholarly publications and speeches emphasized the need for family farms' continued expansion of dairying and root crop cultivation.[21] Thus, the prewar competition for women's labor in Saxony was fueled by increased consumer demand for foodstuffs produced mainly by farm women and both industrial and agricultural experts' stubborn insistence that women workers were irreplaceable.

As elsewhere in Germany, Saxon farmers complained frequently before the war that many young women were unwilling to take on agricultural work and that those who did were often disobedient and disrespectful. These gender and generational tensions emerged most clearly in disputes over the minutely-detailed

---

[18]   Ute Daniel, *The War from Within: German Working-Class Women in the First World War*, trans. Margaret Ries (Oxford: Berg Publishers, 1997), p. 61.

[19]   Benjamin Lapp, *Revolution from the Right: Politics, Class, and the Rise of Nazism in Saxony, 1919–1933* (Atlantic Highlands, NJ: Humanities Press, 1997), pp. 7–8.

[20]   Bruno Moll, *Die Landarbeiterfrage im Königreich Sachsen* (Leipzig: A. Hoffmann Verlag, 1908), pp. 27, 38–9, 41, 43–6, 58.

[21]   Jones, 'Gendering', pp. 311–29.

laws regulating farmhands' employment, the *Gesindeordnungen*.[22] A sample of approximately 70 grievance petitions lodged by *Mägde* or their employers from the Saxon districts of Flöha and Oschatz provides a uniquely intimate view of the squabbles over women's agricultural work in the last quarter of the nineteenth century. These cases also highlight the disagreements between a range of local and regional officials over contract enforcement, and the social tensions between the poorer families of *Mägde* and their better-off employers. The debates over the laws grew more heated after 1900, when even ardent defenders conceded that their complexity might be hindering farmers' efforts to retain hired hands.[23] No matter where they stood on the issue, however, it was clear to Saxon political economists, industrial employers, and farmers that young women faced an array of employment opportunities that they in some measure defined for themselves.[24]

During the war, the pressures on farm women to supply foodstuffs to hungry urban consumers escalated quickly after mid-1915, when the first of many food disturbances erupted in the Saxon city of Leipzig.[25] Indeed, wartime food protests broke out earlier in Saxony than anywhere else in the nation. Meanwhile the farmers who remained angrily reported the disappearance of *Mägde* to nearby munitions factories and vigorously supported the wartime and postwar bans on farm workers' freedom of movement. Like their prewar counterparts, Saxon *Mägde* defied these restrictions, often by exploiting loopholes that allowed them to petition local officials for exemption.[26] Although lawful, many observers warned that young rural women's willingness to voice their preferences about employment signaled an alarming reversal of the prewar status quo. Even more worrisome was the outright refusal of former *Mägde* to return to their positions after the war, and Saxon farmers were particularly disgusted with the Weimar government's decision to continue and even extend benefits to unemployed factory women that often exceeded agricultural wages.[27] For state officials and agricultural experts

---

[22] Wilhelm Kähler, *Gesindewesen und Gesinderecht in Deutschland* (Jena: Gustav Fischer, 1896), pp. 110, 118–19.

[23] Moll, *Landarbeiterfrage*, pp. 27, 109.

[24] Elizabeth Bright Jones, 'Girls in Court: *Mägde* versus their Employers in Saxony, 1880–1914', in M. J. Maynes and Birgitte Soland (eds), *Secret Gardens, Satanic Mills: Placing Girls in European History, 1750–1960* (Bloomington: Indiana University Press, 2004), pp. 224–38.

[25] Sean Dobson, *Authority and Upheaval in Leipzig, 1910–1920: The Story of a Relationship* (New York: Columbia University Press, 2001), pp. 145–7, 167–8; Gerald Feldman, *The Great Disorder: Politics, Economics, and Society in the German Inflation, 1914–1924* (Oxford: Oxford University Press, 1997), pp. 63–4.

[26] Elizabeth Bright Jones, 'A New Stage of Life?: Young Women's Changing Expectations and Aspirations about Work in Weimar Saxony', *German History* 19/4 (2001): 549–70.

[27] Karl-Christian Führer, *Arbeitslosigkeit und die Entstehung der Arbeitslosenversicherung in Deutschland, 1902–1927* (Berlin: Kolloqium Verlag, 1990), pp. 372–3.

determined to recreate prewar stability, it seemed as if the new generation of farm women were abandoning their most important duty, namely advancing the nation's economic, social, and moral reconstruction.

The postwar anxieties about farm women's roles in national reconstruction also attracted the attention of Saxon social welfare reformers, who spearheaded a widely acclaimed rural household rationalization movement. Their most important accomplishment was the 1926 founding of Germany's first rural household management school in the southeastern Saxon village of Pommritz. Pioneered by Dorothea and Georg Derlitzki, the school promoted an extensive network of traveling exhibits and classes throughout the region and sponsored lectures on the "scientific" management of farm households across the nation and abroad. In numerous publications, Dorothea Derlitzki presented a broad array of practical strategies for easing women's productive and reproductive burdens on the family farm. Her advice aimed not only to alleviate the immediate pressures on farm wives but, just as importantly, to persuade farm daughters and *Mägde* to embrace agricultural work as a respected profession. Yet despite experts' optimistic prescriptions, their research also revealed multiple pressures on Saxon farm women that persisted throughout the Weimar period, and a growing recognition that farm wives' overburdening had become a local and national crisis.

Indeed, after the mid-1920s, local Saxon agricultural associations and the Saxon Rural League staged raucous public demonstrations in small district towns where both men and women protested against the state's failure to alleviate family farms' debt and the relentless overburdening of farm dependents, especially women.[28] While similar demonstrations took place throughout Weimar Germany, the Saxon protests were among the largest. By the end of the decade, the complaints about the shortage of women's agricultural labor and the outcry over farm wives' overburdening became part of the litany of grievances enumerated by right-wing agrarian conservatives. In particular, representatives of the new Saxon Rural People's Party [*Sächsisches Landvolk*] and members of the Saxon Rural League often referred to farm wives' mounting physical and psychological burdens in an effort to fuel rising anti-government sentiment in the countryside. Moreover, the Saxon *Landvolk* appealed directly to farm wives for support not only at the ballot box, but also urged them to participate in provincial rallies, celebrations, and marches that underscored rural discontent and demands for radical political change. Thus *Gender and Rural Modernity* also demonstrates the ways that the politicization of women's agricultural labor became central to the radicalization

---

[28]   On rural demonstrations in Weimar Germany, including Saxony, see Jürgen Bergmann and Klaus Megerle, 'Protest und Aufruhr der Landwirtschaft in der Weimarer Republik (1924–1933). Formen und Typen der politischen Agrarbewegung im regionalen Vergleich', in Jürgen Bergmann and Klaus Megerle (eds), *Regionen im historischen Vergleich: Studien zu Deutschland im 19. und 20. Jahrhundert* (Opladen: Westdeutscher Verlag, 1989), pp. 200–87, esp. p. 209.

of Saxon rural politics before the so-called breakthrough elections by the Nazis in 1930.

Historians and the Modern German Countryside

Despite farm women's key role in modern Germany's political economy and the growing recognition of that fact by contemporary observers, historians have paid little attention to their experiences as workers, wives, daughters, and mothers.[29] Instead, scholars have emphasized the ways that urban industrial workers, both men and women, dominated the political, economic, social, and cultural landscape of the Kaiserreich. They also underscore the ways that the First World War accelerated the economic and social transformations that began in the late nineteenth century, and the upheavals in Weimar's urban centers have become synonymous with the modern age and its attendant triumphs and crises.[30] More recently, German historians also have explored the role of provincial middle-class men and women in the Empire's transition to the modern age, whether as members of new political parties, participants in social reform movements, organizers of civic cultural projects, or boosters of the Empire's overseas expansion.[31]

Thus, for most scholars of modern Germany, the countryside is not an obvious place to explore changing definitions of gender and work identities, the interventions of experts, reformers, and bureaucrats, or how rural anxieties about change were manifested in provincial and national politics. Instead the countryside and its inhabitants provide an unchanging backdrop against which the heralded agents of German modernity – scientists, politicians, social welfare experts, factory workers, and "New Women" – jostle for influence. This is despite the fact that over two decades ago historians like Robert Moeller and David Blackbourn turned their attention to the rise of populist movements in the late-nineteenth-century countryside, decisively debunking the stereotype of the "German peasant"

[29] Helene Albers' study of farm wives in Westphalia emphasizes farm women's overburdening also, as well as contemporary scholars' documentation of it, between 1920 and 1960. See Helene Albers, *Zwischen Hof, Haushalt und Familie: Bäuerinnen in Westfalen-Lippe, 1920–1960* (Paderborn: F. Schöningh, 2001), pp. 92–6, 262–75.

[30] See for example Eric D. Weitz, *Weimar Germany: Promise and Tragedy* (Princeton: Princeton University Press, 2007).

[31] See for example Jennifer Jenkins, *Provincial Modernity: Local Culture and Liberal Politics in Fin-de-Siècle Hamburg* (Ithaca: Cornell University Press, 2003); Thomas Lekan, *Imagining the Nation in Nature: Landscape Preservation and German Identity, 1885–1945* (Cambridge: Harvard University Press, 2004); Andrew Lees, *Cities, Sin, and Social Reform in Imperial Germany* (Ann Arbor: University of Michigan Press, 2002); K. Molly O'Donnell et al. (eds), *The Heimat Abroad: The Boundaries of Germanness* (Ann Arbor: University of Michigan Press, 2005).

as the most obstinate opponent of change.[32] Instead they stressed male farmers' shrewd adaptation to increasingly radical economic and political circumstances before, during, and after the First World War.

Moeller's work in particular challenged the *Sonderweg* interpretation of modern German agrarian history, which argued that Wilhelmine farmers, in blind allegiance to the eastern agricultural elite, or *Junker*, staunchly opposed democratic values and liberal capitalism, thus setting the German nation on course to 1933.[33] Since then, numerous studies of German rural politics have appeared, focusing especially on the turbulent final years of the Weimar Republic.[34] Their

---

[32]   Ian Farr, 'Peasant Protest in the Empire – The Bavarian Example', in Robert Moeller (ed.), *Peasants and Lords in Modern Germany: Recent Studies of Agricultural History* (Boston: Allen & Unwin, 1986), pp. 110–39; Jens Flemming, *Landwirtschaftliche Interessen und Demokratie. Ländliche Gesellschaft, Agrarverbände und Staat, 1890–1925* (Bonn: Verlag Neue Gesellschaft, 1978); Dieter Gessner, 'The Dilemma of German Agriculture during the Weimar Republic', in Richard Bessel and Edgar J. Feuchtwanger (eds), *Social Change and Political Development in Weimar Germany* (London: Croom Helm, 1981), pp. 134–54; Robert Moeller, *German Peasants and Agrarian Politics, 1914–1924: The Rhineland and Westphalia* (Chapel Hill: University of North Carolina Press, 1986); Robert Moeller, 'Economic Dimensions of Peasant Protest in the Transition from Kaiserreich to Weimar', in Moeller (ed.), *Peasants and Lords*, pp. 140–67; Robert Moeller, 'Peasants and Tariffs in the Kaiserreich: How Backward were the *Bauern*?', *Agricultural History* 55 (1981): 370–84; Jonathan Osmond, *Rural Protest in the Weimar Republic: The Free Peasantry in the Rhineland and Bavaria* (New York: St. Martin's Press, 1993); Hans-Jürgen Puhle, *Agrarische Interessenpolitik und preussischer Konservatismus im wilhelminischen Reich (1893–1914): Ein Beitrag zur Analyse des Nationalismus in Deutschland am Beispiel des Bundes der Landwirte und der Deutsch-Konservativen Partei*, 2nd edn (Bonn-Bad Godesberg: Verlag Neue Gesellschaft, 1975); Martin Schumacher, *Land und Politik: Eine Untersuchung über politische Parteien und agrarischer Interessen 1914–1923* (Düsseldorf: Droste Verlag, 1972).

[33]   The debate among historians [*Historikerstreit*] over the theory of a German *Sonderweg*, or "special path" is massive. See for example David Blackbourn and Geoff Eley, *The Peculiarities of German History: Bourgeois Society and Politics in Nineteenth-Century Germany* (Oxford: Oxford University Press, 1985); Richard J. Evans, *In Hitler's Shadow: West German Historians and the Attempt to Escape the Nazi Past* (New York: Pantheon Books, 1989); Stefan Berger, 'Historians and Nation-Building in Germany after Reunification', *Past and Present* 148 (August 1995): 187–222; see also James Retallack's review of Robert Moeller (ed.), *Peasants and Lords in Modern Germany: Recent Studies of Agricultural History* (Boston: Allen & Unwin, 1986), *Journal of Modern History* 60/1 (March 1988): 185–8.

[34]   See for example Stephanie Merkenich, *Grüne Front gegen Weimar: Reichs-Landbund und agrarischer Lobbyismus 1918–1933* (Düsseldorf: Droste Verlag, 1998); Guido Dressel, *Der Thüringer Landbund—Agrarischer Berufsverband als politische Partei in Thüringen 1919–1933* (Weimar: Thüringer Landtag, 1998); Dirk Stegmann, *Politische Radikalisierung in der Provinz: Lageberichte und Stärkemeldungen der Politischen Partei und der Regierungspräsidenten für Osthannover 1922–1933* (Hannover: Verlag Hahnsche

detailed attention to the successes and failures of right-wing splinter parties further underscore the contingency of Weimar agrarian politics and the rise of National Socialism in the countryside. Certainly it no longer seems tenable to describe modern rural Germany as unchanging or anti-modern. At the same time, however, defining rural modernity solely in terms of the activities of conservative agrarian leaders or the Nazi electoral triumph tells only part of the story. In particular, farm wives, daughters, and female hired hands remain subsumed under the category of dependents (if they are mentioned at all). Nor do scholars examine how the world of work and conceptions of gender on family farms became central to conservative acclamations of the countryside as the epitome of Germanness, or how worries about the new generation of farm women influenced broader right-wing critiques of the Republic.[35] In contrast, I argue that the conflicts provoked by farm women's shifting motivations and actions shaped some of the most basic transformations in modern German history: the prewar intensification of family farm agriculture, the ongoing shortage of labor in the countryside, official efforts to manage the wartime economy, the deepening of the late Weimar agricultural crisis, and the appeal of right-wing movements, including National Socialism, in the countryside.

My exploration of the links between ordinary rural Germans' experiences of work and broader historical change is inspired by the work of historians like David Sabean and Regina Schulte. Both have used the context of a single German village or region to describe the ways that inhabitants challenged established power relations in the countryside before the dramatic acceleration of German industrialization in the 1880s and 1890s. Sabean, for example, has documented farm wives' changing attitudes about work and family responsibilities between 1700 and 1870 in the Württemberg village of Neckarhausen, stressing how women sought to reconcile new economic and social pressures.[36] Regina Schulte's research on young hired women's astute use of the criminal courts in nineteenth-century Bavaria suggests

---

Buchhandlung, 1999); pp. 17–134; Markus Müller, *Die Christlich-Nationale Bauern- und Landvolkpartei 1928–1933* (Düsseldorf: Droste Verlag, 2001); Andreas Müller, *'Fällt der Bauer, stürzt der Staat': Deutschnationale Agrarpolitik 1928–1933* (Munich: Herbert Utz Verlag, 2003).

[35] See especially Helene Albers, 'Bäuerinnenalltag—Landfrauenpolitik: Das Beispiel Westfalen 1920 bis 1960', and Peter Exner, '"Wenn die Frauen Hosen tragen und die Wagen ohne Deichsel fahren, dann ändern sich die Zeiten": Ländliche Gesellschaft in Westfalen zwischen Weimar und Bonn', in Daniela Münkel (ed.), *Der lange Abschied vom Agrarland: Agrarpolitik, Landwirtschaft und ländliche Gesellschaft zwischen Weimar und Bonn* (Göttingen: Wallstein Verlag, 2000), pp. 39–68, 93–123.

[36] Sabean, *Property, Production, and Family in Neckarhausen*; David Warren Sabean, *Kinship in Neckarhausen, 1700–1870* (Cambridge: Cambridge University Press, 1998). See also Marion Gray's review of Sabean's work, 'Microhistory as Universal History', *Central European History* 34/3 (2001): 419–31.

ways that the youngest and poorest rural girls took advantage of state institutions and public arenas as a means of shaping their own destinies.[37]

Gender and Rural Modernity also traces the links between the diffuse cultural apprehensions that the younger generation of farm women inspired and the growing politicization of rural gender and work identities during the decades of Empire, war, and Republic. In this regard I am indebted to studies of Wilhelmine and Weimar culture that explore the new worries about urban working-class women and their political, economic, and social roles.[38] Atina Grossmann, Katharina von Ankum, and many others have emphasized the complex relationships between New Women, the Weimar metropolis, and state officials determined to quash women's exercise of newly-won political, economic, and sexual rights.[39] In the minds of many Weimar agricultural experts and political economists, New Women were just as omnipresent in the countryside as they were in Berlin, Hamburg, or Leipzig. They warned that the postwar generation of rural female youth, both farm daughters and hired hands, embraced many of the dangerous habits and expectations of their urban sisters. Thus, *Gender and the Politics of Modernity* expands the contemporary historical literature on New Women that inevitably locates her as a department store clerk in the postwar metropolis. Certainly many farm girls were not silent about their expectations of employment and expressed the decision to leave the farm for the factory as a "step up" to cleaner, less strenuous, and more prestigious work.

The historiography of gender and German modernity also includes the voluminous literature on the Wilhelmine and Weimar state's expanding intervention in industrial workers' everyday affairs: as recipients of sickness or unemployment benefits, as debtors, as threats to the national order, and above all as reproducers of the next generation.[40] *Gender and Rural Modernity* asks similar questions about the varied ways that local, provincial, and national officials intervened in farm women's lives. For the prewar period, this intervention centered on ensuring

---

[37] Regina Schulte, *Das Dorf im Verhör. Brandstifter, Kindsmörderinnen und Wilderer vor den Schranken des bürgerlichen Gerichts Oberbayern, 1848–1910* (Hamburg: Rowohlt, 1989).

[38] Alon Confino, *The Nation as a Local Metaphor: Württemberg, Imperial Germany, and National Memory, 1871–1918* (Chapel Hill: University of North Carolina Press, 1997), p. 122.

[39] Renate Bridenthal et al., *When Biology Became Destiny: Women in Weimar and Nazi Germany* (New York: Monthly Review Press, 1985); Atina Grossmann, *Reforming Sex: The German Movement for Birth Control and Abortion Reform, 1920–1950* (New York: Oxford University Press, 1995); Katharina von Ankum (ed.), *Women in the Metropolis: Gender and Modernity in Weimar Culture* (Berkeley: University of California Press, 1997).

[40] George Steinmetz, *Regulating the Social: The Welfare State and Local Politics in Imperial Germany* (Princeton: Princeton University Press, 1993); Young-Sun Hong, *Welfare, Modernity, and the Weimar State, 1919–1933* (Princeton: Princeton University Press, 1998); David Crew, *Germans on Welfare: From Weimar to Hitler* (Oxford: Oxford University Press, 1998).

farmers' control over *Mägde* by tracking down those who had run away and meting out punishment. State authorities' involvement in farm women's lives expanded dramatically during and after the war, when all farm women became the targets of policies on rural social welfare and education, maternal and child health, work and unemployment, mobilization for war, and political participation.

The following chapters trace the feminization of Germany's agricultural sector from multiple points of view. Each explores how tensions over women's labor on family farms shaped contemporary debates about women's work and family duties, the relationships between rural inhabitants and the state, and the efforts of agricultural experts and state policymakers to control the pace and the direction of economic, political, and social change. In particular, the terms used to define the perceptions, motivations, and behavior of young rural women in the prewar decades foreshadowed the future, more widespread conflicts between young women and those who sought to control their labor during and after the war. Taken together, the evidence underscores farm women's centrality to ongoing debates over Germany's future, whether about the food supply for cities or soldiers, the health and well-being of the next generation, or politicians' quest for new national symbols and, eventually, voters. By the end of the First World War, women's labor was no longer viewed as a mere substitute for the shortfall in men's labor, but as fundamental to the survival of family farms in every sense of the word. Indeed, for Weimar agricultural experts, social welfare reformers, state officials, and politicians, mobilizing farm women's labor became a prerequisite for ensuring national stability, moral strength, and unity of purpose between city and countryside. This was no easy task, as *Magd* Frieda Strampe retorted sharply to her employer in 1921, "Let the farmers find someone else!"[41]

---

[41] *Magd* Frieda Strampe, quoted in letter from Otto Petzold to the Saxon *Landeskulturrat*, Luchau bei Glashütte, November 9, 1921, Ministerium des Innern 15933, 'Maßnahmen zur Behebung des Arbeitermangels in der Landwirtschaft', Sächsisches Hauptstaatsarchiv Dresden, p. 168.

Chapter 1
Surviving the Family Farm:
Women, Work, and Agricultural Politics in the German Empire

Early in her study of farm wives' work, completed just before the First World War, rural sociologist Maria Bidlingmaier identified a fundamental dilemma facing German family farms. On the one hand, they were under pressure to produce more and more food for sale to urban consumers. On the other, the shortage of agricultural hired laborers, or *Gesinde*, had become chronic and widespread.[1] Bidlingmaier listed three alternatives for managing the problem but noted that the first two, either to revert to extensive cultivation or to decrease the size of their enterprises, would be excessively risky and might well lead to impoverishment. She described the third option, that family members simply work harder, as the only viable one for the vast majority of family farms. She concluded:

> This means above all the farm wife … Two recent developments, the move toward greater intensification on the one hand, and the labor shortage on the other, shape the fate of farm wives in reciprocal ways. Neither happens in isolation. Both demand an increase in women's labor.[2]

Bidlingmaier was not the only scholar to consider how intensive cultivation practices and the shortage of agricultural labor had transformed the German countryside by the end of the nineteenth century. But her blunt assessment of these changes challenged established expert assumptions about the nature of German family farms, especially the notion that each household member worked equally hard. Indeed, her study is not the "loving little portrait of refreshing earthiness" described by her mentor in the book's foreword.[3] Instead Bidlingmaier's detailed descriptions of farm life, based on months of firsthand observation, revealed that the ability of small and medium-sized family farms to meet the new challenges of producing more food with less labor depended above all on wives' overburdening.[4]

---

[1]   Maria Bidlingmaier, *Die Bäuerin in zwei Gemeinden Württembergs* (Stuttgart: W. Kohlhammer, 1918), pp. 22–3.

[2]   Bidlingmaier, *Die Bäuerin*, p. 23.

[3]   Carl Johannes Fuchs, 'Vorwort des Herausgebers', *Die Bäuerin*, p. v.

[4]   Sabean has called attention to Bidlingmaier's study in his work on the village of Neckarhausen. See David W. Sabean, *Property, Production, and Family in Neckarhausen,*

Blending meticulous empiricism with frank empathy, she argued that many farm women, especially wives, had reached their physical and psychological breaking points. Moreover, Bidlingmaier added that her concern was not only for her subjects but for the future of the German nation if the crisis persisted.

A few years earlier one of Germany's preeminent agricultural economists, Theodor von der Goltz, had described the new pressures on family farms in very different terms:

> Family farms continue to intensify and we are obligated to ensure that this continues. The main prerequisite for this is a greater input of labor. It is unfortunate therefore that the rural population is not expanding, but instead shows an absolute decline.[5]

Thus von der Goltz also recognized that family farms of all sizes struggled to meet their labor demands in the prewar years. Yet his dispassionate allusion to the dilemmas posed by agricultural intensification and the shortage of labor belied the gender tensions at the very center of Bidlingmaier's work.[6] Beyond brief references to "appropriate" gender divisions of labor, farm women were completely invisible in the expert literature on Germany's agricultural economy. Indeed, the largest prewar survey of conditions on family farms, published by the Association for Social Policy in 1883, was almost silent about labor issues.[7] Only one of the 23 questions asked about work, specifically whether overburdening affected the rural population's health, and virtually all of the respondents declared that overburdening was not a problem.[8] Instead the family farm remained the ideal, a "crisis-resistant" production unit whose duty was to supply ever larger numbers of urban consumers with more and better-quality meat, dairy products, fruits, and vegetables. It was in turn the task of agricultural experts to strengthen family farms vis-à-vis consumers

---

1700–1870 (Cambridge: Cambridge University Press, 1990). Helene Albers also uses Bidlingmaier to frame her research on farm wives in Westphalia. Helene Albers, *Zwischen Hof, Haushalt und Familie: Bäuerinnen in Westfalen-Lippe 1920–1960* (Paderborn: Ferdinand Schöningh, 2001).

[5] Theodor von der Goltz, *Agrarwesen und Agrarpolitik*, 2nd edn (Jena: Gustav Fischer, 1904), p. 141.

[6] See also W. R. Lee, 'Women's Work and the Family: Some Demographic Implications of Gender-Specific Work Patterns in Nineteenth-Century Germany', in Pat Hudson and W. R. Lee (eds), *Women's Work and the Family in Historical Perspective* (Manchester: Manchester University Press, 1990), pp. 50–75.

[7] Verein für Sozialpolitik, *Bäuerliche Zustände in Deutschland* vol. 1 (Leipzig: Duncker & Humblot, 1883), pp. 22–4.

[8] Question 23, *Bäuerliche Zustände* vol. 1, X. One exception was agricultural expert Ignaz Kaup, who warned that farm women's overburdening and generally "poor nutrition" were to blame for their failure to breastfeed infants for the recommended nine months. See Ignaz Kaup, *Ernährung und Lebenskraft der ländlichen Bevölkerung: Tatsachen und Vorschläge* (Berlin: Carl Heymanns Verlag, 1910), p. 553.

and the market by identifying the newest, most technologically advanced methods for increasing their "labor inputs."

In objective terms, these experts met with great success. In the last two decades before 1914, both the quantity and the quality of food products produced on family farms rose dramatically and agricultural prices remained stable or increased. As von der Goltz had observed with satisfaction in 1894, "Agricultural production continues and will continue to rise. It produces more plant and animal products than ever before, and can therefore supply a larger population than ever before with foodstuffs."[9] This did not mean, however, that von der Goltz and his colleagues ignored social tensions in the German countryside. But in their view, the most serious disruptions to agricultural labor relations were occurring on large estates in the country's northeastern provinces, whose reliance on seasonal Slavic labor was a source of deepening concern. In contrast, family farms represented a dependable bulwark against the dual threats of potentially restless urban consumers and the equally disquieting, even dangerous, presence of Slavic workers.[10]

What are we to make of the dramatically different perceptions of family farms in the prewar period and how does exploring the tensions between them revise our understanding of the politics of production and consumption in Wilhelmine Germany? The discourse can be divided into two broad categories. The first, exemplified by experts like von der Goltz, emphasized the extraordinary success of family farms in intensifying and diversifying their enterprises and the vital role of expert advice that underpinned these efforts. A less voluminous but equally powerful sociological discourse sought for the first time to measure the costs to individuals of these achievements and, by focusing on women, exposed profound inequities within farm households.[11] But Bidlingmaier and the handful of others who took up the question of farm women's work in the prewar decade did not challenge established gender divisions of labor. Rather than instigating radical social

---

[9]   Theodor von der Goltz, *Die agrarischen Aufgaben der Gegenwart* (Jena: Gustav Fischer, 1894), p. 103.

[10]   Another strand of the discourse linked men's rural–urban migration to the perceived decline in Germany's military readiness. See Kaup, *Ernährung*, pp. 4–15; Georg Bindewald, *Die Wehrfähigkeit der ländlichen und städtischen Bevölkerung* (Halle/Saale: Pierer, 1901).

[11]   On the mission of the Standing Committee and lists of its member organizations see Gertrud Dyhrenfurth, *Ergebnisse einer Untersuchung über die Arbeits- und Lebensverhältnisse der Frauen in der Landwirtschaft* (Jena: Gustav Fischer, 1916), pp. 8–9; Hermann Priester, *Arbeits- und Lebensverhältnisse der Frauen in der Landwirtschaft in Mecklenburg* (Jena: Gustav Fischer, 1914); Elly zu Putlitz, *Arbeits-und Lebensverhältnisse der Frauen in der Landwirtschaft in Brandenburg* (Jena: Gustav Fischer, 1914); Hans Seufert, *Arbeits- und Lebensverhältnisse der Frauen in der Landwirtschaft in Württemberg, Baden, Elsaß-Lothringen und Rheinpfalz* (Jena: Gustav Fischer, 1914); Karl Müller, *Die Frauenarbeit in der Landwirtschaft* (Mönchen-Gladbach: Volksvereins-Verlag, 1913); Marta Wohlgemuth, *Die Bäuerin in zwei badischen Gemeinden* (Karlsruhe: G. Braunsche Hofbuchdruckerei und Verlag, 1913).

change, their aim was to draw attention to the grueling work that fell to women on intensive, diverse family enterprises and to warn of the grave social costs that would accrue if both agricultural experts and state officials failed to acknowledge, and remedy, farm women's overburdening. Thus both discourses employed the language of national crisis when describing the fundamental challenges confronted by family farms, one referring to the diffuse threats posed by unruly industrial workers, demanding middle-class consumers, and the so-called "Polonization" of the northeastern countryside, the other referring to farm women's overburdening.

This chapter emphasizes first the connection between the substantial increase in foodstuffs produced by small- and medium-sized family farms in the prewar decades and the backbreaking work undertaken by farm women documented by rural sociologists. The chapter also explores the discursive construction of the family farm in Germany's prewar political economy and asks how contemporary studies of farm women's work challenged the established wisdom about how to manage the food supply despite the growing shortage of agricultural labor. At the most basic level, the emerging sociological discourse of rural household and gender crisis highlighted the vulnerability of family farm economies during the so-called "golden age" of German agriculture and challenged agricultural experts' conviction that family farms could and would meet the rising demands of urban consumers.[12] Likewise the evidence of farm wives' overburdening revealed the tenuousness of conservative ideologies that portrayed the German family farm as a harmonious, stable, and hierarchical idyll, often extolled as a model for the nation itself.

This chapter also extends the historical debate over food production in Wilhelmine Germany to include the countryside and its inhabitants. Recent research on the food question has focused solely on urban dwellers, the improvement of working-class diets, and the ways in which both working- and middle-class urban consumers began flexing political muscle by demanding lower prices for new "necessities" like meat and butter.[13] But like the Wilhelmine agricultural experts who assumed family farms easily and harmoniously managed the new labor demands, historians have taken family farms' rising contributions to the prewar food supply as a given without asking who was responsible for the work. A closer examination of farm households recasts questions about Germany's transition from an agrarian to an industrial state, and in particular how the various Wilhelmine debates over agricultural intensification on family farms intersected with the new politics of consumer demand. Identifying the continuities and the shifts in these prewar discourses over the nation's food supply, the agricultural labor shortage,

---

[12]   Willi Boelcke, 'Wandlungen der deutschen Agrarwirtschaft in der Folge des ersten Weltkrieges', *Francia* 3 (1975): 498–532, here 498.

[13]   Christoph Nonn, *Verbraucherprotest und Parteiensystem im wilhelminischen Deutschland* (Düsseldorf: Droste Verlag, 1996); Keith Allen, *Hungrige Metropole: Essen, Wohlfahrt und Kommerz in Berlin* (Hamburg: Ergebnisse Verlag, 2002); Hans-Jürgen Teuteberg (ed.), *Durchbruch zum Massenkonsum: Lebensmittelmärkte und Lebensmittelqualität im Städtewachstum des Industriezeitalters* (Münster: Coppenrath Verlag, 1987).

and the overburdening of farm women also offers a new perspective on the crises over food that erupted during the First World War.[14] The tensions in the Wilhelmine discourse, especially over the material and symbolic importance of farm women's labor, reverberated throughout the wartime and postwar debates over the role of family farms in provisioning urban consumers, this time with far higher stakes.[15]

The Kingdom of Saxony, where small and medium-sized family farmers hustled to supply Germany's most densely populated industrial state with potatoes, dairy products, and meat, serves as a case study for exploring the multiple meanings of agricultural intensification in the Kaiserreich. Saxony also had a small number of agricultural estates that concentrated on grain or sugar beet cultivation. But like the national and other regional narratives, the Saxon debates over the practices and the politics of intensification were dominated by worries over the growing producer-consumer rift and the employment of Slavic workers on large estates. At the same time, observers praised Saxon agriculture's overall productivity and heralded Saxon family farms as the most intensive enterprises in the nation. Throughout these decades Saxon farm women, like their counterparts elsewhere in Germany, produced ever more foodstuffs for ever larger numbers of urban consumers.[16] But despite policymakers' acknowledgment that more female dependents were employed full-time on Saxon family farms than ever before, they did not include overburdening in their assessment of the political, economic, and social future of Saxony's agricultural sector. In contrast, rural sociologists exposed not only the growing inequity of men's and women's labor burdens on family farms, but the short-sightedness of agricultural experts and state policymakers who worried about the food supply without any regard for the substantial costs to farm women.

Land and Labor on German Family Farms, 1871–1914

According to the first Imperial German census in 1882, there were just over five million farms in Germany, with dwarf holdings making up almost 60 percent of the

---

[14]   Belinda Davis, *Home Fires Burning: Food, Politics, and Everyday Life in World War I Berlin* (Chapel Hill: University of North Carolina Press, 2000); Keith Allen, 'Sharing Scarcity: Bread Rationing and the First World War in Berlin', *Journal of Social History* 32/2 (1998): 371–93; Avner Offer, *The First World War: An Agrarian Interpretation* (Oxford: Clarendon Press, 1990); Anne Roerkohl, *Hungerblockade und Heimatfront: Die kommunale Lebensmittelversorgung in Westfalen während des Ersten Weltkrieges* (Stuttgart: Franz Steiner Verlag, 1991).

[15]   Elizabeth Bright Jones, 'The Gendering of the Postwar Agricultural Labor Shortage in Saxony, 1918–1924', *Central European History* 32/3 (1999): 311–29; Elizabeth Bright Jones, 'A New Stage of Life?: Young Women's Changing Expectations and Aspirations about Work in Weimar Saxony', *German History* 19/4 (2001): 549–70.

[16]   Leopold Hübel, *Die Gestaltung des landwirtschaftlichen Betriebs mit Rücksicht auf den herrschenden Arbeitermangel* (Dresden: v. Zahn & Jaensch, 1902), pp. 106–8.

total.[17] Just over one-third of all farms were small or medium-sized, ranging from 2–20 hectares. Of the remaining 5.8 percent, the vast majority were classified as large family farms (20–100 hectares), and just 0.5 percent were estates over 100 hectares. But large family farms and estates cultivated more than half the arable land, 31.1 percent on farms of 20–100 hectares and the remaining 24.4 percent on large estates. Small- and medium-sized family farms worked 38.8 percent of arable land and dwarf holdings the remaining 5.9 percent (see Table 1.1).

These basic landholding patterns did not shift dramatically before the last prewar census in 1907. Dwarf holdings less than 2 hectares increased slightly at the expense of small farms and the numbers of medium-sized farms also rose in proportion to large farms and estates. Large family farms in turn increased the amount of land under cultivation at the expense of estates, which shrunk on average by 12 hectares. The mix of estates and family farms of all sizes varied across Germany, with the bulk of large estates located in the northeastern provinces east of the Elbe and in the province of Prussian Saxony [Sachsen-Anhalt], where a large proportion of Germany's sugar beet crop was grown. Agricultural estates were also part of the landscape in the Kingdom of Saxony, but small and medium-sized farms predominated. Further west and south, the balance shifted decisively to small family farms between 2–10 hectares. Medium-sized farms dominated a northern swath that included Schleswig-Holstein, Hanover, Franconia, and the western part of both Saxon territories.[18]

Between 1882 and 1895 the number of full-time farmers increased by 270,000 nationally.[19] Conservative political economists like von der Goltz welcomed this relatively modest increase as a bulwark against the threats of both working-class political radicalism and large-scale "capitalist" farming.[20] But the increase in the numbers of independent family farmers was far outweighed by the decline in the overall size of the agricultural workforce, both in absolute terms and in comparison with employment in the industrial and service sectors. In 1882, 42.52 percent of the German population worked full-time in agriculture, slipping in 1895 to 35.74 percent, and in 1907 to a new low of 28.67 percent.[21] Moreover, the gender balance of those working in agriculture was shifting. While before the war there were still more men employed in German agriculture than women,

---

[17]   For a discussion of German environmental conditions see Heinrich Niehaus, 'Agricultural Conditions and Regions in Germany', *Geographical Review* 23/1 (1933): 23–47. Landholding figures derive from Sigrid Dillwitz, 'Die Struktur der Bauernschaft von 1871–1914', *Jahrbuch für Geschichte* 9 (1973): 47–95, here 54–5.

[18]   See table in Dillwitz, 'Struktur', pp. 58–9.

[19]   Heinrich Dade, *Die landwirtschaftliche Bevölkerung des Deutschen Reichs um die Wende des 19. Jahrhunderts* (Berlin: Paul Parey, 1903), Appendix Tables 21, 51.

[20]   Eduard David, *Sozialismus und Landwirtschaft,* 2nd edn (Leipzig: Quelle & Meyer, 1922), pp. 405–23.

[21]   Müller, *Frauenarbeit,* p. 9.

Table 1.1   Numbers of agricultural establishments in Germany 1882 and 1895; changing proportion of land cultivated by agricultural establishments 1882 and 1895.

Agricultural establishments in hectares	Number of establishments 1882	Number of establishments 1895	Increase or decrease	Cultivated area in hectares 1882	Cultivated area in hectares 1895	Increase or decrease
<2	3,061,831	3,236,367	+174,536	1,825,938	1,808,444	-17,494
2–5	981,407	1,016,318	+34,911	3,190,203	3,285,984	+95,781
5–20	926,605	998,804	+72,199	9,158,398	9,721,875	+563,477
20–100	281,510	281,767	+257	9,908,170	9,869,837	-38,333
100+	24,991	25,061	+70	7,786,263	7,831,801	+45,538

Source: Karl Kautsky, Die Agrarfrage. Eine Übersicht über die Tendenzen der modernen Landwirtschaft und die Agrarpolitik der Sozialdemokratie (Stuttgart: J. H. W. Dietz Nachf, 1899), p. 132.

between 1882 and 1907 the number of men declined continuously compared with a steady rise in full-time women workers (see Table 1.2).

Table 1.2   Number of full-time agricultural workers.

	Female	Male
1882	2,526,633	5,537,333
1895	2,730,216	5,315,225
1907	4,558,718	5,023,084
1925	4,895,701	4,518,219

Source: Elisabeth Baldauf, *Die Frauenarbeit in der Landwirtschaft* (Borna-Leipzig: Robert Noske, 1932), p. 4.

In addition, dependent women working full-time on small and medium-sized family farms was the only category of agricultural worker that increased steadily throughout the prewar period. While this increase was attributable in part to more precise census-taking, contemporary political economists concurred that indeed more women were working full-time on family farms than in previous decades.[22] Their number almost tripled between 1882 and 1907, from just under one million to almost three million. This was the most noteworthy change in the agricultural laboring population before the First World War. The steady drop in the numbers of male family members and hired year-round labor, who were fleeing farms to take higher-paying jobs in industry, meant that the labor of farm wives, daughters, and other female relatives was more highly prized than ever.[23] Between 1882 and 1895 numbers of male and female year-round hired labor (*Knechte* and *Mägde*) declined, adding a greater burden on dependent working women (see Table 1.3).

By 1882 the majority of Saxony's workforce was employed in manufacturing, commerce, and trade and the percentage of the population employed in agriculture was half the national average, or 20 percent of the total workforce.[24] By 1907, the percentage had shrunk to just over 10 percent, a decline from about 290,000 agricultural workers to about 260,000. Between 1882 and 1907, the numbers of farms between 2 and 5 hectares declined, while the numbers of small and medium-sized family farms between 5 and 20 hectares rose modestly. The numbers of large family farms and estates fluctuated only slightly. Table 1.4 shows the distribution

---

[22]   The numbers for both men and women for 1882 are too low, since in Bavaria paid family members were counted as dependents rather than as *Gesinde*, or hired hands. Furthermore, the 1907 census was more precise about how and when to count dependents as full-time workers. Müller, *Frauenarbeit*, p. 10.

[23]   Müller, *Frauenarbeit*, pp. 10–11; Baldauf, *Frauenarbeit*, pp. 7–8.

[24]   O. Wohlfarth, 'Hundert Jahre sächsische Agrarstatistik', *Zeitschrift des Sächsischen Statistischen Landesamtes* 78/79 (Dresden: v. Zahn & Jaensch, 1933): 9–44, here 10.

of Saxon farms by size and percentage of land under cultivation, demonstrating that while Saxony followed national trends in the number of dwarf holdings as a portion of the total (60 percent), a larger than average portion of arable land, about 66 percent, was cultivated by family farms between 5 and 50 hectares.[25]

Table 1.3   Numbers of female [*Mägde*] and male [*Knechte*] year-round hired hands in Germany based on census statistics, 1882–1925.

	Mägde	*Knechte*
1882	615,830	962,994
1895	650,789	1,068,096
1907	625,179	707,538
1925	540,426	574,877

Source: Elisabeth Baldauf, *Die Frauenarbeit in der Landwirtschaft* (Borna-Leipzig: Universitätsverlag Robert Noske, 1932), p. 8.

Table 1.4   Distribution of farms in Saxony according to farm size and land cultivated, 1925.

Farm size in hectares	Percentage of total enterprises	Percentage of total hectares	Percentage of land used for agriculture
< 2	59.79	3.81	5.09
2–5	12.94	5.85	7.75
5–10	9.85	9.6	12.41
10–20	10.16	20.11	25.28
20–50	6.11	23.24	28.42
50–100	0.57	5.16	6.22
100–200	0.3	5.76	6.57
200–1,000	0.21	10.52	7.76
>1,000	0.06	15.95	0.5

Source: O. Wohlfarth, 'Hundert Jahre sächsische Agrarstatistik', *Zeitschrift des Sächsischen Statistischen Landesamtes* 78/79 (Dresden: Zahn & Jaensch, 1933), p. 13.

Geographically Saxony had a wide range of agricultural enterprises scattered throughout all five of the state's districts, but some regional patterns emerged.

---

[25]   On nineteenth-century Saxon landholding patterns see Karl von Langsdorff, 'Die bäuerlichen Verhältnisse im Königreich Sachsen', in *Schriften des Vereins für Sozialpolitik* vol. 54, reprint 1892 ed. (Vaduz: Topos Verlag, 1989), pp. 193–226.

Small and medium-sized family farms were the norm in the southern districts of Zwickau and Chemnitz, dominated by the Erz mountains, and in the southeastern district of Bautzen.[26] Larger family farms between 20 and 50 hectares as well as estates over 200 hectares clustered in the northern district of Leipzig. Almost 80 percent of Saxon farms between 2 and 5 hectares relied solely on family labor, as did 60 percent of the farms between 5 and 10 hectares.[27] Almost 70 percent of farms between 10 and 20 hectares needed hired labor in addition to dependents and about 90 percent of farms between 20 and 50 hectares relied on both family and hired labor. Not surprisingly, family labor was less important on farms over 50 hectares, with family members working on estates over 500 hectares only 11 percent of the time.

Changing the Rural Landscape of Modern Germany

(a) The Pressures to Intensify Family Farm Agriculture, 1871–1914

The conviction that agricultural intensification was absolutely critical for the survival not just of family farmers but the German nation itself contrasted sharply with the attitudes of state policymakers a century earlier, who promoted intensive agricultural practices as long as they posed no threat to the established economic and political order.[28] But the rift between city and countryside had widened during the first decades of the Kaiserreich; by the 1890s steadily falling grain prices together with rapidly rising production costs had mobilized German family farmers to protest their loss of political and economic clout to big business and industrial workers.[29] Even after the recovery of high grain prices in 1902, Wilhelmine agricultural experts, joined by state officials and farmers' associations, emphasized that family farms' efforts to intensify and diversify their operations would protect

---

[26]   Wohlfarth, 'Hundert Jahre', p. 13.

[27]   Wohlfarth, 'Hundert Jahre', p. 10.

[28]   Clemens Zimmermann, 'Bäuerlicher Traditionalismus und agrarischer Fortschritt in der frühen Neuzeit', in Jan Peters (ed.), *Gutsherrschaft als soziales Modell: Vergleichende Betrachtungen zur Funktionsweise frühneuzeitlicher Agrargesellschaften* (München: R. Oldenbourg, 1995), pp. 219–38, esp. p. 231.

[29]   David Blackbourn, *Class, Religion, and Local Politics in Wilhelmine Germany: The Centre Party in Württemberg before 1914* (New Haven: Yale University Press, 1980), pp. 41–53; Robert Moeller, *German Peasants and Agrarian Politics, 1914–1924: The Rhineland and Westphalia* (Chapel Hill: University of North Carolina Press, 1986); Jens Flemming, *Landwirtschaftliche Interessen und Demokratie: ländliche Gesellschaft, Agrarverbände und Staat, 1890–1925* (Bonn: Verlag Neue Gesellschaft, 1978); Hans-Jürgen Puhle, *Agrarische Interessenpolitik und preussischer Konservatismus im wilhelminischen Reich (1893–1914): Ein Beitrag zur Analyse des Nationalismus in Deutschland am Beispiel des Bundes der Landwirte und der Deutsch-Konservativen Partei*, 2nd edn (Bonn-Bad Godesberg: Verlag Neue Gesellschaft, 1975).

the political interests of Germany's farmers by meeting consumer demand for new "necessities," especially meat and milk.[30] In their view, higher yields and a more diverse array of products would ease the tensions between producers and consumers and strengthen the ties between large and small farmers.[31] However, though confident that family farms could and would manage ever larger labor burdens, agricultural experts were pessimistic about the dangers posed by the labor shortage on agricultural estates in Germany's eastern provinces. They viewed estate owners' increased reliance on migrant Polish workers in place of departing Germans as the ultimate threat to the integrity and stability of the countryside. Thus contemporary studies of the agricultural labor shortage focused overwhelmingly on the problem of how to restrict and regulate foreign agricultural workers.[32]

Certainly by the late 1890s, agricultural intensification had transformed the German rural landscape, with both large and small enterprises adopting new cultivation techniques and technology. The steady decline or stagnation in grain prices that had begun two decades earlier meant that farms of all sizes had been forced to rethink their production priorities. While the tendency of family farmers to diversify their operations by purchasing more small livestock and cows as well as by introducing fodder crops into their rotations had been growing in the nineteenth century, these strategies proved critical for their management of the economic depression in the 1870s and 1880s.[33] For while prices for meat, milk, eggs, and butter fluctuated, they did not suffer the protracted downturn that characterized the grain market, which suffered from both Russian and overseas competition.[34] Furthermore, these products could be produced and sold throughout the year, especially in light of much-improved rail transport, providing a more reliable

[30] On rising consumer demand and Wilhelmine food politics see Nonn, *Verbraucherprotest*; Heinz Haushofer, *Ideengeschichte der Agrarwirtschaft und Agrarpolitik im deutschen Sprachgebiet Band II: Vom Ersten Weltkrieg bis zur Gegenwart* (München: Bayrischer Landwirtschaftsverlag, 1958), p. 13.

[31] von der Goltz, *Die agrarischen Aufgaben*, p. 137.

[32] Ulrich Herbert, *A History of Foreign Labor in Germany, 1880–1980: Seasonal Workers, Forced Laborers, Guestworkers*, trans. William Templar (Ann Arbor: University of Michigan Press, 1990), pp. 11–18, 23–30; Klaus J. Bade, '"Billig und willig" – die "ausländischen Wanderarbeiter" im kaiserlichen Deutschland', in Klaus J. Bade (ed.), *Deutsche im Ausland–Fremde in Deutschland: Migration in Geschichte und Gegenwart* (München: Verlag C. H. Beck, 1992), pp. 311–24; Simon Constantine, 'Migrant Labour in the German Countryside: Agency and Protest, 1890–1923', *Labour History* 47/3 (2006): 319–41.

[33] Jones, 'The Gendering of the Postwar Agricultural Labor Shortage', pp. 315–16; Flemming, *Landwirtschaftliche Interessen*, pp. 19–22; Robert Moeller, 'Peasants and Tariffs in the Kaiserreich: How Backward were the "*Bauern*"?', *Agricultural History* 55 (1981): 370–84; Ian Farr, 'Peasant Protest in the Empire – the Bavarian Example', in Robert Moeller (ed.), *Peasants and Lords in Modern Germany: Recent Studies in Agricultural History* (Boston: Allen & Unwin, 1986), pp. 110–39.

[34] von der Goltz, *Die agrarischen Aufgaben*, p. 35; von der Goltz, *Agrarwesen*, p. 4.

income. Increased fodder cultivation spurred expansion of livestock holdings and adding clover, fodder beet, or potatoes to existing rotations also improved grain yields. Put simply, small and medium-sized farms that decreased grain cultivation in favor of root crops and expanded their livestock holdings managed better than those that did not. As von der Goltz noted,

> Regions and enterprises that focus on grain cultivation suffer much more from the present situation than those which focus on livestock-raising. The situation of large estate owners is in general far worse than that of farmers because the former have suffered much more from low grain prices as well as the fact that they tend to carry much larger debts.[35]

Another impetus for agricultural intensification and diversification was rising consumer demand for meat, milk, and dairy products. For state policymakers and agricultural experts, meeting consumer demand for these products was considered absolutely necessary for two reasons. First, Germany's rapidly expanding population of industrial workers purportedly needed a richer, more diverse diet in order to compete with their counterparts in Great Britain or the United States, who consumed "more eggs, cheese, and sugar than German workers, who eat more potatoes and bread."[36] Intensification promised not only better-fed, and thus more competitive, workers but also to reduce Germany's dependence on foreign food imports, which despite all efforts had risen in the last decade before the war.[37] But the goal of food self-sufficiency was never abandoned by conservatives, who often referred to Britain's heavy dependence on imported foodstuffs as excessively risky.[38] As Karl Oldenberg contended in 1897, "Every new export market is a hostage that we hand over to foreigners ... Every import of necessary goods that

[35] Theodor von der Goltz, *Geschichte der deutschen Landwirtschaft, Band 2: Das 19. Jahrhundert*, reprint 1903 ed. (Aalen: Scientia Verlag, 1963), pp. 413–14.

[36] Joseph Bergfried Eßlen, *Die Fleischversorgung des deutschen Reiches: Eine Untersuchung der Ursachen und Wirkungen der Fleischteuerung und der Mittel zur Abhilfe* (Stuttgart: Verlag von Ferdinand Enke, 1912), p. 53. In 1895 agriculture and industry had roughly equal numbers of workers. By 1907 industrial workers outnumbered those in agriculture by over 1 million, 11,256,000 versus 9,883,000 workers. See Gerd Hohorst et al., *Sozialgeschichtliches Arbeitsbuch Band II: Material zur Statistik des Kaiserreichs 1870–1914*, 2nd edn (München: Verlag C. H. Beck, 1978), pp. 66–7.

[37] Friedrich Aereboe, *Der Einfluß des Krieges auf die landwirtschaftliche Produktion in Deutschland* (Stuttgart: Deutsche Verlags-Anstalt, 1927), p. 24.

[38] von der Goltz, *Agrarwesen*, p. 19; Karl Oldenberg, *Deutschland als Industriestaat: Vortrag auf dem Evangelisch-sozialen Kongress in Leipzig am 10. Juni 1897 gehalten* (Göttingen: Vandenhoeck & Ruprecht, 1897), pp. 4–6; Adolf Buchenberger, *Agrarwesen und Agrarpolitik. Erster Band* (Leipzig: C. F. Winter'sche Verlag, 1892), p. 586.

we do not produce ourselves is a chain that binds us to the goodwill of foreigners. Therefore our goal must be: self-sufficiency, that is power, without arrogance."[39]

Agricultural policymakers also worried constantly about balancing the interests of producers with those of working- and middle-class consumers with regard to food prices.[40] One contemporary expert asserted in 1907, "What is important here is meeting consumer demand at fair prices ... If we overstep this boundary we will damage the life interests of a broad section of the population."[41] The emerging political power of Germany's consumers was of real concern to those who fought for the interests of agricultural producers. As Christoph Nonn has observed, consumer protests in the final years of the Kaiserreich were not over shortages of basic foodstuffs like bread, but instead the high price of meat and dairy products. Unlike food riots in the late eighteenth and early nineteenth centuries, these protests were organized, disciplined, and directed not at the so-called middlemen but at farmers themselves.[42] Furthermore, as Nonn has emphasized, consumer protests assumed new meaning in the late nineteenth century in light of the declining agricultural population.[43]

The late-nineteenth-century pressures to intensify production on German agricultural enterprises inspired a multitude of scholarly and scientific studies. Wilhelmine experts painstakingly documented the intensification of German agriculture and debated ways of enhancing the processes and techniques it entailed.[44] By the turn of the century there was a copious literature that aimed to educate farmers of all kinds about crop rotations, livestock breeding and care, scientific bookkeeping, and the like. Likewise, even the most explicitly scientific or practical guides also addressed the role of family farmers in the nation's political economy. As one prominent expert, Friedrich Aereboe, argued, "Questions about feeding the nation and agricultural productivity are above all questions of education and training."[45] His colleague Max Sering posed the challenge even more urgently:

> While unemployment ... resulting from the disproportionate migration to cities like Berlin, Hamburg, and other industrial regions is wreaking havoc, eastern

[39] Oldenberg, *Deutschland*, p. 33.

[40] Buchenberger, *Agrarwesen*, pp. 61–2.

[41] Cited in Eßlen, *Fleischversorgung*, p. 54. See also von der Goltz, *Agrarwesen*, pp. 16–19. On the mass mobilization of urban consumers in the Kaiserreich, see Nonn, *Verbraucherprotest*.

[42] Nonn, *Verbraucherprotest*, pp. 29–30.

[43] Nonn, *Verbraucherprotest*, p. 31.

[44] Sigmund von Frauendorfer, *Ideengeschichte der Agrarwirtschaft und Agrarpolitik im deutschen Sprachgebiet*, vol. 1, 2nd edn (München: Bayerischer Landwirtschaftsverlag, 1963), pp. 472–90; Walter Achilles, *Deutsche Agrargeschichte im Zeitalter der Reformen und der Industrialisierung* (Stuttgart: Verlag Eugen Ulmer, 1993), pp. 214–16.

[45] Cited in Frauendorfer, *Ideengeschichte*, p. 489.

agricultural regions are suffering from a loss of blood ... and this at a time
when technological development and international competition from grain-
exporting states is making the decisive transition to intensive agriculture ever
more necessary.[46]

But agricultural experts emphasized that despite some general guidelines,
intensification was not a one-size-fits-all prescription, and the formulas differed
according to region and farm size. They frequently pointed out that large East
Elbian estates and the family farms characteristic of Saxony and much of southern
and western Germany had different capabilities for intensifying production.
The broad east–west difference in both cultivation patterns and labor relations
was complicated still further by long-established cultivation systems, where
land in individual villages was divided into three or more sections, with each
section's farmers planting, cultivating, and harvesting their crops at the same
time [*Flurzwang*]. This arrangement "worked against virtually every basic step
toward progress in agricultural fieldwork."[47] Between 1821 and the 1880s, these
regulations were dissolved piecemeal by local decrees. The last regions to undergo
this transformation were those southern and western regions still under the
influence of the Napoleonic Code. But as von der Goltz pointed out, the suspension
of *Flurzwang* regulations meant that "each cultivator can use his land according
to nature's laws and which are most appropriate in terms of soil, climate, general
economic conditions, and farm size."[48]

In terms of extra labor, small and medium-sized family farms could rely on the
labor of family members full-time, year-round and if necessary on a *Magd*. Experts
acknowledged that all but the largest family farms lacked the capital to purchase the
latest labor-saving machines and, more importantly, much of the new technology
could not be used practicably on small and medium-sized enterprises.[49] Therefore
manual labor remained the most essential ingredient for intensifying production.
In contrast, large estates had the capital to invest in threshing machines or steam
plows, which could replace increasingly expensive and frequently troublesome
wage laborers. Indeed, at least in theory technology promised a long-term solution
to the problem of labor shortages on large estates and the necessity of importing
foreign labor.

Before turning to the debate over intensification and gender divisions of labor
on family farms, a few general trends that characterized German agricultural
development as a whole should be noted. These trends are important for two
reasons. First and most obviously, the statistics on agricultural productivity in

---

[46]   Cited in Buchenberger, *Agrarwesen*, p. 558.

[47]   von der Goltz, *Agrarwesen*, p. 98.

[48]   von der Goltz, *Agrarwesen*, p. 99.

[49]   Karl Kautsky, *The Agrarian Question*, trans. Peter Burgess (London: Zwan
Publications, 1988), p. 43; Willi Wygodzinski, *Die Landarbeiterfrage in Deutschland*
(Tübingen: J. C. B. Mohr, 1917), p. 17.

the Kaiserreich leave no doubt that intensification expanded dramatically. Even if Germany still relied on imported foodstuffs, family farms' contribution to the nation's food supply was substantial between 1871 and 1914. Second, this achievement may explain why farm women's overburdening was overlooked by the majority of Wilhelmine agricultural experts and state officials. For the language of intensification did not address the role of farm dependents, who were overwhelmingly female, either in terms of its prescriptive scientific advice or in terms of its national political goals. Indeed, as Marion Gray has emphasized, the language used to describe Germany's agricultural economy was implicitly male and no longer took account of women's productive contributions on family farms.[50]

(b) The Impact of Agricultural Intensification and its Results

Between about 1880 and 1914 the total acreage devoted to all major crops increased, replacing pasture and fallow land. Root crops like potatoes and sugar- and fodder beet were introduced into existing crop rotations that had centered on rye, wheat, oats, and other grains. The increased cultivation of root crops permitted a more flexible rotation that "took account of local soil and climatic conditions, of the interrelationships of crops and of price movements for a wider range of crops than hitherto."[51] These new crop rotations produced higher yields, and the market gardening of fruits and vegetables for new urban markets also increased. The number of horses and cows rose, as did the number of small livestock, especially pigs, but also poultry and goats. Only the numbers of sheep declined as foreign demand for German wool slackened in the late nineteenth century and the domestic market never developed a taste for mutton.[52] Machine and chemical fertilizer use increased and access to urban markets improved as the national railway network expanded.[53] Despite regional variations in these trends, Germany's agricultural landscape looked very different in 1900 than it had half a century earlier.[54]

---

[50] Gray argues that this transition in German political economists' thinking was in place by the early nineteenth century, where "agriculture was a capitalist enterprise rather than a household system, and as in other market-oriented undertakings, prescriptive writers largely disregarded females." See Marion W. Gray, *Productive Men, Reproductive Women: The Agrarian Household and the Emergence of Separate Spheres in the German Enlightenment* (New York: Berghahn Books, 2000), p. 15.

[51] J. A. Perkins, 'The Agricultural Revolution in Germany, 1850–1914', *Journal of European Economic History* 10 (1981): 71–118, here 82–3.

[52] Achilles, *Deutsche Agrargeschichte*, pp. 271–2.

[53] Achilles, *Deutsche Agrargeschichte*, p. 242.

[54] von der Goltz, *Geschichte*, pp. 390–6; Achilles, *Deutsche Agrargeschichte*, pp. 220–1; Eric Dorn Brose, *German History 1789–1871: From the Holy Roman Empire to the Bismarckian Reich* (New York: Berghahn Books, 1997), pp. 291–2. On intensification in Saxony see von Langsdorff, 'bäuerliche Verhältnisse', p. 204.

Contemporary experts frequently praised the steady decline in pasturage and fallow as well as in the numbers of sheep, all indicators of extensive rather than intensive agricultural production.[55] In 1878 state governments began collecting yearly statistics on the acreage allotted to the 10 or 12 most important crops, though some states, including Saxony, kept records dating from mid-century.[56] In the last two decades of the Kaiserreich, yields per hectare of the four most important grains – wheat, rye, oats, and barley – rose on average 46.3 percent, potato yields an average of 48.9 percent, and green fodder such as clover and alfalfa 29.4 percent.[57] Although more land was devoted to grains than to root crops throughout the period, the introduction of potatoes, sugar, and fodder beet into existing grain rotations improved the yields of both.[58] As J. A. Perkins has argued, "In terms of more meaningful quantitative and qualitative measures of importance, root crops came to more than rival cereals."[59] Moreover, root crops also provided richer fodder for livestock than hay, allowing the purchase of more livestock. Increased numbers of livestock in turn produced more manure for crop cultivation.[60]

Much of the Wilhelmine literature on intensification highlighted the impact of sugar beet cultivation on large estates, especially in the Prussian province of Saxony and the northeastern districts of the Kingdom of Saxony, where the soil and growing conditions were ideal.[61] The region's estates led the nation in the production and processing of sugar beets and the use of new agricultural technology. By 1895 there were 428 steam plows, 554 broadcast seeders, 31,323 drill machines, 929 manure-spreaders, and 5,637 hoeing machines in Prussian Saxony.[62] This meant for example that one in 10 agricultural enterprises there

---

[55] Friedrich Aereboe, 'Ursachen und Formen wechselnder Betriebsintensität in der Landwirtschaft', *Thünen-Archiv: Organ für exakte Wirtschaftsforschung* 2/3 (Jena: Gustav Fischer, 1907): 363–94, esp. p. 376; Eßlen, *Fleischversorgung*, pp. 33–4.

[56] Walther G. Hoffmann, *Das Wachstum der deutschen Wirtschaft seit der Mitte des 19. Jahrhunderts* (Berlin: Springer Verlag, 1965), p. 270.

[57] Haushofer, *deutsche Landwirtschaft*, p. 254.

[58] Aereboe, 'Ursachen', pp. 379–80.

[59] Perkins, 'Agricultural Revolution', p. 80.

[60] Rudolf Berthold, 'Bemerkungen zu den Wechselbeziehungen zwischen der industriellen Revolution und der kapitalistischen Intensivierung der Feldwirtschaft in Deutschland im 19. Jahrhundert', *Jahrbuch für Wirtschaftsgeschichte* (1972/I): 261–7; Steven B. Webb, 'Tariff Protection for the Iron Industry, Cotton Textiles and Agriculture in Germany, 1879–1914', *Jahrbücher für Nationalökonomie und Statistik* 192 (1977): 336–57, esp. pp. 350–1.

[61] Karl Bielefeldt, *Das Eindringen des Kapitalismus in die Landwirtschaft unter besonderer Berücksichtigung der Provinz Sachsen und der angrenzenden Gebiete* (Berlin: Gebr. Unger, 1910); H. Roth, *Über den Einfluß des Zuckerrübenbaues auf die Höhe der landwirtschaftlichen Kapitalien besonders im Königreich Sachsen* (Ph.D. dissertation: Universität Leipzig, 1892).

[62] Bielefeldt, *Eindringen*, p. 66.

used a drill machine, some 38 times greater than in East Prussia. Perkins also emphasizes that the expansion of root crop cultivation stimulated the use of chemical fertilizers.[63] While sugar beet cultivation expanded rapidly during the Kaiserreich, from 176,000 hectares nationally in 1878 to 569,000 hectares in 1914, the total acreage was always much lower than that of potatoes, which were cultivated in millions of hectares.[64]

In contrast to large estates, small- and medium-sized farmers both intensified and diversified their enterprises, adding new crop rotations, expanding livestock holdings, and investing in new technologies to suit their needs and as their budgets permitted. Sugar beets were not grown widely on family farms in large part because of competition from estates.[65] Instead potatoes, which could be grown on poorer soil and which could be used either for food or as fodder, were central to the intensification of family farms.[66] In particular, German family farmers used potatoes rather than grains for pig fodder, and the sharp rise in the numbers of pigs during these decades reflected the complementarities of production.[67] Nationally, potato cultivation rose from 2,753,000 hectares in 1878 to 3,412,000 hectares in 1913.[68] Potato yields also increased, from an average of about 22.5 million harvested tons per year in the 1880s to about 45.5 million tons in the decade before the war.[69]

In addition to the cultivation of root crops, small- and medium-sized family farms also increased their livestock holdings. One contemporary expert observed in 1912 that since 1816, the production of all meats, including beef, pork, veal, and poultry had increased more than eight-fold, rising 52 percent between 1892 and 1900 alone.[70] While estimates differed on milk production, there is no doubt that it increased markedly, as did the total number of eggs every year between 1880 and 1914.[71] As contemporary agricultural expert Willi Wygodzinski stressed:

> Small- and medium-sized enterprises are the most suitable domain for livestock raising, which absorbs an enormous amount of labor. In 1907 more than 3/4 of all the pigs, more than half the cows, almost all the goats, and 4/5 of chickens were owned by small- and medium-sized farms under 20 hectares. Only with sheep, which demand very little labor, is the relationship reversed. Similarly, a

---

[63]   Perkins, 'Agricultural Revolution', p. 84.

[64]   Hoffmann, *Wachstum*, p. 272.

[65]   Aereboe, *Der Einfluß des Krieges*; Perkins, 'Agricultural Revolution', p. 97.

[66]   Aereboe, *Einfluß*, p. 17.

[67]   Aereboe, *Einfluß*, p. 17; Webb, 'Tariff Protection', p. 350.

[68]   Hoffmann, *Wachstum*, p. 272.

[69]   Hoffmann, *Wachstum*, pp. 84–6.

[70]   Eßlen, *Fleischversorgung*, p. 38; see also Hoffmann, *Wachstum*, pp. 301–3.

[71]   Hoffmann, *Wachstum*, pp. 304–5, 308. On increased milk production and demand see Kaup, *Ernährung*, pp. 46, 545–51, 563–5.

whole array of labor-intensive crops like vegetables and fruit are in large part the
province of small enterprises, though this has begun to expand a bit.[72]

In Saxony a higher proportion of land was devoted to crop cultivation than the
national average, and the proportion of land used as pasturage was less than 20
percent of the national average.[73] The intensification of Saxon agriculture before
the war was evidenced by the steady increase in the acreage devoted to root crops,
fodder crops, and market gardening, while pasturage declined dramatically. Grain
acreage increased steadily between 1878 and 1893, falling off between 1894 and
1900, and then rising again in the decade before the war. Another indicator of
agricultural intensification in Saxony was the increase in the numbers of horses,
cows, and pigs and the simultaneous decline in numbers of sheep. As one Saxon
expert observed, "One important expression of the capability of agricultural
enterprises to adjust to changing economic circumstances is the increase in the
numbers of pigs and the sharp drop in sheep-holding."[74] Indeed, the numbers of pigs
almost doubled during these decades, from about 355,000 in 1883 to 744,000 in
1907. Saxon meat consumption between 1850 and 1900 rose faster than anywhere
else in Germany, annually averaging 4–6 kilos more per person between 1870 and
1895 than its neighbors.[75]

Finally, the Saxon Agricultural Chamber reported that according to the 1907
census, 30 percent of all farms between 1–5 hectares and almost 90 percent of
those between 5 and 20 hectares used some sort of machine.[76] Besides mechanical
(non-steam) threshers, it is worth noting that the milk centrifuge was the most
commonly found machine on farms less than 20 hectares. The centrifuge was also
the only machine to be operated and maintained regularly by women, for churning
butter; all the others, including the drill, mowing, threshing, sowing, and planting
machines increased both men's and women's work.[77]

In 1904 Saxon agricultural economist Bruno Schöne observed many of these
changes in his study of Kühren, a "typical north Saxon village" about 35 kilometers
southeast of Leipzig.[78] Here there was no agricultural estate and the average farm
size was just over 20 hectares.[79] He remarked that:

---

[72]   Willi Wygodzinski, *Die Landarbeiterfrage in Deutschland* (Tübingen: Verlag von
J. C. B. Mohr, 1917), p. 14.

[73]   Wohlfarth, 'Hundert Jahre', p. 19.

[74]   Wohlfarth, 'Hundert Jahre', p. 22.

[75]   Eßlen, *Fleischversorgung*, p. 40.

[76]   Landeskulturrat Sachsen, *Jahres-Bericht über die Landwirtschaft im Königreiche
Sachsen für das Jahr 1909* (hereafter cited as LKR, *Jahres-Bericht* and date) (Dresden:
Kommissionsverlag von Johannes Päßler, 1910), pp. 59–60.

[77]   Lee, 'Women's Work', p. 60.

[78]   Bruno Schöne, *Die wirtschaftlichen und sozialen Verhältnisse der Gemeinde
Kühren* (Dahlen in Sachsen: R. Irrgang, 1904).

[79]   Schöne, *Gemeinde Kühren*, p. 66.

For years the old land use rules [*Flurzwang*] prevented all progress and farmers adhered to the three-field system, using only part of the fallow for root and fodder crops, while today the majority have adopted the new agricultural system that permits more land to be used for these crops. To date 16 [of 37 full-time] farmers have hired the *Oekonomie-Kommissar* in Leipzig to design individual economic plans. The plans follow the principle of crop rotation and generally have a rotation of 7.[80]

Schöne noted that smaller farmers also had adopted the improved three-field system and that only the smallest used a two-crop rotation of rye and potatoes.[81] He observed that almost all the enterprises made use of threshing machines, and that in addition to the manure produced by "more and more livestock" all but three had invested in chemical fertilizers, including sodium nitrate, bone meal, and ammonia super-phosphates. According to Schöne, the village's 37 farmers owned 22 bulls, 286 milk cows, 41 sows, 173 fattened pigs, and 352 young pigs and piglets. Only one household sent its milk to be processed at a cooperative in Leipzig. All the others produced butter and sometimes cheese on the premises; some of the butter was purchased by a middleman for transport to nearby Wurzen or Leipzig, while some sold the butter in Wurzen themselves.

Work in Theory: Agricultural Intensification and Gender Divisions of Labor on Family Farms

How important was farm women's productive labor to the survival of German family farms in the Kaiserreich? Answering this question means sorting out how gender divisions of labor established in the early nineteenth century on family farms, when the practices of agricultural intensification first emerged, shaped decisions about work made generations later by men and women in individual farm households.[82] In other words, to what degree was women's overburdening reinforced by the new imperative of agricultural intensification? As we will see, notions that women were particularly suited to repetitive, painstaking jobs like hoeing potatoes or that their maternal feelings found an ideal outlet in caring for young farm animals overlapped neatly with the dictates of intensive agriculture

---

[80] Schöne, *Gemeinde Kühren*, pp. 66–7; see also Zimmermann, 'Bäuerlicher Traditionalismus', pp. 227–8.

[81] Schöne, *Gemeinde Kühren*, pp. 68–71.

[82] Werner Troßbach, 'Beharrung und Wandel "als Argument". Bauern in der Agrargesellschaft des 18. Jahrhunderts', in Werner Troßbach and Clemens Zimmermann (eds), *Agrargeschichte: Positionen und Perspektive* (Stuttgart: Lucius & Lucius, 1998), pp. 123–30; Zimmermann, 'Bäuerlicher Traditionalismus', pp. 231–6; Sabean, *Property*, pp. 52–60; Sabean, 'Small Peasant Agriculture in Germany at the Beginning of the Nineteenth Century: Changing Work Patterns', *Peasant Studies* 7/4 (Fall 1978): 218–24.

that prescribed increased cultivation of root crops and expanded livestock holdings. Indeed, the statistics on agricultural productivity compiled so assiduously by Wilhelmine policymakers showed the largest increases in precisely those products produced by farm women – potatoes, eggs, milk, butter, and pork – that were considered so essential for meeting new consumer demands.

In that case, why was farm women's productive labor largely ignored by Wilhelmine agricultural experts and state policymakers until the eve of the First World War? The new demographic and political pressures of the prewar period would seem to have enhanced farm women's visibility as economic agents in the eyes of Wilhelmine agricultural experts and state officials. Yet until the studies published by Bidlingmaier, Dyhrenfurth, and a handful of others, neither the authors of practical farm management guides nor those who debated the politics of the agricultural labor shortage addressed the problem of women's overburdening. Part of the answer lies in the fact that while they acknowledged the ongoing need for manual labor, their prescriptions for achieving intensification on family farms ignored the work of dependents, who, as Bidlingmaier pointed out, were overwhelmingly female. Instead their advice for managing the increase in manual labor focused on training the household head in "modern" management practices, which would, in theory, be enhanced by new technology. Farm women's contributions were also obscured by their very success in meeting the new labor demands, as evidenced by the increased productivity of small and medium-sized farms. Indeed, farm families' reputation for ceaseless hard work had become an ideological truth among German agricultural experts as they strove to define family farms' role in the new market-oriented, industrialized economy. In contrast, they worried constantly about assuaging urban–rural tensions and preserving the political power of agricultural producers, or about the dangers of depending on seasonal Polish workers to secure Germany's food supply.

The fact that women's labor filled the widening gap between the new demands of intensive agriculture, a declining pool of labor, and rising consumer demand seemed unremarkable, even natural, to Wilhelmine agricultural experts, state officials, and farmers alike. Much of the manual labor required by intensive cultivation was categorized as women's work, namely milking cows, churning butter, hoeing and weeding root crops, raising pigs and chickens, and growing fruit and vegetables. At the same time, while gender divisions of labor were acknowledged in the scientific literature on agricultural intensification, the fact that women on family farms were assuming ever larger labor burdens as a result went unmentioned. Instead experts' practical advice for attaining intensive cultivation focused on defining the ideal farm size, educating farmers to be more rational and efficient business managers, and urging them to expand root crop cultivation and livestock holdings. The need for extra manual labor was mentioned, but in abstract terms, along with other "inputs" like fertilizer, new technology, or improved construction.[83]

---

[83]   See for example Theodor Brinkmann, 'Kritische Beobachtungen und Beiträge zur Intensitätslehre', *Frühlings landwirtschaftliche Zeitung* 58/ 23 (December 1, 1909): 833–

In terms of strategies for increasing labor productivity, the emphasis was on the role of the household head as farm manager and his anticipated professionalization. In an early article on agricultural intensification, Aereboe discussed the male farmer's need to develop skills in managing relationships with workers "whether with [hired] workers or other workers, but also with trades people, artisans, and many others."[84] He stressed that in contrast to weather or climate, the management of workers offered "individual producers' talents and energy an enormous realm of possibility … but when all is said and done the type and direction of an individual holding's intensity depends on the knowledge, abilities, and conscientiousness of the farmer himself." In a similar vein, his colleague Franz Waterstradt also remarked that achieving intensification depended on each farmer "realizing, guided by practical experience and science, that for every enterprise there is only *one* best approach that must be found, in order for [his/our] economic responsibilities to be fulfilled."[85]

Like the purely management-oriented guides, both conservatives and socialists debating the future of German family farms concentrated on the farmer's role in achieving and maintaining an intensive, profitable enterprise by improving his managerial skills. Once again, von der Goltz summed up the prevailing advice: "Many farmers could increase their net yield if they would reorganize their operations rationally, if they paid equal attention to the results for each sector as to those for the whole, and if they would exercise conscientiousness, thriftiness, and thoughtfulness in their profession."[86] Thus, intensification was always presented as a desirable and necessary goal and, most importantly, an attainable one. On small and medium-sized family farms, this meant an increase in manual labor, for this was the cheapest and most immediate route for small and medium-sized farms to increase productivity.[87] As Wygodzinski noted:

> The increase in labor on smaller farms is due in part to their production emphases. Livestock raising, the domain of small and medium-sized farms, requires an extraordinary amount of labor … as does the cultivation of labor intensive crops like vegetables and fruits. The origins of this increase in labor on smaller enterprises, in this case always manual, is logical.[88]

Women rather than men bore the increased labor burden, for they were considered best suited for livestock care and the arduous manual labor of root crop cultivation:

50, 873–90.

[84]   Aereboe, 'Ursachen', p. 391.

[85]   Franz Waterstradt, 'Ein Beitrag zur Methodik der Wirtschaftslehre des Landbaues', *Landwirtschaftliche Jahrbücher* 33 (1904): 477–515, here p. 486.

[86]   von der Goltz, *Die agrarischen Aufgaben*, p. 123.

[87]   Sabean, 'Small Peasant Agriculture', pp. 218–24.

[88]   Wygodzinski, *Landarbeiterfrage*, p. 14. See also Achilles, *Deutsche Agrargeschichte*, p. 283.

removing stones, weeding, hoeing, digging and sorting, and removing beet tops.[89] Notions that women's sensitivity made them ideally suited for livestock care, and that women's agility was naturally suited to painstaking, manual labor remained a vital part of contemporary agricultural wisdom.[90] Socialist politician and agricultural expert Eduard David's description of agricultural work in 1903 is typical:

> Hoe, scythe, sickle and rake can be used by women, and frequently are. Hoeing, mowing, and hay-baling machines etc. should be guided by a man's hand ... The enlargement and refinement of livestock holdings, especially the raising of young animals, demands increased, individualized nurturing [by women] ... no less important is rationalized poultry raising ... which provides a rich and varied opportunity for women's solicitous care. And finally housework and the raising of children offer farm wives an unending focus for their time and attention.[91]

According to this logic, a small or medium-sized agricultural producer's capacity for intensification depended on an increase in women and children's labor, whether hired or family. As social scientist Karl Müller summarized a decade later, "It is precisely the industrious labor of the farmer's wife and children which ... permits and maintains intensive cultivation on small and medium-sized enterprises."[92]

Although men and women often worked closely together, for instance during planting and harvest time,[93] farms were divided spatially into two domains, the *Innenwirtschaft* and the *Aussenwirtschaft*, which reflected gender divisions of labor.[94]

---

[89]   Lee, 'Women's Work', pp. 55–6.

[90]   Lee, 'Women's Work', p. 59. He observes, "Most of the new crops introduced during this period, in particular commercial crops, such as sugar beet, and root crops, such as potatoes, as well as the expansion in the cultivable area, led to a direct increase in the demand for female outdoor labor."

[91]   Eduard David, *Socialismus und Landwirtschaft. Erster Band: Die Betriebsfrage* (Leipzig: Quelle & Meyer, 1903), pp. 546–7.

[92]   Müller, *Frauenarbeit*, p. 18.

[93]   Kurt Wagner, *Leben auf dem Lande im Wandel der Industrialisierung* (Frankfurt/ Main: Insel Verlag, 1986), pp. 163–4; Ingeborg Weber-Kellermann, *Erntebrauch in der ländlichen Arbeitswelt des 19. Jahrhunderts* (Marburg: N. G. Elwert Verlag, 1965).

[94]   For an exhaustive discussion of gender divisions of labor and the *Innen-* and *Aussenwirtschaft* see Michael Mitterauer, 'Geschlechtsspezifische Arbeitsteilung und Geschlechterrollen in ländlichen Gesellschaften Mitteleuropas', in Jochen Martin and Renate Zoepffel (eds), *Aufgaben, Rollen und Räume von Frau und Mann, Teilband 2* (München: Verlag Karl Alber, 1989), pp. 819–936; K. Wagner, *Leben auf dem Lande*, pp. 163–6; Dyhrenfurth, 'Ergebnisse', p. 54.

Figure 1.1   **"In the Courtyard of Naake's Farm, *c.* 1870" [Source: Emil Hirsch, Matthias Griebel, and Volkmar Herre (eds), *August Kotzsch 1936-1910. Photograph in Loschwitz bei Dresden* (Dresden: VEB Kunstverlag, 1986), p. 209].**

Farmers and agricultural experts alike referred to the *Innenwirtschaft* as the woman's "province," which included stall, garden, and housework.[95] Women fed, watered, and milked dairy cows, raised pigs, chickens, geese, and often rabbits or goats.[96] In contrast, men worked primarily in the *Aussenwirtschaft*, where

---

[95] Siegfried Becker, *Arbeit und Gerät als Zeichensetzung bäuerlicher Familienstrukturen: Zur Stellung der Kinder im Sozialgefüge landwirtschaftlicher Betriebe des hessischen Hinterlandes zu Beginn des 20. Jahrhunderts* (Inaugural-Dissertation, Philipps-Universität Marburg, 1985), p. 202. Becker observes: "Women's role in the household economy of the farm, and for which girls were prepared very early, was divided into domains that were spatially, as well as economically and socially, different [from men's], and these in turn formed the basis for passing on gender divisions of labor across generations." See also Müller, *Frauenarbeit*, pp. 17–20.

[96] Weber-Kellermann, *Landleben im 19. Jahrhundert* (Munich: Verlag C. H. Beck, 1988), p. 150. Weber-Kellermann described late nineteenth-century gender divisions of

they supervised crop cultivation and performed tasks like plowing, sowing grain, operating heavy machines, caring for draft animals, and making repairs.[97] Women assisted men in the *Aussenwirtschaft* seasonally. Again, Karl Müller remarked that on family farms:

> Women are familiar with every aspect of fieldwork ... there are tasks which women do as efficiently as men, sometimes even more so, especially those requiring dexterity, as opposed to brute strength. So we see in springtime women hoeing root crops and grains, planting potatoes, and weeding; in summer harvesting hay and raking and binding sheaves; and in the fall harvesting potatoes and fodder beet.[98]

Thus the increase in livestock raising and expanded root crop cultivation that typified agricultural intensification on small and medium-sized family farms in the decades before the war depended on women's labor.[99]

Even on these farms, the increase in women's manual labor was complemented to some degree by an increase in the use of chemical fertilizers and imported livestock feed. Machine use on family farms increased also, although the limits of mechanization in easing the labor burden on farms under 10 hectares was widely acknowledged.[100] The machines most commonly employed on medium-sized Saxon farms were used in the *Aussenwirtschaft* for harvesting grain. In 1907, 60

---

labor thus, "Everything that had to do with dairying was women's work. Perhaps the farmer or his male hired hand assisted occasionally with fetching water, but working with cows and processing milk was considered unmanly, and was despised [verpönt]."

[97] K. Wagner, *Leben auf dem Lande*, pp. 163–6. See also LKR, *Jahresbericht ... für das Jahr 1912* (Dresden: Verlag des Landeskulturrats Sachsen, 1913), pp. 51–2. The model curriculum for men's agricultural schools, proposed by the Saxon Agricultural Chamber in 1912, emphasized managerial skills such as how to hire workers, give orders, and evaluate their work. In the *Aussenwirtschaft*, men were taught to make decisions about crop rotations based on evaluations of soil, climate, markets, and labor, to understand and operate necessary machines, and to breed and evaluate livestock. As for the *Innenwirtschaft*, men maintained the granary, haylofts, machine sheds, and "supervised its overall orderliness and cleanliness."

[98] Müller, *Frauenarbeit*, p. 22; Sabean, 'Small Peasant Agriculture', p. 221. Sabean concludes, "The history of small peasant agriculture in southern Germany in the nineteenth century is that of the progressive inclusion of women in field work."

[99] Achilles, *Deutsche Agrargeschichte*, p. 283.

[100] Achilles, *Deutsche Agrargeschichte*, pp. 240–52. After comparing the cost of investment in various machines unfavorably with wage rates for hired labor and time saved, etc. (though the gap narrows between 1885–1914), Achilles questions the assumption that farmers were automatically "backward" if they chose not to invest in the latest machines. See also von Langsdorff, 'bäuerliche Verhältnisse', p. 204. He noted the positive influence of large estates on family farms in terms of the spread of knowledge and new technology. He observed that the larger farms surrounding estates tended to make better use of new

percent of farms between 5–20 hectares used threshing machines, and 50 percent used drill plows and reapers.[101]

In terms of the *Innenwirtschaft*, the most widely used machine was the milk centrifuge, and by 1907 nearly 60 percent of all middle-sized and 18 percent of small Saxon farms used one to replace hand-churned butter.[102] However, unlike harvest machines, the vast majority of milk centrifuges used on small and medium-sized farms were hand-powered, which guaranteed a more consistent product but did not decrease women's manual labor.[103] Indeed, Müller conceded that, "Instances of women using agricultural machines is at this point very rare."[104] More recently, W. R. Lee has argued that any displacement of women from certain agricultural tasks by new technology in the nineteenth century was "more than compensated by the rising demand for female labour in many other facets of contemporary agricultural work."[105] In terms of the impact on gender divisions of labor, the adoption of new technology primarily benefited men employed in the *Aussenwirtschaft*. Therefore, although the use of chemical fertilizers and machines on small and medium-sized Saxon farms increased in the decades before 1914, the majority relied first and foremost on greater amounts of women's labor in their efforts to intensify production.

Often the increased labor needs of small and medium-sized farms could not be met by family members alone. Both established gender divisions of labor and considerations of cost meant that the most common form of hired labor was a female hired hand, or *Magd*,[106] as they were less expensive than their male counterparts and considered essential for the care of livestock.[107] The responsibilities of a *Magd* also included assisting the farmer's wife or daughters with seasonal fieldwork and household tasks such as washing, mending, or preparing food. Male hired hands [*Knechte*] were employed mainly on larger enterprises to work with draft animals,

---

tools, methods, etc. than in more mountainous areas where small farms were the rule, such as in Chemnitz and Zwickau districts.

[101]   LKR, *Jahres-Bericht ... für das Jahr 1909*, pp. 59–60.

[102]   LKR, *Jahres-Bericht ... für das Jahr 1909*, p. 60.

[103]   Rudolf Berthold, 'Zur Entwicklung der deutschen Agrarproduktion und der Ernährungswirtschaft zwischen 1907 und 1925', *Jahrbuch für Wirtschaftsgeschichte 1974/ IV*: 83–111, here p. 87.

[104]   Müller, *Frauenarbeit*, pp. 23–4.

[105]   Lee, 'Women's Work', p. 60.

[106]   For an exhaustive comparison of agricultural hired labor's contract conditions, duties, and responsibilities in each German state at the end of the nineteenth century see Wilhelm Kähler, *Gesindewesen und Gesinderecht in Deutschland* (Jena: Gustav Fischer Verlag, 1896), pp. 119, 143, 145.

[107]   Wygodzinski, *Landarbeiterfrage*, p. 22; see also LKR, *Jahres-Bericht ... für das Jahr 1909*, pp. 54–5.

Figure 1.2   "Neubert's Röse with Sheaf, *c.* 1870" [Source: Emil Hirsch, Matthias Griebel, and Volkmar Herre (eds), *August Kotzsch 1936–1910. Photograph in Loschwitz bei Dresden* (Dresden: VEB Kunstverlag, 1986), p. 218].

a task which most small and medium-sized farmers could manage alone.[108] Due to their size and their focus on livestock raising, middle-sized farms between 5–20 hectares employed more *Mägde* than smaller or larger enterprises.[109] Once hired, the laws governing their employment in Saxony specified that the contract last a minimum of one year, with a three-month notice clause.[110]

As Maria Bidlingmaier noted, however, the intensification of family farm agriculture was complicated by the shortage of hired labor, especially of *Mägde*. Yet those who debated the politics of the agricultural labor shortage did not address how German farm families managed the longer hours and increasingly arduous physical work required by intensification. Instead, farm families' seemingly limitless capacity for hard work became an ideological pillar of conservative agrarian politics. Experts were fond of contrasting the contentious urban factory or the ethnically and confessionally divided agricultural estate with the family farm, which they lauded as a smoothly-running production unit founded on a community of shared interests. This image of the family farm found few contemporary critics, even on the left. For example, while Karl Kautsky condemned them as inefficient, Eduard David defended the smaller family farm as a rational, even ideal form of agricultural enterprise.

Despite the prewar idealization of the German family farm some policymakers and state officials warned that rural flight, if left unchecked, would eventually threaten even the smallest agricultural enterprises.[111] But they expressed more irritation than panic over the shortage of *Mägde* in rapidly industrializing regions and attributed the shortage to a selfish desire on the part of young rural women for more "personal freedom" and higher factory wages rather than to larger, more difficult workloads.[112] Nevertheless, in 1902 agricultural economist Leopold Hübel opined that in Saxony "with the growing need for labor demanded by

---

[108]   Elisabeth Baldauf, *Die Frauenarbeit in der Landwirtschaft* (Borna: Universitätsverlag von Robert Noske, 1932), pp. 41–5. See also Rosa Kempf, *Arbeits- und Lebensverhältnisse der Frauen in der Landwirtschaft Bayerns* (Jena: Gustav Fischer Verlag, 1918), p. 21. Kempf, in her study of women's agricultural labor in Bavaria, asserted that "The agricultural labor question is one of permanent, hired labor ... in the case of small and medium-sized farms, this is a *Magd* question."

[109]   For statistics on distribution of *Mägde* in Saxony in 1907 according to farm size see LKR, *Jahres-Bericht ... 1909*, pp. 54–5.

[110]   The laws governing the employment of rural hired hands in the Kingdom of Saxony were revised several times in the nineteenth century, in 1835, 1892, and again in 1898. See Kähler, *Gesindewesen*, p. 119.

[111]   von der Goltz, *Agrarwesen*, p. 313; Franz Mendelson, *Die landwirtschaftliche Arbeiterfrage*, vol. 54 in Karl Steinbrück (ed.), *Bibliothek der gesamten Landwirtschaft* (Hannover: Max Jänecke Verlagsbuchhandlung, 1909); Bruno Moll, *Die Landarbeiterfrage im Königreich Sachsen* (Leipzig: A. Hoffmann, 1908).

[112]   Theodor von der Goltz, *Die ländliche Arbeiterfrage und ihre Lösung* (Danzig: Verlag von A.W. Kasemann, 1872), p. 64; Georg Bindewald, *Sesshaftigkeit und Abwanderung der weiblichen Jugend vom Lande* (Berlin: Deutscher Landwirtschaftsrat, 1905).

intensive agriculture, the labor shortage has become the most serious affliction plaguing every agricultural producer, threatening to lame him completely."[113] Hübel's warning was unusual both in its vehemence and in its inclusion of all agricultural producers. Yet even allowing for some exaggeration, Hübel's remark suggests that Saxon family farms of all sizes struggled to intensify and diversify their enterprises in both prosperous and difficult times. At the same time, the gender politics of agricultural intensification on family farms, encompassing both the increasingly unequal expectations of men and women as workers and the day-to-day management of ever greater labor burdens, remained unexplored until the eve of the First World War.

Work in Practice: Intensification and Women's Overburdening on Family Farms

In the years before 1914, a handful of scholars, many of them women, began to investigate farm women's work and the gendered meanings of intensification. Setting aside both the theoretical concerns of scientific farm management guides and the politics of agricultural wage labor, the authors emphasized instead that the extra work required by agricultural intensification on small- and medium-sized family farms clearly overburdened female dependents. The earliest of these studies was a multi-volume project organized by social welfare reformer Gertrud Dyhrenfurth under the auspices of the Standing Committee on Improving the Interests of Women Workers [*Ständiger Ausschuss zur Förderung der Arbeiterinnen-Interessen*], an umbrella organization founded in 1906 to study women's industrial employment.[114] The project aimed to document the living and working conditions of all women working in agriculture, including seasonal and wage laborers (where relevant), *Mägde*, and farm wives and daughters. The war interrupted its completion, but all the published volumes were based on materials collected before 1914. The authors, many of them active in the prewar social welfare movement, relied on narrative descriptions of farm women's work solicited from prominent local citizens, including pastors, teachers, mayors, local agricultural experts, historians, and the most prosperous farmers. They also used random questionnaires filled out by women themselves. Many of the questions required only yes or no answers, but the study authors also selected excerpts from a handful of open-ended individual testimonies to underscore their arguments.

Two other authors, Maria Bidlingmaier and Marta Wohlgemuth, actually lived among their informants for some months and collected data on farm wives in their

---

[113] Leopold Hübel, *Die Gestaltung des landwirtschaftlichen Betriebes mit Rücksicht auf den herrschenden Arbeitermangel* (Dresden: Zahn & Jaensch, 1902), p. 2.

[114] Dyhrenfurth, *Ergebnisse*, pp. 8–9; Priester, *Arbeits- und Lebensverhältnisse*; zu Putlitz, *Arbeits-und Lebensverhältnisse*; Seufert, *Arbeits- und Lebensverhältnisse*; Müller, *Frauenarbeit*.

respective villages. Wohlgemuth's research on farm wives in Baden, published in 1913, meticulously documented the dramatic increase in women's work on farms that had intensified and diversified their enterprises.[115] Bidlingmaier began her research on wives in two Württemberg villages at roughly the same time, again using firsthand observation and scores of interviews to illustrate that intensification on small and medium-sized family farms depended heavily on women's labor.[116] Both scholars stressed that they knew or came to know their subjects well and while Wohlgemuth did not speculate about farm wives' perceptions of their increased labor burdens, Bidlingmaier emphasized that the new pressures of intensification together with wives' existing household and childcare responsibilities had pushed many of her subjects to the brink of their physical and psychological strength.

All of these authors returned repeatedly to the theme of farm women's overburdening, foreshadowing the explosion of postwar concern about the issue as well as about young women's flight from the German countryside. By focusing exclusively on women rather than farm families, they highlighted women's central role in agricultural intensification in the prewar decades. As Wohlgemuth observed in her introduction, "one can see the importance of farm wives' work for the farm family as well as for supplying broad sections of the population with agricultural products; in socio-political terms an increase and an improvement in their capabilities should be considered."[117] More importantly, by detailing individual women's work on a day-to-day and seasonal basis, as opposed to merely describing gender divisions of labor, these studies demonstrated that women, especially farm wives, were doing more work than anyone else on the farm. Indeed, their findings undermined the notion cherished by many agricultural experts that farm work was shared equally, or at least equitably, among all household members. Moreover, they confirmed that women, including wives, daughters, and female hired hands, in fact performed the labor-intensive tasks that conventional and expert wisdom defined as "women's work." Finally, Bidlingmaier and Wohlgemuth not only acknowledged women's productive contribution to the farm's income but stressed that it often made the difference between prosperity and mere survival. At the same time, all these scholars were acutely aware of farm wives' double burden and explored the ways in which their roles as wives and especially mothers were often incompatible with the increase in their productive work.

The first of the Standing Committee studies, undertaken by Hans Seufert, documented women's agricultural work in the southwestern states of Württemberg, Baden, Alsace-Lorraine, and Rhineland-Pfalz, with particular emphasis on the first two. Published in 1914, Seufert's study synthesized a total of 133 narrative

---

[115] Wohlgemuth, *Bäuerin*.

[116] It is unclear whether Bidlingmaier and Wohlgemuth were acquainted, despite the proximity of their universities, Tübingen and Karlsruhe respectively, but Bidlingmaier cites Wohlgemuth's work.

[117] Wohlgemuth, *Bäuerin*, p. v.

surveys on women's agricultural work.[118] Seufert also selected answers from a total of 277 individual questionnaires completed by women themselves, 74 of them from *Mägde*, 103 filled out by farm wives and daughters, and the remainder by casual or seasonal day laborers. All of the informants were asked about work, living conditions, and wages, if relevant. Seufert repeatedly discussed the influence of intensification on family farms, and especially the increase in women's work. Commenting on both the changes in production and the growing shortage of hired labor, Seufert concluded,

> The work must get done somehow, if it can't be lessened through the use of machines or a change in production, it is carried by fewer shoulders and becomes more burdensome than ever. Each individual's results must improve, whether female wage laborer, farm wife, or daughter, or the enterprise suffers. This is both expected and demanded by the farmer or employer. Everything reported in the surveys about the burdening of farm women through agricultural work, housework, and childcare bears repeating here.[119]

While these remarks refer to farm women in Württemberg, Seufert also raised the problem of intensification and women's overburdening in the narrative reports from Baden.[120] Quoting from women's individual questionnaires, Seufert stressed that *Mägde* as well as farm wives and daughters worked on average 15.5 hours daily in summer and 12.5 in winter and in addition to more stall and garden work often did "men's work," which included mowing, collecting and loading manure, pitching hay, plowing, harrowing, driving teams, and carrying heavy sacks of fruit.[121]

In her research for the Standing Committee, social scientist Rosa Kempf drew on 68 narrative reports from Bavarian regions with both medium-sized and small family farms.[122] In terms of changes in the organization of women's work, the most commonly reported cause was a shift in production emphasis, followed by the shortage of male hired labor.[123] Although the changes in production were not specified, respondents cited them as the reason for more female dependents working full-time on family farms than in previous decades. Kempf's report on farm wives and daughters was based on 88 questionnaires, 65 from wives and 33 from daughters. Based on their replies about work, Kempf constructed a table breaking down the various tasks in the *Innen-* and *Aussenwirtschaft*: of the 65 wives, 24 were responsible for all stall work and 25 only for milking and feeding

[118] Seufert, *Arbeits-und Lebensverhältnisse*, pp. x–xii.
[119] Seufert, *Arbeits-und Lebensverhältnisse*, p. 103.
[120] Seufert, *Arbeits-und Lebensverhältnisse*, pp. 164–6.
[121] Seufert, *Arbeits-und Lebensverhältnisse*, pp. 28, 43, 317.
[122] Kempf, *Arbeits- und Lebensverhältnisse*, pp. 12–13.
[123] Kempf, *Arbeits- und Lebensverhältnisse*, p. 26.

cows.[124] Sixty-three reported that they did all the work of caring for pigs and poultry. In terms of fieldwork, 30 noted that they participated fully, including mowing, haying, spreading manure, harvesting, loading wagons, and all aspects of root crop cultivation; 16 plowed using cattle. The remaining 26 who answered questions about field work did only haying, mowing, and harvest work. All 33 daughters were responsible for stall work, 20 reported that they had plowed in addition to helping out with all aspects of field work.[125] Overall, wives worked the longest hours on the farm and Kempf argued that the only way to combat wives' overburdening was to regulate their working hours as had been done with industrial work.[126]

In the conclusion to her introductory chapter, Kempf lamented "The entire expert, official assistance has supported male farmers, livestock, or crops. Up until now all official measures have bypassed the one at the center of the family farm, the one who ensures both the survival and the joyfulness of the farm family, the farm wife."[127] Kempf added pointedly that the lack of support for farm wives' work had led to a "rift" on family farms, where the interests of men superseded more than ever those of women. She also warned that if family farms were to survive in the future, more would have to be done to celebrate farm women's vital role in agricultural enterprises.

Wohlgemuth's study described the experiences of farm wives in two very different farming communities in Baden. Her stated goal was to describe the "ideal-type" of farm wife. Thus her observations and comparisons were purely descriptive and less critical of farm women's work than Bidlingmaier's. But her careful documentation of her subjects' daily and monthly routines nevertheless offers a clear perspective on the gendering of intensification on family farms in prewar Germany. In the first section, Wohlgemuth compared family farms in the village of Wolfenweiler, which had benefited both from mild climatic conditions and its close proximity to the provincial city of Freiburg-im-Breisgau, with the much larger farms in the Black Forest village of St. Märgen. Wolfenweiler's family farms, most of them under 10 hectares, derived their incomes primarily from the sale of wine grapes, but Wohlgemuth emphasized that families balanced the unpredictability of vineyard harvests by selling fruit, vegetables, potatoes, eggs, milk, and butter, which always ensured a "quick, certain source of income."[128] In contrast, the St. Märgen enterprises were much larger, between 20 and 100 hectares, and their relative isolation from local markets and harsher climatic conditions

---

[124]   Kempf, *Arbeits- und Lebensverhältnisse*, p. 105.

[125]   Kempf, *Arbeits- und Lebensverhältnisse*, p. 107.

[126]   Kempf, *Arbeits- und Lebensverhältnisse*, p. 108; see also Kempf, *Das Leben der jungen Fabrikmädchen in München* (Leipzig: Duncker & Humblot, 1911); Sabine Schmitt, *Der Arbeiterinnenschutz im deutschen Kaiserreich: Zur Konstruktion der schutzbedürftigen Arbeiterin* (Stuttgart: Verlag J. B. Metzler, 1995).

[127]   Kempf, *Arbeits- und Lebensverhältnisse*, p. 53.

[128]   Wohlgemuth, *Bäuerin*, p. 5.

precluded the cultivation of labor-intensive grapes, fruits, and vegetables grown by women in Wolfenweiler. Wohlgemuth pointed out that St. Märgen farmers used only 25 percent of their land to grow oats, summer rye, and potatoes and used the rest for pasturage, rather than relying on stall feeding, which saved a great deal of women's labor.[129]

In the second section, entitled "the organization of work on family farms," Wohlgemuth argued that although farm wives in both villages had been relieved of some productive work for the household, such as weaving, their new task of producing foodstuffs for the market, especially in Wolfenweiler, more than compensated for the "extra" time.[130] She explained that the farmer and his wife had distinct productive realms and that work was assigned:

> according to capabilities based on physical strength and the physical characteristics of gender and age, so that men do work requiring brute strength and women perform tasks that require greater agility and a more delicate touch, while young children and the aged serve occasionally as light helpers.[131]

While Wohlgemuth reminded readers that conventional understandings of men's and women's work could at times be flexible and that these characterizations were schematic rather than absolute, her detailed descriptions of men's and women's work mirrored established notions of gender appropriateness. For example, separate sections follow that described women's arduous manual labor by season in the vineyard, in the fields, in the garden, in the barns, in the dairy, and in the marketplace.

With regard to the market, Wohlgemuth was quick to mention that while Wolfenweiler farmers occasionally sold large livestock, their wives loaded fresh butter, eggs, cheese, vegetables, and flowers in baskets every week and transported them by train to the Freiburg suburbs for sale.[132] Wohlgemuth noted the careful consideration each woman gave to her prices, based on her own household needs and her sense of customers' desires. "Through her own efforts, she [the farmer's wife] can produce quality products to sell, with a combination of luck and friendliness, to great advantage on the market."[133] Thus Wohlgemuth's major contribution was to highlight the indispensable role farm wives played both in the prosperity of German family farms and the satisfaction of urban consumer demand in the Kaiserreich.

In her introduction, Bidlingmaier laid out two goals for her research: to explore the influence of economic development on local agriculture, and, more importantly, to evaluate the impact of agriculture's rationalization [*Rationalisierung*] on the

---

[129]   Wohlgemuth, *Bäuerin*, pp. 9–10.
[130]   Wohlgemuth, *Bäuerin*, p. 17.
[131]   Wohlgemuth, *Bäuerin*, p. 15.
[132]   Wohlgemuth, *Bäuerin*, pp. 50–1.
[133]   Wohlgemuth, *Bäuerin*, p. 57. Emphasis in the original.

character, the economic value, and the amount of work performed by farm wives, also in two very different agricultural landscapes. The study's three parts traced farm wives' multiple roles as economic producers, as household workers and consumers, and as wives and mothers.

Bidlingmaier's first case study was the village of Kleinaspach, where she attributed family farms' extensive production to the less than ideal climatic conditions, the lack of local industry, and their remoteness from rail transport.[134] Almost all the farms were under 10 hectares and produced foodstuffs primarily for their own needs, including grains, potatoes, pulses, fruit, milk, butter, and eggs. Their meager cash income came from the sale of dairy products, and the money was used primarily for household goods not produced by the farm wife. In the village of Lauffen, Bidlingmaier argued that easy access to urban markets and the rise of local industries had had a dramatic impact on small family farms and noted that climatic conditions were optimal for labor-intensive crops, including grapes, root crops, vegetables, industrial crops, and fodder crops.

Bidlingmaier concluded that the intensification of agricultural production in Lauffen had indeed brought prosperity to the farming community, but at the cost of extreme hardship for farm wives.[135] She blamed the pressure to produce more and varied products for the market, complicated by the lack of technology, for farm wives' overburdening. In this case, farm wives were forced to work harder to meet the increased demand for their labor, while still trying to maintain the household and be devoted and attentive mothers.[136] In contrast, Bidlingmaier noted that the extensive cultivation practices that persisted in the more isolated village of Kleinaspach, and the ready availability of hired labor, allowed farm wives more time for the household, their children, and themselves. While the Kleinaspach households were not as "well-to-do" as those in Lauffen, Bidlingmaier described them as more "private and peaceful."[137]

In terms of their intensive cultivation practices and easy access to trade networks, family farms in Lauffen as well as those in the Baden village of Wolfenweiler closely resembled family farms in Saxony in 1914. At the same time, the majority of Saxon family farms were medium-sized, but unlike those in the Württemberg village of Kleinaspach, the demand for hired women's labor had for decades exceeded the supply. The harsh consequences of agricultural intensification for farm wives observed by Bidlingmaier and Wohlgemuth offers some idea, then, of the dilemmas confronting many Saxon farm wives. While Bidlingmaier clearly favored the model of farm wives in Kleinaspach, she conceded that "there are a

---

[134]   Bidlingmaier, *Bäuerin*, pp. 4–13.

[135]   Bidlingmaier, *Bäuerin*, p. 23.

[136]   Bidlingmaier, *Bäuerin*, pp. 18–25. More recently, see Sabean, 'Small Peasant Agriculture', who uses Bidlingmaier's study as a starting point for his own analysis.

[137]   Bidlingmaier, *Bäuerin*, p. 199.

number of deficiencies in their work practices. One wishes, in spite of oneself, that they would use their energies in a different way and increase production."[138]

Yet despite their different methods, all the authors agreed that farm women's work had changed dramatically as a result of the new exigencies of intensification, shifting consumer demand, and the growing shortage of hired workers. Most importantly, their studies catalogued the harmful effects on farm women of work that had characterized prosperous, "modern" family farms for decades, namely expanded livestock-raising, market gardening, and root crop cultivation. Finally, each author stressed that the increased expectations of women as workers also coincided with higher standards for farm women as wives, mothers, and housekeepers. Bidlingmaier summed up the mounting burdens on farm wives succinctly:

> The clear, uncomplicated division of labor between farmer and wife is possible only when the enterprise practices extensive cultivation or, alternatively, when there is enough cheap, hired labor ... As soon as cultivation becomes more diverse, the wife is drawn into ever more field work, for a variety of crops demands more work, and due to the accompanying refinement of care, both bodily strength and agility ... Therefore every such change in the enterprise is felt directly by the farm wife: they determine her destiny [*Frauenschicksal*].[139]

Conclusion

There was no shortage of debate in the prewar period over how to enhance the productivity of German family farms and the diffuse dangers posed by the growing shortage of agricultural labor. Yet despite the shrinking rural population, Germany's agricultural productivity rose dramatically in the prewar decades, especially in the foodstuffs produced almost exclusively by women. This tension went unexamined by Wilhelmine agricultural experts and state officials, who assumed that family farms, or more precisely farmers themselves, would manage the demands of intensive agriculture, encouraged and assisted by local and national agricultural associations. Furthermore, state policymakers and agricultural experts viewed the labor shortage almost exclusively as a problem plaguing large eastern estates and lionized the German family farm as a model for the nation.

In short, Wilhelmine experts, whether celebrating German agriculture's successes or warning of potential crises, ignored the feminization of agricultural work in the decades before the First World War and the growing evidence of farm women's overburdening. Instead agricultural economists, state and regional officials, and farmers' associations used the positivist, progressive language of intensification to ease the multiple tensions between producers and consumers,

---

[138]   Bidlingmaier, *Bäuerin*, p. 198.
[139]   Bidlingmaier, *Bäuerin*, pp. 19–20.

rural and urban inhabitants, Germans and non-Germans. Contemporary observers documented the dramatic changes in the rural landscape and praised the results, creating the "modern" German family farmer. Indeed, to have emphasized the increasingly unequal labor burdens borne by farm men and women would have undermined agricultural policymakers' careful construction of the family farm as a model for the German nation.

The optimistic tone of the scholarly literature on intensification was challenged only by experts who analyzed the labor of farm women. The descriptions of farm women's work presented by Wohlgemuth, Bidlingmaier, Seufert, and Kempf revealed a strikingly different and often pessimistic view of agricultural intensification on German family farms. While not challenging the boundaries and definitions of women's productive responsibilities, these authors recognized that intensive farming did not take place without unequal costs to individuals, and that the emphasis on root crop cultivation and livestock-raising translated most often into more work for women. In Saxony, the tensions over farm women's overburdening were also rising, as evidenced by the grievances lodged by runaway *Mägde* against their masters. Many of these young women cited the increased workloads expected of them as their reason for fleeing family farms in the decades before the First World War. Testimonies about their working conditions and future aspirations, as well as those of farm wives and daughters, are explored in the following chapter.

Chapter 2

Contesting the Family Farm:
Young Women's Challenges to the Rural
Ideal during the Kaiserreich

In May 1875, farmer Braune in the Saxon village of Frankenstein wrote to the district authorities in Flöha to report that a few nights earlier, his unmarried *Magd* Julie Reihsig had "secretly run away without legal grounds."[1] He added that she was now living with her foster father, a factory worker in the village of Erdmannsdorf, who informed him that she had taken another position at a higher wage. Braune demanded her severe punishment and that she be returned to him immediately. The official replied that although this appeared to be a case of simultaneous hiring, he could not impose a jail sentence since she had not received a bonus [*Mietgeld*] from both employers, and suggested that the local magistrate in Erdmannsdorf look into the matter. Several days later, Julie appeared before the magistrate and testified that she had run away because she had not been hired for heavy work, but instead for housework, laundry, and milking; that she had been forced to do every sort of heavy job, "like a stall maid," which was unsuited to her physical strength; that she had given proper notice; that Braune had verbally insulted and mistreated her constantly; and that he had withheld part of her wage. After some debate between the magistrate and the district official, the Flöha authorities informed Braune that, based on her testimony regarding timely notice and poor treatment, they had decided not to pursue his grievance. The fact that the case record ends there suggests that Julie Reihsig managed to leave a job she disliked in order to search for employment elsewhere.

While not terribly dramatic, the testimonies, formal procedures, and results of this grievance case offer a vivid example of the labor disputes that disrupted farming operations in the Kaiserreich and one young woman's spirited response to what she considered unfair demands and inappropriate treatment. Julie Reihsig's case was not an isolated one. Including hers, 68 disputes between *Mägde* and their employers from the Saxon districts of Flöha and Oschatz between 1875 and 1897 suggest that some young women's expectations about employment did not conform to the established ideal of the subservient, hard-working, and

---

[1] Sächsisches Hauptstaatsarchiv Dresden [hereafter SäHStA], Akten der königlichen Amtshauptmannschaft Flöha [hereafter AH Fl.] 2506, 'Über Gesinde-Differenzen', case of Julie Reihsig, May 10–16, 1875, no page numbers. Translation mine and all those hereafter.

loyal *Magd* enshrined in the regulations governing agricultural hired hands, or *Gesindeordnungen*, and idealized by agricultural experts.[2] Furthermore, *Mägde* lodged 47 of the 68 grievances against their employers. Many young women alleged overwork or being made to do jobs for which they were not hired. Others cited abusive treatment, withheld wages, sexual harassment, "superficial" or "unfair" work references, and the withholding of their reference books, or *Dienstbücher*.[3] Over half of them, like Julie, ultimately succeeded in changing the terms and conditions of their employment. Indeed, as Siegfried Becker has argued, "Taken together, the impact of [individual challenges] to the master's authority may have been comparatively minor, but it was precisely these points of friction that cost energy."[4] In addition, the case narratives frequently exposed the social tensions between the poorer households from which these young women came and those in which they worked, where the collective decisions made by *Mägde* and their families about their work and future prospects often clashed with farmers' rising demand for hired women's labor.[5]

In almost every instance, the various actors' testimonies contradicted each other. On the one hand, local magistrates and policemen, as the recorders of statements, fit young women's testimonies and those of other witnesses into established narrative structures that reflected their own understandings of the grievance process, their knowledge of the *Gesindeordnungen*, and above all their previous experience with the law's enforcement.[6] But as in the Reihsig case, state officials did not invariably side with employers or bow to their demands for punishment of runaway or recalcitrant *Mägde*. Instead, officials' private deliberations about how to approach these grievances revealed the multiple pressures they faced. Their immediate duty was to weigh the individual rights and claims of generally poor, often very young women against those of their more powerful employers. These disputes also forced local state officials to grapple

---

[2]   In addition to AH Fl. 2506, see AH Fl. 2507, 'Über Gesinde-Differenzen', SäHStA; AH Oschatz 1114, 'einzelne Gesindepolizeisachen betreffend', Sächsisches Staatsarchiv Leipzig, hereafter StL.

[3]   Also referred to as a *Zeugnißbuch*.

[4]   See Siegfried Becker, 'Der Dienst im fremden Haus: Sozialisation und kollektive Identität ehemaliger landwirtschaftlicher Dienstboten', in Siegfried Becker et al. (eds), *Gesindewesen in Hessen* (Marburg: Jonas Verlag, 1989), pp. 241–70, here pp. 260–1. In contrast, Austrian ethnologist Maria Woitsche found only two disputes between *Mägde* and their employers that had been recorded in three localities. See Woitsche, *Gesindewesen in Tirol im 19. Jahrhundert: Dienstbotenlieder, Dienstbotenrecht – mit einem Versuchen über das Verhältnis zwischen Dienstboten und Gemeinde* (unpublished MA thesis, University of Innsbruck, 1989), pp. 100–7. She instead uses folk songs to analyze disputes between *Mägde* and their employers.

[5]   S. Becker, 'Dienst', p. 247.

[6]   See especially Peter Becker, 'Randgruppen im Blickfeld der Polizei: Ein Versuch über die Perspektivität des "praktischen Blicks"', *Archiv für Sozialgeschichte* 32 (1992): 283–304.

with more abstract questions about rural youth's freedom of movement; young women's changing aspirations about work and family life; and how to negotiate the competition between agrarian and industrial interests over women's labor in the Kaiserreich.[7]

Although the Saxon grievance cases represented unusually public, often vehement, displays of young rural women's dissatisfaction with their fates, the voices of some farm daughters and *Mägde* in Bavaria, Baden, and Württemberg emerged indirectly in the studies by Bidlingmaier and Seufert discussed in Chapter 1. They are included here to complement the testimonies of Saxon *Mägde*, and because farm daughters are otherwise virtually silent in the historical sources from the prewar period. Their remarks reinforce the evidence from the grievance cases about the growing frustration among some young rural women about their everyday lives and their prospects for the future in the prewar decades. While some farm daughters seemed satisfied with or resigned to their fates, others expressed unwavering determination to learn a trade or to marry outside the farming community.

A variety of contemporary observers reacted with growing uneasiness to young rural women's mobility after 1900 and speculated endlessly about their motivations for resisting agricultural work and the implications of these attitudes for the nation's stability. Certainly young rural women's spatial mobility was not a new phenomenon. As Regina Schulte has pointed out, throughout the nineteenth century young women who entered agricultural service between school and marriage were very likely to leave one job for another every year or so.[8] What *was* new, however, was experts' growing conviction that young rural women's mobility, both away from farm work and away from the countryside, had to be stopped and their intense frustration with officials who seemed unwilling or unable to control unruly *Mägde*. While we cannot presume that Julie Reihsig later moved away from her home village or left agricultural work for the factory, contemporary observers interpreted both the actions and the stated motivations of runaway *Mägde* as a serious challenge to established gender, social, and labor relations in the countryside. The fact that most young rural women remained on family farms as working dependents failed to assuage their anxieties. Instead, they were convinced that some young women's expressions of dissatisfaction with the rural status quo would inspire the restlessness of the entire prewar generation of rural female youth.

---

[7]   For a fascinating discussion of labor conflicts between *Gesinde* and their employers in Bavaria during the Nazi era that raises many of the same issues, see Falk Wiesemann, 'Arbeitskonflikte in der Landwirtschaft während der NS-Zeit in Bayern 1935–1938', *Vierteljahresheft für Zeitgeschichte* 25 (1977): 573–90.

[8]   Regina Schulte, *Das Dorf im Verhör: Brandstifter, Kindsmörderinnen und Wilderer vor den Schranken des bürgerlichen Gerichts, Oberbayern 1848–1910* (Reinbeck bei Hamburg: Rowohlt Verlag, 1989), p. 130.

The broader context of experts' new worries about the implications of the mobility and outspokenness of rural female youth was the Empire's shifting rural-to-urban demographic profile. Especially after the census of 1895, the first to record an absolute decline in the German rural population, political economists of every stripe assessed rural flight's impact on everything from the nation's food supply, to its future health and military readiness, to the more nebulous but equally pressing problem of preserving German culture.[9] Most agreed that if left unchecked, rural flight would threaten the hard-won gains in agricultural productivity and completely undermine the social hierarchies essential for maintaining harmonious rural labor relations.[10] Extreme conservatives amplified the threat still further by framing rural flight as a destructive impulse symptomatic of the entire younger generation of poorer rural inhabitants, thereby endangering the nation's future demographic and moral strength. In 1872, conservative political economist Theodor von der Goltz singled out agricultural servants' growing disrespect for "patriarchal authority" and their "inappropriate expectations" with regard to wages, workload, food, and lodging.[11] Certainly these sorts of complaints about *Gesinde* were also not new.[12] Still, by the prewar decade virtually every local and national report on agricultural labor conditions implied that the new generation of rural youth was no longer committed to the hard work and sacrifice so essential for maintaining family farm prosperity. The prewar census statistics substantiated expert fears about the waning of the institution. While the numbers of *Knechte* and *Mägde* peaked between 1882 and 1895, to about one-quarter of the agricultural workforce, thereafter their numbers declined steadily.[13]

---

[9]   For overviews of the debate see Sigmund von Frauendorfer, *Ideengeschichte der Agrarwirtschaft und Agrarpolitik im deutschen Sprachgebiet. Band 1: Von den Anfängen bis zum Ersten Weltkrieg*, 2nd edn (München: Bayrischer Landwirtschaftsverlag, 1963), pp. 386–402; Kenneth Barkin, *The Controversy over German Industrialization* (Chicago: University of Chicago Press, 1970), pp. 131–85.

[10]   *Gesinde* is always plural and gender neutral.

[11]   Theodor von der Goltz, *Die ländliche Arbeiterfrage und ihre Lösung* (Danzig: Verlag von A.W. Kasemann, 1872), pp. 64–7.

[12]   See for example Ulinka Rublack, *The Crimes of Women in Early Modern Germany* (Oxford: Clarendon Press, 1999), pp. 99–107. Rublack cites a 1652 Swabian report complaining that many *Mägde* "behaved in a masterless and bold manner, and if told or forbidden anything in response to their crime [sic!] they immediately became angry" (p. 100). On urban servant girls see Dorothee Wierling, *Mädchen für alles: Arbeitsalltag und Lebensgeschichte städtischer Dienstmädchen um die Jahrhundertwende* (Berlin: Dietz Verlag, 1987); Dagmar Müller-Staats, *Klagen über Dienstboten: eine Untersuchung über Dienstboten und ihre Herrschaften* (Frankfurt/Main: Insel Verlag, 1987).

[13]   Elisabeth Baldauf, *Die Frauenarbeit in der Landwirtschaft* (Borna-Leipzig: Universitätsverlag Robert Noske, 1932), p. 8; Rosa Kempf, *Die deutsche Frau nach der Volks-, Berufs-, und Betriebszählung von 1925* (Mannheim: Bensheimer Verlag, 1931), p. 48. Nor were these trends particular to prewar Germany. See T. M. Devine, 'Women

Village and regional agricultural associations sharpened these still rather vague anxieties about rural youth by repeatedly emphasizing the shortage of *Mägde* and condemning young rural women's new awareness of their value on the agricultural labor market. Local complaints about young rural women's "unruliness," as well as expert predictions about the possible ramifications of these trends, did not fall on deaf ears. But as the Saxon grievance cases underscored, the anxieties about managing young rural women's mobility raised new questions about established liberal economic and social principles that had no easy answers, specifically concerning the freedom-of-movement and freedom-of-employment laws passed in the 1860s.[14] While most agricultural experts agreed that these freedoms were at least in part to blame for the labor shortage, they generally conceded that restricting youth's mobility would be impossible. State and local officials concurred, particularly those who struggled to manage the prewar agricultural labor shortage. But extreme conservatives condemned these more-or-less pragmatic attitudes and warned that young rural women's mobility was a primary cause of the rural population's deteriorating physical health and, increasingly, of the destruction of German rural culture.

In the final prewar years, social welfare experts dedicated to preserving German rural culture and conservative social values transformed these diffuse anxieties about rural female youth into a multi-faceted agenda for reform.[15] By 1905 at least one prominent agricultural expert and various members of the burgeoning rural social welfare movement were explicit about the economic and social dangers of young women's resistance to agricultural work and their flight from the German countryside.[16] In contrast to their antipathy for industrial work and its negative influences on working-class youth, however, they approached the task of reforming rural girls with the firm conviction that farm work was the most appropriate work for women. Like agricultural experts, rural social welfare advocates viewed the

---

Workers, 1850–1914', in T. M. Devine (ed.), *Farm Servants and Labour in Lowland Scotland, 1770–1914* (Edinburgh: John Donald Publishers, 1984), pp. 98–123, esp. p. 113; Nicola Verdun, *Rural Women Workers in 19th-Century England: Gender, Work and Wages* (Woodbridge, Suffolk: Boydell Press, 2002), pp. 95–7.

[14] Thomas Kühne, 'Imagined Regions: The Construction of Traditional, Democratic, and other Identities', in James Retallack (ed.), *Saxony in German History: Culture, Society, Politics, 1830–1933* (Ann Arbor: University of Michigan Press, 2000), pp. 51–62, esp. p. 60; George Steinmetz, *Regulating the Social: The Welfare State and Local Politics in Imperial Germany* (Princeton: Princeton University Press, 1993), pp. 88–9, 114–18.

[15] Klaus Bergmann, *Agrarromantik und Großstadtfeindschaft* (Meisenheim: Verlag Anton Heim, 1970), pp. 63–70. Thomas Vormbaum's study of the changing politics of the *Gesindeordnungen* includes lengthy critiques of the laws by contemporary legal experts. See Vormbaum, *Politik und Gesinderecht im 19. Jahrhundert (vornehmlich in Preußen 1810–1918)* (Berlin: Duncker & Humblot, 1980); see also Heinrich Scheller, *Das Gesinderecht und seine Aufhebung* (Borna-Leipzig: Universitätsverlag Robert Noske, 1919).

[16] Derek Linton, *"Who has the Youth, has the Future": The Campaign to Save Young Workers in Imperial Germany* (Cambridge: Cambridge University Press, 1991), p. 1.

nurturing of plants and animals and the raising of a family as analogous, promising a seamless combination of work and motherhood. While a few admitted that farm women's overburdening might explain the younger generation's growing alienation from their proper roles, most asserted that it was not young rural women's work so much as their negative attitudes toward it and toward rural life more generally that needed changing.[17]

This chapter explores the increasing tensions between the ideal young rural woman envisioned by experts and prescribed in the *Gesindeordnungen* and the challenges to these expectations by both *Mägde* and farm daughters in the Kaiserreich. In particular, the grievance cases reveal that many young rural women were willing to contest their employers' expectations of them and were adept navigators of official procedures that facilitated the public airing of their grievances.[18] In this regard, a Bavarian commentator's comfortable remark in 1895 that "[with respect to the old patriarchal structures] things in the countryside follow their peaceful, time-honored course" was, if not an illusion, then a pattern that some young women purposefully sought to remake.[19] Moreover, exploring these conflicting ideals recasts the contemporary social-scientific discourses about rural flight, agricultural labor demands, and female youth that converged at the end of the nineteenth century. Nor were these tensions resolved. Instead they set the stage for the crisis over rural female youth that erupted during and after the First World War, as young rural women's search for new employment opportunities, expert worries about the demise of rural Germany, and state officials' efforts to meet the increased demand for women's agricultural labor collided.

Gesinde as a Social and Economic Institution in the Kaiserreich

By the early 1890s, agricultural experts like von der Goltz, Buchenberger, and others were lamenting the decline in the numbers of *Gesinde* and characterized

---

[17]   K. Bergmann, *Agrarromantik*, p. 94; Max Matter, '"Ech stohn net ob – ech treck net us – leck mech em Asch – me Johr os us": Gesindeverhältnisse, Gesindeordnungen und Wechseltermine in Hessen und der ehemaligen preußischen Rheinprovinz', in S. Becker (ed.), *Gesindewesen in Hessen*, pp. 12–34, esp. p. 18. Matter argues that contemporary experts' observation that certain rural traditions "still persisted" was more wishful thinking than a reflection of reality.

[18]   In contrast, Ingeborg Weber-Kellermann argues that late nineteenth-century *Gesinde* did not challenge the established rural hierarchy, but instead "took more pride in their [subservient] status than the highest aristocrat." See Weber-Kellermann, 'Land-Stadt-Bewegungen als Kontext für das Gesindewesen im 19. Jahrhundert', in S. Becker, *Gesindewesen in Hessen*, pp. 65–84, here p. 73.

[19]   Untersuchung der wirtschaftlichen Verhältnisse in 24 Gemeinden des Königreiches Bayerns (Munich, 1895), pp. 231–2, cited in Schulte, *Dorf im Verhör*, p. 131.

the institution of service, or *Gesindewesen*, in increasingly nostalgic terms. The shrinking numbers of *Mägde* triggered particular unease, for they embodied the quintessential hired agricultural workers: submissive, hard-working, and loyal.[20] To experts' way of thinking, service provided not only vital female labor for family farms; it also bridged the time between school and marriage for poorer girls and the social distance between struggling and more prosperous farm families.[21] Most importantly, the institution promised to strengthen the future economic, social, and demographic vitality of rural communities, since the years spent in service ostensibly enhanced poorer girls' chances of becoming farm wives, or at the very least of marrying rural artisans and remaining in the countryside.[22] In contrast, young rural men's resistance to agricultural service after completing military duty had been noted with growing resignation since the 1850s. But by 1900 young rural women's reluctance to enter agricultural service and their mobility – both between jobs and away from the countryside – was perceived as both entirely new and deeply threatening to rural, and even national, stability.

In each German state, the *Gesindeordnungen* outlined the unique social and moral functions of the institution and the strict expectations about servants' behavior in exhaustive detail. In particular, experts extolled the benefits for *Mägde* of living and working under the constant discipline of the household head and his wife, where alongside farm daughters they could learn the productive skills and domestic duties necessary for later life. Thus agricultural service was seen as infinitely preferable to the precarious existence of casual agricultural wage laborers or to the immoral, spendthrift life of the factory girl.[23] Experts conceded that girls could learn some of these skills as household servants in large cities, but emphasized the dangers of urban life for their spending habits and future aspirations, as well as the temptation to fall into prostitution. By the eve of the First World War, experts viewed the declining numbers of *Mägde* as a clear symptom of rural disintegration and young rural women as a key population contributing to the larger crisis of rural flight.[24] Above all they worried that the restlessness and

[20] Wilhelm Kähler, *Gesindewesen und Gesinderecht in Deutschland* (Jena: Gustav Fischer, 1896), pp. 60–1.

[21] Adolf Buchenberger, *Agrarwesen und Agrarpolitik. Erster Band* (Leipzig: C. F. Winter'sche Verlag, 1892), p. 559; Theodor von der Goltz, *Agrarwesen und Agrarpolitik* (Jena: Gustav Fischer, 1904), p. 147.

[22] Schulte, *Dorf im Verhör*, pp. 13–40; Ingeborg Weber-Kellermann, *Landleben im 19. Jahrhundert*, 2nd edn (Munich: C. H. Beck, 1988), p. 164.

[23] Buchenberger, *Agrarwesen*, pp. 570–4.

[24] E. Hurwicz, 'Kriminalität und Prostitution der weiblichen Dienstboten', *Archiv für Kriminalanthropologie* 65 (1916): 185–251, esp. pp. 205, 234.

inappropriate aspirations of a few young women might inspire an entire generation of rural female youth to flee the countryside.[25]

In Germany as a whole *Gesinde* comprised approximately one-quarter of all hired agricultural workers in 1882 and were 3.5 percent of the total population, totaling 1,569,957.[26] The Kingdom of Bavaria was the exception, with almost 22 percent of the total number of *Gesinde,* constituting 6.6 percent of that state's total population. In Prussia, other districts in north-central Germany, and in the southwest, *Knechte* outnumbered *Mägde*, sometimes by almost 2:1. This was in part due to the inclusion of estate foremen in the census numbers. Significantly, *Mägde* outnumbered *Knechte* in only two states: in Bavaria, where they made up just over one-half of all *Gesinde,* and in Saxony, where *Mägde* were three-fifths of the total number. Between 1882 and 1907, the numbers of *Mägde* declined nationally from 55,488 to 42,762, or 23 percent; *Knechte* declined from 42,822 to 37,684, or just 12 percent.[27] The relatively large numbers of *Mägde* in comparison to *Knechte* in Saxony may be explained by several factors. First, as Chapter 1 stressed, they were highly sought after to help manage the rising workloads on the small- and medium-sized family farms that predominated there. Second, Saxon agricultural estates were smaller on average than those further north and east, so that while some estate owners began to hire specially-trained men to oversee the care of livestock by the end of the nineteenth century, many others continued to rely on *Mägde* for the actual work of milking, cleaning out stalls, etc. Above all, the overwhelming success of intensification efforts in Saxony might explain why *Mägde* so far outnumbered *Knechte* by the end of the nineteenth century and also why their numbers declined more precipitously than those of *Knechte* between 1882 and 1907.

A brief overview of the *Gesindeordnungen* is helpful for understanding the diverse prewar discourses about *Mägde* and the "problem" of rural female youth more generally. Experts of all kinds referred to the ideal *Magd* depicted in the *Gesindeordnungen* as a starting-point for their critique of the new generation of young rural women, and to suggest new strategies for reforming their attitudes and behavior.[28] Again, in contrast to daily wage laborers, experts stressed that

---

[25]   Doris Tillmann, *Der Landfrauenberuf: bäuerliche Arbeit, Bildungsstätten und Berufsorganisationen der Landfrauen in Schleswig-Holstein, 1900–1933* (Neumünster: Wachholtz Verlag, 1997), p. 39.

[26]   Kähler, *Gesindewesen*, pp. 61–2. Agricultural [*landwirtschaftliches*] *Gesinde*, sometimes referred to as *Dienstboten*, were in a different category than household [*häusliches*] *Gesinde/Dienstboten.* Hereafter *Gesinde* refers only to year-round agricultural hired hands.

[27]   For 1882 statistics, see Kähler, *Gesindewesen*, p. 61. For 1907 statistics see *Jahres-Bericht über die Landwirtschaft im Königreich Sachsen für das Jahr 1909* (Dresden: Kommissionsverlag von Johannes Päßler, 1911), p. 55.

[28]   Hurwicz repeatedly observed that the young women most likely to commit crimes in large cities came from poorer rural origins. Hurwicz, 'Kriminalität', pp. 205, 211, 234.

living and working in such close extended contact with the farm family offered an unprecedented opportunity for *Mägde* to become acquainted with the skills and the sacrifices that eventually would fall to them as farm housewives and mothers.[29] Thus the *Gesindeordnungen* were unique in that they provided a detailed set of social and moral expectations for *Mägde*, in contrast to other forms of women's employment, such as home work, which was not regulated by the state, or even factory work. Above all the agricultural service laws aimed to shape young women's attitudes toward work, working relationships, and leisure time that reflected the ideals of the 1820s and 1830s, when many of the modern *Gesindeordnungen* were revised, with some additional revisions in some states, including Saxony, in the 1890s and 1910s. As such they were rooted firmly in the paternal labor relations characteristic of the early nineteenth century and earlier. The respect for "patriarchal relations" so revered by experts was exemplified by the employer's right to punish disobedience as he saw fit.[30] This was precisely the ideal that so many young rural women appeared to reject by the end of the nineteenth century and which provided endless fodder for conflicts between *Mägde* and their employers throughout the Kaiserreich. Even if a formal contract were not signed, and this was not required, in the disputes between *Mägde* and their masters, the *Gesindeordnungen* acted as an all-important reference point for official deliberations and virtually every grievance case cited one or more ways in which the laws had been violated by one party or the other.

The *Gesindeordnungen* regulated all aspects of the master–agricultural servant relationship. The term master, or *Dienstherr*, was used very explicitly in the laws as opposed to employer, although occasionally the "master" was a widow. Each state had its own laws, but many of the statutes were similar, with local modifications.[31] All had statutes covering contract negotiation; mutual duties and responsibilities; giving notice; unlawful behavior; grounds for breaking the contract, for both masters and servants; grounds for immediate dismissal; the conferring of references; and dispute procedures, including the jurisdiction of the police.[32] The Saxon *Gesindeordnungen* dated from 1835 and were revised in 1892, 1898, and again in 1906.[33]

Furthermore, whether or not the contract itself was in writing, the employer was required to enter the starting date of service into the servant's reference book

---

[29] von der Goltz, *Agrarwesen*, p. 449; Schulte, *Dorf im Verhör*, pp. 139–40. Schulte observes that a maid's knowledge of farm and housework was an essential part of her dowry, at least as important as cash and household items.

[30] "Patriarchal" and "paternal" were often used interchangeably by contemporary experts.

[31] For a detailed, state by state history of the laws' genealogy, see Kähler, *Gesindewesen*, pp. 107–28.

[32] Kähler, *Gesindewesen*, pp. 128–95.

[33] Landeskulturrat Sachsen, *Jahres-Bericht über die Landwirtschaft im Königreiche Sachsen für das Jahr 1906* (hereafter cited as LKR, *Jahres-Bericht* and year).

[*Dienst-* or *Zeugnißbuch*] along with the amount of the bonus paid either to the servant or to the labor broker or both.[34] The bonus was to be negotiated between the two parties, but local custom was to take precedence. In Saxony, throughout the decades in question it was 3 Marks and was not considered part of the yearly wage, which ranged between 120 and 150 Marks. If the length of the contract was not specified in writing, then it was considered a yearly contract, with three-months' notice required.[35] Apart from giving proper notice, a contract could only be terminated without dispute in cases of either party's death or if the employer became bankrupt. If the farm were sold, then the servant was required to abide by the original contract unless both parties agreed to end it.[36]

The regulations about servants' proper behavior and required duties were detailed and specific. Not only was the *Magd* required to perform all tasks ordered by the employer, she was to devote all her time and energies to the household.[37] This was also the case when off duty, and in Saxony the master was to provide the servant with three free hours a week in order to take care of personal matters, including mending or attending a fair.[38] A *Magd* was to be god-fearing and moral; modest and respectful; pleasant to fellow servants and family members; avoid extravagance; not gossip about the household to strangers; never leave the premises without permission from the employer; and allow the employer to search her personal possessions at any time, although a witness was to be present.[39]

The statutes on servants' behavior also included prohibitions whose violation could lead to immediate dismissal, including "persistent and willful" disobedience of the master or those charged with his authority; insulting the master or his dependents; lack of industriousness that incurred losses for the employer; a proclivity to gamble, drink, or quarrel; staying out late at night without permission; and misrepresenting the skills necessary for the job.[40] More serious grounds for dismissal included carelessness about the use of fire and lighting; stealing or telling lies, or encouraging another servant to do so; falsifying a reference; making a loan in the name of the master; seducing a child or the master's dependent into immoral

---

[34]   Kähler, *Gesindewesen*, pp. 117, 138, § 17, *sächsische Gesindeordnungen* (hereafter listed by paragraph). *Miethsgeld* or *Angeld* were also used.

[35]   Kähler, *Gesindewesen*, p. 143, § 2, 19. Only if the wages were paid monthly was the required notice shortened, in which case it corresponded to the wage payment schedule.

[36]   Kähler, *Gesindewesen*, p. 145, § 81–2.

[37]   Kähler, *Gesindewesen*, p. 147, § 32–4.

[38]   Kähler, *Gesindewesen*, p. 153, § 59, 61.

[39]   Kähler, *Gesindewesen*, pp. 148–50, § 30, 42, 44, 46, 99.

[40]   Kähler, *Gesindewesen*, pp. 146–50, 175–8, § 15, 16, 17, 84. Kähler noted that many states' *Gesindeordnungen* included epilepsy in the list of "disgusting or contagious diseases."

behavior; catching a "disgusting or contagious" disease; or being prevented from working because of a jail sentence lasting more than eight days.[41]

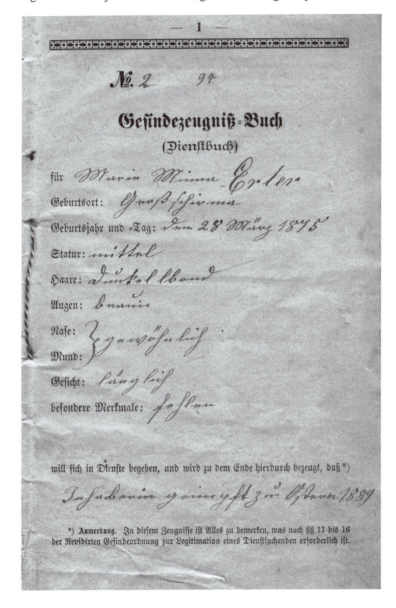

Figure 2.1 "Reference Book of a Saxon *Magd*, 1889" [Source: author's collection].

---

[41] Kähler, *Gesindewesen*, pp. 175–80, § 7, 8, 10, 13, 18, 19, 84.

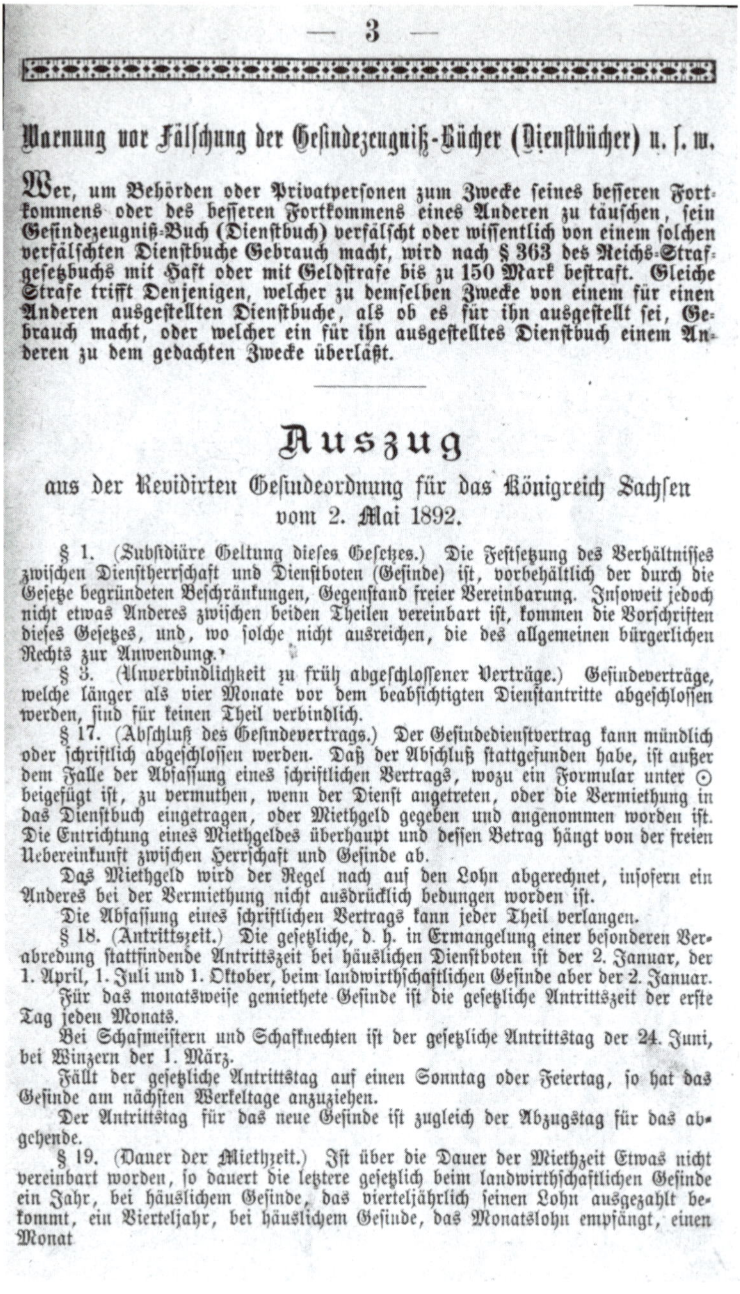

— 3 —

Warnung vor Fälschung der Gesindezeugniß-Bücher (Dienstbücher) u. s. w.

Wer, um Behörden oder Privatpersonen zum Zwecke seines besseren Fortkommens oder des besseren Fortkommens eines Anderen zu täuschen, sein
Gesindezeugniß-Buch (Dienstbuch) verfälscht oder wissentlich von einem solchen
verfälschten Dienstbuche Gebrauch macht, wird nach § 363 des Reichs-Straf-
gesetzbuchs mit Haft oder mit Geldstrafe bis zu 150 Mark bestraft. Gleiche
Strafe trifft Denjenigen, welcher zu demselben Zwecke von einem für einen
Anderen ausgestellten Dienstbuche, als ob es für ihn ausgestellt sei, Gebrauch macht, oder welcher ein für ihn ausgestelltes Dienstbuch einem Anderen zu dem gedachten Zwecke überläßt.

Auszug

aus der Revidirten Gesindeordnung für das Königreich Sachsen
vom 2. Mai 1892.

§ 1. (Subsidiäre Geltung dieses Gesetzes.) Die Festsetzung des Verhältnisses
zwischen Dienstherrschaft und Dienstboten (Gesinde) ist, vorbehältlich der durch die
Gesetze begründeten Beschränkungen, Gegenstand freier Vereinbarung. Insoweit jedoch
nicht etwas Anderes zwischen beiden Theilen vereinbart ist, kommen die Vorschriften
dieses Gesetzes, und, wo solche nicht ausreichen, die des allgemeinen bürgerlichen
Rechts zur Anwendung.

§ 3. (Unverbindlichkeit zu früh abgeschlossener Verträge.) Gesindeverträge,
welche länger als vier Monate vor dem beabsichtigten Dienstantritte abgeschlossen
werden, sind für keinen Theil verbindlich.

§ 17. (Abschluß des Gesindevertrags.) Der Gesindedienstvertrag kann mündlich
oder schriftlich abgeschlossen werden. Daß der Abschluß stattgefunden habe, ist außer
dem Falle der Abfassung eines schriftlichen Vertrags, wozu ein Formular unter ⊙
beigefügt ist, zu vermuthen, wenn der Dienst angetreten, oder die Vermiethung in
das Dienstbuch eingetragen, oder Miethgeld gegeben und angenommen worden ist.
Die Entrichtung eines Miethgeldes überhaupt und dessen Betrag hängt von der freien
Uebereinkunft zwischen Herrschaft und Gesinde ab.

Das Miethgeld wird der Regel nach auf den Lohn abgerechnet, insofern ein
Anderes bei der Vermiethung nicht ausdrücklich bedungen worden ist.

Die Abfassung eines schriftlichen Vertrags kann jeder Theil verlangen.

§ 18. (Antrittszeit.) Die gesetzliche, d. h. in Ermangelung einer besonderen Ver-
abredung stattfindende Antrittszeit des häuslichen Dienstboten ist der 2. Januar, der
1. April, 1. Juli und 1. Oktober, beim landwirthschaftlichen Gesinde aber der 2. Januar.

Für das monatsweise gemiethete Gesinde ist die gesetzliche Antrittszeit der erste
Tag jeden Monats.

Bei Schafmeistern und Schafknechten ist der gesetzliche Antrittstag der 24. Juni,
bei Winzern der 1. März.

Fällt der gesetzliche Antrittstag auf einen Sonntag oder Feiertag, so hat das
Gesinde am nächsten Werkeltage anzuziehen.

Der Antrittstag für das neue Gesinde ist zugleich der Abzugstag für das ab-
gehende.

§ 19. (Dauer der Miethzeit.) Ist über die Dauer der Miethzeit Etwas nicht
vereinbart worden, so dauert die letztere gesetzlich beim landwirthschaftlichen Gesinde
ein Jahr, bei häuslichem Gesinde, das vierteljährlich seinen Lohn ausgezahlt be-
kommt, ein Vierteljahr, bei häuslichem Gesinde, das Monatslohn empfängt, einen
Monat

Figure 2.2   "*Gesinde* Ordinance in Reference Book, *c.* 1880s" [Source:
author's collection].

The *Gesindeordnungen* contained equally detailed statutes about the employer's responsibilities toward the servant but were, perhaps predictably, much less specific about the circumstances under which a servant might resist mistreatment without penalty. In the first instance, the master was responsible for wages and food. The value of both was to be determined by both parties but, as with the *Mietgeld*, local custom was to take precedence.[42] The Saxon statutes were unusual with regard to the provision of food, and specified that meals must be satiating and not detrimental to the servant's health. However, a servant's complaints about the food could be settled if it were demonstrated that the master and the servants shared the same food.[43] The master was also responsible for instructing the servant in "civic virtues" and moral behavior, encouraging church attendance, and for exercising "parental discipline" with those under 18.[44]

The regulations regarding the master's use of discipline were vague, and one observer noted in 1896 that the issue of servants' self-defense in response to harsh treatment had recently sparked "lively theoretical and practical debate."[45] Specifically, the regulations stated that "invective and minor violent punishments provoked by the improper behavior of the servant are not to be considered punishable and are not to be pursued through legal redress."[46] At the same time, the master was not to overburden the servant beyond his or her physical capabilities. Furthermore, the servant could break the contract without notice if the master overstepped his power of command by "mishandling" or treating the servant with "unusual harshness or cruelty."[47] By 1907, the master's right to physical punishment had been limited by many states' *Gesindeordnungen*, although some experts pointed out that employers "were not always clear" about the changes that had been made with regard to boxing ears and other mistreatment.[48]

Finally, the *Gesindeordnungen* guided the state's oversight of the entire system, the settlement of disputes between *Gesinde* and their employers, and the tracking down and return of runaway hired hands by local police, or *Gesindepolizei*. The *Gesindepolizei* was also charged with issuing servants' reference books and keeping a running record of all relevant information on servants' employment records.[49] The reference book itself was often kept at the local police station, but in Saxony the employer oversaw its safekeeping. After the contract ended and if proper notice had been given, the employer was required to enter a "completely

---

42 Kähler, *Gesindewesen*, p. 151.
43 Kähler, *Gesindewesen*, pp. 151–2, § 52, 53.
44 Kähler, *Gesindewesen*, pp. 154–5, § 43, 59.
45 Kähler, *Gesindewesen*, p. 155.
46 Kähler, *Gesindewesen*, p. 156.
47 Kähler, *Gesindewesen*, pp. 153, 180, § 46, 85.
48 A. Stumpfe, 'Zur Dienstbotenfrage: die soziale Lage der weiblichen Dienstboten', *Soziale Revue: Zeitschrift für die socialen Fragen der Gegenwart* 7 (Essen, 1907): 428–38, esp. p. 431.
49 Kähler, *Gesindewesen*, p. 182, § 100.

truthful" reference, which would then be presented to subsequent employers.[50] If the servant felt the reference were somehow unfair, however, he or she had the right to appeal to the *Gesindepolizei* about obtaining another. At the same time, any employer who knowingly entered false information in a reference book was liable for any damages incurred by a future employer as a result.[51] Without a reference book, a *Magd* could no longer legally find another position and a master often informed authorities that he was withholding it in order to compel his *Magd* to return to service. Like the issue of physical discipline, the requirement that all *Gesinde* must have reference books was hotly debated after the turn of the century, with many experts arguing that a poor reference unduly harmed a servant's future chances of getting ahead while others clung to this regulation as the only way for employers to protect themselves against dishonest or criminal behavior on the part of *Gesinde*.[52]

The local policeman, or gendarme, was often summoned to locate the runaway *Magd* and to return her, by force if necessary, to her employer. But *Gesinde*, and agricultural workers more generally, had no special courts to hear their disputes with employers, unlike workers in industry or other trades.[53] Instead the village magistrate, or *Gemeindevorstand*, and the gendarme worked together to locate and communicate with the two parties and gather witness statements. The mediation of disputes as well as their formal reporting to the district authorities was undertaken by the *Gemeindevorstand*, who in turn often requested guidance from the district official in charge of these cases. Finally, if the *Gemeindevorstand* ruled that a *Magd* had run away "without grounds and of her own volition," then the gendarme would be responsible for escorting her back, by force if necessary.[54] Occasionally she would be given a jail sentence, served at the local police station, or a fine, or both, especially if she ran away more than once.

The only other actors not yet mentioned were the *Gesindevermittler*, or private labor brokers paid by agricultural employers for referrals of *Gesinde*.[55] One historian has observed that in regions of small and medium-sized family farms, there were virtually no demands for state intervention in the agricultural labor market as a means of addressing the growing labor shortage, either because agricultural experts believed that industrialization was merely a temporary phenomenon or because it

---

[50]   Kähler, *Gesindewesen*, p. 184, § 100. On the heated disputes in the Hamburg government [*Senat*] over the wisdom of introducing mandatory *Dienstbücher* see Müller-Staats, *Klagen*, pp. 129–31.

[51]   Kähler, *Gesindewesen*, p. 185, § 100, 108.

[52]   Hurwicz, 'Kriminalität', pp. 240–4.

[53]   See the December 3, 1909 Reichstag petition by Albrecht et al. to create courts to hear disputes between agricultural workers and their employers like those designated for industry. SäHStA, Ministerium des Innern 15876, 'Das Gesindewesen', p. 42.

[54]   Kähler, *Gesindewesen*, p. 188, § 22, 96.

[55]   Also referred to as *Gesindemakler*, *Gesindevermieter*, or *Gesindeagent*.

was simply impracticable.[56] For example, Wilhelm Kähler's encyclopedic 1896 study of the evolution of *Gesindewesen* in the nineteenth century has nothing to say about labor brokers. In stark contrast, the state began to implement regulations of labor brokers who specialized in the importation of foreign labor in 1890, due to fears that Poles would settle permanently in the eastern provinces if the state did not intervene.[57] Certainly the debate over state intervention in the agricultural labor market, including the placement of *Gesinde*, heated up considerably as the shortage of rural labor worsened after 1900, but state-run labor exchanges charged with locating and placing local workers were established in Saxony only in 1913, and were prefaced by increasingly anxious debates about the disappearance of *Gesinde* and the role of rural youth in Germany's new political economy.[58]

A Disappearing Ideal? Critiques of *Gesinde* and Rural Youth Before 1900

In two lengthy speeches about *Gesinde* in 1873, Theodor von der Goltz did not address their economic importance for family farms, but instead framed the institution and experts' fears about its decline as part of the so-called "social question." In his opening remarks, he observed that "although this might seem to be a lesser link in the large and complicated [social] chain, it is nonetheless central to its existence, and of much greater importance for the whole than one might think. I am referring to that section of the population that we call '*Dienstboten*' or '*Gesinde*.'"[59] Von der Goltz was quick to point out the differences between agricultural hired hands and urban household servants, but stressed that both categories of *Gesinde* worked under long-term contracts that could not be ended "at any convenient time;" that they received a yearly, rather than a weekly or daily, wage; and above all that they were members of the household.[60] Another key aspect of the institution, he added, was its association with a distinct age cohort, since the vast majority of *Knechte* and *Mägde* were single and between the ages of 15 and 25.[61]

Yet von der Goltz followed his praise of *Gesinde* as a vital rural institution with lengthy diatribes on the new and unreasonable demands made by agricultural servants, including their laziness, their lack of trust in their employers, and their

---

[56]   von Frauendorfer, *Ideengeschichte*, p. 402.

[57]   Klaus Bade, '"Billig und willig" – die "ausländischen Wanderarbeiter" im kaiserlichen Deutschland', in Klaus Bade (ed.), *Deutsche im Ausland-Fremde in Deutschland: Migration in Geschichte und Gegenwart* (Munich: C. H. Beck, 1992), pp. 311–24.

[58]   LKR, *Jahres-Bericht 1913*, pp. 46–50.

[59]   Theodor von der Goltz, *Die sociale Bedeutung des Gesindewesens. Zwei Vorträge* (Danzig: Verlag von A. W. Kasemann, 1873), p. 6.

[60]   von der Goltz, *sociale Bedeutung*, p. 7.

[61]   von der Goltz, *sociale Bedeutung*, p. 14.

immorality, especially their lust for new entertainments and finery. Above all he condemned the tendency of *Gesinde* to change employers frequently and hastily "for the smallest reason."[62] Von der Goltz concluded his second speech with the assertion that the good of the whole was being damaged by the "principle of self-interest," and that at least some noteworthy political economists had begun to conclude that the "one-sided emphasis of this principle is not justifiable either in theory or in practice."[63]

Twenty years later, agricultural expert Adolf Buchenberger summarized the dual economic and social significance of *Gesinde* and hinted at the younger generation's threat to rural, and therefore national, stability:

> Servants are mostly at an age where ... the power of the master and of the police is justified by the lack of parental authority, and further because contract-breaking especially among agricultural servants may lead to enormous disadvantages that harm not only the interests of the employer, but also appear to endanger the interests of the entire society.[64]

A local state official in Schleswig-Holstein complained in 1894 that *Knechte* and *Mägde* were no longer willing to do whatever was asked of them.[65] He added, "The young maids, despite higher wages, tend to leave their positions at the slightest provocation or they behave themselves so badly that the master has no objections if they leave before their contracts end." By 1897, Buchenberger noted that many employers as well as his fellow experts viewed contract-breaking among *Gesinde* as a "public calamity."[66] Nevertheless, the idealization of the institution and strong faith in its power to preserve the social and moral stability of the countryside persisted. In 1902 Saxon agricultural expert Leopold Hübel's manual for reorganizing agricultural enterprises in response to the labor shortage suggested strategies for remedying the problem. He urged his readers to ponder that:

> [The dependent status of *Gesinde*] offers certain educational opportunities for younger workers if the master considers their economic and moral needs ... We need to reexamine the *Gesinde* relationship so that ... it is viewed by both master and servant as a manifestation of Christian family life; that is, good will from the one side, submission on the other, and loyalty from both: selfless devotion to the present and future well-being of the other party now and for all time.[67]

---

[62]   von der Goltz, *sociale Bedeutung*, p. 31.

[63]   von der Goltz, *sociale Bedeutung*, p. 64.

[64]   Buchenberger, *Agrarwesen. Erster Band*, pp. 578–9.

[65]   Cited in Tillmann, *Landfrauenberuf*, p. 38.

[66]   Adolf Buchenberger, *Grundzüge der deutschen Agrarpolitik* (Berlin: Paul Parey, 1897), p. 164.

[67]   Leopold Hübel, *Die Gestaltung des landwirtschaftlichen Betriebes mit Rücksicht auf den herrschenden Arbeitermangel* (Dresden: v. Zahn & Jaensch, 1902), pp. 21–3; Johannes

Nevertheless, the numbers of *Gesinde* declined steadily throughout Germany and, by the early twentieth century, agricultural experts began to frame the shortage of *Mägde* as a particularly ominous threat to the future prosperity of family farms and the social and moral stability of the countryside. Although it never overshadowed the dangers posed by migrant Slavic workers, the perception that poorer rural women were no longer choosing to serve as *Mägde*, and especially those who migrated to towns and cities in search of alternative employment, attracted ever closer scrutiny from Wilhelmine political economists. In 1904, von der Goltz returned to the agricultural labor question and singled out the shortage of *Mägde* as a pressing issue in the contemporary debate over the agricultural labor shortage: "The shortage of *Gesinde* is especially serious, namely of female *Gesinde*, whose lack is felt more or less throughout the entire nation ... With regard to the decision to stay put or to leave, mostly it is a feeling, an impression, and not cool, rational considerations that play a part."[68] Several years later agricultural economist Franz Mendelson addressed the worsening agricultural labor shortage, basing his observations on local agricultural associations' reports.[69] Once again, he highlighted the risks of replacing German agricultural workers with Polish migrants, although he conceded that this was the only way for large estates to manage their labor demands.[70] But in his discussion of local labor supplies, he stressed that the problem lay with the shortage of *Gesinde*.[71]

Yet while Buchenberger, von der Goltz, Mendelson, and others viewed the migration of young people from rural to urban areas with alarm, all of them agreed that restricting the freedom-of-movement laws would have no impact whatsoever on the problem.[72] At the same time, while experts disagreed about its extent, there was consensus that if rural flight persisted, disastrous consequences for the nation would follow.[73] Indeed, debates over citizens' freedom of movement took place at the highest levels of government and in both the scholarly and popular presses throughout the Wilhelmine period. For example, between mid-1899 and 1901, officials in the Interior, War, Finance, and Agricultural Ministries in Berlin all weighed in against a proposal to alleviate the rural labor shortage that would have required youth under

---

Corvey, 'Der Arbeitermangel in der sächsischen Landwirtschaft', *Der Arbeiterfreund* 40 (1902): 395–404, esp. pp. 400–1.

[68] von der Goltz, *Agrarwesen*, pp. 152–3.

[69] Franz Mendelson, *Die landwirtschaftliche Arbeiterfrage*, vol. 54 in Karl Steinbrück (ed.), *Bibliothek der gesamten Landwirtschaft* (Hannover: Max Jänecke Verlagsbuchhandlung, 1909).

[70] Mendelson, *landwirtschaftliche Arbeiterfrage*, pp. 17–20.

[71] Mendelson, *landwirtschaftliche Arbeiterfrage*, p. 7.

[72] Buchenberger, *Agrarwesen. Erster Band,* pp. 551, 560; von der Goltz, *Agrarwesen*, p. 161; Mendelson, *landwirtschaftliche Arbeiterfrage*, p. 21.

[73] Peter Becker, *Verderbnis und Entartung: eine Geschichte der Kriminologie des 19. Jahrhunderts als Diskurs und Praxis* (Göttingen: Vandenhoeck & Ruprecht, 2002), pp. 186–93.

18 to obtain written permission from their parents or guardians to leave their residences, as well as proof of employment at their intended destinations.[74] Despite his ministry's obvious sympathy for the proposal, the Agricultural Minister ended up agreeing with his colleagues that the regulations simply would not work:

> Like the Interior Minister, I believe that these regulations will not help us keep rural inhabitants in their villages. The subjects in question will have no trouble obtaining permission from their legal guardians to leave. Most [youth] emigration occurs in any case with the permission and often even the encouragement of their adult family members. That's in the nature of things. It's the desire to improve their economic situation, to obtain cash wages and, they fancy, better living conditions, which is luring the rural working population, including youth, to large cities and industrial centers.[75]

He added that these sorts of regulations had failed miserably with respect to youth employed in industry, where "dwindling parental authority, lack of savings, frequent visits to dance halls and bars, and hasty marriages" persisted among those young workers who no longer lived at home.[76] Despite their general commitment to the principle of freedom of movement, however, Wilhelmine officials did not tamper with the contract regulations of agricultural hired hands, which required them to commit to a minimum of one-year's service. And complaints about contract-breaking among young agricultural workers punctuated virtually every official and scholarly report on the subject of agricultural labor.

Farmers too echoed these fears about the new and unreasonable demands made by *Gesinde*: their resistance to hard work; their growing unavailability; and especially their tendency to run away. Once again, reports from local agricultural associations frequently singled out the shortage of *Mägde* and their unruly behavior as a particular problem. By the early 1890s, the Association for Social Policy had completed its massive study of rural labor relations, including *Gesinde*, daily wage laborers, and migrant laborers.[77] In his summary of the survey, agricultural economist Kuno Frankenstein reported complaints about the

---

[74]   Official reactions to the Gamp-Arendt proposal to alleviate the agricultural labor shortage by amending freedom-of-movement regulations. Bundesarchiv Berlin (hereafter BAB) R1501, no. 115485, Aug. 1899 – Dec. 1900, pp. 1–2, 7, 25–7, 33–4, 37–40, 48–52, 54–6, 86–94; Elizabeth Bright Jones, 'The Gendering of the Postwar Agricultural Labor Shortage in Saxony, 1918–1924', *Central European History* 32/3 (1999): 311–29, esp. p. 324.

[75]   Sterneberg, Ministerium für Landwirtschaft, Domänen und Försten, 'Abänderung der Gesetze über Freizügigkeit und den Unterstützungswohnsitz', Berlin, July 9, 1900; BAB, R1501, no. 115485, p. 37.

[76]   Sterneberg, 'Abänderung', p. 2.

[77]   Verein für Sozialpolitik, *Die Verhältnisse der Landarbeiter in Deutschland*, vols 53–5 (Leipzig: Duncker & Humblot, 1892).

shortage of *Gesinde* across Germany.[78] Complaints about the shortage of *Mägde* in particular were voiced in Upper Silesia, Schleswig-Holstein, northwest Germany, and both Prussian Saxony [Sachsen-Anhalt] and the Kingdom of Saxony.[79] Sometimes the shortage of *Mägde* was merely mentioned, but Frankenstein was more expansive on the problem in middle Germany, including the Kingdom of Saxony, where he had acted as lead investigator for the Association's survey.[80] He observed that, "Female *Gesinde* in middle Germany are disappearing more and more, and sometimes they will only work in the household, while some of the stall work is handled by *Knechte*, and the milking must be done by their wives or the wives of daily wage laborers. The shortage of female *Gesinde* has led here and there to enormous wage increases."[81] He added that the increasingly high wages commanded by *Mägde* were the result of the "dismal situation whereby daughters of rural workers only seldom turn to agricultural work. Whenever possible, they seek a position in the city instead, or they marry the first decent man that presents himself." In conclusion, Frankenstein glumly echoed his colleagues' lament about the deterioration of rural social relations: "The earlier patriarchal relations between employer and worker in middle Germany are as good as gone. Employers do what they can for their workers and they take into account their increased self-esteem; nevertheless a loosening of discipline continues and contract-breaking persists."[82]

In Saxony, the shortage of *Mägde* drew comment and complaint from experts and local agricultural associations alike. Frankenstein's summary was amplified by Saxon agricultural experts and by yearly reports on labor conditions by the Saxon Agricultural Chamber between 1901 and 1913. In almost all of the reports, special mention is made of the younger generation's growing unwillingness to accept agricultural work and the worsening shortage of women's labor, especially of *Mägde*. For example, the 1901 report observed, "It is significant for the state of [Saxon] agriculture that young workers seem to be more and more inclined to turn away from agriculture in order to pursue other kinds of work."[83] In the section on labor relations more specifically, the report continued, "There is a shortage of agricultural servants, especially of *Mägde*, that is at least as bad as in the previous year. Some districts report *that female agricultural servants are no longer to be*

---

[78]   Kuno von Frankenstein, *Die Arbeiterfrage in der deutschen Landwirtschaft. Mit besonderer Berücksichtigung der Erhebungen des Vereins für Sozialpolitik über die Lage der Landarbeiter* (Berlin: Robert Oppenheim, 1893), pp. 46, 72, 135, 175, 191, 236, 259–60, 271.

[79]   von Frankenstein, *Arbeiterfrage*, pp. 159, 196, 218, 224, 236, 242.

[80]   Kuno von Frankenstein, 'Königreich Sachsen', in *Die Verhältnisse der Landarbeiter in Deutschland, Schriften des Vereins für* Sozialpolitik 54 (Vaduz: Topos Verlag, 1989), pp. 321–63.

[81]   von Frankenstein, *Arbeiterfrage*, p. 236.

[82]   von Frankenstein, *Arbeiterfrage*, p. 242.

[83]   LKR, *Jahres-Bericht 1901* (Dresden: M. Schönfeld's Verlagsbuchhandlung, 1902), p. 7.

had at all ... Agricultural workers' wage demands remain stable ... but their demands with regard to meals are rising everywhere."[84] The summation for 1903 is even gloomier:

> The labor shortage that we've complained about for years remains unchanged ... The shortage of *female agricultural servants* has grown worse everywhere ... In some districts *Mägde* are completely unavailable. In others, girls' tendency to prefer industrial work or to be employed as an urban housemaid has had the effect of shrinking the numbers of girls willing to be *Mägde* ... It's not at all uncommon for some to complain that their daughters stubbornly resist working in the field or in the stall, and prefer instead cleaner industrial work and the free city life with its expected pleasures.[85]

In 1909, the Saxon Agricultural Chamber chronicled the declining numbers of *Gesinde* in Saxony between 1895 and 1907, where the numbers of *Mägde* and *Knechte* fell at virtually the same rate, about 15 percent, and faster than any other category of paid agricultural worker.[86] By 1911, the yearly report lamented,

> With respect to *local workers*, the shortage of labor, namely of female agricultural servants, is becoming worse than ever. [Small and medium-sized] farms are suffering from this the most ... In many places they are trying to substitute male for female workers to work in the stall and in the household. Naturally due to the uniqueness of these enterprises, this is only a stop-gap measure, but it has to be attempted in order to keep these farms going. Of course only foreign boys will do this sort of work; only in a few cases have local boys been willing to do it.[87]

Returning to the question of managing the shortage of *Gesinde* in the prewar period and the role of *Gesinde* brokers, there was much more debate in the last prewar decade about the state's role in regulating the agricultural labor market and how to prosecute dishonest brokers. In 1904, von der Goltz remarked that "With reason there have been complaints about the bad business practices of some *Gesindevermittler* in the last few years and demands for state intervention by passing stricter laws for their regulation are justified. As in many other things, the state can only address the worst offenses, but is not in a position to effect overall positive change that would remedy the situation."[88] Von der Goltz underscored the efficacy of self-help remedies in

[84] LKR, *Jahres-Bericht 1901*, pp. 56–7. Emphasis in the original.

[85] LKR, *Jahres-Bericht 1903* (Leipzig: Verlagsbuchhandlung Richard Carl Schmidt & Co., 1904), pp. 54–5. Emphasis in the original.

[86] LKR, *Jahres-Bericht 1909* (Dresden: Kommissionsverlag von Johannes Päßler, 1910), pp. 54–5. *Mägde* in Saxony declined from 50,022 to 42,663; *Knechte* from 39,793 to 34, 519. LKR, *Jahres-Bericht 1911*, p. 46.

[87] LKR, *Jahres-Bericht 1911*, p. 50.

[88] von der Goltz, *Agrarwesen*, p. 160.

this respect, and referred to the efforts of some agricultural associations to organize local labor exchanges that would support employers. He conceded that private *Gesindevermittler* would not be made obsolete by such efforts, but that they "might create more solid business practices."[89] Other experts also raised concerns about unethical *Gesindevermittler*, who were accused of turning a blind eye to contract-breaking since they could always collect fees for new placements. The detailed qualifications for the official appointed to run the main Saxon agricultural labor exchange in Dresden as well as the planned branches in Großenhain, Lommatzsch, Meißen, Löbau, and Wurzen suggested that there were undoubtedly brokers who took advantage of the system for their own gain.[90] The proposed regulations focused overwhelmingly on the appointee's necessary organizational skills, his "strict commitment to confidentiality," and his liability for damages if he placed a known contract-breaker in another position. He also was forbidden to make any private placements or use the office for other purposes, and if he violated any of these regulations he would be subject to a fine of 1,000 Marks.

The Problem of Rural Female Youth and the Search for Solutions after 1900

Perhaps the earliest study of rural female youth's flight from the land was commissioned by the German Chamber of Agriculture and authored by agricultural expert Georg Bindewald.[91] Completed in 1905, *The Rootedness and the Emigration of Rural Female Youth* set the tone for much of the subsequent discourse before 1914, both about young women's motivations for leaving the countryside as well as the dire consequences of these shifting attitudes. By identifying a specific female cohort as his focus, Bindewald not only broke with the existing Wilhelmine literature on rural flight; he proposed an entirely new way of conceptualizing the problem. First, making women the subject of scrutiny focused the vague worries about the demographic and biological dangers of rural flight that had surfaced in the 1880s and offered a specific target for reforms aimed at preserving the family farm as the foundation of the nation's political economy.[92] As Saxon agricultural expert Johannes Corvey had observed mildly a few years earlier, "This broad perspective regarding social hygiene should be shared by the average farmer, that is, the concern that a substantial proportion of a state's population remains in agriculture and that the transition from work on family farms to other forms of

---

[89]   von der Goltz, *Agrarwesen*, p. 160.

[90]   LKR, *Jahres-Bericht 1913*, pp. 46–8.

[91]   Georg Bindewald, *Sesshaftigkeit und Abwanderung der weiblichen Jugend vom Lande* (Berlin: Sonderabdruck aus dem Archiv des Deutschen Landwirtschaftsrats, 1905), pp. 103–214, here p. 213.

[92]   Barkin, *Controversy*, p. 107; see also Elizabeth Bright Jones, 'Pre- and Postwar Generations of Rural Female Youth and the Future of the German Nation, 1871–1933', *Continuity and Change* 19/3 (2004): 1–19.

employment does not overstep certain boundaries."[93] By this time, conservatives had begun to argue that the hiring of Polish women, who made up the majority of imported agricultural labor, tainted agricultural work irrevocably for Germans. Bindewald made this point tirelessly, noting that this was one important reason that rural girls and their parents viewed agricultural work with disdain.[94] Others warned that the rural-to-urban population shift would have a negative impact on the nation's birthrate, emphasizing that rural mothers had more and healthier children than their urban working-class counterparts.[95]

Second, Bindewald's careful focus on women between 16 and 20 years old signaled to social policymakers that Germany's youth problem was not limited to urban working-class boys. Instead, he sought to persuade his audience that rural female youth was an equally volatile population in need of expert attention. Like the members of the Standing Committee on Improving the Interests of Women Workers, Bindewald relied on a lengthy questionnaire distributed to prominent local citizens, mostly pastors and male teachers. Specifically, his informants were asked to report on young women born between 1884 and 1888 whose movements were traceable, focusing especially on those who left the countryside for the Saxon city of Leipzig and the nearby city of Halle, in Prussian Saxony. Based on these reports, he found that of 100 subjects, two-thirds had chosen to leave both the countryside and agricultural work.[96]

Bindewald was especially bothered by the explanations given for young women's decisions to abandon family farms. While he dutifully reported that the high wages and lighter, cleaner work offered by factory jobs certainly played a role, he repeatedly referred to girls' alienation from the homeland, or *Heimat*, as a significant source of the problem.[97] Bindewald often blamed parents for this deficit and asserted that young women who refused positions as *Mägde* were driving many family farmers into selling or leasing their enterprises.[98] In particular, his repeated observation that rural girls' aspirations were both more ambitious and more ambiguous than those of their mothers provoked deep consternation in his audience. Responding to Bindewald's report, one of the Chamber's delegates exclaimed, "Gentlemen, a direct result of the disdain for agricultural work, of the flight of female inhabitants, of girls' rush to leave the countryside, is that umpteen farmers are compelled to sell part or even all of their enterprises."[99] At the same time, Bindewald described medium-sized family farms as "insurers of

---

[93]   Corvey, 'Der Arbeitermangel', p. 397.

[94]   Bindewald, *Sesshaftigkeit,* pp. 118, 122, 131, 132–3, 149, 165; see also Katrin Roller, *Frauenmigration und Ausländerpolitik im Deutschen Kaiserreich: polnische Arbeitsmigrantinnen in Preußen*, 2nd edn (Berlin: Dieter Bertz Verlag, 1994).

[95]   Barkin, *Controversy*, pp. 157–60.

[96]   Bindewald, *Sesshaftigkeit*, p. 107.

[97]   Bindewald, *Sesshaftigkeit*, pp. 107, 122.

[98]   Bindewald, *Sesshaftigkeit*, p. 124.

[99]   Bindewald, *Sesshaftigkeit*, pp. 202–3, remarks of Cetto-Reichertshausen.

rural rootedness and stability," a label that suggested both their present importance and future potential for preserving a settled rural population based on family farm agriculture. He added:

> From numerous reports … it is absolutely clear that large and especially medium-sized family farms are of the utmost significance in retaining female rural youth in their places of birth [*Heimatsort*]. Here [the farmer] relies on the labor not only of his daughters but also on that of one or more local girls, all of whom are retained for the *Heimat* … on the basis of patriarchal relationships, which secure a social place for these girls on the farm.[100]

Like the connection Bindewald made between young women's resistance to agricultural work and the collapse of many agricultural enterprises, his constant affirmation of the positive effects of patriarchal social relations between young farm women and their fathers and/or employers was echoed by social welfare reformers. Bindewald portrayed rural parents who encouraged their daughters to leave the farm for the factory not only as materially grasping but as "climbing the social ladder."[101] In conclusion, Bindewald urged his colleagues to take the problem of girls' rural flight very seriously and warned that if the present rate of outmigration in the region were representative, "grave political consequences for the Kaiser and the Reich" would result.[102] He concluded gloomily that soon only the stupid or physically unfit would remain in the countryside.[103] Bindewald also noted that some were not farmers' daughters but instead daughters of "transients."[104] In contrast, Bindewald argued that the "pièce de résistance of rootedness" was the medium-sized family farm which had the potential to employ either dependent or hired women year-round.[105]

Bindewald's concerns did not go unheeded. Yet many of the new social welfare reformers approached the task of reforming rural female youth with much greater optimism. Their first aim was to minimize the differences between better-off farm daughters and rural girls from poorer families, including *Mägde*, and to address the problems allegedly shared by rural female youth as a whole. Once rural female youth learned to appreciate the value of their work as producers and mothers, the new generation would be the backbone of a socially cohesive countryside. At the same time, Wilhelmine social welfare reformers disagreed about precisely

---

[100]   Bindewald, *Sesshaftigkeit*, p. 131.
[101]   Bindewald, *Sesshaftigkeit*, pp. 117–18, 133, 164.
[102]   Bindewald, *Sesshaftigkeit*, p. 171.
[103]   Bindewald, *Sesshaftigkeit*, p. 160.
[104]   Bindewald, *Sesshaftigkeit*, p. 107.
[105]   "Er bildet die pièce de résistance der Seßhaftigkeit." Bindewald, *Sesshaftigkeit*, p. 120. In this case, he stressed the key minimum was 5 hectares, p. 109.

what rural girls needed most.[106] Some authors favorably compared them to their urban counterparts, emphasizing their superior health and moral integrity. Others declared that rural girls were just as unruly and unprepared as their working-class sisters for their future responsibilities as wives, mothers, and workers. The prewar discourse about rural female youth reflected but did not address these tensions, with some reformers advocating training or education, while others favored strict bans on rural girls' freedom of movement.

Yet whatever their differences, both conservative and liberal reformers agreed with Bindewald that young rural women's growing spatial, economic, and social mobility had tremendous political implications. By the prewar decade much of the discourse on rural female youth linked young women's resistance to agricultural work directly to myriad ills, including a "Polonized" countryside, population decline, the breakdown of the gender and social order of rural households, and youth rebelliousness. German farmers and their representatives also confirmed expert worries that the aspirations of the new generation of young rural women threatened the prosperity and even the survival of family farms, and by extension the nation itself. Conversely, there was broad consensus that if the future generation of farm women learned to balance work and family duties with ease, their positive social, cultural, and moral influence on the nation would be inestimable.

The majority of rural social welfare reformers therefore stressed the merits of special training as a means of keeping German girls in the countryside. This emphasis had grown out of their experiences with working-class adolescent boys and their threats to the nation's economic, political, and social stability. Just as the family farm encapsulated all that was "traditional" and stable about German society for many middle-class reformers, urban male youth was a problem symptomatic of industrial modernity and symbolized all that was wrong with the nation. Soon urban working-class girls too came under scrutiny. Prewar social welfare reformers like Alwine Reinald, Hertha Siemering, and Rosa Kempf, who authored a study of Munich factory girls before turning to her study of women's agricultural work in Bavaria, worried increasingly about the health, values, habits, and morals of Germany's urban female youth.[107]

Many of these same concerns, especially the defiance of established authorities, also began to surface in the new discourse about the prewar generation of rural female youth. Above all it emphasized experts' dangerous lack of knowledge about rural girls and especially their vulnerability to corrosive outside, i.e. urban, influences. For example, in 1909 the Central Office for Social Welfare held the first scholarly conference dedicated exclusively to the social problems posed by

---

[106]   By contrast, there was much more consensus among social welfare reformers about the threats posed by working-class girls. See Elizabeth Harvey, *Youth and the Welfare State in Weimar Germany* (Oxford: Clarendon Press, 1993), esp. p. 33.

[107]   Derek Linton, 'Between School and Marriage, Workshop and Household: Young Working Women as a Social Problem in Late Imperial Germany', *European History Quarterly* 18/4 (1988): 387–408, here p. 389.

female youth.[108] While the participants focused overwhelmingly on working-class girls' social and moral deficiencies, the report warned that rural girls were also ill-prepared for household duties and motherhood. "Even if [agricultural work] is not completely separate from the household, due to the incredibly heavy physical labor girls are doing during the day, one cannot speak of any sort of real household training that would prepare them for their later responsibilities."[109]

A few years later, social welfare reformer Elisabeth Gnauck-Kühne painted a much rosier picture, contrasting rural girls and their work to the dire existence of their urban sisters.[110] While she cautioned that women's factory employment threatened both the next and subsequent generations' ability to become mothers as well as workers, she repeatedly qualified her warnings when referring to young rural women, "whose blooming rosy cheeks" contrasted with those of their "sallow, emaciated" urban counterparts.[111] Gnauck-Kühne also celebrated the physical and psychological benefits of agricultural work for young women, and called for the "inoculation" of city girls from the "bacterias" that surrounded them by sending them out to work on family farms.[112] However, she hastened to add that despite their natural advantages, rural girls needed special guidance in order to preserve their attachment to the countryside, guidance that they sorely lacked. Soon admonitions about the dangerous consequences of young women's flight from the countryside were stated unequivocally. In 1913 Karl Müller argued that farm wives' overburdening threatened not only the strength of their future children but also "dampened the younger generation's desire to begin farm families of their own."[113] A report on rural women in Brandenburg also framed the problem of women's rural flight and the shortage of labor in generational terms:

> Spreading manure, milking cows, hoeing beets is all beneath the young lady in her modern attire. Rural flight is widespread. More finery, more dancing, more money drives young women into the city and most come to a bad end ... Married

---

[108] Anon., 'Die Förderung und Ausgestaltung der hauswirtschaftlichen Unterweisung für die gesamte weibliche Jugend. Verhandlungen der 2. Konferenz am 11. und 12. Mai 1908 in Berlin', *Schriften der Zentralstelle für Volkswohlfahrt* 2 (Berlin: Carl Heymanns Verlag, 1909): 1–42; Hertha Siemering, 'Pflege der schulentlassenen weiblichen Jugend', *Schriften der Zentralstelle für Volkswohlfahrt* 10 (Berlin: Carl Heymanns Verlag, 1914): 1–48; Frida Gräfin zur Lippe-Oberschönfeld (ed.), *Die Frau auf dem Lande. Ein Wegweiser für Haus-, Guts- und Gemeindepflege* (Berlin: Deutsche Landbuchhandlung, 1908).

[109] Anon., 'Förderung und Ausgestaltung', p. 21.

[110] Elisabeth Gnauck-Kühne, 'Die allgemeine Bedeutung und Notwendigkeit des Ausbaus der weiblichen Jugendpflege', *Schriften der Zentralstelle für Volkswohlfahrt* 9 (Berlin, 1912): 186–98, here p. 187.

[111] Gnauck-Kühne, 'Die allgemeine Bedeutung', p. 193.

[112] Gnauck-Kühne, 'Die allgemeine Bedeutung', p. 191.

[113] Karl Müller, *Die Frauenarbeit in der Landwirtschaft* (Mönchen-Gladbach: Volksvereins-Verlag, 1913), p. 44.

women don't complain too much, the unmarried complain of too little change
and not enough fun in the countryside. The spirit of the modern has permeated
even these districts.[114]

Like Bindewald and the local expert quoted above, many observers brooded at length
about the perceived motivations of individual young women for resisting agricultural
work and leaving the countryside. Experts also were concerned about the messages
that poorer rural parents might be sending their daughters, especially their approval
of daughters' abandonment of agricultural work for another occupation in order to
enhance the economic and social prospects of the family's next generation.

Gertrud Dyhrenfurth was the first to suggest that young women's refusal
to work in agriculture might lie not merely in their fantasies about other kinds
of work, especially the promise of higher wages and more leisure, but in the
conditions that they had already observed and experienced on the farm.[115] Here
too, although from a completely different point-of-view, Dyhrenfurth constructed
the problem of women's rural flight as a generational one, and underscored that a
daughter's strategies for getting ahead often precluded following in her mother's
and grandmother's footsteps.[116] She remarked, "If we ask most girls what they
would like to be, they say 'like my mother.' Most farmers' daughters don't have
this wish anymore!"[117] Another rural social welfare expert concurred, noting that

> In every corner of Germany, we see rural girls turn to other kinds of work after
> confirmation than that which busied their mothers and grandmothers: kitchen,
> stall, barnyard, field do not tempt them anymore – they want to be factory
> workers, or, if that's not possible, a servant, not on a farm, but in the big city.[118]

At the same time, Dyhrenfurth's primary goal was to educate both state officials
and the general public about the conditions that promoted rural women's flight and
to promote concrete remedies for their mental and physical fatigue.

---

[114]   Elly zu Putlitz, *Arbeits-und Lebensverhältnisse der Frauen in der Landwirtschaft
in Brandenburg* (Jena: Gustav Fischer, 1914), p. 157.

[115]   Gertrud Dyhrenfurth, *Ergebnisse einer Untersuchung über die Arbeits- und
Lebensverhältnisse der Frauen in der Landwirtschaft* (Jena: Gustav Fischer, 1916), p. 25.

[116]   Dyhrenfurth, *Ergebnisse*, p. 50.

[117]   Dyhrenfurth, *Ergebnisse*, p. 50.

[118]   Arete Gogarten, 'Die hauswirtschaftliche Ausbildung der Töchter der ärmeren
Landbevölkerung', in Gräfin zur Lippe-Oberschönfeld (ed.), *Die Frau auf dem Lande*, pp.
67–74, here p. 68.

Wishes for the Future: Individual "Profiles" of Rural Female Youth

What precisely did young rural women themselves have to say about their futures, other prospects, and their opinions of rural life? Not only did girls often describe their move from farm to factory as a "step up" to better-paid, cleaner employment, but their parents also often spoke in terms of wanting "something better" for their daughters or not wanting them to share the same fate as their mothers. From the perspective of some young farm women and their families, spatial, occupational, and generational mobility often were tied together, to the growing alarm of contemporary social welfare reformers and political economists.

Before turning to the Saxon cases, it is worth exploring the evidence of young rural women's future plans and goals reported in the Standing Committee and Bidlingmaier's studies. Although fragmentary and sometimes cited secondhand, this evidence suggests that some young women had indeed set their sights beyond the farm, whether with respect to their decisions about marriage or their desires for alternative training and employment. Moreover, some clearly understood that their answers broke with established expectations and life courses, whether in response to queries about themselves in the case of young, single women or about what mothers wanted for their daughters.

Under the heading "Reasons for Leaving the Countryside," the Standing Committee authors occasionally quoted young women directly, including *Mägde*, farm daughters, and seasonal workers; these were often referred to as "individual profiles." In a wide-ranging appendix, Bidlingmaier reported the results of her survey of 33 farm daughters over the age of 29 about why they had remained single.[119] I have included this evidence in order to round out the portrait of runaway *Mägde* in the following section and to make the point that even better-off farm daughters occasionally expressed discontent with their lot even as others appeared more sanguine about the prospect of remaining on the farm. The same ambivalence emerges in the statements of older women, who may have been reluctant to make changes in their own lives but wanted something different for their daughters. Certainly the "individual profiles" paint a more complex and varied portrait of young rural women's hopes and aspirations for the future than that of worried expert observers.

Hans Seufert began his discussion of women's flight from the countryside in southwest Germany with a clear warning that women's testimonies were mediated by his local experts. But he hastened to add that he had included any and all direct quotes contained in his reports, all of them from either Württemberg or Baden, and underscored their importance for understanding women's flight from the countryside. While most of the quotes confirmed expert fears about the reasons for women's dissatisfaction, especially about the burdens of agricultural work, some young women expressed ambivalence about what they might lose if they chose to

---

[119] Maria Bidlingmaier, *Die Bäuerin in zwei Gemeinden Württembergs* (Stuttgart: W. Kohlhammer Verlag, 1918), Table 47, p. 261.

leave the countryside. In Württemberg, a 20-year-old farm daughter testified that city life was "less exhausting and more varied in terms of leisure" and that she would find "a better place."[120] A 25-year-old *Magd* admitted that she "knew rural life was healthier and that she could save more, but that her sister, who had married a state official and lived in the city was still better off [than she]. Stall work and field work in bad weather are not tempting."[121] An 18-year-old farm daughter wanted to "get out from under parental authority." Another 18-year-old *Magd* from Baden planned "to go to the city like everyone else; more pleasures and more freedoms."[122]

Somewhat older women, like a 34-year-old day laborer from Württemberg, asserted that she "won't permit her daughter to work in agriculture," but instead expressed the desire that she should work in the factory or as a maid in the city, "where everything is better and nicer."[123] A 51-year-old farm wife from the same region remarked that in the city, "You don't have to get up at 4:00 a.m., you finish by 8 p.m., higher wages, not so much work and you're a 'wife' not a 'woman' [*ist "Frau" nicht "Weib"*]." But a 42-year-old day laborer, also from Württemberg, observed that "In the city everything would surely be better and nicer, but one is really at home in the countryside."

Rosa Kempf included far fewer direct quotes from her women respondents than Seufert and those that she selected offered either overwhelmingly positive or very bitter perspectives of Bavarian farm life. Describing the feelings of *Mägde* about their work and the future, Kempf noted that only a handful expressed negative sentiments about their fates and that these few were physically weak; the majority wanted to marry within the farming community.[124] When quoting the reasons given by those who wanted to remain, Kempf switched from the first to the third person, while still retaining the quotation marks: "The reasons that they [*Mägde*] prefer rural life are simple enough: 'because I'm at home here;' 'because I love my home;' 'because she could never leave the mountains'; 'because she knows and loves the work;' 'because she grew up here;' 'because she is healthy and wants to remain so;' or as another *Magd* put it, 'Because I like the food and the work.'" Some, according to Kempf, even expressed their distaste for urban life, observing that it was "hectic," "they'd had enough of it from visiting relatives," or "that you could go crazy from the noise."

However, in her section on farm daughters Kempf included some of the most damning judgments recorded anywhere, all of them from farm daughters who grew up on larger farms and "who experienced their mother's overburdening and

---

[120]   Hans Seufert, *Arbeits- und Lebensverhältnisse der Frauen in der Landwirtschaft in Württemberg, Baden, Elsaß-Lothringen und Rheinpfalz* (Jena: Gustav Fischer, 1914), p. 97.

[121]   Seufert, *Arbeits- und Lebensverhältnisse*, p. 97.

[122]   Seufert, *Arbeits- und Lebensverhältnisse*, p. 216.

[123]   Seufert, *Arbeits- und Lebensverhältnisse*, p. 97.

[124]   Rosa Kempf, *Die Arbeits- und Lebensverhältnisse der Frauen in der Landwirtschaft Bayerns* (Jena: Gustav Fischer Verlag, 1918), p. 78.

whose own bodies suffered in their youth."[125] Again, Kempf employed the third person, but cited their comments as direct quotes: "She is newly aware of her rights as a human being; she is repelled by the raw despotism of the farmer;" "The men here desperately need education. He [the farmer] only knows what his wife is worth after she's dead." Kempf ended the volume with two quotes from farm daughters, presumably about their mothers, "'She's so numb that she doesn't even realize how unworthy her position has become.' 'But the daughters see, hear, and feel – and they go to the city.'"[126]

While Bidlingmaier focused mainly on the fate of farm wives in two Württemberg villages, she reported the reasons that 33 single women from farms in Lauffen had given for their failure to marry. Bidlingmaier noted that 20 of them were either "weak" or "sickly," and of these, three were physically or mentally handicapped and four reported that they had chosen to look after an elderly parent. At the same time, nine of them, among them several who had reported themselves "too weak to be a farm wife," had "ruled farmers' sons out" and had wanted to marry an official (the most desirable profession), a teacher, a minister, or a railroad conductor. A few gave no reasons for their decision, and Bidlingmaier noted simply "Reason unknown, healthy." Four of the women who had rejected offers of marriage from farmers were characterized as coming from "wealthy" farm families, and described themselves as "choosy" or "wanting something better;" two well-off sisters, of "better social standing" ruled out "many suitors." Again, while not necessarily representative, these farm daughters' reasons for refusing to become farm wives were precisely those which so troubled experts concerned about the next generation of rural inhabitants.

Contesting the Family Farm: *Mägde* and Masters in Prewar Saxony

Before turning to the specifics of individual cases, a brief synopsis of the sample, including some common patterns in these disputes and the ways in which they were handled by local and district officials, are worth noting. The case of Julie Reihsig that opened the chapter was one of three recorded by village officials in the district of Flöha in 1875, and the earliest among the 68 grievance petitions in the sample. Of the 68 cases under consideration, 49 occurred in the south-central Saxon district of Flöha, northeast of Chemnitz, and the remaining 19 from the more remote north-central district of Oschatz, roughly equidistant between Leipzig and Dresden. The last petitions were submitted in 1897. Of the 68 complaints, 47 were lodged by *Mägde* or their parents or guardians about their employers. The young women's ages were not often given; however, in the 16 instances where a father or, less frequently, a mother, signed the complaint, several of them were as young as 15. Seven young women were either pregnant or had an illegitimate child. By

---

[125]   Kempf, *Arbeits- und Lebensverhältnisse*, p. 132.
[126]   Kempf, *Arbeits- und Lebensverhältnisse*, p. 143.

far the most frequent grievance among *Mägde* was about their employers' refusal to return their reference books, and often their clothes, after they had run away or even if they had left with proper notice (27). An additional six disputed the references that they had been given and sought new ones because they alleged the originals were inaccurate, superficial, or untruthful.

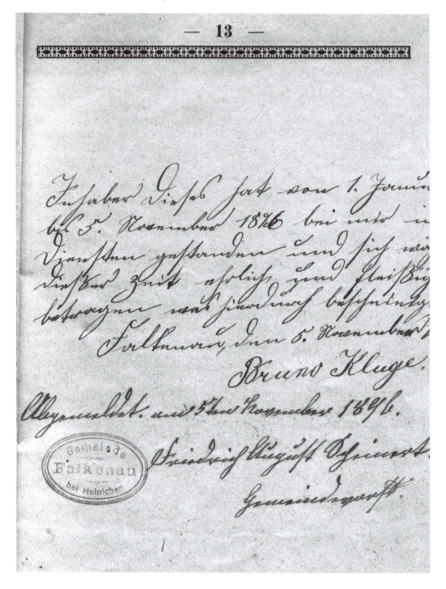

Figure 2.3 **"Employer's Reference, *c.* 1896" [Source: author's collection].**

Many of these complaints also cited their reasons for running away in the first place, most often because of alleged mistreatment like insults and beating (14); overwork (10); meager or inedible food (7); or sexual harassment (6). In the allegations of sexual harassment or "threatened morals," *Mägde*, or more usually their fathers, complained about harassment from either their employers or employers' sons, or a *Knecht*. Several grievances cited having to share a bed with another *Magd* who had nightly visits from a "boyfriend;" another came from a father who explained that his daughter was forced to work so hard that she had no time to attend church.

Of the 68 grievance petitions, 21 were lodged by employers against *Mägde*, the vast majority for running away without grounds, many "secretly," and either "of her own volition" or because a parent was preventing her return (16). Employers also asserted that girls often lied about their treatment or about medical conditions that made it impossible for them to fulfill their duties (8). Others complained of disobedient, rude, or lazy behavior (6), stealing or embezzlement (6), inciting other hired hands to leave (5), not appearing as promised after agreeing to a contract (3), and mistreating animals in their care (3). Finally, one employer complained of a *Magd's* heavy drinking and her application for a new reference book under false pretenses. Employers also occasionally lodged grievances against local magistrates, accusing them of less than zealous application of the *Gesindeordnungen*, or against another employer for luring a *Magd* away from her position before the original contract had ended.

The standard procedure for each case was a formal statement by the complainant recorded by the village *Gemeindevorstand*, and signed by both parties. The *Gemeindevorstand* then notified the district authorities in charge of ruling on these petitions about the case details, often adding his own commentary about what he believed the truth of the matter to be, asking specific questions about how to proceed, and often whether a particular paragraph of the *Gesindeordnungen* might be relevant to his decision about who was in the right (or wrong). Invariably the district official issued brief instructions about how the *Gemeindevorstand* should proceed, either by referring the matter to the *Gesindepolizei*, or more often by requesting that the *Gemeindevorstand* or the gendarme collect additional testimonies from both parties and/or from relevant witnesses. The *Gemeindevorstand* therefore mediated many of the testimonies submitted by *Mägde*, although most employers and occasionally one of the young women's fathers wrote their own petitions. Despite this, all but a few of the *Mägde* in question signed their names indicating that they had sworn to the version of events and to the content of the verbal exchanges presented by the local magistrate. With few exceptions, the complaints were resolved relatively quickly, in a matter of several days or sometimes weeks, although some of the petitions lack responses or are fragmentary, with no evidence of a resolution.

It is noteworthy that just over half the time, in 37 of 68 cases, *Mägde* succeeded in leaving their positions without a mark on their records; a handful could not be located. Another 19 might be considered inconclusive or ending in compromise, that is, instances where young women agreed to return to their masters if working conditions were improved or if a physical condition were accommodated. A few admitted to substantial wrongdoing, like stealing or embezzlement, and agreed to return to their masters in exchange for criminal charges being dropped. Of the remaining cases, only three served jail sentences for running away, another was sent home, and the rest were forced to return to their masters over their strong objections.

Another pattern in many of the cases was the clear social tension between the *Mägde* and their families and the young women's employers. Very often the *Magd* or a parent mentioned in their appeals to the authorities that they lacked means, or that the girls' futures would be jeopardized if the dispute were not resolved in their favor. Fathers often stated their professions in their requests for official assistance, including agricultural worker; miner (or mining invalid); artisan; and factory worker. These tensions often came to a head when the parents or parent went to see the employer about a dispute. They described being "put off," "sent away," or "treated coldly." In other instances the confrontations became violent or threatened to become violent, as with one father who repeatedly stressed to the authorities that he "had kept his temper," and "spoken humbly." One dispute that lasted for several months in 1878 arose because the employer refused to allow the *Magd,* Marie Arnold, to bring her 10-month-old illegitimate child with her and insisted instead that she leave the child with her mother and return alone.[127] Marie explained that her mother was ill, as verified by a doctor's certificate, and that her sister could not look after the child either since she had gone to work in a factory. After being turned away when she showed up a second time with the child, she eventually found agricultural day work with an employer who allowed her to bring the baby along. In this case the local magistrate sided with the *Magd,* to the outrage of her original employer, who accused her of "outrageous behavior" and "chicanery" since she had originally stated in her one-year contract that her mother would care for the child. The clearly contradictory expectations about work and working conditions that emerge in these grievances are certainly not surprising. More striking are the ways in which *Mägde* and their families contested how young women's grievances were handled by their employers and the authorities, and their appeals for justice despite their relative lack of power and means.

The reason most employers gave for withholding the *Dienstbuch* and often personal belongings was in order to force a *Magd* to return or as punishment, knowing full well that without her reference book she could not legally find another position. This was the case with one Emma Schubert.[128] In early 1880, the *Gemeindevorstand* in her home village of Grünhainchen wrote to the Flöha authorities that her employer in the village of Zschopau had reported to him that she had run away in early January and demanded that the local magistrate force her to return. The *Gemeindevorstand* continued that in response to his inquiry her

---

127   Case of Marie Arnold, begun July 12, 1878, AH Fl. 2506, SäHStA.

128   Case of Emma Franziska Schubert, begun January 4, 1880, AH Fl. 2506, SäHStA.

father, an "agricultural worker and householder," and his wife refused to allow their daughter to return to her position under any circumstances, alleging that her employer beat her for things "she did not do." He explained further that when her mother and sister went to the employer to see about the return of her *Dienstbuch* and personal belongings, he at first treated them "very coldly and told them that they had no business there." According to the mother, the encounter had escalated quickly thereafter with her "being thrown from one corner to the other" and the daughter becoming "very anxious that she would be hit [by the employer] for telling her parents about what was going on." A few days later Emma's brother, a furniture maker, appeared before the district magistrate in Flöha to defend his sister's allegations, reporting that she "was afraid if not for her life then for her health ... he [the employer] had threatened her with the whip and insulted her ... She wants her *Dienstbuch* back and a suitcase full of clothes."

In response, the employer testified to the local magistrate in Zschopau that Emma had in the last year mentioned to his wife that "she wanted to learn sewing and therefore wanted to leave service, but was firmly discouraged." He added that she made all kinds of mistakes and therefore that his wife had hit her once or twice "very casually." He further alleged that the testimony of her brother "was all lies and very insulting." He admitted to shouting at her mother, sister, and brother, and that he was "perhaps threatening" and "regretted disturbing the peace," but demanded that Emma be returned to his employ. A few days later, the Zschopau magistrate reported to the district authorities in Flöha that on closer questioning, Emma had admitted that she had not given proper notice according to Paragraph 55 of the *Gesindeordnungen* and that the mistreatment was not as bad as she had maintained. He therefore ordered her to return or face criminal charges. He added that her brother, apparently accompanying her, "who was not familiar with the relevant paragraph of the *Gesindeordnungen*," became so upset "that he had to be shown out." Emma's parents contested the ruling once more, but ultimately she was forced to return to her employer.

By 1895, however, district officials were warning employers that they could no longer withhold the reference book as a means of forcing a *Magd* to return after she had run away, no matter what her reasons. For example in April 1895, Maria Traglauer came to the local magistrate in Gönnsdorf and testified that she had worked for her employer since January but that "the work was too heavy" and so she had run away.[129] She testified that she had a problem with her uterus and at Easter had returned home to see a doctor who had "urgently advised her to avoid heavy work and to find another position. I reported this to my master and thereafter requested the return of my reference book." According to Maria, her employer and his wife refused and "threw her out of the courtyard." She added that she was "completely without means and without my reference book, I cannot find another, lighter job" and requested the magistrate's assistance in securing its return.

---

[129] Case of Maria Traglauer, begun April 30, 1895, AH Fl. 2507, SäHStA.

In response, Maria's employer testified that she had not reported her medical condition to him or his wife at the time of hiring and that another *Magd* who was no longer in his employ said it was a lie. He retorted that he had not thrown her out as she had alleged and that if she could not produce a doctor's certificate he would press criminal charges against her. The district official in Flöha wrote back and reminded the local magistrate that the employer no longer had the right to withhold the reference book as "a way to ease the filing of grievance charges" even if she did not have a medical certificate. He concluded:

> In any case, the contract must now be considered dissolved. Even if [Maria] T. left of her own volition and without legal grounds, we cannot at this point oversee her return by force according to Paragraph 96 of the revised *Gesindeordnung* of 2 May 1892, which states that the grievance has to be filed within one week if a position is left without grounds. In order to avoid a legal battle, we recommend that her things and her reference book be returned.[130]

A note made by the *Gemeindevorstand* in the margin of her original testimony noted that she had received her reference book and other belongings on May 7. Similarly, Emilie Arnold appeared before the local magistrate in the district of Oschatz in 1894 to complain that her master refused to return her *Dienstbuch*, even though she had given proper notice.[131] She added that she had run away because a *Knecht* had regularly entered her room at night, which she could not lock, "taken over her bed," and lit matches; furthermore, she had reported the problem to her master to no avail. In this case the district authority in Oschatz ordered her employer to return her reference book and insurance card within two days, warning that the law stated that he could no longer withhold these items, and that they were absolutely necessary in order for her to "get ahead." In subsequent cases, the district authority in Oschatz warned local magistrates ever more vehemently that the employer was not permitted to withhold the *Dienstbuch* under any circumstances and often requested a written confirmation from the *Gemeindevorstand* that the return had taken place properly.[132]

Like Maria Traglauer and Emilie Arnold, the cases of 11 other *Mägde* or their parents raised concerns about the return of the reference book as a means of ensuring future employment or "getting ahead," often referred to as "*Fortkommen*,"

---

[130]   Case of Maria Traglauer, District official in Flöha to Gemeindevorstand Eichler in Gönnsdorf, May 6, 1895, AH Fl. 2507, SäHStA.

[131]   Case of Emilie Arnold, begun May 22, 1894, AH Oschatz 1114, SSL, p. 24.

[132]   All from AH Oschatz 1114, "Gesindepolizeisachen betreffend," SSL; case of Ida Konrad, begun June 3, 1895, p. 46; case of Anna Zaspel, begun July 1, 1895, p. 55 folio; Ida Kastner, begun August 7, 1895, p. 67 folio; case of Maria Bain, begun February 23, 1896, p. 96; case of Linna Marschner, begun June 22, 1896, p. 116 folio; case of Wilhelmine Hering, begun April 4, 1897, p. 162 folio; case of Auguste Bernhardt, begun mid-May 1897, p. 175 folio.

whether as a *Magd* or elsewhere.[133] The testimonies where these worries emerged often acknowledged the young woman's wrongdoing, such as the case of 14-year-old Anna Herkner, who was accused of setting a fire out of homesickness (quickly extinguished), others admitted to embezzlement, harming the animals in her care, and even using the wrong pitchfork.[134] One *Magd*, Emma Windemann, lodged a complaint against her master because his reference was "superficial," with no mention of her honesty, and insisted that this would prevent her from "getting ahead."[135] The employer agreed to change the reference, but added that although she was honest, she was also "stubborn and disobedient."

One Anna Koehler lodged complaints against two different masters, in 1881 and again in 1884, both times expressing concern about her future prospects if the authorities did not come to her aid.[136] In the first case, she explained to the magistrate that she had left because her master had admonished her for using the wrong pitchfork, thereby harming an ox, which she said was untrue. According to her testimony, he then retorted "Either I'll box your ears or hunt you out of the courtyard," and since she "had endured enough boxing of her ears," and once before he had torn her jacket, she left. She added that he had refused to return her *Dienstbuch* and her back wages, and demanded that she find him another *Magd*. Since her parents were "without means," she pleaded that the magistrate assist her in the return of her reference book in order that she might "get ahead."

As in many of these disputes, Anna's employer gave a drastically different version of events, noting that his ox was still lame where she had injured him, that he had told her repeatedly not to use a particular pitchfork for cleaning out stalls, and finally that Anna had told the other maids, "He can do whatever he wants to me, but I'm going to use that pitchfork anyway." He admitted to threatening to chase her off his property and conceded that "this may be the reason that she secretly ran away," but that he had never withheld her reference book. He also admitted that he had boxed her ears a few times but had never torn her jacket, as she alleged. In this case the dispute was settled quickly and the reference book returned so that she could find other employment.

In Anna Koehler's second complaint, against a different employer in 1884, she appeared before the local magistrate and testified that she had left service "with the prior knowledge of her master because he treated her badly." However, now

---

[133] Kähler made just one reference to *Fortkommen*, whereby youth under 18 could enter into contracts as *Gesinde* without their parents' or guardians' permission "if by explicit or implicit consent of the same they were no longer living at home and therefore were forced to see to their own affairs [*Fortkommen*]." Kähler, *Gesindewesen*, p. 137.

[134] Setting a fire, case of Anna Rosalie Herkner, begun April 13, 1877, AH Fl. 2506; mistreating animals, case of Anna Laura Koehler aus Kleinwaltersdorf, 1881, AH Fl. 2506; embezzlement, case of Amalie Schiffner, 1877, AH Fl. 2506; case of Anna Laura Koehler aus Kleinwaltersdorf, 1884 AH Fl. 2507.

[135] Case of Emma Windemann, begun September 5, 1882, AH Fl. 2507, SäHStA.

[136] Case of Emma Franziska Schubert, begun January 4, 1880, AH Fl. 2506, SäHStA.

he was withholding her *Dienstbuch* and other things and in order that she might "get ahead," she requested the authorities' assistance in settling the matter. In this instance, her employer testified that he had not mistreated her and that she had only lodged a complaint in order to avoid charges of theft and embezzlement. He also refused to release her from service or to return her things unless he hired a new *Magd*. In the end, the *Gemeindevorstand* reported to the Flöha authorities that Anna had agreed to drop her complaint and return to her master if he dropped the charges against her, which both had done, resolving the dispute.

In cases where *Mägde* alleged that they had been overworked, the issue, as with Julie Reihsig, was usually that they felt they had been asked to perform tasks that were not part of the job description. In July 1883 Anna Seifert complained to the authorities in Flöha that she had been hired as a stall maid, but gave notice because the food was not enough to sustain her while doing such hard work.[137] She explained that her employer had refused to accept her notice, so she left anyway. Since her complaint had also been rebuffed by the local magistrate in the village of Plaue, she appealed directly to the district official to help with the return of her reference book. The official noted that in this case Anna was referring to Paragraphs 20, 90, and 98 about inadequate food, and that in general she had been poorly treated. He added that at present she could be found at her artisan father's house.

In this instance, both Anna Seifert and her employer appeared a few days later before the magistrate in Plaue, who reported that her employer insisted that he could not afford to let her go. She retorted that she was "too weak for all the work assigned to her," and that given how little food there was, she was afraid of becoming ill. The magistrate continued, "After a little negotiation she said she would return, and in response her master agreed that he would in the future respect her weak physical constitution, so that her fears of becoming sick were allayed." The statement was signed by both parties and the *Gemeindevorstand*.

Sometimes, however, these disputes about overwork and mistreatment were not resolved so peacefully. In 1892, "miner and homeowner" Schreiber wrote directly to the authorities in Flöha to report that his daughter Clara had complained to him frequently about being overworked, given very meager food, and permitted no time to mend her personal belongings.[138] He added, "As a father I am concerned about my daughter's weak physical state," noting that previously he had written her two letters about his concerns. However, after no reply, he suspected that the letters had been intercepted by the master's son. Finally, he had resolved to go and see her employer himself and "I asked him very politely to let her go after her notice was up." Schreiber explained that the employer said he would release Clara "only if I brought him another girl, and otherwise would refuse to consider it. I kept my temper and told him in a very humble way that this was impossible and that I would not let my daughter work there any longer." During this encounter the master's son appeared and grabbed Clara's arm, "raising his hand as if to strike

---

137   Case of Anna Seifert, begun July 2, 1883, AH Fl. 2507, SäHStA.

138   Case of Clara Schreiber, begun March 1, 1892, AH Fl. 2507, SäHStA.

her. I said she's my girl not yours," to which they had threatened to throw him out. Schreiber ended his appeal by repeating again that he had kept his temper and told the master that he and his daughter were leaving and would report his outrageous behavior to the authorities. In a long postscript, he informed the authorities that two more *Mägde* from Clara's employer had appeared suddenly at his house, "still in their work clothes and having walked there," saying that they could not stand to work there anymore. The girls complained that they had not been allowed to do laundry for a month and that when they asked for their other belongings they were threatened with beatings and ear boxing. Schreiber concluded, "It's no wonder if skin diseases and other contagious ills spread as a result."

In response to his appeal, the *Gemeindevorstand* reported to the authorities in Flöha that the employer's wife had explained that they kept the girls clothes locked up only to keep them from running away, but confided that "the place is known for bad treatment. The son mishandled the *Mägde* brutally and beat them." The magistrate also reported that the master had told him if he had known the two *Mägde* would run away secretly that "on the night in question he would have locked the gate so that they fell on their asses; this shows that basic human rights are not respected here." The *Gemeindevorstand* subsequently collected statements from the postman, who swore that he had delivered Schreiber's letters to the farm, and from a *Knecht*, who testified that conditions were bad and that he was leaving after a thrashing from the master's son. The records for Anna Schreiber's case end there, but one of the other *Mägde*, Emilie Ilbrig, nevertheless ended up being prosecuted for running away and spent three days in jail.[139]

Occasionally a complaint by a *Magd* would be refuted by other witnesses, as in the case of two sisters in 1896. Minna and Auguste Spiegel sought out the local magistrate and testified that their employer and his wife beat them and that "the food is terrible. We've found hair in the soup and the meat tastes like petroleum."[140] They appealed to the authorities to investigate these "awful conditions." The local magistrate subsequently reported to the authorities in Oschatz that, according to the testimonies of their employers and other servants, Auguste was an inveterate liar who behaved "intolerably toward the other servants. She always treated the livestock hurriedly and didn't milk the cows completely. Her sister Therese Minna … is reputed to be just as forward and disobedient and without a doubt was behind the idea of running away." The *Magd* responsible for the meals and others employed there insisted that no hair had ever been found in the soup and "if the meat tastes like petroleum it's because they hadn't washed their hands properly." In sum, everyone was "thoroughly delighted" that the girls had left.

---

[139]   Case of Emilie Ilbrig, begun March 21, 1892, AH Fl. 2507, SäHStA.

[140]   Case of Auguste and Minna Spiegel, AH Oschatz 1114, SSL, p. 100 folio.

Conclusion

Mägde who challenged established gender, generational, and labor relations in the German countryside attracted growing scrutiny from a variety of agricultural experts and social welfare reformers in the decades before the First World War. Especially after the turn of the century, as the rural-to-urban demographic shift continued unabated, Bindewald and others expressed concerns about the loyalty and the commitment of rural female youth to the ongoing prosperity of family farms. For them, young rural women had become dangerously autonomous and utterly selfish individuals who did not respect their proper places. Thus, by 1914 rural female youth from all social backgrounds, whether *Mägde* from impoverished rural families or the daughters of better-off farm families, had become a new social category in desperate need of reform and regulation. At the same time, very few of these observers mentioned the specter of overburdened and underappreciated farm wives as the reason that young rural women might search for alternative employment.

In framing the problem of rural female youth, the new social-scientific discourse used older models of rural social behavior, especially the submissive, industrious *Magd* idealized in the *Gesindeordnungen*, to critique the mobility and the aspirations of the prewar generation of young rural women. But this discourse also drew on new ideas about how to maintain the nation's biological and demographic health and its political stability. Nevertheless, Wilhelmine conservatives frequently contrasted the combative and costly battles between urban workers and industrial employers with a portrait of the countryside as unmarred by social tensions, anchored by the hard-working farm family and their loyal *Gesinde*. In this light, young rural women's movement away from agricultural work and the countryside appeared to threaten the delicate balance between agrarian and industrial interests promised by the steady intensification of family farm agriculture in the last few decades of the Kaiserreich. Farmers' associations added their complaints about the shortage of *Mägde* to the growing chorus of concern about rural female youth, and pressed state officials to punish all those who ran away more harshly.

Certainly the decline in the numbers of *Mägde* by the end of the nineteenth century suggests that many young rural women were ready to trade the long, unregulated hours, filthy conditions, and heavy physical labor required of them in all seasons and weather, as well as the constant supervision of either the farmer or his wife, for any other kind of work. Some of the remarks by *Mägde* and farm daughters certainly offered hints of growing dissatisfaction with their fates among rural female youth. Likewise the Saxon grievance cases offer especially compelling evidence of the ways in which young rural women publicly challenged rural social ideals and expert expectations in the prewar decades. With a few exceptions, these cases were not about young women's out-and-out rejection of agricultural work, but instead about their perceptions of fair treatment and their expectations of justice if their employers violated the rules as they understood them. Clearly families, especially fathers, often shaped young women's decisions to lodge a complaint, and in many instances their involvement amplified the confrontations between *Mägde* and their masters. The cases also reveal how hard local state officials worked to manage these contradictory claims and to negotiate solutions that satisfied both employers' and young women's demands, even if they did not often succeed. The gender, social, and generational tensions that permeated these disputes were not enough to disrupt German agriculture's golden age, but they do substantiate expert concerns about social fissures in the Wilhelmine countryside. These fissures would come yawning open after August 1914, when the battles over young women's agricultural labor, state officials' constant struggle to manage the food supply, and young women's willingness to take matters into their own hands escalated beyond all predictions.

Chapter 3
"Compelling Duty?":
The First World War and the Crisis of Rural Female Youth, 1914–1922

The First World War immediately and profoundly transformed labor relations in the German countryside. After its outbreak in August 1914, hordes of eager volunteers responded to last-minute appeals for help with the fall harvest, temporarily allaying worries about food shortages.[1] But in the ensuing months, civil officials, with the strong support of women's organizations, launched a formal campaign to mobilize farm women. This made sense not only because so many farmers had left for the front, but also because large estates could continue to rely on seasonal foreign workers now trapped within the nation's borders.[2] State authorities and agricultural experts proudly declared that German soldiers and urban consumers would have nothing to fear: farm women – young and old, hired and family – would dedicate their utmost to guarantee the nation's food supply. Moreover, the new patriotic rhetoric of cheerful self-sacrifice in the service of the collective national interest dampened any lingering concerns about female youth's defiance or the overburdening of farm wives.

But as everywhere else, spirits in the countryside had plummeted by Christmas as the prospect of a long war became reality. Even as plans to mobilize farm women expanded, it was clear that they would not be able to compensate for the shortages of male labor, horses, fuel, fertilizer, and other supplies necessary for the smooth running of agricultural enterprises. Meanwhile, the tightening of the Allied blockade made German farm women's contributions to the food supply doubly vital.[3] New job opportunities for rural youth in the war industries made matters even worse, and by the spring of 1915 the farmers who remained had begun to clamor for a strict ban on all agricultural workers' freedom of movement. In particular, they

---

[1] See for example Bruno Schöne, *Die sächsische Landwirtschaft. Ihre Entwickelung bis zum Jahre 1925* (Dresden: Verlag des Landeskulturrats Sachsen, 1925), p. 421.

[2] Avner Offer, *The First World War: An Agrarian Interpretation* (Oxford: Clarendon Press, 1989), p. 62.

[3] In general, see Offer, *First World War*; August Skalweit, 'The Maintenance of the Agricultural Labour Supply during the War', *International Review of Agricultural Economics* [hereafter *IRAE*] 12/12 (1922): 836–90; Jochen Oltmer, *Bäuerliche Ökonomie und Arbeitskräftepolitik im Ersten Weltkrieg* (Emsland, Bentheim: Verlag der Emsländischen Landschaft e.V., 1995), pp. 22–3.

warned of dire consequences for the food supply if young women continued to flee family farms for more lucrative jobs in munitions factories. Their grievances were supported by an array of social welfare experts, who asserted that the proposed ban was the only way to combat the "unbridled living-for-oneself" that now seemed to pervade the entire generation of rural youth, especially young women.[4]

Rapidly worsening material conditions on the home front during late 1915 and early 1916, punctuated by violent food riots in Germany's major cities, increased the pressure on state officials to intervene decisively in the agricultural labor market, culminating in the imposition of the so-called "exception laws" of April 1917.[5] Mirroring an emergency ban decreed in Bavaria two years earlier, the Prussian and Saxon Ordinances Concerning Labor Assistance in Agriculture and Forestry prohibited rural minors of either sex from accepting paid work outside the agricultural sector, and any male or female agricultural worker from changing jobs without official permission.[6] Of course, by this time coercive regulations were commonplace in many German industries and the most comprehensive of these, the Patriotic Auxiliary Service Law, had taken effect in December 1916.[7] Still, the agricultural ordinances were the only compulsory labor laws that included women as well as men, and represented a major victory for farmers and their supporters. In the context of a war for national survival, policymakers across the political spectrum had concluded that the use of force was the most expedient way to ensure that young women fulfilled their duties to German agriculture. But official and expert debates over the laws lingered, in large part because young women defied them with abandon, either by ignoring them altogether or by challenging state authorities directly over their right to work where they pleased.

---

[4]   *"schrankenloses sich Ausleben"*. Irmgard von Thering, 'Wie arbeiten wir durch ländliche Jugendpflege auf den Dörfern gegen die Landflucht?', in *Die Landfrauenarbeit im Kriege. Dreiundzwanzig Vorträge (2. Kriegslehrgang)* (Berlin: Deutsche Landbuchhandlung, 1916), pp. 211–16, here p. 211.

[5]   On wartime urban food shortages and riots see Belinda Davis, *Home Fires Burning: Food, Politics, and Everyday Life in World War I Berlin* (Chapel Hill: University of North Carolina Press, 2000).

[6]   'Verordnungen über Arbeitshilfe in der Land- und Forstwirtschaft', *Leipziger Zeitung* (April 1917); *Sächsischer Staatszeitung*, April 21, 1917, Ministerium des Innern [hereafter MdI] 15925, 'Verbot des Arbeitswechsels der landwirtschaftlichen Arbeiter und Dienstboten', Sächsisches Hauptstaatsarchiv Dresden [hereafter SäHStA], pp. 73, 78.

[7]   Ute Daniel, *The War from Within: German Working-Class Women in the First World War*, trans. Margaret Ries (Oxford: Berg, 1997), pp. 65–70; Gerhard Albrecht, 'Soziale Probleme und Sozialpolitik in Deutschland während des Weltkrieges', *Jahrbücher für Nationalökonomie und Statistik* 144 (1936): 96–107, 215–32; Gerald Feldman, *Army, Industry, and Labor in Germany, 1914–1918* (Princeton: Princeton University Press, 1966), pp. 173, 188, 197–249, 301–49; Günther Mai (ed.), *Arbeiterschaft in Deutschland 1914–1918: Studien zu Arbeitskampf und Arbeitsmarkt im Ersten Weltkrieg* (Düsseldorf: Droste Verlag, 1985), p. 17.

This chapter explores the explosive social conflicts ignited by the competing demands of agriculture and industry for young women's labor during and after the First World War, and the herculean dilemmas that confronted state authorities charged with maintaining order in the countryside. In particular, it traces young rural women's canny navigation of the tightening restrictions on their freedom of movement, and how vague prewar anxieties about rural female youth's rebelliousness were transformed into a full-blown gender crisis. Likewise, the bitter conviction shared by many observers that young women's resistance to agricultural work had fatally undermined the war effort persisted into the early years of postwar reconstruction. Thus, despite the repeal of the *Gesindeordnungen* and the wartime freedom-of-movement bans after the war ended in November 1918, Weimar officials reintroduced similar coercive measures just ten weeks later, yielding to farmers' outraged protestations that the shortage of *Mägde* was paralyzing agricultural enterprises.[8] If anything, however, the March 1919 ordinances met with even stiffer opposition from young women, inciting endless wrangling between farmers, agricultural experts, social welfare reformers, and Weimar officials over the proper remedy for the shortage.

Although the exact number of challenges to the laws is unknown, 49 petitions for exemption submitted by young women in Saxony between 1917 and 1921 reveal in detail how the circumstances of war and revolution multiplied existing social and gender tensions in the countryside. To their intense frustration, state authorities charged with the bans' enforcement came under fire both for upholding them and for granting exemptions. For while the petitions to leave agriculture were lawful, they highlighted young women's discontent with agricultural work and their "flaunting" of duties to community and nation in very public ways. Most importantly, like the grievance cases of previous decades, the petitions forced state officials to debate the ethics and practicalities of intervention into the minutiae of ordinary Germans' affairs, this time amid the seemingly endless turmoil of war and revolution. Moreover, the debate over the use of coercion as a means of controlling rural female youth persisted throughout the Weimar years, as did the panicked laments over young women's flight from farms to factories and its ominous implications for national stability. Indeed, for many observers, the gloomy predictions of prewar experts like Georg Bindewald had come nowhere close to describing the calamitous impact of young women's abandonment of family farms and the rebelliousness of those who remained.

Their petitions also make clear that even if young women's resistance to agricultural work was driven by their own desires and aspirations, these were rarely distinct from the pressing need to support parents, siblings, husbands, and sometimes children. Most of all, however, they objected not to a particular

---

[8]   Reichsgesetzblatt, March 19, 1919, Nr. 6764, 'Verordnung zur Behebung des Arbeitermangels in der Landwirtschaft vom. 16. März 1919', MdI 15925, SäHStA, p. 191; Elizabeth Bright Jones, 'The Gendering of the Postwar Agricultural Labor Shortage in Saxony, 1918–1925', *Central European History* 32/3 (Fall 1999): 311–29.

situation or employer, as was often the case before the war, but to the notion that their obligation to agricultural work was limitless. Many insisted that they had "already done their duties," and deeply resented the implication that they had not done enough. In this respect, the wartime encounters between young rural women and state officials over the terms of their mutual obligation are evidence not merely of coercion's failure, but of the need for other, more lasting remedies to the crisis of young women's rural flight.

Defining Duty: the Agricultural Labor Shortage and the Mobilization of Farm Women during the First World War

Recalling the war's impact on labor relations in German agriculture, one observer commented,

> We have no completely accurate statistics, but over half of all agricultural enterprises are being run by women, mostly with very little help from men … They have nevertheless succeeded, with energy and perseverance, to overcome these difficulties. The woman at the plow will remain the symbol of the war.[9]

A few years after the conflict ended, in 1922, economist August Skalweit estimated that approximately 64 percent of men had been withdrawn from the agricultural sector at one time or another.[10] But in August 1914, the widespread expectation that the war would end by Christmas together with the rush of citizens who volunteered to assist with the harvest briefly postponed anxieties about the food supply. As one Saxon agricultural expert later recounted,

---

[9]   Cited in Marie Elisabeth Lüders, *Das unbekannte Heer: Frauen kämpfen für Deutschland 1914–1918* (Berlin: Verlag von E. S. Mittler, 1936), p. 126, fn. 1.

[10]   Skalweit carefully explained how he arrived at the national estimate in 'Maintenance', pp. 850–2. Achter estimated that 70 percent of Bavarian family farms had one or more men at the front. Franz Achter, 'Die Einwirkung des Krieges auf die bäuerliche Wirtschaft in Bayern' (Dissertation, München: 1920), p. 53. Historians' estimates vary by region. Bessel cites a contemporary Karlsruhe source that reported roughly 89 percent of the farms there were being run by women. Richard Bessel, 'Mobilizing German Society for War', in Roger Chickering and Stig Förster (eds), *Great War, Total War: Combat and Mobilization on the Western Front, 1914–1918* (Cambridge: Cambridge University Press, 2000), pp. 437–51. For the Rhineland and Westphalia, Moeller gives an estimate of 23–50 percent. Robert Moeller, *German Peasants and Agrarian Politics, 1914–1924: The Rhineland and Westphalia* (Chapel Hill: University of North Carolina, 1986), pp. 47, 442. For Schleswig-Holstein, Tillmann estimates that 45 percent of male labor was withdrawn. Doris Tillmann, *Der Landfrauenberuf: Bäuerliche Arbeit, Bildungsstätten und Berufsorganisationen der Landfrauen in Schleswig-Holstein 1900–1933* (Neumünster: Wachholtz Verlag, 1997), p. 97.

The call for volunteers met with unanticipated success. Volunteers from every age group and every profession streamed into application offices so that in no time we had 14,000 people available. Of those, only 350 were used ... The Central Labor Exchange left no stone unturned trying to place the remaining volunteers in other parts of Germany. They had no success. The need for [agricultural] workers was met everywhere.[11]

By the following spring, however, reports of agricultural labor shortages were widespread across Germany and the outlook for spring planting was gloomy.[12]

All agricultural enterprises suffered from wartime labor shortages, but not equally; at least some large family farms and estates retained Polish seasonal workers. Larger enterprises were also in a better position to use prisoners-of-war, who most often were assigned to work in teams that required constant supervision.[13] Thus, as Robert Moeller has emphasized, the labor shortage on small and medium-sized family farms was especially acute.[14] In 1915, the War Ministry in Berlin began granting temporary exemptions to rural recruits during planting and harvest time, and one year later mandated the use of schoolchildren, war orphans, and dissolved border units for the same purpose.[15] By the fall of 1917, the national War Labor Office even entertained the idea of importing "coolies" from China.[16] In Saxony, estate owners pressed immediately and successfully to prohibit the departure of imported Polish workers between the ages of 17 and 45.[17] Just before the war ended, the number of prisoners-of-war working in Saxon agriculture

---

[11]   Schöne, *Die sächsische Landwirtschaft*, p. 421.

[12]   For Saxony see Landeskulturrat [hereafter LKR] an das königliche Ministerium des Innern [hereafter MdI], February 15, 1915; MdI 16599, 'Arbeiter und Hilfskräfte für die Landwirtschaft', SäHStA, p. 8. In general see Hans Fuhrmann, *Die Versorgung der deutschen Landwirtschaft mit Arbeitskräften im Weltkriege* (Würzburg: Verlag wissenschaftlicher Werke Konrad Triltsch, 1937), pp. 12–13.

[13]   Ernst v. Wrisberg, *Heer und Heimat, 1914–1918* (Leipzig: Koehler Verlag, 1921), p. 102; Friedrich Aereboe, *Der Einfluß des Krieges auf die landwirtschaftliche Produktion in Deutschland* (Stuttgart: Deutsche Verlags-Anstalt, 1927), pp. 33–4. See also Skalweit, 'Maintenance', pp. 868–75; Richard Bessel, *Germany after the First World War* (Oxford: Clarendon Press, 1993), pp. 22–3.

[14]   Moeller, *German Peasants*, p. 47.

[15]   Wrisberg, *Heer und Heimat*, pp. 108, 211–13. On foreign workers and prisoners-of-war in agriculture see also Jürgen Rund, *Ernährungswirtschaft und Zwangsarbeit im Raum Hannover 1914 bis 1923* (Hannover: Hahnsche Buchhandlung, 1992), pp. 219–97.

[16]   Königliches Sächsisches Kriegswirtschaftsamt, 'Rundschreiben', Dresden, September 19, 1917, MdI 15849, 'Arbeitsverhältnisse bei der Landwirtschaft', SäHStA, pp. 35–7. On Wilhelmine proposals, all eventually rejected, to import African and Chinese labor to Germany see Arnulf Huegel, *Kriegsernährungswirtschaft Deutschlands während des Ersten und Zweiten Weltkrieges im Vergleich* (Konstanz: Hartung-Gorre Verlag, 2003), p. 44.

[17]   Skalweit, 'Maintenance', pp. 852–68. For Saxony see Schöne, *Die Sächsische Landwirtschaft*, p. 422.

numbered approximately 22,000. The Saxon Interior Ministry provided subsidies for their wages, food, and lodging, as well as for guards to oversee them.[18]

The ongoing search for stop-gap remedies to the wartime agricultural labor shortage did not prevent authorities from recognizing that much more needed to be done. From the start it was clear to state officials, agricultural experts, and women's groups that women were not only the most numerous, but also the most important of the nation's agricultural workers, and unleashing their productive and patriotic energies became a top priority. Richard Bessel's recent observation that "success, if it was to come, rested on mobilizing a society that was predominantly female" was nowhere more true than in the countryside.[19] Of course, the campaigns to maximize farm women's contributions to the war effort were part of broader initiatives to manage the huge disruptions to the labor market caused by male workers' sudden departure, the slowdown in the production of consumer goods, and the rising demand for munitions and war materiel.[20] But while widespread ambivalence about women's factory work greatly complicated the task of recruiting them to work in mining and heavy industry, the mobilization of farm women appeared to be a far more straightforward matter, at least initially.[21]

The assumption that rallying farm women for the war effort would not disrupt established economic, social, and political structures was based in part on the knowledge that many women had been hard at work on the land for decades.[22] Commenting on the agricultural labor crisis after the war, political economist Friedrich Aereboe noted that women on small and medium-sized family farms were "already familiar with the various details [of production]" and furthermore were "invested in the preservation and in the continued output of the enterprise."[23]

---

[18]   LKR an das MdI, Dresden, April 18, 1918, MdI 15849, SäHStA, p. 68; Schöne, *Die Sächsische Landwirtschaft*, pp. 422–3. In 1917 just over half (11,042) were Russians, followed by French (5,456) and Serbs (2,366).

[19]   Bessel, 'Mobilizing German Society', p. 447.

[20]   On German mobilization campaigns during 1914 see Roger Chickering, *Imperial Germany and the Great War, 1914–1918* (Cambridge: Cambridge University Press, 1998), p. 16. Horne describes "self-mobilization" among European combatants as citizens' often enthusiastic participation in state-led mobilization campaigns, especially during the war's first two years. See John Horne, 'Mobilizing for "Total War", 1914–1918', in John Horne (ed.), *State, Society and Mobilization in Europe during the First World War* (Cambridge: Cambridge University Press, 1997), p. 4.

[21]   On Germany's piecemeal approach to economic mobilization during the war see Gerald Feldman, *The Great Disorder: Politics, Economics, and Society in the German Inflation* (New York: Oxford University Press, 1997), p. 55.

[22]   von Delbrück argued that mobilization's primary goal was minimal economic disruption in order to ensure a swift return to the status quo ante bellum. Clements von Delbrück, *Die wirtschaftliche Mobilmachung in Deutschland 1914. Aus dem Nachlaß herausgegebenen, eingeleitet und ergänzt von Joachim von Delbrück* (München: Verlag für Kulturpolitik, 1924), p. 117.

[23]   Aereboe, *Einfluß*, pp. 34–5.

The director of the Committee for Women's War Work [*Frauenarbeitszentrale*] Marie-Elisabeth Lüders concurred, pointing out that "Farm women had no time to ponder ... The farm woman was burdened with work from the first hours of the war ... double and triple the labor was expected from these women, more than from any other."[24]

Other observers were just as adulatory, but also acknowledged the tremendous physical and psychological costs to women of maintaining family farms under such difficult conditions. Agricultural economist Hans Fuhrmann conceded that family farms' survival during the war depended on women's extra work: "Even though women on small and medium-sized family farms were already doing the lion's share of the work, the man's labor was still essential for the orderly management of the enterprise ... nevertheless the labor contract on family farms seems to have proven itself more resilient [than that on large enterprises] for managing the war's agricultural labor demands."[25] Similarly, political economist Franz Achter recalled that "Those who were left in the countryside saw their workloads double, especially women and family dependents as well as non-family labor. Here working hours had no limits, like in industry; if one worked 10 or 12 hours before, now it was 14 or 16 hours in order to manage the extra work."[26]

In contrast, state efforts to recruit women to work in war industries began in earnest only in the fall of 1916, when the introduction of the Hindenburg program made their labor in munitions, chemicals, and metals appear indispensable.[27] Indeed, as before the war, organizers frequently touted the health and moral

---

[24]   Lüders, *unbekannte Heer*, p. 34. The wartime recasting of women's agricultural work as vital to the national interest was not unique to Germany. For France see Anon., 'Women and Farm Labour', *IRAE* LXX/10 (October 1916): 115–18. For Britain see Anon., 'Women Workers on the Farm', *IRAE* 8/4 (April 1917): 106–8. For Italy see Anon. ("G. C."), 'Measures adopted during the War to Maintain the Supply of Agricultural Labour', *IRAE* 13/3 (May 1922): 337–66, esp. pp. 360–1. See also Margaret H. Darrow, *French Women and the First World War: War Stories of the Home Front* (Oxford: Berg, 2000), pp. 178–90. For Russia see Peter Gatrell, *Russia's First World War: A Social and Economic History* (Harlow, England: Pearson Longman, 2005), p. 73.

[25]   Fuhrmann, *Versorgung*, p. 39.

[26]   Achter, 'Einwirkung', p. 44.

[27]   See Kriegsministerium Berlin, 'Anlage a zu Anlage 1 der Richtlinien für die K. W. A. und K. W. St.', January 3, 1917, MdI 16614, 'Verpflichtung von Landarbeitern im Krieg: Kriegszustand', SäHStA. See also Walter Chemnitz, *Frauenarbeit im Kriege* (Berlin: Verlag von Emil Ebering, 1926), pp. 19, 28–54; Ute Daniel, 'Women's Work in Industry and Family: Germany, 1914–1918', in Richard Wall and Jay Winter (eds), *The Upheaval of War: Family, Work and Welfare in Europe, 1914–1918* (Cambridge: Cambridge University Press, 1988), pp. 267–96, esp. pp. 278–81; Susanna Dammer, *Mütterlichkeit und Frauendienstpflicht: Versuche der Vergesellschaftung 'weiblicher Fähigkeiten' durch eine Dienstverpflichtung (Deutschland 1890–1918)* (Weinheim: Deutscher Studienverlag, 1998), esp. ch. 7; Matthew Stibbe, 'Anti-Feminism, Nationalism and the German Right, 1914–1920: A Reappraisal', *German History* 20/2 (2002): 185–210, esp. pp. 193–8.

benefits of agricultural work for women as opposed to the dangerous and unhealthy conditions in factories. Moreover, although many experts now acknowledged farm women's overburdening, such concerns were brushed aside by the grim reality that as a result of the Allied blockade, consumers were now more reliant than ever on domestically-produced food supplies. Under the circumstances, then, agricultural experts and state officials approached the task of increasing and "improving" women's labor on family farms with determined optimism.

In the introduction to his 1915 manual entitled *War Work in the Countryside*, prominent rural social welfare expert Heinrich Sohnrey outlined the new thinking about farm women's expanded role in the German political economy as a result of the war:

> Above all it is essential that we fulfill our responsibilities in the arenas of *agriculture and household* so that victory is guaranteed. Agricultural and household management are, more than ever, no longer purely private economic matters, but instead are of the utmost importance for preserving the nation's well-being ... The duties of maintaining rural social welfare fall first and foremost on women, many of whom also bear the whole burden of work that used to be shared with men.[28]

Sohnrey's insistence on the links between production, reproduction, and consumption in rural households and his claim that women's proper management of all these spheres was the key to victory marked a dramatic shift in the Wilhelmine discourse about family farms.[29] From this perspective, farm women were no longer invisible dependents subject only to the authority of the household head and whose labor (merely) complemented his. Instead, Sohnrey and his colleagues had designated farm women as vital stewards of Germany's wartime mobilization, both as agricultural workers and as preservers of domestic morale.[30] His counterpart Ernst von Strebel announced the heightened expectations of farm women in more melodramatic terms: "How will things go this spring when most estate owners, leasers, farmers, and farm hands [*Knechte*] are at the front? It will be difficult ... but the primary burden will fall on the already busy wives and daughters of small and medium-sized farmers ... they will preserve the hearth and

---

[28]   Heinrich Sohnrey, *Kriegsarbeit auf dem Lande. Wegweiser für ländliche Wohlfahrts- und Heimatpflege in Kriegszeit* (Berlin: Deutsche Landbuchshandlung, 1915), p. 6. Emphasis in original.

[29]   See also Tillmann, *Landfrauenberuf*, pp. 102–12. Of course, the wartime emphasis on thrifty household consumption extended to all housewives. See Willi Wygodzinski, *Die Hausfrau und die Volkswirtschaft* (Tübingen: J. C. B. Mohr, 1916).

[30]   Doris Tillmann, *Früh aufstehen, arbeiten und sparen: Landfrauenleben zwischen 1900 und 1933* (Heide: Boyens & Co., 1997), p. 69.

at the same time plant the soil. Honor these brave German women!"[31] Yet despite its laudatory tone, this discourse also made it clear that it was up to agricultural experts, social welfare reformers, and state officials to ensure that farm women understood and fulfilled their new national duties.

Figure 3.1   **"Women with Agricultural Machines during World War I" [Source: Marie-Elisabeth Lüders, *Das unbekannte Heer. Frauen kämpfen für Deutschland 1914–1918* (Berlin: E. S. Mittler, 1936), p. 128].**

Of course, wives and daughters were not the only ones responsible for maintaining family farms. Above all, Sohnrey sternly cautioned *Mägde* that "now was not the time to make unreasonable demands on employers or to take advantage of the situation" and outlined various strategies for reducing conflicts over work and boosting rural inhabitants' patriotic spirit more generally.[32] These included the distribution of educational fliers and posters, training traveling social welfare reformers, and regular village "war evenings" where the latest regulations and advice about agricultural production could be discussed and which all rural inhabitants were encouraged, or even required, to attend.[33] In many respects, then,

---

[31]   Ernst von Strebel, *Der Krieg und die deutsche Landwirtschaft* (Stuttgart: Eugen Ulmer, 1915), p. 24.

[32]   Sohnrey, *Kriegsarbeit*, p. 34.

[33]   Sohnrey, *Kriegsarbeit*, pp. 87–91.

War Work in the Countryside advocated (and itself epitomized) official efforts during the war's first two years to "frame the process of persuasion in highly directive ways."[34]

The exhortations of Sohnrey and his colleagues did not go unheeded: farm women, or *"Landfrauen,"* became the targets of a broad mobilization campaign that included local and national conferences, traveling exhibits, posters and pamphlets, professional manuals, newspaper articles, and a flood of expert literature.[35] Indeed, the frequent use of the term *"Landfrau,"* as opposed to more specific ones like *"Bäuerin"* (farm wife) or *Magd*, clearly signaled that the new expectations applied to *all* women working in agriculture, young and old, hired and family. Most of this propaganda combined practical guidance about crop cultivation and farm management with fervent affirmations of the nation's new dependence on women's agricultural labor. Under the supervision and sponsorship of state authorities, numerous private women's organizations enthusiastically took up the mission of educating traveling agricultural instructors, rural social welfare reformers, and farm wives and daughters about "the special challenges posed by the war to the economic situation and to the general management of rural households."[36] Fuhrmann described the campaigns as gradual at first, "but eventually [they] assumed such tremendous importance that civil and military authorities moved from giving [them] direction to a deliberate consideration [of all their facets]. No other issue inspired such close collaboration."[37]

The most prominent initiative was a yearly conference on farm women's work convened in Berlin between 1915 and 1917 and attended by women from all regions of rural Germany. At the first "War Instruction Course" in January 1915, the participants numbered about 650, including 192 professional rural social welfare experts and 458 civilians, almost all of them women.[38] Warmly welcomed

---

[34]   Horne, 'Introduction', in Horne, *State, Society and Mobilization*, p. 5.

[35]   Fuhrmann, *Versorgung*, p. 42.

[36]   *Zur Erinnerung an den Kriegs-Lehrgang für landwirtschaftliche Haushaltungs-und Wanderlehrerinnen und für Hausfrauen und Töchter auf dem Lande mit Unterstützung des Herrn Landwirtschaftsminister Dr. Freiherr von Schorlemer-Leiser von Montag den 18. bis Sonnabend den 23. Januar 1915*, Berlin, Abgeordnetenhaus [hereafter *Kriegs-Lehrgang* 1915]. Organizers included the landwirtschaftlicher Hausfrauenverein; Evangelischer Frauenbund; Vaterländischer Frauenverein; Deutscher Landpflege-Verband; Ständiger Ausschuß zur Förderung der Arbeiterinnen-Interessen; Evangelischer Verband zur Pflege der weiblichen Jugend; Verband zur Hebung der hauswirtschaftlichen Frauenbildung; and the Centralstelle für Volkswohlfahrt Weibliche Jugendpflege. See also Helene Albers, *Zwischen Hof, Haushalt und Familie: Bäuerinnen in Westfalen-Lippe (1920–1960)* (Paderborn: Ferdinand Schöningh, 2001), pp. 247–50; Christina Schwarz, *Die Landfrauenbewegung in Deutschland. Zur Geschichte einer Frauenorganisation unter besonderer Berücksichtigung der Jahre 1898 bis 1933* (Mainz: Gesellschaft für Volkskunde in Rheinland-Pfalz e. V., 1990), pp. 72–4, 204–9.

[37]   Fuhrmann, *Versorgung*, p. 41.

[38]   *Kriegs-Lehrgang* 1915, p. 56.

by national Agricultural Minister von Schorlemer-Leiser, they spent the next five days listening to advice about the basics of farm management, especially decisions about cultivation; how to navigate the complex and ever-changing regulations of the controlled economy; and other practical matters like renewing hail and fire insurance. Presenters also repeatedly stressed farm women's key role in bolstering morale on the home front and praised their constant hard work and cheerful self-sacrifice. Thus, early campaigns to mobilize farm women constantly reminded them that their actions and attitudes were under close expert and official scrutiny, and also reassured them that their productive and patriotic contributions to the nation were widely appreciated.

At the same time, the wartime construction of the ideal *Landfrau* also underscored the fact that not all farm women were devoting their utmost to the national cause.[39] For example, some observers had begun to chide farm wives for withholding food from state authorities, participating in the black market, and complaining of war weariness or the demands of urban consumers.[40] As social reformer Fritz Cassel sharply reminded them in a 1917 speech, "You, farm women, are responsible not merely for your own pantry but for the nation's pantry, your nation's pantry ... do you understand that? ... You are the nourishers ... of the whole nation; therefore hand over all the provisions that you do not immediately need."[41]

The new combination of urgent appeals to farm women's patriotism and the thinly-veiled criticism of their misplaced priorities was exemplified by a slideshow produced in the same year by the Image and Film Office in Berlin, part of a short-lived initiative to persuade women who had left family farms to work in the war industries to return to the countryside.[42] The War Ministry sent 131 copies of "Women's Agricultural Work " to officials as far west as Strasbourg and as far east as Vienna.[43] The accompanying text repeatedly emphasized how healthy and satisfying farm work was for women, and maintained that those who now worked in munitions factories "look back to the land with silent envy and secret regret."[44]

---

[39]   This did not mean the end of state-led initiatives to mobilize farm women. The *Zentrale der deutschen Landfrau* was founded in November 1917. See Annie Juliane Richert, 'Die "Zentrale der deutschen Landfrauen" und ihre Aufgaben', *Land und Frau* 1/32 (10 November 1917): 249–50, here p. 249. See also Fuhrmann, *Versorgung*, p. 41.

[40]   Darrow argues that the same shift occurred in France: "In 1914, the French peasant woman was a war heroine; by 1917 she was a potential deserter." Darrow, *French Women*, p. 180.

[41]   Fritz Cassel, *Die Landfrau im Weltkriege*, vol. 2 in series *Im Dienste der Zeit* (Straßburg i. Els.: Straßburger Druckerei und Verlagsanstalt, 1917), p. 8.

[42]   For details of the initiative '*Frauen aufs Land*' see Huegel, *Kriegsernährungs-wirtschaft*, pp. 195–6; Oltmer, *Bäuerliche Ökonomie*, pp. 248–61.

[43]   Kriegsministerium Berlin, betrifft: Werbearbeit für Gewinnung weiblicher Arbeitskräfte für die Landwirtschaft, June 16, 1917, MdI 15849, SäHStA, p. 29.

[44]   Vortragstext Landwirtschaft, 'Frauenarbeit auf dem Lande' [hereafter 'Frauenarbeit auf dem Lande'] MdI 15849, SäHStA, p. 31 folio, p. 4.

Meanwhile, the wartime agricultural labor shortage was ascribed to farm women's "striving for social and cultural improvement, to get ahead, to take their places in the so-called better circles of society," and their desire for "a freer, more personal development."[45]

Rural Female Youth and the Debate over Coercion, 1915–1917

Sohnrey's early warning to young rural women not to take advantage of the situation fell on deaf ears. Indeed, the wartime anxieties about farm women in general paled in comparison to the panicked laments over rural female youth, whose attitudes, actions, and priorities became the subject of heated debate. Not surprisingly, farmers were the first to complain about young women's increased mobility and to call for a strict ban on *all* agricultural labor's freedom of movement. In March 1915, farmer Böhme in the Saxon village of Kleinopitz wrote to the Interior Ministry to report that:

> Recently a certain restlessness among young workers has become apparent, causing many to abandon their positions. Since victory is predicated on maintaining the general population's food supply, farmers must be empowered to meet their obligations ... Therefore the undersigned is requesting that the so-called freedom-of-movement restrictions be tightened by prohibiting workers from leaving their positions without permission. It should also be forbidden for them to leave the agricultural sector ... The matter is urgent! This is no time to be doctrinaire.[46]

In the same week, another farmer, this time from a village near the Bavarian border, wrote to the Deputy Commanding General in Leipzig to inform him that "Keeping hired hands at their work has become a terrible plague and spring planting will be severely endangered if people continue to leave."[47] He also enclosed clippings from two newspapers about a decree by the Deputy Commanding General in Bavaria that prohibited all hired hands from leaving their positions until the fall harvest ended and politely requested a similar ordinance for Saxony.[48] A few

---

[45] 'Frauenarbeit auf dem Lande', MdI 15849, SäHStA, p. 31 folio, p. 3.

[46] K. Böhme an das Kgl. MdI, March 27, 1915, MdI 15925, SäHStA, p. 4.

[47] M. Schuster-Stengel an das stellvertr. Königl. Generalkommando des 19. Armeekorps, March 26, 1915, MdI 15925, SäHStA, p. 7.

[48] Stellvertretende Generalkommando III. Armeekorps, Betreff: Sicherung der Frühjahrsbestellung, Nürnberg, March 19, 1915, MdI 15925, SäHStA, p. 26. See also the bitter exchanges over the law in the press between the local unions and the Bavarian Interior, Justice, and War Ministries. 'Der Dienstbotenerlaß in Bayern', *Münchener Post* no. 91, April 20, 1915, MdI 15925, SäHStA, p. 12; 'Zum Dienstbotenerlaß in Bayern', *Münchener Post* no. 92, April 21, 1915, MdI 15925, SäHStA, p. 13.

weeks later, both the Saxon Agricultural Chamber, or *Landeskulturrat*, and the German Agricultural Council [*Deutscher Landwirtschaftsrat*] in Berlin expressed their warm support for the Bavarian restrictions.[49]

In contrast, the Bavarian decree created considerable consternation among Saxon and Prussian civil authorities. However, those who opposed compulsion did so not because they disagreed with the principle that young rural women belonged on family farms or that their flight from the countryside threatened national security. Instead their misgivings were both political and eminently practical, and the two were closely linked. Reacting to the news, the Saxon Interior, War, and Justice Ministries expressed deep uneasiness about the prospect of turning over the regulation of the agricultural labor market to military authorities.[50] In their view, such a move would send a clear signal to the public that state officials had failed to manage the agricultural labor crisis. In a memo to the Deputy Commanding Generals in Leipzig and Dresden, the Saxon Interior Ministry observed sharply that "placing the regulation of agricultural labor contracts under the coercive authority of the military is far more apt to stir up mistrust and to discourage people from accepting agricultural work in the first place ... this is especially likely to be the case in the Kingdom of Saxony."[51]

Civil officials in Berlin were equally concerned about the precedent set in Bavaria. In a secret communication to military authorities in September 1915, the Prussian War Minister advised them to proceed cautiously, because such a move might "quickly awaken fears among workers that they are being repressed [and] ... prepare the ground for undesirable agitation."[52] Indeed, left-leaning political representatives in the Bavarian *Landtag* already had voiced staunch opposition to "what amounts to a grave restriction on agricultural workers' and hired hands' freedom of movement."[53] Later that year, a *Reichstag* commission headed by moderate socialists Eduard David and Friedrich Ebert proposed a law

---

[49] LKR an das Königliche MdI, April 14, 1915, MdI 15925, SäHStA, p. 8; Antrag des Deutschen Landwirtschaftsrats an das Königl. Sächsische MdI, June 5, 1915, MdI 15925, SäHStA, p. 22.

[50] On the wartime bureaucratic "maze" see Chickering, *Imperial Germany*, pp. 32–5. Significantly, only Bavaria had a law that mandated cooperation between the Commanding General and the War Minister, who was a civilian official. See Feldman, *Army*, p. 32.

[51] MdI an das stellvertretende Generalkommando des XII. Armeekorps Dresden, August 16, 1915, MdI 15925, SäHStA, p. 50.

[52] Kriegsministerium an sämtliche Königliche stellvertretenden Generalkommandos, sämtliche Kaiserlichen und Königlichen Gouvernements und Kommandaturen im Inlande und das Königliche Oberkommando in den Marken; an das Königliche Sächsische Kriegsministerium zu Dresden, Berlin, September 10, 1915, MdI 15925, SäHStA, p. 53.

[53] 'Der Dienstbotenerlaß in Bayern', *Münchener Post* no. 91, April 20, 1915, MdI 15925, SäHStA, p. 12.

guaranteeing the right of agricultural workers and *Gesinde* to give notice.[54] Even more worrisome was the prospect of overseeing the ban's judicious enforcement even as their authority waned, and endless debate arose over whether the proposed restrictions on rural labor's freedom of movement would supersede existing law or not, and how that would complicate the forcible return or punishment of runaway hired hands.[55]

While over the course of 1916 civil officials in Saxony and Prussia successfully deflected pressure to enact a law similar to the Bavarian measure, farmers' complaints about the labor shortage grew increasingly loud. Moreover, they were now more likely to single out young women as the source of the crisis. For example, in July farmers in the Saxon district of Kamenz informed the Interior Ministry that adolescent workers were earning up to 90 Marks weekly in local munitions factories and that "a certain element among them are reportedly spending those wages on completely unseemly things."[56] By the following year, farmers in both Kamenz and Großenhain districts reported that knowledge of the high wages young women were earning in local munitions factories was making their female workers "disobedient" and deterring young women from accepting agricultural work in the first place.[57] The Kamenz report also expressed concern that such high industrial wages would disrupt the postwar agricultural labor market. Moreover, farmers not only blamed heavy industry for the worsening shortage of female hired labor. In a raucous February 1917 meeting, Dresden district farmers singled out the local artificial flower industry for stealing their female agricultural workers and demanded that young rural women be prohibited from accepting such work between April 1 and the end of October.[58]

Local officials like the magistrate in the Saxon village of Erdmannsdorf often agreed with farmers that young rural women were becoming increasingly disruptive. In May 1916 he reported to his superiors in Flöha that "Recently many

---

[54]   Beilage 1137, Antrag submitted by Gentner et al., Kammer der Abgeordneten, XXXVI Landtagsversammlung, Munich, September 20, 1915, MdI 15925, SäHStA, p. 55; Nr. 160 und 161, Reichstag, 13. Legislatur-Periode II. Session 1914/15, Gesetzentwurf betreffend Landarbeiter und Gesinde submitted by Ebert et al., Berlin, December 7, 1915, MdI 15925, SäHStA, p. 56.

[55]   Abschrift des stellvertr. Generalkommando XII. an das MdI, Dresden, June 2, 1915, MdI 15925, SäHStA, p. 40; MdI an das Justizministerium, Dresden, August 6, 1915, MdI 15925, SäHStA, p. 43.

[56]   AH Kamenz an das königliche MdI, July 17, 1916, MdI 15849, SäHStA, p. 9.

[57]   AH Großenhain an das königliche Kriegsministerium zu Dresden, April 20, 1917, MdI 15849, SäHStA, p. 47; der Vorsitzende der Kriegswirtschaftsstelle Kamenz an das Kriegswirtschaftsamt Dresden, April 14, 1917, MdI 15849, SäHStA, p. 49.

[58]   AH Dresden-Neustadt an die königliche KH Dresden, February 12, 1917, MdI 15849, p. 16. The Saxon Interior Ministry decided that there was not enough of a problem to pass such an ordinance. See KH Dresden an das MdI, February 27, 1917, MdI 15849, SäHStA, p. 15.

of us have found it completely unacceptable that young people under 18 years old, *especially girls from better circles*, have been roaming around the streets after 9:00 at night without chaperones. It would be appreciated if you would repeat the announcement of the ordinance forbidding such behavior."[59] A month earlier, echoing a report from the Hessian district of Kassel, many Saxon newspapers had printed a story pleading with youth in rural districts not to waste the high wages they were earning in munitions on "frivolities;" instead, rural youth were urged to rein in their spending and to help out their parents.[60]

Echoing their urban counterparts, rural social welfare reformers and a wide array of experts on women's work also decried the growing unruliness of rural female youth, and linked the problems they observed to the broader social and moral upheavals of the war.[61] In general they stressed that young rural women were uniquely ill-equipped to manage the tension *all* women were experiencing between their collective duty to the nation and their individual aspirations.[62] While they reproached young rural women for flaunting patriotic appeals to remain in agriculture, they also blamed themselves and German society more generally for ignoring what they described as rural girls' profound social, moral, and educational

---

[59]   Gemeindevorstand [hereafter GV] in Erdmannsdorf an die königliche AH in Flöha [hereafter Fl.], May 25, 1916, AH Fl. 2431, 'Maßnahmen gegen die Jugendlichen', SäHStA, p. 30. Emphasis mine.

[60]   'An die Tageszeitungen des Bezirks zur gefälligen Aufnahme in redaktionellen Teile', n.d., AH Fl. 2507, SäHStA, p. 19. Story reprinted in *Leipziger Zeitung* no. 82, April 4, 1916, AH Fl. 2507, no page number.

[61]   On social welfare reformers' worries about young urban workers see Elizabeth Harvey, *Youth and the Welfare State in Weimar Germany* (Oxford: Clarendon Press, 1993), pp. 57–61.

[62]   The contemporary and historical literature on the war and changing notions of women's national duties versus citizenship rights is vast. For Germany see Georg Schwiening, *Die Dienstpflicht der Frauen* (Cassel: Ernst Hühn, 1900); Maria Cauer, *Frauendienstpflicht* (Tübingen: J. C. B. Mohr, 1916); Fritz Giese, *Die Idee einer Frauendienstpflicht* (Langensalza: Wendt & Klauwell, 1916); Institut für soziale Arbeit München (ed.), *Die weibliche Dienstpflicht* (München: Verlag des Aerztlichen Rundschau Otto Gmelin, 1916); Leo Hohmann and Ernst Reichel, *Die Dienstpflicht der deutschen Frauen* (Berlin: Mathilde-Zimmer-Haus, 1917); Rosa Kempf, 'Das weibliche Dienstjahr', *Archiv für Sozialwissenschaft und Sozialpolitik* 41 (1916): 422–37; Rosa Kempf, 'Schriften vom weiblichen Dienstjahr und Verwandtes', *Archiv für Sozialwissenschaft und Sozialpolitik* 44 (1917/1918): 854–66. The German historical literature includes Dammer, *Mütterlichkeit*; Daniel, *War from Within*, pp. 65–89; Ute von Gersdorff, 'Frauen im Kriegsdienst', *Wehrkunde: Organ der Gesellschaft für Wehrkunde* 14 (1965): 576–80. See also Darrow, *French Women*, pp. 53–97; Claire A. Culleton, *Working-Class Culture, Women, and Britain, 1914–1921* (New York: St. Martin's Press, 1999); Susan Grayzel, *Women's Identities at War: Gender, Motherhood, and Politics in Britain and France during the First World War* (Chapel Hill: University of North Carolina, 1999); Nicoletta F. Gullace, *'The Blood of Our Sons': Men, Women, and the Renegotiation of British Citizenship during the Great War* (New York: Palgrave MacMillan, 2002).

deficiencies and their longing for firm guidance and professional training. As one local youth advocate in the Silesian district of Breslau observed, "[Before the war] anyone interested in the reform [of rural female youth] was advised against it – I know this from my own experience … it was considered superfluous."[63]

Two lectures given at the second "War Instruction" conference in January 1916 were among the earliest public discussions of young women's wartime flight from the countryside. The first, given by the secretary of the Hanover Agricultural Association's young women's club, Irmgard von Thering, began by enumerating the reasons young women were fleeing family farms, namely their desire for "higher wages, lighter … work, and unlimited freedom, as well as their understandable desire for sociability, variety, and intellectual stimulation."[64] In conclusion, she implored her colleagues to teach rural girls the "true, inner meaning of freedom, and to show them that real freedom does not mean the unbridled living-for-oneself." Von Thering insisted that "achieving this inner freedom will tie rural female youth more firmly to the *Heimat*."[65] Her colleague Frau von Druffel took a completely different tack, blaming "misunderstood, thoughtless performance of agricultural tasks" for provoking young women's distaste for farm work and poorer rural parents for sending their daughters into service in big cities rather than to work as *Mägde*.[66] She also castigated her audience for complaining about village life and agricultural work and warned that all the training in the world would be useless unless they themselves provided the proper example.

However, by 1917 reformers' sympathy for young rural women as victims of benign neglect had waned. Increasingly they portrayed young rural women as clever and determined navigators of a chaotic labor market, eager to abandon family farms at a moment's notice in their quest for high-wage jobs in munitions and other war industries. That year reformer Maria Kerkerink delivered several speeches that articulated the new concerns, blaming rural female youth's increased "wildness" on their lack of continuing education. She added that the problem was especially acute among the "simpler rural classes."[67] Kerkerink described rural flight as "a gaping wound on the nation's body" and warned that it was "high time

---

[63]   Frl. von Roeder, *Wie sammelt und fesselt man die weibliche Jugend auf dem Lande?* vol. 2 in series *Unsere weibliche Landjugend. Beiträge zur Förderung evangel. Jugendpflege auf dem Lande* [hereafter *Unsere weibliche Landjugend*] (Berlin: Evangel. Verband zur Pflege der weiblichen Jugend Deutschlands, 1917), p. 1.

[64]   von Thering, 'Wie arbeiten wir …?', p. 211.

[65]   von Thering, 'Wie arbeiten wir …?', p. 216.

[66]   Frau von Druffel, 'Weibliche Jugendpflege auf dem Lande', in *Die Landfrauenarbeit* (*2. Kriegslehrgang*), pp. 227–32.

[67]   Maria Kerkerink, *Was erwarten wir von der ländlichen Fortbildungsschule für Mädchen und welche Anforderungen sind an sie zu stellen?* vol. 7 of *Schriften der Provinzialabteilung Rheinprovinz des Deutschen Vereins für ländliche Wohlfahrts- und Heimatpflege* (Bonn: Verlag der Provinzialabteilung Rheinprovinz des Deutschen Vereins für ländliche Wohlfahrts- und Heimatpflege, 1917), p. 5; Maria Kerkerink, 'Landflucht und

to undertake energetic measures against this evil ... before it is too late."[68] She concluded that she was well aware that imposing required training for girls older than 14 would mean raising "certain barriers to their freedom-of-movement; but I don't think unlimited freedom of movement for our least-experienced youth is a good thing, and it certainly is not a natural right [*Naturrecht*] for which our vital rural interests should be sacrificed."[69]

But it was physician and conservative social welfare reformer Malita von Rundstedt who summed up the crisis most dramatically: "*We can rescue the nation only if we refuse to allow, at any price, our German rural population – above all rural girls – to slip away from German agricultural work without a thought, or worse, to abandon it scornfully.*"[70] While conceding that some farm women were overburdened, von Rundstedt remained convinced that on the whole agricultural work transformed "physically and morally average or even below average" women and girls into productive citizens.[71] Even more vital than the benefits to individuals, however, was the importance of women's agricultural work for the nation. The war, von Rundstedt declared, had taught everyone this lesson. Returning to the theme of rural girls' resistance to agricultural work, she insisted that they must perform their "patriotic *duties*, now and in peacetime – whether they like it or not. The more we can make them all aware of their obligations through clear, specific guidelines, the better."[72] The simplest means of "sharpening their consciences," she continued, were compulsory regulations that prohibited their freedom-of-movement. But while von Rundstedt supported such measures wholeheartedly, she insisted that they should not substitute for long-term educational guidance as a strategy for reforming rural female youth.[73]

Thus, it was not merely young women's abrupt disappearance from agricultural enterprises that provoked such outrage, for after all the problem of runaway *Mägde* was not new. More alarming by far was their apparently willful disregard for the messages of moral and national duty defined so explicitly by wartime experts, state officials, and local youth activists. Certainly it was not clear how the programs that reformers advocated could succeed in renewing young women's commitment to family farms where previous mobilization efforts had failed or, just

---

Fortbildungsschule für Landmädchen', in *Die Landfrauenarbeit im Kriege. Zweiundzwanzig Vorträge (3. Kriegslehrgang)* (Berlin: Deutsche Landbuchhandlung, 1917), pp. 156–65.

[68]   Kerkerink, *Was erwarten wir?*, pp. 7–8.

[69]   Kerkerink, *Was erwarten wir?*, p. 9.

[70]   Malita von Rundstedt, *Die Arbeit des Landmädchens*, vol. 4 in *Unsere weibliche Landjugend* (Berlin: Burckhardthausverlag, 1917), pp. 1–16, here p. 7. Emphasis in the original. Stibbe notes that von Rundstedt also played an active role in mobilizing women's support for the ultra-conservative German Fatherland Party [*Deutsche Vaterlandspartei*]. Stibbe, 'Anti-Feminism', p. 200.

[71]   von Rundstedt, *Arbeit*, p. 9.

[72]   von Rundstedt, *Arbeit*, p. 10. Emphasis in the original.

[73]   von Rundstedt, *Arbeit*, pp. 11–12.

as importantly, how they would be financed. Other practical obstacles included the training of enough teachers and whether rural girls could be spared from family farms long enough to attend such programs regularly. So while the wartime crisis of rural female youth inspired a host of suggestions and ambitious proposals that emphasized education, all of these ideas, prefaced as they were on the anticipated return of peace and prosperity, remained on paper. In the meantime, most rural youth experts were ready to concede that coercion in the form of a ban on young rural women's freedom of movement was the only remedy for the current crisis.

The Failure of Coercion, 1917–1922

The Allied blockade; ongoing shortages of male labor, fuel, fertilizer, and horses; record cold temperatures; and state authorities' inept and often corrupt management of the food supply all contributed to the catastrophic "turnip winter" on the home front in 1916–1917.[74] In addition to being on the receiving end of farmers' furious reports about the shortage of agricultural labor and the increasing waywardness of rural female youth, officials were acutely aware of the food riots roiling Germany's cities, including Leipzig, Dresden, and Berlin.[75] As agricultural economist Fuhrmann later admitted, by the middle of the war "propaganda alone was not sufficient to combat the dangers of rural flight. It was time to add official intervention."[76] Moreover, there were by now numerous precedents for the forced mobilization of the civilian population by the military. For one thing, military authorities in East Prussia and Pomerania had followed Bavaria's lead and passed strict prohibitions on all agricultural workers' freedom of movement in the

---

[74]   For precise statistics on wartime declines in agricultural production see Aereboe, *Einfluß*, pp. 84–92. On the state's mismanagement of the controlled economy see Davis, *Home Fires Burning*; Moeller, *German Peasants*, pp. 43–67; Robert Moeller, 'Dimensions of Social Conflict in the Great War: A View from the Countryside', *Central European History* 14/2 (June 1981): 142–68; Offer, *First World War*, pp. 21–78.

[75]   In general see Karsten Rudolph, *Die sächsische Sozialdemokratie vom Kaiserreich zur Republik (1871–1923)* (Weimar: Böhlau Verlag, 1995), pp. 129–49; Feldman, *Great Disorder*, pp. 63–4; Stephan Pfalzer, 'Der "Butterkrawall" im Oktober 1915. Die erste größere Antikriegsbewegung in Chemnitz', in Helga Grebing et al. (eds), *Demokratie und Emanzipation zwischen Saale und Elbe: Beiträge zur Geschichte der sozialdemokratischen Arbeiterbewegung bis 1933* (Essen: Klartext Verlag, 1993), pp. 196–213. For Berlin see Davis, *Home Fires Burning*. For the wartime and postwar periods, see Martin H. Geyer, 'Teuerungsprotest und Teuerungsunruhen 1914–1923: Selbsthilfegesellschaft und Geldentwertung', in Manfred Gailus and Heinrich Volkmann (eds), *Der Kampf um das tägliche Brot: Nahrungsmangel, Versorgungspolitik und Protest 1770–1990* (Opladen: Westdeutscher Verlag, 1994), pp. 319–45.

[76]   Fuhrmann, *Versorgung*, p. 42.

summer of 1915.[77] A year later, the launch of the Hindenburg Program a protracted and contentious debate in Berlin between the High Con officials, and labor representatives over the use of compulsion in all s. labor market, specifically over the proposed Patriotic Auxiliary Service Law.[78]

One major point of dispute over the Auxiliary Service Law was General Hindenburg's insistence that, "'He who does not work shall not eat' is, *also pertaining to women*, more justified than ever before in our present situation."[79] But in the end, the military was unable to overcome civil officials' stiff opposition to women's inclusion in the law. As State Secretary of the Interior Karl Helfferich countered "The introduction of universal compulsory service for women would … be an inappropriate measure, to which the most serious reservations, also in economic, moral, and social respects, stand in the way."[80] Instead, in its final form the December 1916 law stated that every German youth and male between the ages of 15 and 60 not serving at the front could be compelled by the War Minister to perform "Patriotic Auxiliary Service" in whatever economic sector deemed most appropriate.[81] Describing the law's impact on agriculture in 1920, Franz Achter stressed above all that it "was no use when it came to women … masses of them continued to take jobs in the city and in munitions factories."[82] Similarly, Günther Mai and Ute Daniel have stressed that women's exclusion from the Auxiliary Service Law meant that they continued to "mobilize themselves," especially if they were young and single, for high-paying jobs in munitions, above all at agriculture's expense.[83]

In sharp contrast, none of the debates that preceded the March 1917 decree of the Ordinance Concerning Labor Assistance in Agriculture and Forestry touched on the issue of women's exclusion. The first Saxon ordinance, published in the *Leipziger Zeitung* on April 5, announced that beginning immediately:

---

[77]   Kriegsministerium Berlin. Dem stellvertretenden Königlichen Sächsischen Herrn Militärbevollmächtigten, July 3, 1915, MdI 15925, SäHStA, p. 35. See also Albrecht, 'Soziale Probleme', p. 105; Oltmer, *Bäuerliche Ökonomie*, p. 206.

[78]   Feldman gives a detailed overview of compulsory mobilization in general and the debates over the *Hilfsdienstgesetz*. Feldman, *Army*, pp. 76–7, 88–9, 168–249, 301–49.

[79]   Quoted in Feldman, *Army*, p. 173. Emphasis in the original.

[80]   Quoted in Daniel, *War From Within*, p. 67. See also Lüders, *unbekannte Heer*, pp. 116–17; Feldman, *Army*, pp. 173, 188, 198, 219; Mai, *Arbeiterschaft*, p. 17.

[81]   Frieda Wunderlich, *Farm Labor in Germany, 1810–1945* (Princeton: Princeton University Press, 1961), p. 30.

[82]   Achter, 'Einwirkung des Krieges', p. 54.

[83]   Mai calls young, single women "the most mobile" category of war worker. Mai, *Arbeiterschaft*, pp. 17–18. See also Daniel, *War from Within*, p. 87. She observes, "The Auxiliary Service Law did nothing to change the fact that the wartime female labor market remained a free labor market, in which women 'mobilized' themselves according to the law of supply and demand."

no male or female person now employed in agriculture or forestry may leave their jobs for non-agricultural work without formal permission from the local authorities. Likewise youth in rural districts who have never worked [for wages] are banned from accepting anything other than agricultural employment without official authorization. Permission will be granted only if the authorities deem that the acceptance of other work will not harm the Fatherland's interests with respect to agricultural production and if the War Office in Leipzig ... formally confirms that there is a shortage of labor in the place [of proposed residence] and in the economic sector in question.[84]

The ordinance also specified that local authorities could order every male or female to accept agricultural work "appropriate to their strength and abilities" at the established local wage if it did not pose "undue personal hardship." Punishment for violators included imprisonment for up to one year or the payment of a 1,500 Mark fine.[85] In a handwritten letter to the Deputy Commanding General for Dresden district, the Saxon Interior Ministry finally admitted that coercion was the only way to hinder rural youth's continued movement into munitions factories, and recommended the immediate adoption of the Leipzig ordinance.[86] Ten days later, on April 21, 1917, the decree appeared in the *Sächsische Staatszeitung* in Dresden without modifications. In early October, at the urging of the *Landeskulturrat* and the Interior Ministry, the Saxon Deputy Commanding Generals extended the ordinances "indefinitely."[87] Thus, amid the welter of compulsory wartime legislation aimed at regulating the German labor market, what became known as the agricultural "exception laws" set a unique precedent by targeting women and female adolescents as well as men.

At the same time, civil officials' persistent concerns about "stirring up" agricultural workers and poorer rural parents, not to mention the objections of Social Democrats, meant that the ordinance also contained several provisions

---

[84]   *Leipziger Zeitung*, April 5, 1917, MdI 15925, SäHStA, p. 73. For Prussia see Rundschreiben Kriegsministerium Berlin an Stellvertretende Generalkommandos, Nr. 278/3. 17. E.D. II, Berlin, March 27, 1917, MdI 15925, SäHStA, p. 64; *Sächsische Staatszeitung*, April 21, 1917, MdI 15925, SäHStA, pp. 77–8; Feldman, *Army*, p. 307.

[85]   Such compulsory ordinances were not peculiar to wartime Germany. For Austria see Hermann Kallbrunner, 'Measures Taken during the War to Maintain the Supply of Agricultural Labour', *IRAE* XIII/3–4 (March–April 1922): 219–33. For Italy see G. C., 'Measures', p. 363. For Switzerland see Anon., 'The Food Supply Crisis and State Action to Overcome It (1914–1919)', *IRAE* XI/3 (March 1920): 207–21, esp. p. 217.

[86]   MdI an das stellvertr. Generalkommando des XII. Armeekorps, April 11, 1917, MdI 15933, SäHStA, p. 76.

[87]   LKR an das MdI, August 16, 1917, MdI an das stellvertr. Generalkommando des XII. und des XIX. Armeekorps, August 23, 1917, MdI 15933, SäHStA, pp. 82–3.

for appeal.[88] Its final paragraphs noted that exemptions would be granted with the presentation of a doctor's note certifying unfitness for agricultural work, and that local authorities, whose decisions would be final, would settle grievances. So while the ordinance aimed to appease those who demanded decisive state intervention in the agricultural labor market, it also strove to dampen the potential for social and political conflict in an already chaotic and war-weary countryside. This compromise was unavoidable under the circumstances, but it opened up a new arena where young women could debate and even challenge publicly the new definitions of farm women's national duty.

Several weeks after the Saxon ordinance was announced, the Interior Minister replied to yet another complaint from Kamenz district that many young women and girls who formerly worked in agriculture were now employed at the Artillery Factory in Radeberg.[89] He noted confidently that the recent decrees by the Deputy Commanding Generals "should give us sufficient means to combat the problem." But it was not long before reports surfaced that rural youth were disregarding the ban, despite penalties. By September, officials were discussing proposals for additional restrictions on rural youth's freedom of movement, specifically targeting adolescent boys and girls between the ages of 14 and 17, in order to combat their continued employment in munitions factories. According to the War Economic Office in Dresden, which summarized the new debate, the war industries' high wages "were pernicious and a sin against youth."[90] By the spring of 1918, the Saxon Interior Minister directed officials in every Saxon district to "enforce the ordinances of the Deputy Commanding Generals very strictly in order to ease the anticipated labor shortages for planting and harvest, which could prove extremely dangerous for the nation's food supply."[91] That same month the *Landeskulturrat* informed the Interior Ministry that:

---

[88]   On the wartime negotiations between labor, the military, and industry over the creation of arbitration committees [*Schlichtungsauschüsse*] in connection with compulsory wartime legislation in heavy industry and the *Hilfsdienstgesetz* see Feldman, *Army*, pp. 74, 77–80, 87, 92, 203–4, 210–13; Frieda Wunderlich, *German Labor Courts* (Chapel Hill: University of North Carolina Press, 1946), pp. 31–3.

[89]   Der Vorsitzende der Kriegswirtschaftstelle Kamenz an das Kriegswirtschaftsamt zu Dresden, April 14, 1917, MdI 15849, SäHStA, pp. 48–9. See also AH an das Königliche Kriegsministerium zu Dresden, Großenhain, April 20, 1917, MdI 15849, SäHStA, p. 47.

[90]   Abzügsweise Abschrift, K. S. Kriegswirtschaftsamt Dresden, September 19, 1917, MdI 15849, SäHStA, no number [p. 63].

[91]   MdI an die AH und die Stadträte der Städte mit rev. Städteordnung, March 27, 1918, MdI 15925, SäHStA, p. 98. See also Kriegswirtschaftsamt an das Kgl. Sächs. MdI, March 1, 1918, MdI 15925, SäHStA, p. 89; Stellv. Generalkommando XII. Armeekorps, Abschrift an das Kriegswirtschaftsamt Dresden, February 25, 1918, MdI 15925, SäHStA, p. 90; MdI an die AH Dresden, April 8, 1918, MdI 15925, SäHStA, p. 101.

Despite the April 1917 ordinance … young male and female agricultural workers are still finding industrial jobs. Many employers now decline to report offences because they assume that the authorities will not enforce the law with the necessary zeal or they fear that such a complaint might provoke revenge.[92]

Moreover, farmers expressed intense frustration not merely with district officials' inconsistent enforcement of the ban, but also with military authorities' reluctance to strengthen the measures by allowing employers to force runaway hired hands who had accepted industrial work to return. This was the case in February 1918, when the Deputy Commanding General in Dresden rebuffed farmers with the observation that while moving from agriculture to industry was punishable under the 1917 ordinance, it superseded the *Gesindeordnungen* with respect to forced returns.[93] He added that to threaten or to oversee forced returns were special cause for concern since "the right to personal freedom in the district has not been suspended." The general's observation sparked another flurry of exchanges between the Saxon Interior and Justice Ministries over the ban, with Justice officials finally concluding that the general was correct, since the *Gesindeordnungen* stated that runaways "could be forced to return *or* be punished, but not forced to return *and* be punished."[94] However, the memo also observed that breaches of contract were "beside the point. Even those whose contracts have ended cannot seek other work and are punishable if they do. On the other hand, according to the ordinance, those who leave their positions illegally for other agricultural work or who do not work at all are not breaking the law."

Just days after the collapse of the Wilhelmine government in November 1918, the new provisional government rescinded the *Gesindeordnungen*; the 1917 agricultural ordinances were suspended two weeks later.[95] The new Saxon Ministry for Labor and the Economy sent word to all military and civil authorities that "The [1917] ordinance contradicts the view of the present government with respect to contractual freedom as well as the spirit of the declarations of the People's Deputies, which under Paragraph 8 suspended all of the exception laws regarding agricultural workers."[96] However, by late January 1919, heated discussions

---

[92]   LKR an das Königliche MdI, Dresden, March 28, 1918, MdI 15925, SäHStA, p. 99. For similar complaints see K[önigliches] S[ächsisches] Kriegswirtschaftsamt an das Kgl. Sächs. MdI, March 1, 1918, MdI 15925, SäHStA, p. 89.

[93]   Abschrift! Stellv. Generalkommando XII., Dresden, Feb. 25, 1918, SäHStA, p. 90.

[94]   Ministerium der Justiz 777I/18 zu Nr. 564 III L/18, Dresden, March 21, 1918, MdI 15925, SäHStA, pp. 92–4. Emphasis mine.

[95]   Beschluß des Arbeits- und Wirtschaftsministerium, Dresden, December 5, 1918, MdI 15925, SäHStA, p. 138; on the lifting of the *Gesindeordnungen* see Bessel, *Germany*, p. 201.

[96]   Arbeits- und Wirtschaftsministerium an das stellvertretende Generalkommando XII. Armeekorps, das stellvertretended Generalkommando XIX, die KH, die AH und Stadträte der Städte, den LKR, December 11, 1918, MdI 15925, SäHStA, no number [p. 141a].

between the head of the National Demobilization Committee Joseph Koeth and his colleagues had begun in Berlin about the introduction of a nationwide ban on agricultural workers' freedom of movement.[97] The Saxon government's formal objections to such proposals were overruled by Koeth's frustrated insistence that:

> The current situation in agriculture is such that we need a minimum of 1,000,000 workers … If spring planting does not take place in an orderly fashion we will find ourselves in a most severe food crisis. It is clear to me that we cannot manage without coercion. Some of my colleagues … believe that the use of force seems impossible, but none of you has suggested a better solution.[98]

This time the discussions over what became the March 1919 "Ordinance to Relieve the Agricultural Labor Shortage" addressed women's inclusion in the law at length. While several officials expressed misgivings about the use of coercion on unemployed men, there was unanimous support for compelling women, especially former *Mägde* and those between the ages of 14 and 30, to return to the countryside.[99] As representative Keiser from the Demobilization Committee warned, "There is no other way than to force those who formerly worked in agriculture to return. We're even considering sending girls now in domestic service (for example in Berlin) en masse back to the land, most of them are from the countryside anyway. We cannot hesitate, we cannot have too many misgivings, and spring planting will not wait."[100] In February the *Sächsische Staatszeitung* exclaimed that "The shortage of *Mägde* is catastrophic. The availability of unemployment benefits means that young women who formerly worked in agriculture are staying in the cities."[101] German farmers also faced the loss of prisoners-of-war and many of the approximately 14,000 Polish seasonal workers in Saxony and elsewhere had

---

[97] Der stellvertretende Bevollmächtigte zum Bundesrat von Holtzendorff an das Ministerium der auswärtigen Angelegenheiten, January 20, 1919, MdI 15925, SäHStA, pp. 143–4.

[98] 'Demobilmachungsbesprechung vom 20.1.: Arbeitskräfte für Landwirtschaft und Bergbau', January 21, 1919, MdI 15925, SäHStA, pp. 155–7, here p. 155; Arbeitsministerium Sachsen, Beschluß des Wirtschaftsministerium, V. Abteilung, Dresden, February 7, 1919, MdI 15925, SäHStA, pp. 159–60.

[99] This was certainly part of postwar leaders' determination to re-establish a "normal gender hierarchy." See Susanne Rouette, 'Nach dem Krieg: Zurück zur normalen Hierarchie der Geschlechter', in Karin Hausen (ed.), *Geschlechterhierarchie und Arbeitsteilung: Zur Geschichte ungleicher Erwerbschancen von Männern und Frauen* (Göttingen: Vandenhoek & Ruprecht, 1993), pp. 167–90.

[100] Ökonomierat Keiser, 'Vermerk über die Sitzung am 14. Januar 1919 … über Beschaffung von Arbeitern für Landwirtschaft und Kohlenbergbau', January 15, 1919, MdI 15925, SäHStA, pp. 163–7, here p. 165.

[101] Anon., 'Der Stand des Arbeitsmarktes im Reiche', *Sächsische Staatszeitung* no. 37, February 14, 1919, MdI 15849, SäHStA, p. 141.

returned home.[102] At the same time, the *Landeskulturrat* conceded that farmers were extremely reluctant to hire former soldiers and urban unemployed men, even when they could be persuaded to accept agricultural work.[103]

The March 1919 ordinance obligated the newly-organized public labor exchanges to refer "any person seeking work who had previously been employed in agriculture back to agriculture." Furthermore, as long as agricultural jobs "with appropriate wages and working conditions were available, the labor exchange should not refer anyone who worked in agriculture since the war's outbreak to a job outside the agricultural sector."[104] It also forbid industrial employers from hiring anyone who had worked in agriculture since the beginning of the war unless they were "no longer suitable." Employers who violated the law could be fined up to 3,000 Marks. It also noted that the ban would be suspended "as soon as the agricultural labor emergency ends." In October, officials approved an addendum to the ordinance which stated that local demobilization committees could approve exemptions "on the grounds of serving the public good."[105]

Almost immediately, farmers began complaining that the ordinance was having no effect.[106] They were also outraged at the repeal of the *Gesindeordnungen*, although that was no great surprise, and at the regulation of working hours, conditions, and wages under the provisional agricultural labor law.[107] By January 1920, a representative from the demobilization committee in the Saxon district of Flöha informed his superior that,

> Farmers are extremely worried about procuring and retaining enough agricultural
> labor to guarantee the people's food supply in the coming year ... It is therefore

---

[102]   Niederschrift aus der Sitzung des Ausschusses für Arbeiterwesen am 22. Januar 1919, MdI 15849, SäHStA, p. 136 folio. The reimportation of Polish seasonal workers resumed by the early 1920s. See Ulrich Herbert, *A History of Foreign Labor in Germany: Seasonal Workers, Forced Laborers, Guestworkers*, trans. William Templer (Ann Arbor: University of Michigan Press, 1990); Kathrin Roller, *Frauenmigration und Ausländerpolitik im Deutschen Kaiserreich: polnische Arbeitsmigrantinnen in Preußen*, 2nd edn (Berlin: Dieter Bertz Verlag, 1994).

[103]   LKR an das Arbeits- und Wirtschaftsministerium, Dresden, December 11, 1918, MdI 15849, SäHStA, p. 113; see also Jones, 'Gendering'.

[104]   *Reichs-Gesetzblatt*, 'Verordnung zur Behebung des Arbeitermangels in der Landwirtschaft', MdI 15925, SäHStA, p. 191; published in the *Sächsische Landwirtschaftliche Zeitschrift* 13, March 29, 1919, MdI 15925, SäHStA, p 194.

[105]   Abschrift. Reichsarbeitsminister an alle Landesregierungen, Berlin, November 6, 1919, MdI 15925, SäHStA, p. 257.

[106]   Arbeitsministerium an die Handelskammern, die Gewerbekammern, den Verband Sächsischer Industrieller, Dresden, July 26, 1919, MdI 15925, SäHStA, p. 234.

[107]   According to Saxon labor exchange officials, many farmers "paid no attention" to the new regulations. See Jones, 'Gendering', p. 321; Elizabeth Bright Jones, 'A New Stage of Life?: Young Farm Women's Changing Expectations and Aspirations about Work in Weimar Saxony', *German History* 19/4 (Fall 2001): 549–70, esp. pp. 557–8.

necessary to prevent as strenuously as possible any illegal job-changing from agriculture to industry. Recently there have been reports of a huge number of hired hands leaving their positions. For example, in Großolbersdorf, every girl and in Drehbach 51 girls have left their positions in agricultural service. In other localities it is reputed to be the same.[108]

The following month, farmers in the district of Meißen expressed their strong desire to "fulfill their duty to maintain the food supply," but they also pressed the government to employ "every available legal and pragmatic remedy to halt the shocking and ever-increasing flight of our young female workers. If the government is not in a position to do so, livestock production on family farms will be severely endangered and we will not be responsible for the consequences."[109] Anguished reports about the shortage of *Mägde* were not unique to Saxony. Describing the postwar agricultural labor market in Bavaria, Kurt Königsberger observed that "Here we find a positive development with respect to men's labor and an extremely negative one with respect to women ... [Of the districts reporting a labor shortage] complaints about the shortage of *Mägde* are the most common."[110]

Between the fall of 1921 and the spring of 1922, Saxon farmers' complaints about the shortage of young women reached a crescendo: the shortage of *Mägde* was mentioned in virtually all communications between farmers, their representatives, and state officials about labor relations in the countryside. For example, in October 1921, the Saxon *Landeskulturrat* cautioned the Economics Ministry in Dresden that the imminent suspension of demobilization controls must not include the March 1919 ordinance. It continued, "We remind you that an extremely grave shortage of labor persists and agricultural workers continue to leave for industry ... the shortage of *Mägde* is so severe that it has been impossible to maintain livestock, etc."[111] Soon after, the Economics Ministry called a special meeting to discuss the crisis.[112] In his opening remarks, representative Sala brooded that young women avoided the demobilization regulations successfully by remaining at home for a few weeks after leaving agriculture, then taking a job in industry. He insisted that, "We must solve this problem, which poses such a grave danger for

---

[108] Der Staatskommissar für Demobilmachung an die AH Flöha, Dresden, January 13, 1920, AH Fl. 2509 'Behebung des Arbeitermangels in der Landwirtschaft', SäHStA, p 26.

[109] Landwirtschaftlicher Bezirks-Verband Meißen an das Wirtschaftsministerium des Freistaates Sachsen, Meißen, February 7, 1920, MdI 15850, 'Arbeitsverhältnisse bei der Landwirtschaft', SäHStA, p. 127.

[110] Kurt Königsberger, 'Die wirtschaftliche Demobilmachung in Bayern während der Zeit vom November 1918 bis Mai 1919', *Zeitschrift des bayrischen Statistischen Landesamtes* 52 (1920): 193–226, here pp. 213–14.

[111] LKR an das Wirtschaftsministerium, 5. Abteilung, Dresden, October 13, 1921, MdI 15933, SäHStA, p. 7.

[112] Wirtschaftsministerium, Abteilung Landwirtschaft, 'Sitzung über *Mägdenot*', Dresden, November 3, 1921, MdI 15850, SäHStA, pp. 217–18.

domestic agriculture, especially for small and medium-sized enterprises, and which threatens to grow out of control ... The repeated suggestion that the demobilization committees should intervene to stem the crisis has proven a failure." While there was widespread agreement that the 1919 regulations "remained largely on paper," his colleague commented perceptively that "It is not only a question of wages but of working and living conditions, especially those of farm wives, whose existence is so harsh that they often advise their daughters not to share their fate ... This can only be addressed through social welfare programs." Another put in that "The shortage of *Mägde* has its roots in the social environment ... farmers must hire more of them so that there is less overburdening. As [our] inquiries have established, their work often begins at 4:00 a.m. and ends at 10:00 p.m." The press and politicians also entered the fray.[113] In early December 1921, Saxon *Landtag* Representatives Schreiber, Friedrich, and Pietsch of the German National People's Party [*Deutschnationale Volkspartei*, or *DNVP*] interpellated, "What does the government propose to do about the ever-more-threatening shortage of female workers on small and medium-sized agricultural enterprises?"[114]

All through the spring of 1922, farmers in districts across the former Kingdom, now the Freestate, of Saxony, responded to surveys about the agricultural labor shortage. Their responses were filled with bitter laments about young women, even though the statistics they reported reflected shortages of both male and female labor.[115] Asked to comment on the numbers, they complained that young women were either "completely unavailable," "leaving in mid-harvest for factory work," "100 per cent missing," or "all going to the factory." Again and again, farmers asserted that the shortage of women's labor made it impossible to farm intensively, to maintain livestock holdings, to harvest root crops, and the like.[116] At the same time, to the great chagrin of labor exchange officials, farmers refused to substitute men for women, or even boys for girls.

In late March 1922, the Weimar government finally suspended the 1919 ordinance. By this time even Germany's largest agricultural interest organization, the newly-organized Rural League [*Reichs-Landbund*], admitted wearily that "The 1919 ordinance did not have great success ... [nevertheless] on March

---

[113] 'Das Elend der Landarbeiter', *Zeitung der unabhängigen sozialdemokratischen Partei* 254, November 29, 1921, MdI 15933, SäHStA, p. 12; 'Der Arbeitermangel in der Landwirtschaft', *Volksstimme Chemnitz*, December 27, 1921, MdI 15933, SäHStA, p. 54.

[114] Berichte usw. des Landtags. Nr. 470, Anfrage eingegangen am 7. Dezember 1921, MdI 15933, SäHStA, pp. 91, 95; Sitzung des sächsischen Landtags, February 9, 1922, MdI 15933, SäHStA, p. 95.

[115] Antworten auf die Anfragen bei den landwirtschaftlichen Vereinen betr. Arbeiternot; Feststellung über Arbeiternot in der Landwirtschaft im Kreisbezirk Dresden; Statistik über Arbeitermangel in der Landwirtschaft; Landwirtschaftlicher Kreisverein Leipzig an das Generalsekretariat des LKR, January 11, 1922; Bericht über die Arbeiternot, n.d., MdI 15933, SäHStA, pp. 127, 128–31, 133–4, 137, 138–43, 216–23.

[116] Jones, 'Gendering', pp. 312–13, 321–3.

31, 1922 it was suspended over the protests of large numbers of agricultural organizations."[117] Complaints about the shortage of women's agricultural labor persisted in Saxony throughout the decade.[118] At the same time, the head of the Saxon labor exchange argued vigorously against the reintroduction of coercive regulations in light of the experience with the 1919 demobilization laws: "At the time, nobody paid any attention to the regulations. It is just not feasible to single out one particular profession for control, while all the others are not subject to coercion. That made people very upset, and provoked a lot of resistance that was only counterproductive." But as the testimonies of young women who contested the ordinances underscored, the "rush to personal freedom" was only part of the story.[119]

Compelling Duty? Young Rural Women's Appeals to the Ordinances of 1917 and 1919 and New Definitions of Citizenship in Saxony

Between 1917 and 1921, both men and women contested the ordinances banning agricultural labor's freedom of movement and freedom of employment in Saxony. As with the prewar grievance cases, the most detailed Saxon records available contesting the 1919 demobilization regulations are from the district of Flöha.[120] Here young women made roughly half of all the appeals between December 1919 and February 1921, 45 in total.[121] This is not surprising, given the district's proximity to Chemnitz, where numerous textile factories continued to rely on women's labor after the war. The evidence of challenges to the 1917 regulations is much more fragmentary, and includes two cases from the district of Borna, south of Leipzig, and two from Großenhain district, north of Dresden. However, in all four instances, district officials' private correspondence either referred to "countless" other cases or reminded one another that clear precedents in favor of the ban should be set in anticipation of future appeals. Like their counterparts before the war, many young women continued to rely on family members, especially fathers but also widowed mothers, to intercede for them in their dealings with state authorities. This was especially the case if the initial request were denied.

In some respects, the petitions clearly recall elements of the grievance cases of *Mägde* in previous decades. Like their prewar counterparts, young rural women

---

[117]   'Der Arbeiternot in der Landwirtschaft', Reichs-Landbund, Berlin, May 5, 1922, MdI 15933, SäHStA, p. 225.

[118]   'Zur Landtags-Anfrage 1207 der Abgeordneten Schreiber/Pagenstecher ... vom 26. Februar 1925', MdI 15933, SäHStA, pp. 307–9, 132; Sitzung des sächsischen Landtags, April 7, 1925 [hereafter 132. Sitzung], MdI 15933, SäHStA, p. 310.

[119]   132. Sitzung, MdI 15933, SäHStA, p. 311.

[120]   However, even here the evidence is complicated by the fact that many cases are incomplete or that only the last name is given with no subsequent references to gender.

[121]   This number represents case records that are more or less complete.

during and after the war determinedly sought to improve the circumstances of their employment. Many also echoed longstanding complaints by *Mägde* about the poor wages and strenuous, unrelenting work on family farms. Village officials, especially the magistrate, continued to play a key role in mediating these encounters between young women, agricultural employers, and provincial officials, corroborating the "facts" of a particular case for their superiors and offering opinions based on firsthand or prior knowledge of the participants. Finally, ongoing official and expert debates over the wisdom or even the possibility of restricting agricultural labor's freedom of movement meant that the outcomes of individual cases were unpredictable.

Yet unlike the grievance cases of *Mägde*, young women's wartime and postwar petitions for exemption from agricultural work rarely named a specific employer as the source of discontent. Instead these appeals underscored young women's resistance to agricultural work under any circumstances and their resentment of state-imposed restrictions on both their freedom-of-movement and freedom-of-employment rights. Moreover, while many of them still voiced longstanding complaints about low wages or heavy work on family farms, they also outlined very specific plans for the future that did not include remaining on the farm. Most significantly, they frequently justified their requests for exemption in terms of having already fulfilled their duty to agriculture and maintained that the switch to other employment was the only way to meet their ongoing, and much more pressing, obligations to parents, siblings, in-laws, and (future) husbands. Thus, while contemporary observers invariably claimed that young rural women who abandoned agriculture were merely "out for themselves," the evidence reveals that their calculations and aspirations were rarely so one-dimensional.

In early May 1917, just weeks after the wartime ordinance was decreed, 19-year-old Martha Ruder contacted the Borna district authority requesting permission to move from the village of Altmörbitz to the city of Leipzig, where she intended to take a job in one of the munitions factories.[122] She explained that she had tried to find "suitable agricultural work" since October 1914, but that there was "already enough labor available." She concluded her appeal by saying that she no longer wished to burden her parents in such difficult times and that the munitions job "will allow me to earn what I need to support myself independently."[123] While her testimony about the adequacy of the rural labor supply provoked outraged incredulity from the Borna official in charge of the case, the newly-designated

---

[122]   Martha Ruder an die Königliche AH Borna, May 4, 1917, AH Borna 3857, 'Allgemeine landwirtschaftliche Angelegenheiten', Sächsisches Staatsarchiv Leipzig [hereafter SSL], pp. 72–3.

[123]   '*damit ich mir die nötigen Lebensbedürfnisse selbst verdienen und beschaffen kann*'.

agricultural expert in Altmörbitz confirmed brusquely that there were "enough female agricultural workers in the locality" and her request was granted.[124]

Others were not so fortunate. In the same week of May 1917, Anna Ziegner also sought approval from the Borna authorities to leave her job as *Magd*.[125] In her statement, she explained that she had worked for a farmer in the village of Auligk for several years, but claimed that her wages together with the subsidy she received as a soldier's wife were not enough to support herself and her young children. She insisted that she no longer could do the heavy work required, and in the meantime had found "lighter and better-paid employment" at the local canteen. In response, the Borna official first inquired abruptly of the local magistrate, "Has Frau Z. given proper legal notice? Or was no notice given (?)."[126] The magistrate replied that according to her employer, Anna had worked there for two years, most recently in the cow stalls, but that "Suddenly, on May 4th, she announced that she would no longer do such strenuous work."[127] He claimed that she also had refused lighter tasks and had not given proper notice. The village agricultural expert also chimed in, asserting that her wages, even had she accepted the lighter work, together with her state subsidy, were "clearly adequate."[128] He concluded anxiously that such appeals:

> undoubtedly harm the Fatherland's interests with regard to the food supply. Moreover, we must fear that this will not be an isolated case. The authorities are not even aware of most of them. People seem to think that they can leave their jobs without penalty and without considering how they are contributing to the already grave agricultural labor shortage. Therefore, in order to sharpen people's consciences in these difficult times, paragraph 1 of the 1917 ordinance should be followed.

A few weeks later, Anna's request was denied.[129]

By 1918, young women's challenges to the ordinance aroused even more controversy. Between December 1917 and April 1918, Emma Bernstein from the

---

[124] By the middle of the war, each village had a designated agricultural expert who oversaw and reported on labor issues and other matters. Königliche AH Borna an den landw. Sachverständigen Herrn Rothe, May 5, 1917, AH Borna 3857, SSL, no page number [p. 73a]; Rothe an die AH Borna, May 6, 1917, AH Borna 3857, [p. 74]; Stengel an Martha Ruder, Altmörbitz, May 9, 1917, AH Borna 3857, no page number [p. 75].

[125] Anna Lina Ziegner an die königliche AH Borna, May 7, 1917, AH Borna 3857, SSL, p. 114.

[126] Sala an den Herrn GV in Auligk, May 9, 1917, AH Borna 3857, SSL, p. 114a.

[127] GV Beumert an die königliche AH Borna, May 13, 1917, AH Borna 3857, SSL, p. 115.

[128] P. Wirth an die königliche AH Borna, May 16, 1917, AH Borna 3857, SSL, p. 115a.

[129] Die königliche AH an Frau Anna Ziegner, May 24, 1917, AH Borna 3857, SSL, p. 116.

Saxon village of Colmnitz repeatedly contested the ban.[130] The Großenhain district official overseeing the case reported that Emma first had sought release from her position by maintaining that agricultural wages were "too low." In response to the village magistrate's observation that she was "fit and healthy," Emma "retorted that she knew how to get a doctor's certificate and would do so in order to achieve her goal." Six weeks later, she indeed presented a doctor's note stating that her rheumatism "recommended a change in employment."[131] However, "after a thorough investigation" the magistrate determined that "she was perfectly capable of working as a *Magd* and ordered her to remain." The final affront came in April 1918, when after finally securing permission to stay at home to help her ailing parents with agricultural work, the district official learned that she had applied for a job at the state factory works in Zeithain. He concluded sternly that "The shortage of agricultural labor, especially of *Mägde*, is enormous. Many positions in the district are vacant. Thus the district is forced to recommend that a strict standard be applied to all cases of *Mägde* who wish to leave agricultural work." A few days later, her final appeal was denied.[132]

The case of Anna Gaudlitz, who applied for an exemption from agricultural work only after she ran into trouble with local authorities for leaving her position, illustrates the ongoing tension over the law's enforcement and how some young women used it to their advantage.[133] In her August 1918 testimony, the 23-year-old told the provincial court in Dresden that she had served as a *Magd* "for ages" and left her position in order to assist her future father-in-law with his small plot and to work for the local locksmith. She assured the authorities that she had had "no idea that the 1917 ban applied to her," and added that, in any case, the wage had not allowed her to save for a dowry. In conclusion, Anna staunchly maintained that she had been unable to find another position. The court found her tale entirely persuasive, noting that it must be shown that a person had "recklessly ignored the law" when in fact she had applied for exemption after being informed of her violation. In its summation, the court exonerated her of the charge, concluding that, "The [enforcement of the] ordinance must respect individual circumstances because it contains an exemption provision … In the normal course of things, individual workers must be permitted to leave agriculture for personal reasons without committing a crime and without harming the law's intention." In a furious rebuttal, the Großenhain district official who oversaw the case expressed outrage over the ruling, arguing that the law could only be interpreted in the context of the

---

[130]   August Bernstein an das MdI, May 7, 1918, MdI 15925, SäHStA, p. 102.

[131]   AH Großenhain an das Königliche MdI, May 13, 1918, MdI 15925, SäHStA, p. 103.

[132]   MdI an Herrn August Bernstein in Colmnitz, May 17, 1918, MdI 15925, SäHStA, p. 104.

[133]   Abschrift. Im Namen des Königs. Die Angeklagte Anna Gaudlitz wird von der Anklage freigesprochen, MdI 15925, SäHStA, p. 132.

present national emergency.[134] He also accused the court of ignoring local officials' tireless efforts to publicize the decree, adding that "Every case ... where the ban was imposed was quickly known to the rest of the rural population." In conclusion, the official declared that Anna's testimony that she could not find another position as *Magd* after being ordered to return was "worthless ... Her demands were intentionally so extreme that no employer would honor them."[135]

Young women's appeals to the 1919 demobilization regulations followed similar patterns, and the vast majority were successful in their quest for exemptions. Most mentioned a long period of prior service and displayed an intimate knowledge of the law, despite Anna Gaudlitz's protestations to the contrary. For example, in over half of all the cases under consideration, young women addressed one or both exemption provisions directly, providing evidence of illness or, less often, of extreme personal hardship. In 16 instances, young women procured the requisite doctor's certificate confirming their unsuitability for agricultural work. Most of the time, it seems that doctors gave their consent readily, whether because of missing fingers, a poorly-healed broken arm, lung or bladder infections, frostbite damage, or a bout of typhoid.[136] Occasionally the doctor confirmed that while the injury or illness made agricultural work "inadvisable," it should not prevent the young woman from working in food processing or, in several cases, at the local spinning mill or stocking factory.[137] Sometimes a young woman's pregnancy or young children, both legitimate and illegitimate, were enough to secure approval of an exemption.[138] One exception was the case of Anna Lehmann in April 1920, who was granted a temporary exemption because of her impending delivery but informed that she would have to reapply for release in the fall.[139]

Others, like Elisabeth Neubauer, Martha Köhler, and Frida Börner, were able to persuade the local magistrate to testify that agricultural wages were insufficient to

---

[134]   die Königliche Amtshauptmannschaft [hereafter AH] Großenhain an die Königliche Staatsanwaltschaft beim Landgericht zu Dresden, August 28, 1918, MdI 15925, SäHStA, p. 130.

[135]   die AH Großenhain an die Königliche Staatsanwaltschaft beim Landgericht zu Dresden, August 28, 1918, MdI 15925, SäHStA, p. 130.

[136]   AH Fl. 2509, SäHStA, see cases of Liddy Kempe, December 1919, pp. 17–19; Arnold, Jan. 1920, p. 60; [Martha] Dora Kirchhübel, Jan. 1920, p. 174–5; Hedwig Hoffmann, April 1920, pp. 187–8; AH Fl. 2510, SäHStA, case of Johanna Wagner, July 1920, p. 226.

[137]   AH Fl. 2509, SäHStA, cases of Liddy Kempe, December 1919, pp. 17–19; Ella Neubert, March 1920, p. 39–40; Arnold, January 1920, p. 60; [Martha] Dora Kirchhübel, January 1920, pp. 174–5; AH Fl. 2510, cases of Erna Kuhn, February 1920; Helene Bauer, April 1920, p. 108; Johanna Wagner, July 1920, p. 226.

[138]   AH Borna 3857, SSL, case of Anna Ziegner, pp. 114–16; AH FL. 2509, SäHStA, cases of Maria Hofbauer, January 1920, pp. 62–8; Johanna Neuber, January 1920, pp. 77–9.

[139]   AH Fl. 2510, SäHStA, case of Anna Lehmann, April 1920, p. 183.

prevent either them or their families from destitution; all were approved.[140] Another successful petitioner, Johanna Schulze, testified to the magistrate in Falkenau in June 1921 that she had worked in agriculture since leaving school in 1917, and had left only to care for her sick mother at home.[141] She added that her two sisters also worked in agriculture. In light of her family's "impoverished circumstances," she requested permission to work at the spinning mill in Plauen, "where I have been promised a job." After confirming her story with the local magistrate, her appeal was approved.[142] Or, as 18-year-old Elisabeth Kluge, who had already found a factory job at a cotton spinning mill in nearby Schellenberg, pleaded,

> If I must return to agriculture, I will be in a very bad way. My parents are
> impoverished and cannot provide for my future. They have spent a great deal
> on my fourteen-year-old brother, who has tuberculosis … I earned very little in
> agriculture and could barely clothe myself … In the future I had hoped to earn
> enough for my own survival and to save a little … If I must return to agriculture
> this will cause me and my parents great anxiety. Also, I am much too weak to do
> the heavy work that agriculture requires.[143]

Once again, the village magistrate corroborated her tale, noting that "the facts she gives are true. The petitioner's parents find themselves in a very unenviable state," and reassured authorities that, "Miss K. is a very sickly girl and is hardly up to agricultural work."[144]

Sometimes, too, an industrial employer interceded on the young woman's behalf. In the case of Liddy Kempe, the owner of the spinning mill in Sachsenberg explained that due to the loss of three fingers in an agricultural accident two years before, she was "unable to perform agricultural work appropriate to her age," yet apparently her handicap did not affect her ability to work in the factory.[145] Similarly, in January 1920, the director of a stocking firm wrote to the district authorities about Ella Weißbach.[146] In his letter, he recounted that he had hired her at the behest of her parents, and that her weekly agricultural wage of 3.50 Marks "would hardly allow her to purchase a pair of wooden shoes, much less clothing or other things."

---

[140]   AH. Fl 2509, SäHStA, case of Elisabeth Neubauer, January 1920, pp. 77–9; AH Fl. 2510, SäHStA, cases of Martha Köhler, March 1920, pp. 68; Frida Börner, June 1920, p. 194.

[141]   Johanna Schulze testimony certified by GV in Falkenau, July 1, 1921, AH Fl. 2509, SäHStA, p. 1.

[142]   GV Falkenau an die AH Fl., July 6, 1921; die AH Fl. an Fräulein Johanna Schulze, July 12, 1921, AH Fl. 2509, SäHStA, p. 3.

[143]   Elisabeth Kluge an die AH Fl., Marbach, May 25, 1920, AH Fl. 2510, SäHStA, pp. 187–8.

[144]   GV testimony, Marbach, May 28, 1920, AH Fl. 2510, SäHStA, p. 188.

[145]   C. G. Reichelt an die AH Fl., December 6, 1919, AH Fl. 2509, SäHStA, p. 19.

[146]   Weißbach an die AH Fl., January 5, 1920, AH Fl. 2510, SäHStA, p. 2.

Later that year the same employer worked with the local magistrate to establish that five young women whom he had hired were not "professional agricultural workers."[147] He noted that several of them, all in their late teens, had only "helped out" and also had previous experience with factory work. Therefore, he reasoned, they should not be forced to return. After the Chemnitz demobilization commission ruled to the contrary, three of the girls refused to return and opted to go to court.[148] One of them, Martha Kräusel, lodged an impassioned protest arguing that

> I left agriculture because I was ill ... Agricultural work is notoriously heavy
> and one cannot take care of one's health. I got rheumatism because I could not
> take care of myself and was forced to return to my parents. So I am asking that
> you allow me to continue in the factory. I'm content there and my rheumatism
> is better ... I willingly and cheerfully gave two years to agriculture and I would
> not hesitate to return. But under the circumstances *I refuse to allow my personal
> freedom to be curtailed with respect to my work.*[149]

In this case, however, since she was unable to obtain a doctor's certificate confirming her illness, Martha was returned to agriculture.[150]

Conclusion

The upheavals of the First World War greatly magnified the late-nineteenth-century trends in the gender balance of the agricultural labor force and, by extension, the delegation of more and more work to farm women. On the one hand, German state authorities' tireless campaigns to mobilize farm women of all ages for the war effort affirmed the importance of their productive contributions to the nation's food supply, permanently reversing their previous invisibility on family enterprises. On the other hand, this same scrutiny also revealed the limits of the German state's wartime mobilization of the countryside, and highlighted the fact that not all farm women embraced the new rhetoric of unending self-sacrifice for the collective good. Moreover, it was not only young women, especially *Mägde*, who bristled under the new burdens imposed by the war. By 1916 even farm wives, now celebrated as the bedrock of German agricultural production and the established

---

[147]   GV Lindner an die AH Fl., Dittmansdorf, May 12, 1920, AH Fl. 2510, SäHStA, p. 72; Mitteilung F. W. Weißbach, May 11, 1920, AH Fl. 2510, p. 74; GV an die AH Fl., Gornau, July 8, 1920, AH Fl. 2510, SäHStA, p. 82.

[148]   Demobilmachungs-Kommissar Chemnitz an die AH Fl., June 3, 1920, AG Fl. 2510, p. 76; F. G. Weissbach an die AH Fl., June 18, 1920, AH Fl. 2510, SäHStA, p. 80.

[149]   Martha Kräusel an die AH Fl., Dittmannsdorf, June 21, 1920, AH Fl. 2510, SäHStA, p. 87. Emphasis mine.

[150]   Beschluß des GV Lindner, July 29, 1920, AH Fl. 2510, SäHStA, p. 88.

rural social order, were criticized for putting their families' needs before those of the nation.

In many respects, the April 1917 ordinances represented a victory for those who sought to reinforce new understandings of farm women's duties and the naturalness of agricultural labor for rural female youth, as did the reintroduction of a similar ban during the early Weimar years. Despite criticism that such measures would never provide a lasting solution to the crisis, by late 1916 the precedents for the use of force to regulate the labor market and the rising panic over Germany's food supply temporarily silenced the ban's opponents. Similarly, the chaotic months of violent revolution that marked the birth of the Weimar Republic quickly suppressed any objections to new restraints on agricultural workers' freedom-of-movement and freedom-of-employment rights. At the same time, young farm women's challenges to prohibitions on their mobility and choice of employment exemplified the passionate and often contentious clashes that erupted during the war over the balance between individual rights and the duty to the collective national interest in a state of emergency. While the debates over the merits and drawbacks of women's compulsory service in agriculture lingered, the failure of the 1917 and 1919 ordinances inspired an extended search for other remedies to ensure that *all* farm women met their productive and reproductive duties to the nation, which is the subject of Chapter 4.

Chapter 4

The Campaigns to Rationalize Farm Women's Work in Weimar Germany

Many rational moments will transform family farms and farm women's lives. A new type of farm wife will emerge from this transitional phase who will adapt herself more harmoniously to the new times ... who in particular will possess practical knowledge. This is the challenge presented by my findings.[1]

By the early 1920s, Maria Bidlingmaier's vision of a new, "rational" farm wife had captured the imaginations of numerous observers dedicated to solving the crisis of women's agricultural labor that had emerged so dramatically during the war. The leaders of what became a broad nationwide campaign to rationalize farm women's work included agricultural experts, rural social welfare reformers, and state officials. Their goals were far-reaching and their messages targeted both wives and daughters. As workers, rationalized farm women would help Germany attain food self-sufficiency, while as wives and mothers they would restore the health and morals of their families and communities. Moreover, experts reasoned that if farm wives won public recognition and respect as skillful, modern household managers, their daughters would be less likely to flee the countryside at the earliest opportunity and instead remain to act as disciples of rationalized work methods and techniques.[2] Therefore rationalization was pitched not only as an antidote to the overburdening of farm wives, but also as a remedy for the chronic shortage of women's labor on family farms, and the accompanying economic and social chaos.[3]

---

[1]　Maria Bidlingmaier, *Die Bäuerin in zwei Gemeinden Württembergs* (Stuttgart: W. Kohlhammer Verlag, 1918), p. 199.

[2]　Dorothea Derlitzki, *Arbeitsersparnis im Landhaushalt. Eine zusammenfassende Darstellung der "Arbeitslehre im Landhaushalt" unter Berücksichtigung der haushaltswissenschaftlichen und hauswirtschaftlichen Bestrebungen der Jetztzeit für Landfrauen, wirtschaftliche Frauenschulen, Haushaltungsschulen, usw* (Berlin: Paul Parey, 1926), p. 9; Georg Derlitzki, 'Die Forschungsarbeit der hauswirtschaftlichen Abteilung Pommritz unter Berücksichtigung der Hygiene der Landfrauenarbeit', *Land und Frau* 16/34 (August 1932): 571.

[3]　Elizabeth Bright Jones, 'Landwirtschaftliche Arbeit und weibliche Körper in Deutschland, 1918–1933', in B. Binder, S. Göttsch, W. Kaschuba, and K. Vanja (eds), *Ort. Arbeit. Körper: Ethnographie Europäischer Modernen* (Münster: Waxmann Verlag, 2005), pp. 477–84. For a detailed overview of the rural housewives' movement

In a nutshell, the new science of agricultural home economics emphasized that saving time, energy, and cash depended more on educating farm wives to think "economically" than on the purchase of the latest labor-saving devices.[4] Indeed, while German home economists frequently lauded American farms as models of progress, they also acknowledged that the American vision of farm wives as enthusiastic consumers of expensive appliances was unrealistic given the average farm family's perennially tight budget and shortage of cash.[5] Thus,

---

see Christina Schwarz, *Die Landfrauenbewegung in Deutschland. Zur Geschichte einer Frauenorganisation unter besonderer Berücksichtigung der Jahre 1898 bis 1933* (Mainz: Gesellschaft für Volkskunde in Rheinland-Pfalz, e.V., 1990); Helene Albers, *Zwischen Hof, Haushalt und Familie: Bäuerinnen in Westfalen-Lippe (1920–1960)* (Paderborn: F. Schöningh, 2001), pp. 262–83.

[4]   On industrial rationalization see Mary Nolan, 'Das Deutsche Institut für technische Arbeitsschulung und die Schaffung des neuen Arbeiters', in Dagmar Reese et al. (eds), *Rationale Beziehungen? Geschlechterverhältnisse im Rationalisierungsprozeß* (Frankfurt/ Main: Suhrkamp, 1993), pp. 189–221; Mary Nolan, *Visions of Modernity: American Business and the Modernization of Germany* (New York: Oxford University Press, 1993); Detlev Peukert, *The Weimar Republic: the Crisis of Classical Modernity* (New York: Hill and Wang, 1992), pp. 107–26; Nancy Reagin, 'Comparing Apples and Oranges: Housewives and the Politics of Consumption in Interwar Germany', in Susan Strasser et al. (eds), *Getting and Spending: European and American Consumer Societies in the Twentieth Century* (Washington, DC: German Historical Institute, 1998), pp. 241–62; J. Ronald Shearer, 'Talking About Efficiency: Politics and the Industrial Rationalization Movement in the Weimar Republic', *Central European History* 28/4 (1995): 483–506. On the rationalization of sexuality see Atina Grossmann, 'The New Woman and the Rationalization of Sexuality in Weimar Germany', in A. Snitow et al. (eds), *Powers of Desire: The Politics of Sexuality* (New York: Monthly Review Press, 1983), pp. 153–761; Cornelie Usborne, *The Politics of the Body in Weimar Germany: Women's Reproductive Rights and Duties* (Ann Arbor: University of Michigan, 1992), pp. 69–101. On farm household rationalization in Europe during the 1920s see Maurice Beaufreton, 'Farm Household Management Travelling Schools', *International Review of Agricultural Economics* [hereafter *IRAE*] 3I (1925): 147–64; G. C., 'Belgium: The Caravan Farm Household Management School', *IRAE* 4 (1926): 315–17; S. L. Loewes, 'Farm Household Management Instruction in the Netherlands', *IRAE* 4 (1926): 518–31.

[5]   See Irene Witte's enthusiastic descriptions of American home economics in *Heim und Technik in Amerika* (Berlin: VDI Verlag, 1928); Anina Klebe, 'Das wirtschaftliche Amerika', *Land und Frau* 9/29 (July 18, 1925): 359–60; see also Nolan, *Visions of Modernity*, p. 9. Mary Neth, Katherine Jellison, and other historians of American farm women during the same period nevertheless emphasize that American farm wives *did not* absorb the overwhelmingly consumerist message promoted by agricultural experts and extension services without question, but instead made decisions about investing in new technology according to budget, generation/age, geographic location, and community disapproval. Katherine Jellison, *Entitled to Power: Farm Women and Technology, 1913–1963* (Chapel Hill: University of North Carolina Press, 1993), pp. 33–65; Mary Neth, *Preserving the Family Farm: Women, Community, and the Foundations of Agribusiness in the Midwest, 1900–1940* (Baltimore: The Johns Hopkins University Press, 1995), pp. 187–213; see also

discussions about new machines and gadgets often were prefaced by caveats about their limited labor-saving potential in the German farm household. For example, in her 1926 manual for farm wives, Agnes Brirup-Lindemann introduced the discussion of household technology with her "Golden Rule" of machines: *"Using simple machines saves energy and time, but not labor."*[6] Instead, German home economists and agricultural experts emphasized the labor-saving potential of planning, analyzing, and evaluating each task, and stressed that farm wives could implement many of their guidelines and suggestions without cost.

This chapter explores how Weimar agricultural and home economics experts defined rationalization on family farms with respect to farm wives' work, and the perceived opportunities for reform due to the overlapping of farm women's productive and reproductive tasks. It traces how the new standards of efficiency and the latest technology were evaluated and promoted through rural home economics manuals, farm periodicals, and both state-sponsored and independent agricultural organizations. While the high cost of new labor-saving devices for the farm household and the priority given to the *Aussenwirtschaft* continually stymied these rationalization efforts, reformers noted that notions of "housewifely honor" and established traditions also slowed the adoption of their prescriptions.[7] Much of the advice addressed the working conditions of farm wives across Germany, but special attention is given here to the rationalization campaign in Saxony, the site of the nation's most prominent rural home economics school. Founded in 1925 by Dorothea and Georg Derlitzki in the southeastern village of Pommritz in Upper Lusatia [Oberlausitz], it was a sub-department of the Pommritz state-sponsored experimental farm. Statistics on Saxon family farms' investment in new technology and the weekly diary entries of one farm daughter from the district of Dresden between 1930 and 1932 offer several measures of the rationalization movement's impact on Saxon farm households and individual girls at the end of the Weimar period.

The Weimar campaign to rationalize farm wives' work was above all a quest for order through lessons in careful planning, economy of movement, and concentration on the task at hand. In that sense, the experiences of deprivation and upheaval during and after the war were fundamental to the campaign's shape and direction. Glowing advertisements for the latest labor-saving appliances were tempered by experts' cautionary advice to farm wives about the cost and practicalities of owning new appliances such as electric washing machines, stoves, or milk separators. As one prominent activist warned:

Jane Adams, *The Transformation of Rural Life: Southern Illinois, 1890–1990* (Chapel Hill: University of North Carolina Press, 1994).

[6]   Agnes Brirup-Lindemann, *Der Arbeits- und Pflichtenkreis der ländlichen Hausfrau in Westfalen und Lippe* (Warendorf I. Westf.: Heimatverlag der J. Schnellschen Buchhandlung, 1926), p. 180. Emphasis in original.

[7]   G. Derlitzki, 'Forschungsarbeit', p. 570.

Rationalization will become merely a slogan, and will subsequently disappear, if it is branded falsely as Americanization and mechanization, stigmatized as flat and lifeless ... Housework [on the farm] is in crisis ... Change is necessary, and that change must come through rationalization.[8]

Defining Farm Women's Work and the Scope of Rationalization

The context of the farm household, where productive and reproductive work overlapped, profoundly shaped the goals of the rationalization campaign. In this respect, Weimar experts had come a long way from the prewar agricultural management guides that ignored the farm household, and the labor of dependents, altogether. Indeed they sought to integrate the postwar goal of increasing food production on family farms with those of the broader campaign to modernize all German women's housework, which sought to relieve women of the most onerous domestic responsibilities.[9] As agricultural home economics experts were fond of pointing out, the saving of farm women's reproductive labor in the form of housework translated into tangible benefits for the nation in the form of readily accessible and better-quality food supplies. Virtually all the prescriptive literature on rationalizing farm wives' work argued that the overlapping of farm women's productive and reproductive work must serve as the starting point for reform. In a speech at a Paris conference on the rationalization of work, rural home economist Liselotte Kueßner-Gerhard echoed Heinrich Sohnrey's wartime assertion that:

The farm household is inseparable from the economy of the farm. The organic connection is so strong that the business of the normal family farm would be unthinkable without the household ... Every sort of household waste, whether it be in material, time, or energy, drags the whole farm down; in contrast, every savings in time, energy, and material benefits the farm through the increase in production and the improvement in quality, in short, boosts the profitability of the farm.[10]

---

[8] Helene Wenck, 'Landfrauenarbeit "Grüne Woche" 1928', *Land und Frau* 12/7 (February 1928): 124. Quote is cited from the speech by G. Derlitzki under a sub-heading 'Rationalisierung der Landfrauenarbeit'.

[9] On the German housewives' movement more generally see Nancy R. Reagin, *Sweeping the German Nation: Domesticity and National Identity in Germany, 1870–1945* (Cambridge: Cambridge University Press, 2007).

[10] Liselotte Kueßner-Gerhard, 'Arbeitserleichterungen im Landhaushalt und ihre Auswirkung auf den landwirtschaftlichen Betrieb', IV Congrés International de L'Organisation Scientifique du Travail, Paris, 1929 (Bordeaux: Imp. Delmas, 1929): cxi–2. See also Heinrich Sohnrey, *Kriegsarbeit auf dem Lande. Wegweiser für ländliche Wohlfahrts- und Heimatpflege in Kriegszeit* (Berlin: Deutsche Landbuchhandlung, 1915),

Similarly, in a 1931 article on plans for building new farmhouses, the author emphasized that in contrast to urban household planning, where maximizing the efficiency of household work was the sole objective, farmhouse plans must heed both the demands of its members as consumers "as well as the more important role of production, the processing of foodstuffs, and the use of food unsuitable for sale. Thus a sensible farmhouse plan first takes into account the *demands of production*."[11]

The campaign to rationalize farm wives' productive work focused on ways to increase their output of eggs, milk, butter, fruits, and vegetables. Agricultural home economics experts asserted that farm wives' increased efficiency in the *Innenwirtschaft* would boost urban food supplies and decrease Germany's dependence on food imports, while at the same time reinforcing their femininity through the constant nurturing of plants and animals. One author, lamenting the rising imports of butter, cheese, eggs, vegetables, and fruit between 1913 and 1926, exhorted German farm wives to "take back domestic foodstuff markets."[12] At the same time, experts were optimistic that women's heavy, dirty work assisting men in the fields, or *Aussenwirtschaft*, would become increasingly unnecessary.[13] The deluge of advice targeting farm women reinforced the primacy of the *Innenwirtschaft* as the target of the rationalization campaign. Articles on gardening, small livestock (pigeons, rabbits, sheep, etc.), dairying, poultry, beekeeping, and garden equipment dominated the pages of women's farm journals.[14] Much of the advice focused on the most cost-effective strategies for expansion, how to recycle and reuse materials for other purposes, and gave explicit instructions on how to build simple labor-saving devices at home.

The postwar idealization of farm women's productive work in the rationalized *Innenwirtschaft* contrasted with the persistent ambivalence about married women's industrial work, and the prescribed transformation of the working-class household from separate sphere to rationalized factory as a means of easing their reproductive

---

p. 6; Fritz Klare, *Untersuchung über Einsatz und Ausnutzung der menschlichen Arbeitskräfte in bäuerlichen Betrieben* (Dessau: Gutenberg, 1932), p. 121.

[11]   Aenne von Strantz, 'Betriebs- und arbeitswirtschaftliche Betrachtungen zur Grundriß- und Raumgestaltung von Bauernhäusern', *Land und Frau* 15/22 (May 30, 1931): 415–16. Emphasis mine.

[12]   Tasch, 'Die Landfrau und die aktuellen agrarpolitischen Problemen', *Land und Frau* 12/3 (January 1928): 35. See also Anon., 'Die Bedeutung der Frauen im Obst und Gartenbau', *Land und Frau* 4/7 (February 1920): 41–2; Frau P. in Polen, 'Nochmals: Wege zur Gewinnung des Marktes für deutsches Obst', *Land und Frau* 12/32 (August 1928): 600; Anon., 'Die Stellung der Frau in der Landwirtschaft', *Die Praktische Landwirtin. Blätter für die Hausfrau des Landwirts* 14/7 (Magdeburg, August, 1922): 1.

[13]   See *Schriftensammlung der Zentrale der deutschen Landfrauen*, no. 2 (1918), p. 15.

[14]   See the tables of contents [*Inhaltsverzeichnisse*] for *Land und Frau* 1918–1933; also for *Die Gutsfrau:Halbmonatschrift für die gebildete Frau auf dem Lande* (Berlin: Deutscher Schriftenverlag).

labor.[15] Indeed, many of the recent arguments about the limits of household rationalization in Weimar focus on the campaign's new, and problematic, equation of the working-class household with the factory.[16] Barbara Orland and others point out that reformers never resolved the tensions between industrial rationalization, where success could be measured in terms of time, energy, or resources saved, and the rationalization of housework, where success was defined in terms of creating "better" mothers.[17] In contrast, agricultural home economists lauded the farm household as the ideal workplace for married women, and could measure the effectiveness of their strategies in liters of milk, bushels of fruit, and dozens of eggs.

Easing the arduous, and, above all, time-consuming reproductive work of farm wives, including cooking, cleaning, washing, mending, and childcare was viewed as the best means of increasing food production. The effort to reform farm wives' housework was not limited to the promotion of new technology in the form of consumer goods like washing machines or vacuum cleaners, although by the early 1930s, advertisements for these items appeared alongside those for canning equipment, piglets, fertilizers, strawberry plants, and the like.[18] Numerous prescriptive articles and household manuals urged farm wives to think not only about saving cash and stretching budgets, but above all in terms of saving time and energy. As Kueßner-Gerhard declared, "By saving time on housework, one can increase milk production through more careful feeding, more hygienic milking, and more efficient handling and shipping, all of which brings a higher market price."[19] She added that the same time-saving lessons could be applied to the production of eggs, vegetables, and fruit. Another agricultural home economist observed that although the laundry, or *Große Wäsche*, was done only periodically, the time spent on this task when spread out over the whole year

---

[15]   Mary Nolan, "'Housework Made Easy": The Taylorized Housewife in Weimar Germany's Rationalized Economy', *Feminist Studies* 16/3 (Fall 1990): 549–77, here p. 560.

[16]   Leonore Davidoff observes the same contradiction between middle- and upper-class households and the campaign to rationalize housework in late-nineteenth and early-twentieth-century Britain. Leonore Davidoff, 'The Rationalization of Housework', in Leonore Davidoff (ed.), *Worlds Between: Historical Perspectives on Gender and Class* (New York: Routledge, 1995), pp. 73–102, esp. p. 95.

[17]   See Nolan, 'Housework'; Barbara Orland, 'Emanzipation durch Rationalisierung? Der "rationelle Haushalt" als Konzept institutionalisierter Frauenpolitik in der Weimarer Republik', in Reese, *Rationale Beziehungen?*, pp. 222–50; Barbara Orland, 'Effizienz im Heim: die Rationalisierungsdebatte zur Reform der Hausarbeit in der Weimarer Republik', *Kultur und Technik: Zeitschrift des deutschen Museums München* 4/7 (1983): 221–7.

[18]   For example, see *Land und Frau* 16/34 (August 1932): 568, 580–6.

[19]   Kueßner-Gerhard, 'Arbeitserleichterungen', pp. cxi–4.

averaged the same amount of time daily as that spent on milking, "a task that is surely more valuable to the farm."[20]

The discussion of rationalization in farm households often acknowledged that the shortage of cash prevented investment in the latest household technology, as well as in farm machinery for the *Aussenwirtschaft*.[21] As one rural rationalization expert commented in 1925, "The majority of [farm] household budgets have suffered from the years of war, inflation, and deflation (and our efforts, if we want them to be worthwhile, should target the majority)."[22] In her 1926 manual, *Saving Labor in the Farm Household*, Dorothea Derlitzki complained that family farmers were slow to invest in even the simplest labor-saving conveniences to assist farm wives with their housework, even as they prided themselves on their use of new machines and management techniques.[23] Nevertheless, Derlitzki optimistically affirmed the potential of small-changes:

> In these hard times we must not leave the smallest means untried to make housework more economic (*wirtschaftlich*) ... "A little goes a long way" is more valid in this case than anywhere else.[24]

Her husband, nationally-acclaimed agricultural labor expert Georg Derlitzki, elaborated on this theme in a 1932 article for *Land und Frau* [*Land/Nation and Woman*], the national journal for farm women. Derlitzki argued that it was not merely the *amount* of housework that burdened farm wives but also the "irrational organization of work."[25] He added that the rationalization of farm work meant "the preservation of a healthy soul and body," which the farm wife could achieve immediately, and without cost, by avoiding heavy lifting, bending, stretching, and carrying. Derlitzki warned farm wives not to confuse rationalization with mechanization, giving them an excuse to reject the advice before even trying it. Instead, he encouraged farm women, if they still wanted labor-saving devices, to choose small, inexpensive machines with great care, following home economists' guidelines for selection. Others, like his colleague Eva Förster, exhorted farm women to adopt strict bookkeeping methods as a way of rationalizing their spending and scolded wives for not making time to draw up detailed household

---

[20]   Aenne von Strantz, 'Bericht über die Arbeiten der hauswirtschaftlichen Abteilung der Versuchsanstalt für Landarbeitslehre Pommritz', *Land und Frau* 16/34 (August 1932): 574.

[21]   G. Derlitzki, 'Die Forschungsarbeit', pp. 570–2; Kueßner-Gerhard, 'Arbeits-erleichterungen', pp. cxi–2.

[22]   Anon., 'Hauswirtschaftlichkeit', *Land und Frau* 9/29 (July 18, 1925): 363.

[23]   D. Derlitzki, *Arbeitsersparnis*, pp. 8–9. Similar observations appear in contemporary American farm journals, see Jellison, *Entitled to Power*, pp. 11, 19.

[24]   D. Derlitzki, *Arbeitsersparnis*, p. 1.

[25]   G. Derlitzki, 'Forschungsarbeit', p. 571.

budgets.[26] She demanded, "How else will you account for the valuable resources entrusted to you? How can you *save* – and that you must do in these difficult times – if you cannot display the figures that you begin with and which later prove what you have saved?"

In addition, Georg Derlitzki asserted that any program to rationalize farm women's housework should consider "physiological, psychological, hygienic, social, pedagogical, household, and national economic factors."[27] While their proposals seemed overwhelmingly ambitious (or diffuse), the Derlitzkis were not alone in their insistence that rationalized farm wives would simultaneously propel Weimar Germany's economic recovery and repair the nation's badly torn social and moral fabric. Social reformer J. B. Dieing conceded that the fears raised by some that rationalizing farm women's work would transform them into "pure materialists" with no "spiritual connection" to their work was best combated by balancing technical and cultural training.[28] In his view, a farm wife that felt less burdened with unpleasant tasks would contribute more to the agricultural economy *and* promote the happiness and the industriousness of her household and her community.

Agricultural home economists acknowledged that changing women's behavior would not be easy, especially in terms of how to perform certain tasks. Georg Derlitzki complained that farm wives consistently resisted his advice about performing many tasks sitting down, despite the fact that doing the same task standing up did not yield better results and caused backaches and varicose veins.[29] While rationalization experts frequently chided older women for clinging to their grandmothers' ways, they emphasized that if the younger generation adopted the new techniques, girls would be less likely to leave the countryside.

Despite rationalization experts' assurances that the new science of home economics would enhance the economic and social status of farm women, their agenda grappled with the same tensions that plagued the movement to rationalize urban women's housework. On the one hand, the movement promised that household rationalization would win new respect from their families and the public for farm wives' reproductive work, and reinforce the common bonds between rural and urban housewives. On the other hand, increasing farm wives' productive work remained the clear, overarching goal of agricultural home economics experts, which reinforced the low status of everyday household tasks like cooking, cleaning, and laundry.

---

[26]   Eva Förster, 'Buchführung im Landhaushalt', *Land und Frau* 15/1 (January 8, 1931): 7.

[27]   G. Derlitzki, 'Forschungsarbeit', p. 572.

[28]   J. B. Dieing, *Landfrauennot!* (Freiburg i. Br.: Verlag der Arbeitsgemeinschaft für Dorfcaritas, 1928), p. 12.

[29]   G. Derlitzki, 'Forschungsarbeit', p. 570.

Still, the campaign never aimed to revise established gender divisions of labor as a means of easing farm wives' burden.[30] While experts sought to break down, analyze, and reconfigure every task according to Taylorist principles, there was no question that wives bore primary responsibility for the profitability of the *Innenwirtschaft* and the everyday maintenance of the farm household.[31] Furthermore, experts often assumed that the farmer, not his wife, decided whether a particular purchase for the house or dairy was necessary. An article on the financial crisis in a 1929 Saxon agricultural calendar urged the farmer to think about the work of his "loyal life-partner," and to consider investing in an electric milk separator, for "a rationally-run dairy is not only a reliable and consistent source of income, it is often the only reserve when crops fail."[32] One contemporary labor psychology expert argued explicitly that, "The gender division of labor, which is present even in the most primitive economies, must be researched according to its psychological principles so as to make it optimally productive for the multitude of agricultural tasks."[33] Agricultural efficiency studies published throughout the Weimar period invariably, and uncritically, referred to women in their examples of manual labor, such as hoeing beets or sorting potatoes, while men used the latest plows, cultivators, and harrows.[34] The blend of conservatism and innovation that characterized the campaign's efforts reinforced established gender divisions of labor, even as it sought to transform farm wives from harried beasts of burden into confident, efficient household managers.[35]

---

[30]   A rare exception is Dieing's suggestion that men and boys, however unwillingly, be trained to do stall work to relieve farm wives. Dieing, *Landfrauennot!*, p. 11.

[31]   Von Saldern, describing the 1920s campaigns to rationalize German and American women's housework, argues, "Thus, the gender division of labor was neither given up nor did it remain traditional, but it was reconstructed and renewed, i.e., 'regendered,' but on the basis of modern social rationalization." Adelheid von Saldern, 'Social Rationalization of Living and Housework in Germany and the United States in the 1920s', *The History of the Family* 2/1 (1997): 73–97, here p. 83.

[32]   'Etwas über die Geldnot und ihre Beseitigung! Es gibt einen Ausweg aus der Geldnot!', *Der landwirtschaftliche Kalender für den Freistaat Sachsen* (Dresden: Verlag des Landeskulturrates Sachsen, 1929), p. 141.

[33]   Friedrich Sander, 'Die Bedeutung der Arbeitspsychologie für die Land-arbeitslehre', in G. Derlitzki (ed.), *Berichte über Landarbeit 1* (Stuttgart: Franck'sche Verlagsbuchhandlung, 1927), p. 103.

[34]   G. Derlitzki, 'Die Landarbeitsforschung: dargestellt an den Arbeiten des Versuchsanstalt für Landarbeitslehre Pommritz im Sachsen', *Berichte über Landarbeit*, illustrations on pp. 26–30, 44–5.

[35]   Gertrud Dyhrenfurth, *Ergebnisse einer Untersuchung über die Arbeits- und Lebensverhältnisse der Frauen in der Landwirtschaft* (Jena: Gustav Fischer, 1916), p. 51.

Leaders of the Campaign

The movement to rationalize farm women's work was broad-based, promoted by agricultural home economists, the National Agricultural Housewives' Association [*Reichsverband landwirtschaftlicher Hausfrauen-Vereine* – hereafter RLHV], provincial agricultural chambers, and regional associations of farm wives throughout Germany. In Saxony, the Home Economics Department of the state-sponsored experimental farm in Pommritz, overseen by the Derlitzkis, tested new household gadgets and promoted their standardization, devised more efficient work methods based on time/motion studies, and broadcast their findings to farm wives through published manuals, traveling exhibitions, films, and radio.[36] The home economics research experiments at Pommritz had far-reaching influence in Germany, and also attracted the attention of other European rationalization experts.[37] Numerous articles and advertisements from farm journals like *Land und Frau*, as well as agricultural calendars for women published by its regional branches, attempted to educate and inform women about the latest tools and techniques designed to ease their productive and reproductive labor. In 1928, the Saxon Agricultural Chamber described its recent efforts to educate farm women, a program that included traveling classes in nutrition and cooking, sewing and ironing, cheese-making, fruit processing, gardening, and poultry-raising. In addition, the Agricultural Chamber also sponsored seminars to train teachers for home economics classes, and approved the election of a representative from the teachers' committee to attend meetings of the Chamber in order to promote "close cooperation" between the two organizations.[38]

The Pommritz Experimental Farm was founded in 1919 along with similar institutions in the Saxon village of Möckern, near Leipzig, and in Dresden.[39] While the Möckern research station focused on livestock breeding and Dresden on plant cultivation, Pommritz conducted studies of agricultural labor, which included farm

---

[36]   D. Derlitzki, *Arbeitsersparnis*, p. 10; see also L. Kueßner-Gerhard, 'Arbeits-erleichterungen', pp. cxi–3; D. R. Kleinhans, 'Die Bedeutung des landwirtschaftlichen Lehrfilms', *Vorträge gehalten anläßlich der zweiten sächsischen landwirtschaftlichen Woche in Dresden vom 23. bis 27 Januar 1922* (Dresden: Verlag des Landeskulturrates Sachsen, 1922), pp. 58–60.

[37]   Anon., 'The Rationalization of the Work of Farm Women in Germany', *International Labour Review* 26 (1932): 707–9.

[38]   'Abteilung Frauenarbeit', *Bericht über die Tätigkeit der Landwirtschaftskammer für den Freistaat Sachsen im Jahre 1927 und amtlicher Bericht über die 6. Gesamtsitzung am 27. März 1928* (Dresden: Selbstverlag der Landwirtschaftskammer für den Freistaat Sachsen, 1928), p. 96.

[39]   For a detailed description of the Saxon *Versuchsanstalten*, see Sächsische Wirtschaftsministerium an den Herrn Reichsminister für Ernährung und Landwirtschaft, April 1923, Ministerium des Innern [hereafter MdI] 15498/2, 'Anfragen auswärtiger Regierungen über hiesigen landwirtschaftliche Verhältnisse und Einrichtungen', Sächsisches Hauptstaatsarchiv [hereafter SäHStA], pp. 59–62.

management, work techniques, and developing new labor-saving technology. In a 1920 speech given to the Saxon Economics Society in Dresden, Georg Derlitzki argued that the science of farm management needed drastic rethinking, and that the institute's research on the theory and practice of agricultural work would establish "the elusive boundary between maximal intensity and diminishing returns."[40] In 1923, the Saxon Economics Ministry in Dresden reported with satisfaction that the experiments and films produced at Pommritz had aroused great interest in farm communities, and that "countless agricultural associations and schools had visited [Pommritz], because they have an especially strong interest [in research on work]."[41]

Georg and Dorothea Derlitzki also zealously promoted household rationalization as a strategy for easing the physical burdens of farm wives' labor and boosting the productivity of family farms. The establishment of the Pommritz Home Economics Department in 1926, with financial support from the Saxon and Reich governments, attested to the Derlitzkis' success at promoting their philosophy that farm wives' productive work constituted a "national economic factor: for the skill with which a farm wife carries out her work, her 'household management,' determines the prosperity of her family, the entire household, the economy, and therefore the nation."[42] At the same time, the Derlitzkis' emphasis on creating rationalized farm wives who would "cleanse" and "refresh" family life, in turn fostering "community and a sense of belonging," elevated them from industrious producers to reassuring cultural symbols of maternity and national strength.

In *Saving Labor in the Farm Household*, Dorothea Derlitzki credited the influence of Pommritz presentations and films, as well as conversations with her husband, for inspiring her to extend the study of farm management to the household. The manual is divided into two sections, "The Creation of Optimal Working Conditions" and "Work Techniques." Under "Working Conditions," Derlitzki included chapters on the relationship of rooms to one another, the practical furnishing of work rooms, a guide to the most useful household tools and machines, the planning and preparation of work, work rhythms and breaks, and maintaining steady concentration.

The reorganization of rooms was the first prerequisite for much of Derlitzki's labor-saving advice. She urged farm women to make sketches of their kitchens, pantries, cellars, eating areas, laundry rooms, cow stalls, milk-processing rooms, pig pens, and chicken coops, noting how the rooms related to one another, and

[40] G. Derlitzki, *'Versuchsanstalt Pommritz'*, *Vorträge: Die Neuorganisation der landwirtschaftlichen Versuchsanstalten in Sachsen und ihre Aufgaben, in Schriften der Oekonomischen Gesellschaft im Freistaat Sachsen* (Leipzig: Reichenbach'sche Verlagsbuchhandlung, 1920), pp. 12–22, here p. 15.

[41] Wirtschaftsministerium an den Herrn Reichsminister, April 1923, MdI 15498/2, SäHStA, p. 61.

[42] D. Derlitzki, *Arbeitsersparnis*, p. 8.

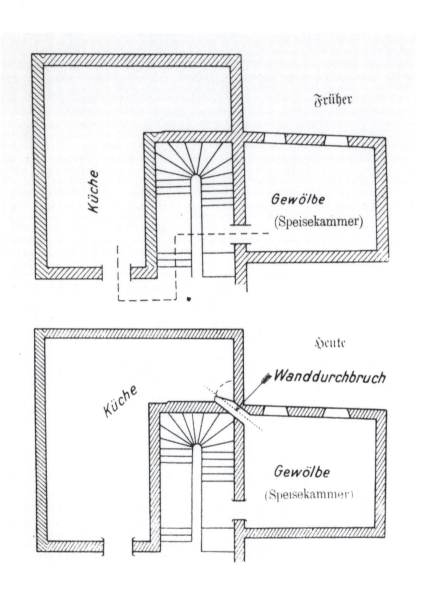

Figure 4.1   **"Correct Arrangement of Doors between Kitchen and Pantry,
               c. 1925" [Source: Dorothea Derlitzki, *Arbeitsersparnis im
               Landhaushalt* (Berlin: Paul Parey, 1926), p. 14].**

informed them that "small, often astonishingly simple changes can be made that make an enormous difference in lightening the workload."[43] Derlitzki provided simple illustrations of the right and wrong placement of rooms, with suggestions for making improvements that shortened distances between kitchen and pantry, stall and shed, laundry and bleaching room, primarily by removing walls or adding doors. She also offered detailed advice, acknowledging her debt to American home economist Christine Frederick, on how to arrange individual rooms, again offering diagrams of practical and impractical arrangements, with lines illustrating how the number of back-and-forth movements decreased when equipment was arranged "functionally."[44]

Derlitzki continued with a discussion of recent innovations in equipment used by farm wives, all developed and tested at Pommritz, often with illustrations for do-it-yourself construction, such as a wheelbarrow for transporting laundry from bleaching to drying room or a cheese-making table designed by a Saxon farm wife. None of the machines and tools she described used electricity or other fuel. Instead, Derlitzki emphasized improving the efficiency of everyday items. She queried, for example, "Why industry, which has given us the most complicated machines, has not come up with a milk can or a coffee pot that doesn't drip, or a collapsible shelf on the stove to put down our mixing bowls? Why is there no thermometer in the oven? ... Every housewife could name these and many other examples from their own experience."[45] Derlitzki also criticized industry for its failure to standardize everything from bedsteads and sheets to milk pails, sewing machines, and canning equipment. She praised the local rural housewives' association in Hamburg for pioneering this effort by inviting engineers to a 1924 exhibition of household machines and tools, encouraging farm wives to express their wishes directly to the manufacturers.[46] Derlitzki ended with the declaration that, "We housewives must never give up the efforts to make our wishes known; only tenacity will achieve the goal."

---

[43]   Derlitzki, *Arbeitsersparnis*, pp. 14–16.

[44]   Derlitzki, *Arbeitsersparnis*, p. 17. See also Irene Witte, *Die rationelle Haushaltsführung. Betriebswissenschaftliche Studien* (Berlin: Julius Springer, 1920, 1922), a translation of Christine Frederick, *The New Housekeeping; Efficiency Studies in Home Management* (Garden City, NY: Doubleday, Page & Co., 1913, 1916); Irene Witte, *Taylor, Gilbreth, Ford: Gegenwartsfragen der amerikanischen und europäischen Arbeitswissenschaft*, 2nd edn (Berlin: Verlag von R. Oldenbourg, 1925); Aenne von Strantz, 'Betriebs- und arbeitswirtschaftliche Betrachtungen zur Grundriß und Raumgestaltung von Bauernhäusern', *Land und Frau* 15/22 (May 30, 1931): 415–16; Theda Behme, 'Ländliche Wohnungseinrichtung der Gegenwart', *Land und Frau* 15/22 (May 30, 1931): 417–18. On the influence of American ideas on the German housekeeping movement and the "new household" see Nicholas Bullock, 'First the Kitchen: Then the Façade', *Journal of Design History* 1/3–4 (1988): 177–92.

[45]   Derlitzki, *Arbeitsersparnis*, p. 36.

[46]   Derlitzki, *Arbeitsersparnis*, p. 10.

In addition to publishing rationalization manuals, the home economists at Pommritz also conducted numerous experiments at their model farmhouse on 25 hectares of land. In one two-year experiment, all the tasks associated with the farm household were observed and logged according to sequence and the time required to complete them.[47] In the second year, a plan of tasks for each week was drawn up by the farm wife (unnamed) and the home economist, and the impact of the plan on the farm wife's work measured according to time saved. With evident pride, the reporter Aenne von Strantz noted:

> The results were very gratifying. While [during the first year] the farm wife's days were hectic and nervous, with work constantly being interrupted by much back-and-forth, the following year went more smoothly, first because tasks were organized more efficiently and second because the farm wife was calmer now that she had a plan that assured her that all the work would be completed.

Von Strantz also commented that the weekly plan had saved the farm wife an average of 78 minutes per day, but that instead of using it as free time, she added the cleaning of milk bottles to her duties, which in turn allowed the *Magd* more time for field work.[48]

While the Home Economics Department was charged with researching and reforming all aspects of farm wives' work in the *Innenwirtschaft*, Pommritz experts also conducted experiments using tools and techniques designed to lighten farm women's burden in the *Aussenwirtschaft*. For example, new tools and techniques for more efficient potato planting, weeding, and harvesting were developed specifically for women workers. Georg Derlitzki enthusiastically described the introduction of a rake designed for potato harvesting: "The success of the new tool was, despite its unfamiliarity, immediately apparent. The women eagerly adopted the new rake ... especially since they did not have to bend so deeply when harvesting."[49] He also described a table designed at Pommritz for potato harvesting, tilted to make the work of sorting less strenuous because women could work sitting down. In conclusion, Derlitzki declared that in addition to being in the interests of the farm manager,

---

[47]   von Strantz, 'Bericht', pp. 573–5.

[48]   von Strantz, 'Bericht', p. 573. Von Strantz's observations echo those of Schützhold in his study of Saxon farm wives, where women unfailingly used timed saved on one task to complete another. See Gerhard Schützhold, *Die sächsische Landfrau: ihr Aufgaben- und Pflichtenkreis im bäuerlichen Landwirtschaftsbetrieb* (Dresden: Theodor Steinkopff, 1934).

[49]   G. Derlitzki, 'Die Landarbeitsforschung dargestellt an den Arbeiten der Versuchs- anstalt für Landarbeitslehre Pommritz i. Sachsen', in Derlitzki, *Berichte über Landarbeit*, p. 29.

> The psychological effects of these improvements cannot be underestimated. In this case, it was particularly noticeable, since the women reported for work gladly and punctually, even women who had previously avoided potato harvesting because their girth made it difficult to bend over. We try through such measures to strengthen the desire to work.[50]

In later experiments, Pommritz researchers measured how much oxygen and how many calories women used to plant potatoes, first with a specially-designed basket that allowed them to stand up straight, and then using the conventional method of bending over to reach baskets on the ground.[51] They concluded that the lesser amount of oxygen and fewer calories women used when planting with the new basket reinforced their previous assertion that women appeared less tired when using the new techniques.

The Derlitzkis' guidelines on task planning, preparation, timing, and methods were intended mot merely to simplify and expedite the farm wife's work. Indeed, they predicted confidently that the calmness and order the farm wife created when following their models would spur other members of the household to work more efficiently and with greater zeal than before. Thus the farm wife was responsible both for reevaluating and reorganizing her own work and workplace, and ensuring that the mood of the farm household remained "high-spirited."[52] Dorothea Derlitzki opined that the farm wife's rational management of the household was valuable "not just in monetary terms, like that of her husband, but also in terms of ideal values ... The farm wife's efficient household management has the power to ... preserve family life as the source of the nation's strength."[53] Aenne Gausebeck, a representative of the Rhenish Rural Social Welfare Office, carried this responsibility even further, claiming that a good farm wife should be synonymous with a good neighbor, and that farm wives bore responsibility for the tone of the community and for promoting its emotional well-being.[54]

Wilhelm Wagner, who published an exhaustive manual for "new farm wives" in 1926, also gave advice about the most efficient arrangement of rooms in the farmhouse, and offered guidance on household cleaning and on the use of new hand-powered kitchen gadgets for slicing, grinding, straining, etc.[55] While Wagner claimed that "every farmhouse should have an electric motor and

---

[50]   G. Derlitzki, 'Landarbeitsforschung', p. 31.

[51]   Dr. Huxdorff, 'Arbeitsphysiologische Aufgaben bei der Untersuchung der Arbeiten von Landfrauen', *Land und Frau* 16/34 (August 1932): 575–6.

[52]   D. Derlitzki, *Arbeitsersparnis*, p. 57.

[53]   D. Derlitzki, *Arbeitsersparnis*, p. 8.

[54]   Aenne Gausebeck, 'Vom Landmädchen zur Landfrau', published speech in *Wohlfahrt und Wirtschaft: Bericht über die 29. Hauptversammlung des deutschen Vereins für ländliche Wohlfahrts- und Heimatpflege am 25. und 26. Februar 1926 in Berlin* (Berlin: Deutscher Verein für ländliche Wohlfahrts- und Heimatpflege, 1926), pp. 19–27, here p. 24.

[55]   Wilhelm Wagner, *Die Schule der Jungbäuerin* (Berlin: Paul Parey, 1926), pp. 1–30.

therefore a vacuum cleaner," his meticulous cleaning directions nevertheless recommended sweeping carpets daily, "first to the left, then to the right, then once more against the grain" with a solution of vinegar and water or damp tea leaves. He also recommended using a mixture of soap and sand in lukewarm water for the weekly scrubbing of bare floors.[56] Furthermore, while he gave very explicit instructions about the proper height for the kitchen tap, Wagner reminded readers that "One should remember to boil enough hot water for washing up while one is cooking."[57] For laundry, he noted that a copper kettle was best, since it could be used in the fall for making preserves, but that less expensive enamel or tin kettles were acceptable. Also requisite were "buckets, basins, washing boards, washing baskets, and a clothesline."[58] In a subsequent section, Wagner recommended that farm wives consider purchasing an electric washing machine if they had access to cheap electricity, but otherwise suggested that hand-cranked washers were a good alternative. However, he warned that "if you do acquire a washing machine, you cannot avoid the purchase of a wringing machine."[59]

Like other Weimar experts on rural rationalization, Wagner also aimed to increase the efficiency and productivity of farm women's work in food production and gave advice about livestock care, preparing milk and milk products, and vegetable gardening. Yet very few of these sections mentioned labor-saving devices or machines, with the exception of milk preparation, where he provided a detailed illustration of the "Alfa-Caval Milk Centrifuge" that could be powered by hand or by electricity.[60] Wagner emphasized that the machine was more efficient at separating the milk fat when run by electricity, but also pointed out that each time it was used, all the (disassembled) parts had to be scrubbed with a mixture of baking soda and hot water, rinsed, and allowed to air dry.[61] Directions for making butter included illustrations of recommended hand churns, notably "the Triumph" and "the Viktoria," which required "steady and uninterrupted turning. After 25–45 minutes (of turning), the butter is ready."[62] His instructions for vegetable cultivation outlined garden plans and proper cellar storage to ensure that the household had a steady supply of vegetables all year, while he advised on the use of fertilizers, eradication of garden pests, and precisely how many centimeters should separate rows of plants. In addition to hand tools, he recommended that wives have two watering cans.[63]

According to Wagner, farm wives' work also included their duties as "members of the political economy," or *Volkswirtschaft*, which for him encompassed the family, village, province, and nation. Furthermore, he insisted that the sole purpose

---

[56]   W. Wagner, *Schule*, pp. 14–17.

[57]   W. Wagner, *Schule*, pp. 18, 26.

[58]   W. Wagner, *Schule*, p. 30.

[59]   W. Wagner, *Schule*, p. 36.

[60]   W. Wagner, *Schule*, p. 246.

[61]   W. Wagner, *Schule*, p. 247.

[62]   W. Wagner, *Schule*, pp. 248–9.

[63]   W. Wagner, *Schule*, p. 261.

of farm wives' civic and practical education was the preservation of the German *Heimat*.[64] This meant not only improving farm women's productive and household work, but even the family's leisure time. Wagner urged farm wives and especially daughters to find ways of making Sunday "a real family holiday" instead of "reserving time for one's own pleasures."[65] Besides local agricultural chambers, the German Agricultural Council [*Deutscher Landwirtschaftsrat*], and Heinrich Sohnrey's Association for Rural Social Welfare and *Heimat* Preservation [*Verein für ländliche Wohlfahrts- und Heimatpflege*], Wagner singled out rural housewives' associations, led by Elisabet Boehm, as the linchpin of the campaign to educate farm women to become better workers, mothers, and community members.[66]

Indeed rural housewives' associations were at the forefront of grassroots efforts to rationalize farm wives' productive and reproductive work. Elisabet Boehm, the wife of an East Elbian estate owner, founded the first rural housewives' association in 1898 in Rastenburg, East Prussia, and by 1914 there were rural housewives' associations in West Prussia, Posen, Brandenburg, Silesia, and Schleswig-Holstein.[67] By 1932 there were 2,195 rural housewives' associations throughout Germany, with 129 in Saxony alone.[68] In the same year, the Saxon associations reported that 620 lectures and films had been presented, including 65 on poultry-raising, 62 on gardening, 51 on milking and dairy production, 50 on general agriculture, 83 on housework, 34 on economics, 103 on health and nutrition, 37 on culture and pedagogy, and 135 "miscellaneous."[69] In addition, 104 courses were taught, with over half devoted to housework, 70 fields trips were sponsored, and 13 exhibitions mounted.

At the national level, representatives of the RLHV, including Boehm and Kueßner-Gerhard, worked closely with the German Agricultural Association [*Deutsche Landwirtschafts-Gesellschaft*, or DLG] on projects like the formation in 1921 of a sub-committee on household appliances within the larger DLG Committee on Agricultural Machines, and the participation of the RLHV in annual national farm exhibitions like the *Grüne Woche* in Berlin, beginning in 1925.[70] In 1924, the DLG also created the Committee for Housework, to "improve the overall functioning of the farm," and sub-committees that addressed the question

---

[64]   W. Wagner, *Schule*, p. 319.

[65]   W. Wagner, *Schule*, pp. 325–6.

[66]   W. Wagner, *Schule*, p. 319.

[67]   Christina Schwarz and Friederike v. Natzmer, '"Frauen im Zeichen der Biene" – die Geschichte der deutschen Landfrauenbewegung', in Ostpreußisches Landesmuseum, Lüneburg (ed.), *Elisabet Boehm und die Landfrauenbewegung*, museum catalog (Husum: Husum Druck- und Verlagsgesellschaft, 1998), p. 34.

[68]   Schwarz and Natzmer, 'Frauen', p. 34. Saxony's first association was founded in 1917.

[69]   'Übersicht über die Tätigkeit in den Verbänden', in *Land und Frau* (ed.), *Landfrauen-Kalender 1932* (Berlin: Paul Parey, 1932), p. 40.

[70]   Schwarz and Natzmer, 'Frauen', p. 48.

of kitchen lay-out, laundries, and agricultural education. That the representative of the Housework Committee for the RLHV also filled the same post for the DLG testifies to the close cooperation of the two organizations.[71] Together, the DLG committees and the Rural Agricultural Housewives' associations published numerous pamphlets and manuals on the rationalization of farm women's work.[72]

Abb. 144. Vom dritten Lehrgang für Schweinefütterung und -haltung in Ruhlsdorf: 5 weibliche Kursusteilnehmer. — Zu nebenstehendem Beitrage.

Figure 4.2   "Participants in a Pig-Raising Seminar, Ruhlsdorf/Brandenburg, c. 1925" [Source: *Land und Frau*, July 4, 1925, p. 331].

One early sign of their cooperation was an exhibit of farm household gadgets at a larger DLG-sponsored exhibition in Nürnberg in 1922.[73] In addition, numerous regional rural housewives' associations presented Pommritz films on the correct method of ironing, washing dishes, doing laundry, and canning, as well as longer feature films like, "Women's Work in the Garden, Stall, and Fields," and "How the

---

[71]   Eva Förster, 'Landfrauenarbeit und D.L.G.', in *Sonderbeilage zur Grünen Woche 1929,* MdI 16426, 'Ausstellung landwirtschaftlicher Gegenstände', SäHStA, no page number.

[72]   Förster, 'Landfrauenarbeit', MdI 16426, SäHStA.

[73]   Beate Krieg, *'Landfrau, so geht's leichter!' Modernisierung durch hauswirtschaftliche Gemeinschaftsanlagen mit Elektrogroßgeräten im deutschen Südwesten von 1930 bis 1970* (Munich: tuduv-Verlagsgesellschaft, 1996), p. 35.

Farm Wife Can Lighten Her Workload."[74] In 1925, a rural housewives' association in Württemberg organized an exhibit of a "model farm house" for the "newfangled farm wife" at the DLG exhibition "Electricity and Agriculture" in Stuttgart. There farm wives (and their husbands) could see an electric iron, hot water heater, oven, and an apparatus for processing fodder, and the electricity costs per unit were posted.[75] According to the Württemberg rural housewives' association, the exhibit was inspired by the awareness that "today women are the representatives of smaller family enterprises" and that farm women had a responsibility despite the "devastating impact of rural flight" to represent rootedness to the land and to "build and strengthen professional pride."[76] In conclusion, one organizer declared,

> We do not need to discover "the farm wife," the numbers alone attest to that: 300,000 small enterprises in Württemberg, each with at least a farm wife, not to mention young daughters. We want to keep them together, to create a whole, to rescue them from their isolation … We want to discover their needs and lessen their burdens, and expose them to the latest technical achievements and scientific insights.[77]

The two organizations also coordinated the effort to increase farm women's "visibility" in the occupational census of 1925, exhorting their members to "make sure that on 16 June not a single (farm) housewife allows the enumerator to categorize her merely as 'wife.'"[78]

In early 1917, the RLHV in Berlin published the first issue of *Land und Frau*, a weekly periodical offering news and advice about poultry-raising, gardening, and other market-oriented work, as well as articles on housework, childcare, and social questions such as how farm women might ease urban/rural tensions or the ongoing crisis of rural flight.[79] While early issues of *Land und Frau* devoted most of their coverage to the rationalization of farm wives' productive work, by the late 1920s, the number of articles on productive work had declined. Now a substantial portion of the content was devoted to new categories like "Mother and Child," while the previous heading of "Miscellaneous Household" had expanded into "Kitchen and

---

[74]   von Strantz, 'Bericht über die Arbeiten', p. 575.

[75]   Krieg, *'Landfrau, so geht's leichter!'*, pp. 38, 58. See also the "model kitchen" presented by the rural housewives' association in Wismar (Mecklenburg). Anon., 'Märkischer Landfrauentag', *Land und Frau* 9/29 (July 18, 1925): 365–6.

[76]   Toni Kuessner, 'Die Ausstellung des Reichsverbandes landwirtschaftlicher Hausfrauenvereine in Stuttgart', *Land und Frau* 9/24 (June 13, 1925): 285.

[77]   Kuessner, 'Ausstellung', p. 285.

[78]   Liselotte Kueßner-Gerhard, 'Die Berufszählung am 16. Juni 1925', *Land und Frau* 9/21 (May 23, 1925): 244–5, here p. 245.

[79]   *Land und Frau: illustrierte Wochenschrift für deutsche Frauenarbeit* was published weekly between January 1917 and March 1943, and resumed publication between August 1948 and 1974.

Cellar" and "Household Machines and Tools." Between 1929 and 1933, *Land und Frau* added a special monthly section that "advised women about housework and the latest innovations in household technology, reports about product-testing, and measures to simplify and rationalize the household."[80]

In addition to advice about rationalizing production and household work, *Land und Frau* also provided book reviews, reports from regional branches of the RLHV, and news about market prices and national politics. Recommended books included not only cookbooks and gardening books but also adventure novels, books about exotic travels, and songbooks. Stories from regional branches of the RLHV included reports of newly-founded associations, local exhibitions of interest to farm women, and special meetings about various subjects ranging from goat-raising to selling eggs to infant care.[81]

Land und Frau also discussed recent innovations in electric heating, plumbing, and lighting on family farms. The first comprehensive article in *Land und Frau* on electricity in the farm household was published in January 1920 in response to "an outpouring of requests for information" about an electric stove mentioned briefly in a previous issue.[82] The article began by referring to the "mysterious energy source," whose applications had expanded from electric lighting to recent innovations like cooking and heating. The author rhapsodized, "Nothing sounds more wonderful than the idea of hot water at a moment's notice without the least amount of trouble. And the boiler can also be hooked up to the bath." The author also observed that increased prices of coal, wood, and gas due to the war made electricity an economical alternative to these energy sources. But the bulk of the article informed farm wives about the possible drawbacks of electric stoves, such as the need for new pots and pans with flat bottoms, the inability to cook over high heat, and, above all, the high cost of the stove, all of which, the author cautioned, had to be weighed against its acknowledged labor-saving potential.

Almost a decade later, another *Land und Frau* article, "Electricity as Helper of the Farm Wife," immediately raised the question of farm wives' overburdening, and declared that farm wives' desire to ease their labor did not imply that they had become lazy or weary of work.[83] The author added that not only farm wives but also their husbands were asking how time, energy, and money could be saved in the household in light of their success with rationalized work methods in the *Aussenwirtschaft*. Electricity would ease farm wives' work in three areas, namely with "daily cooking, cleaning, and the dreaded laundry." The author concluded with the warning that farm husbands might grumble loudly about the prices, but

---

[80]   Christina Schwarz, 'Zur Geschichte der Landfrauenbewegung in Deutschland', *Zeitschrift für Agrargeschichte und Agrarsoziologie* 40/1 (1992): 28–42, here p. 35.

[81]   Vereine, Versammlungen, Ausstellungen, 'Inhaltsverzeichnisse', *Land und Frau*, 1920–1933.

[82]   'Eine elektrische Küche', *Land und Frau* 4/6 (February 7, 1920): 44.

[83]   Frau A. Conrad, 'Die Elektrizität als Helferin der Landfrau', *Land und Frau* 12/7 (February 1928): 125.

she urged farm wives to use every spare penny and every opportunity for a gift to acquire items piece by piece. The author confided to readers, "I know that in your striving to be modern you will not rest until you have acquired a fully-electrified kitchen."

While the article enthusiastically endorsed the purchase of various new appliances such as the electric stove, washing machine, and iron, the author also conceded that the financial difficulties of most farms prevented the purchase of anything new, and, in a shift from the earlier article, that the high price of electricity posed an even greater problem. But she ended by offering readers "things to tempt and spoil them," suggesting that they consider purchasing an electric teakettle, egg cooker, or toaster "to prepare small, appetizing meals for the family." Here the acknowledgment that the new technology might not be accessible to most farm wives did not overshadow the message that the most thrifty, modern, and nurturing farm wives would afford them somehow, representing a new, more consumerist vision of household rationalization and the farm family. Later articles on the subject cannily framed the new technology in terms that aimed to reassure farm wives that the apparent diminution of their labor did not make them less capable housewives than their mothers. For example, an article in March 1931 by a female engineer opened with the guarantee that "Electric washing machines do not abandon the old tried-and-true laundry methods of our mothers and grandmothers. Instead they rely on the experiences of generations and follow time-honored methods, then simplify and improve them."[84]

Invariably, the lessons of household rationalization were couched in familiar terms, and its proponents urged farm wives to relate their own experiences and advice as a means of strengthening and popularizing the rationalization campaign. Derlitzki and others strove to foster intimacy between home economics experts and rural housewives, regularly soliciting suggestions from readers and using informal forms of address (*ihr* as opposed to *Sie*). *Land und Frau* also employed this strategy for educating readers about new techniques, appliances, and products, especially in the question box, or *Fragekasten*, where four or five questions were asked and answered by readers each week.[85] The questions ranged from how to expand your poultry business to fighting garden pests to the best recipe for pumpernickel or other regional specialties. Readers were assured that their contributions would cost them nothing, and "practical-minded farm wives" were encouraged to send in their questions and/or answers; indeed, many questions began with, "Can any of my dear fellow readers inform me about...?" Throughout the journal, there

[84]   Käthe Böhm, 'Volt X Ampère (gleicht) Watt, das 1 x 1 der Elekrotechnik für die Frau. Elektrische Waschmaschinen', *Land und Frau* 15/9 (March 1931): 153.

[85]   Hüchtker makes a similar observation about contemporary periodicals aimed at Polish farm women. See Dietlind Hüchtker, 'Die Bäuerin als Trope: Sprache und Politik in der polnischen Frauen- und Bauernbewegung an der Wende vom 19. zum 20. Jahrhundert', *Werkstatt Geschichte* 37 (2004): 49–63, esp. p. 57.

were prominent requests for readers' wish-lists and suggestions in response to the articles.[86]

Another facet of the RLHV's rationalization efforts was the development of cooperatives where farm women could sell their products directly to the consumer. By 1932, the RLHV had a network of roughly 150 cooperatives and 90 egg cooperatives.[87] Of these, 98 were located in the eastern states of East Prussia, Mecklenburg-Schwerin, and Pomerania, the center of the RLHV movement. Saxony was typical of other southern and western states, with four: three in Leipzig district and one in Dresden district.[88] The RLHV made a particular effort to improve the distribution of eggs and introduced their own "seal of approval" with the symbol of a honeybee, stamped on eggs and other products that met the RLHV's strict guidelines for sale. The regulations specified that eggs could not be more than three days old in summer or six days old in winter, that they be clean, stored in a cool place, must fall within a certain weight, and be as uniform in size and color as possible.[89] Furthermore, farm women who were members of the RLHV were required to sell all their products that received the seal of approval through the local cooperative.[90] A 1926 *Land und Frau* article emphasized the importance of greater systematization in local and regional foodstuff distribution so that farm wives could compete successfully with imported goods, as well as avoid the long trips back and forth to market:[91]

> It should be possible in every [farm] household to bake bread one week, and in another week make cheese, to deliver butter every week, twice a month to butcher a pig and make sausage etc. The cooperative must guarantee that specific foodstuffs are delivered on specific days, and that these goods are all of the same excellent quality.[92]

In order to encourage farm women's participation, local branches of the RLHV also offered courses in sorting and packing fruit, vegetables, and the like.[93] In 1898, the first cooperative in Rastenburg posted sales of 4,000 Marks; in 1929, East Prussia's 57 cooperatives boasted sales of 4,000,000 Marks.[94]

---

[86]   See for example Toni Kueßner, 'Gedankenaustausch über hauswirtschaftliche Maschinen und Geräte', *Land und Frau* 7/10 (May 1923): 155.

[87]   *Landfrauenkalender* 51 (1932) (Berlin: Paul Parey, 1932), pp. 42–6.

[88]   *Landfrauenkalender 1932*, p. 44.

[89]   Schwarz, *Landfrauenbewegung*, p. 105.

[90]   Schwarz, *Landfrauenbewegung*, p. 106.

[91]   On the efforts to standardize agricultural products in general see v. Dietze, 'Die Lage der deutschen Landwirtschaft', pp. 676–7.

[92]   *Land und Frau* 25, 1926; cited in Schwarz, *Landfrauenbewegung*, p. 88.

[93]   Schwarz, *Landfrauenbewegung*, p. 90.

[94]   Schwarz, *Landfrauenbewegung*, p. 93. While I do not have similar statistics for Saxony's rural housewives' cooperatives, detailed statistics on the expansion of fruit and

The Weimar campaign to rationalize farm women's work also encompassed the curriculums of girls' agricultural schools, some of which were founded in the decades before the First World War.[95] A 1924 report on classes for farm women and girls in Prussia observed with satisfaction that "The opportunity of further education along suitable lines is now within reach of the daughters of small farmers, or other persons engaged in rural occupations, by the recent establishment in certain districts of special classes for women in the existing schools of agriculture."[96] In Saxony, four agricultural schools for farm girls from better-off families had existed since the turn of the century, two in Leipzig district, one in Lusatia, and one in Dresden district.[97] In 1921, the Saxon Agricultural Chamber took over the administration and funding of the schools, and by 1925, 11 Saxon agricultural schools had added departments for girls in addition to the existing schools that catered solely to farm girls.[98]

Bruno Schöne, the head of the Saxon Agricultural Chamber, observed that it was not merely the new law specifying that girls must attend some sort of vocational school until age 17 behind the recent growth, but also the enthusiasm of farm communities for the project.[99] He cited several towns that had collected and donated large amounts of kitchen equipment for girls' education, or which had even found a suitable building to establish all-girls agricultural schools. In the winter of 1924/1925, there were 1,455 boys and 939 girls enrolled in all Saxon agricultural schools, making girls almost 40 percent of the total student body. Moreover, the number of boys enrolled remained more or less steady between 1919/1920 and 1924/1925, while the number of girls increased almost 12-fold.[100] Schöne asked rhetorically whether the rapid growth in Saxon agricultural schools would diminish the popularity of traveling courses, concluding, "In a word, no ... There is certainly no other state in Germany that has so many educational opportunities for agriculture in relation to the size of its farming population as Saxony."[101]

---

vegetable cultivation, and on the growing numbers of small livestock according to farm size are reported in O. Wohlfarth, 'Hundert Jahre sächsische Agrarstatistik', *Zeitschrift des sächsischen statistischen Landesamtes* 78/79 (Dresden: Zahn & Jaensch, 1932/1933): 9–44, esp. pp. 22, 33–7.

[95] See the list of girls' agricultural schools in Josephine Levy-Rathenau and Lisbeth Wilbrandt, 'Landwirtschaft und Nebengebiete', in Josephine Levy-Rathenau and Lisbeth Wilbrandt (eds), *Die deutsche Frau im Beruf. Praktische Ratschläge zur Berufswahl*, vol. 5 of *Handbuch der Frauenbewegung*, ed. Helene Lange and Gertrud Bäumer (Berlin: W. Moeser Buchhandlung, 1906), pp. 5–16.

[96] F. J. R., 'Germany: State subsidized Special Classes for Women and Girls in Schools of Agriculture', *IRAE*, new series II (1924): 627–8, here p. 627.

[97] Levy-Rathenau and Wilbrandt, 'Landwirtschaft', pp. 5–7.

[98] Bruno Schöne, *Die sächsische Landwirtschaft: ihre Entwicklung biz zum Jahre 1925* (Dresden: Verlag des LKR Sachsen, 1925), p. 177.

[99] Schöne, *Die sächsische Landwirtschaft*, pp. 177–8.

[100] Schöne, *Die sächsische Landwirtschaft*, pp. 180–1 (Table).

[101] Schöne, *Die sächsische Landwirtschaft*, pp. 185–6.

Both the location and the curriculums of Saxon agricultural schools testified to the impact of the Weimar rationalization campaigns in agriculture and housework.[102] The Saxon Agricultural Chamber reported in 1923 that agricultural schools and model farms were closely affiliated, often sharing the same space, and that a deliberate attempt had been made to choose "typical family farms" for this purpose.[103] It noted that 21 model farms had been created in the last two years, all between 10 and 60 hectares, and assured constituents that, "The Saxon Agricultural Chamber will continue to create new model farms, especially in regions that have no agricultural school. Without a doubt, model farms offer the best means of increasing production." In the same year, the Saxon Economics Ministry reported to the national government about the new agricultural schools. The representative observed that while classes took place only in winter, so that students could work at home during the busiest times of the year, summers were used also for field trips to students' family farms.[104] The class visits to individual farms would not only give the teacher an opportunity "to get a feel for the sort of economic advice that might be given at the end of the term, but also to gather valuable teaching material for the following winter's lessons."

The consensus among Weimar agricultural experts and home economists that farm girls would benefit far more from "practical" education in subjects like cooking, gardening, and dairying than from theoretical instruction in agronomy or botany was reflected in the curriculum of girls' agricultural schools. Here too, there was a dual emphasis on farm girls' future responsibilities as workers and as mothers. In 1922, social scientist Rosa Kempf spoke about the future of German agricultural education at the Second Saxon Agricultural Week in Dresden. She began with a lament about the postwar overburdening of farm wives, and exclaimed, "Every unnecessary task, every thoughtless bustling about, every wasteful production method must disappear."[105] Likewise she was unusual in maintaining that girls' agricultural schools should not separate general education from practical training:

> In the first year, housework should be at the center of their education, in the
> second year, livestock raising … in the third year, training in pedagogy and

---

[102]   For an official history of the rural housewives' movement in Saxony, see Maria Braune et al. (eds), *Geschichte der Landfrauenbewegung in Sachsen* (Freistaat Sachsen: Staatsministerium für Landwirtschaft, Ernährung und Forsten, 1996).

[103]   LKR an das Wirtschaftsministerium, Abt. Landwirtschaft, betrifft Schreiben des Reichsministerium für Ernährung und Landwirtschaft; Dresden, August 17, 1923, MdI 15498/2, SäHStA, p. 76.

[104]   Wirtschaftsministerium Sachsen an den Herrn Reichsminister für Ernährung und Landwirtschaft in Berlin; Dresden, June 2, 1923, MdI 15498/2, SäHStA, Bl. 69.

[105]   Rosa Kempf, 'Aufgaben und Ziele der ländlichen Pflichtfortbildungsschule', *Vorträge anläßlich der zweiten sächsischen landwirtschaftlichen Woche in Dresden vom 23. bis 37 Januar 1922* (Dresden: Verlag des Landeskulturrats Sachsen, 1922), pp. 45–57, here p. 48.

hygiene that addresses both of women's work spheres; that is, training for both kinds of nurturing, namely for the health of her family and herself as bearer of the next generation, and also for the health of the farm and its livestock ... so that the young girl learns her importance as a mother, and how to care for babies, the sick ... as well as how to prevent disease in the household and the stall.[106]

Kempf's remarks illustrated, once again, that rationalization as an antidote to farm wives' overburdening – in this case the education of their daughters to become more efficient producers, housekeepers, and mothers – idealized, and reinforced, women's established roles on German family farms. Following this model, the girls' curriculum for agricultural schools in Saxony devoted almost half the total class time to "practical" instruction in cooking and laundry, and less time than boys to hard sciences, bookkeeping, and math.[107] The Arwedshof Housekeeping and Agricultural School for Young Women in Leipzig district, which enrolled approximately 50 young women annually between 1920 and 1930, also emphasized the practical in their approach to farm girls' education, with courses in cooking, canning, housework, sewing, laundry, milking, the care of pigs, sheep, and goats, gardening, and poultry-raising.[108] Classes spent 45 minutes on the "theoretical," and the following three hours on "practice."[109] Afternoons were reserved for "Theoretical Courses," but all with a focus on women's work in the house, garden, and stall.

In addition to supervising the expansion of girls' agricultural education in the early 1920s, the Saxon Agricultural Chamber also promoted the education of farm wives, working closely with regional branches of the RLHV. In 1923, the Chamber formed a Committee for Women's Work, "in recognition that the farmer's wife is the farmer's closest business partner."[110] The Committee organized public lectures, exhibitions, conferences, and advice centers, observing that "farm wives' production as well as their households can only be administered *rationally* if farm wives become familiar with the latest innovations in science and technology."[111] In 1927, at the behest of the Saxon Rural Housewives' Association, the Committee sponsored six three-day, six-hour-per-day courses in "Modern Cooking."[112] The

---

[106]   Kempf, 'Aufgaben und Ziele', p. 51.

[107]   Stieger and Willi Wagner recommend similar school curriculums for farm girls. See Georg Stieger, *Der Mensch in der Landwirtschaft: Grundlagen der Landarbeitslehre* (Berlin: Paul Parey, 1922), pp. 352–3; Wagner, *Die Schule der Jungbäuerin*.

[108]   Arved Roßbach, 'Lehrgänge und Ziele', *Haus- und landwirtschaftliche Frauenschule Arvedshof in Elbisbach*, MdI 15798/1, 'Haus- und landwirtschaftliche Schule Arvedshof', SäHStA, Bl 20, folio, S. 6.

[109]   'Stundenplan, Winterhalbjahr 1921/22', MdI 15798/1, Bl. 17.

[110]   Bruno Schöne, 'Die Frau in der sächsischen Landwirtschaft', in Schöne, *Die sächsische Landwirtschaft*, p. 505.

[111]   Schöne, *Die sächsische Landwirtschaft*, p. 508. Emphasis mine.

[112]   'Abteilung Frauenarbeit', *Bericht über die Tätigkeit der Landwirtschaftskammer für den Freistaat Sachsen im Jahre 1927*, pp. 95–7.

report noted sternly that the course was not intended to instruct farm wives and daughters in the preparation of "so-called fine cuisine, but instead to demonstrate how the new nutritional knowledge can be put into practice." In the same year, the Committee also organized five-week cooking courses in regions without girls' agricultural schools to teach young women about the "latest cooking techniques and correct work methods, and address related questions of milking, poultry-raising, and gardening."[113] These courses also included festivals that taught folk dancing and singing. The Committee made special note of the popularity of classes in ironing, cheese-making, fruit processing, and gardening.

In 1928, the Committee for Women's Work observed that since milking and milk processing continued to be women's work, it had sponsored the training of 66 "female milking advisors."[114] The training took place on farms with "model stalls" in the Leipzig, Chemnitz, and Meißen districts, and the report commented that since the course would be offered continually, "the constant complaints from the [cooperative] dairies about the poor quality of milk and milk handling gradually should diminish." The report also observed pointedly that if the Saxon Economics Ministry, the State Milk Committee, and the Agricultural Chamber would offer more financial support so that such courses could be offered free of charge, production would increase even more.

Also in 1928, the Committee for Women's Work reported on its initial efforts to educate farm wives about housework, and noted the training of 82 housework advisors, in conjunction with the Saxon Rural Housewives' Association and Pommritz. In 1929, a model farmhouse was established in the village of Paudritzsch bei Leisnig, between Grimma and Döbeln, to encourage visits from the general public.[115] Two years later, the Committee reported that their educational program to reform housework had expanded despite financial difficulties, and that their purpose was "above all to instruct farm wives in the lessons of work simplification and to educate her to purchase only the most useful, thoroughly tested tools and machines."[116] In April 1931 one of the occasional instructors at Paudritsch described the enthusiastic participation of local women who attended regular lectures and demonstrations that inspired "lively interest and discussion, as well as exchange of experiences ... [Teaching] took up a lot of my energy ... but one is delighted with the interest in the subject that each participant brings; often our time is up before the discussion has ended."[117]

[113] 'Abteilung Frauenarbeit', *Bericht über die Tätigkeit der Landwirtschaftskammer für den Freistaat Sachsen im Jahre 1927*, p. 96.

[114] *Bericht über die Tätigkeit der Landwirtschaftskammer für den Freistaat Sachsen im Jahre 1928* (Dresden: Verlag des Landeskulturrats Sachsen, 1929), p. 98.

[115] *Bericht über die Tätigkeit ... im Jahre 1929*, p. 95.

[116] *Bericht über die Tätigkeit ... im Jahre 1930*, p. 122.

[117] M. Schuler, 'Hauswirtschaftliche Beratungsarbeit', *Land und Frau* 3/4 (April 4, 1931): 261.

Abb. 133. Von der Mecklenburgischen landwirtschaftlichen Ausstellung zu Güstrow: Bild aus dem Festzuge der Trachtenschau. Phot. Emil Walter, Güstrow. — Zu dem Beitrage auf Seite 313.

**Figure 4.3   "Farm Girls' Parade, Mecklenburg Agricultural Exhibition, *c.*
1925" [Source: *Land und Frau*, June 17, 1925, p. 311].**

In keeping with rationalization's emphasis on maintaining household calm, the Committee also addressed the question of recreation and relaxation possibilities for Saxon farm families.[118] The Saxon rural housewives' association and the Committee for Women's Work founded the first "vacation home" [*Erholungsheim*] for farm wives in Germany in 1927, and reported the next year that 252 guests stayed at the Oswald-Friedrich-Heim in Bad Elster, in the southern Erz mountains, at a cost of 3–4 Marks per day.[119] The majority of guests were farm wives from small and medium-sized Saxon farms, all listed according to district and farm size. Between February and December, 141 farm wives, 20 farmers, 19 farm daughters, 12 female hired hands, 29 urban housewives who were members of the rural housewives' association, and a handful of farm managers (male and female) stayed; 11 visitors were fully funded, and 49 received partial funding from the housewives' association and the district.[120] The attendance figures for 1929 and 1930 increased, but by far the largest numbers of visitors were wives from farms between 2–20 hectares.[121] The Committee also sponsored numerous rural festivals throughout Saxony as well as radio broadcasts of the festivals, and segments on rural art and culture. The purpose of

---

[118]   See also Neubert-Maevers report on vacation opportunities for farm wives in Minnesota. Hedwig Neubert-Maevers, 'Ferienlager für Farmfrauen in den Vereinigten Staaten', *Land und Frau* 15/6 (February 7, 1931): 97.

[119]   *Bericht über die Tätigkeit ... im Jahre 1928*, pp. 100–1. See also Schwarz, *Landfrauenbewegung*, p. 202.

[120]   The table does not specify who received funding by gender.

[121]   *Bericht über die Tätigkeit ... im Jahre 1929, 1930*, pp. 98 and 124 respectively.

these efforts was "to encourage rural inhabitants to form joyful communities, to give them an example of the simplicity and purity of such events, and to inspire them to initiate their own festivities."[122]

The Impact of Rationalization on Family Farms

Based on the evaluations of German rationalization experts, the campaign to rationalize farm women's work met with great success, despite women's initial misgivings. At the same time, widespread laments about the overburdening of farm women and the shortage of young women's labor persisted throughout the Weimar period. In contrast to his German colleagues, contemporary American economist Robert Brady's assessment of the campaign to rationalize German agriculture was decidedly mixed, and hints at the tensions and obstacles confronted by reformers.[123] On the one hand, he observed German farmers' resistance to the new methods and techniques, and the financial difficulties that prevented most family farms from investing in the latest technology. On the other, Brady described, in a footnote, the runaway popularity of 83 experimental farms in Prussia:

> Once the project was well under way, and the principal fears of the peasants had been settled, the main difficulty to be faced was the large number of visitors. These crowded around the machinery, trod over the fields, raised hosts of questions, and vented their curiosity in so many different ways and so continuously and insistently at times as to bring all work to a standstill.[124]

Although Brady's comments about agricultural rationalization addressed efforts to educate male farmers about new cultivation methods and farm technology, farm wives appeared briefly in his account of another experiment, where, in addition to pooling village land and resources, a new electric bakery and laundry were constructed for communal use:

> The women, in their turn, insisted upon the right to use the new facilities as they saw fit. Despite the fact that the kilowatt-hour rate was held as low as 4 pfennigs ($.00952), both laundry and bakery expenses remained prohibitively high until the women could be persuaded to specialize the labor among them.[125]

---

[122] *Bericht über die Tätigkeit ... im Jahre 1928*, p. 102.
[123] Robert A. Brady, 'The Status of Rationalization in other Industries: the Case of Agriculture', in Robert A. Brady (ed.), *The Rationalization Movement in German Industry: A Study in the Evolution of Economic Planning* (Berkeley: University of California Press, 1933), pp. 271–81.
[124] Brady, *Rationalization*, p. 277, fn. 67.
[125] Brady, *Rationalization Movement*, p. 276, fn. 65.

In this instance, the mixed reactions to rationalized farming Brady observed in male farmers were shared by their wives. While the author chided farm women for resisting the rationalization of work through a communal division of labor, he does not indicate that women rejected the new technology out of hand.[126] Indeed, Brady's observations reveal that ambivalence, rather than wholehearted acceptance, might best characterize farm wives' responses to new programs, technology, and advice designed to lighten their workload. Like his German counterparts, Brady emphasized the barriers to rationalization imposed by "rigid and patterned" attitudes, and implied that once these were unlearned, agricultural rationalization would proceed smoothly.[127]

More recently, Karen Hagemann has explored the question of women's responses to household rationalization and the limits of the campaign in urban working-class households. She argues that working women in Weimar Hamburg viewed many of the new recommendations about simplifying housework with skepticism, and that the single most important barrier to household rationalization was the high cost of new gadgets and appliances.[128] Hagemann also highlights the persistence of established notions of thrift among working-class wives, where, "a good 'reputation' in their own women's network of relatives, friends, and neighbors weighed more than all the sage advice of the proponents of rationalization."[129]

Although it is difficult to gauge farm women's reactions to the new home economics firsthand and the ways in which they adapted the advice of experts to their own needs, the statistics on machine ownership and electrification offer one means of measuring rationalization on family farms. The statistics for machines and tools owned by Saxon family farms after the war support home economists' observations that the *Aussenwirtschaft* was a priority in terms of investment. A 1924 inventory of 239 Saxon farms between 5 and 30 hectares revealed that 40 percent of investment was in power or horse-drawn machines, the highest

---

[126]   On the debate over working-class women's negative reactions to proposed collective kitchens before and after the war, and the response of the various women's movements, see Hiltraud Schmidt-Waldherr, 'Rationalisierung der Hausarbeit in den zwanziger Jahren', in Gerda Tornieporth (ed.), *Arbeitsplatz Haushalt: Zur Theorie und Ökologie der Hausarbeit* (Berlin: Dietrich Reimer Verlag, 1988), pp. 32–54; Nolan, '"Housework made Easy"', pp. 563–4; Orland, 'Emanzipation durch Rationalisierung?', p. 232.

[127]   Brady, *Rationalization*, p. 271.

[128]   Karen Hagemann, 'Of "Old" and "New" Housewives: Everyday Housework and the Limits of Household Rationalization in the Urban Working-Class Milieu of the Weimar Republic', *International Review of Social History* 41 (1996): 305–30. Bullock points out that in 1927, 53 percent of residents in the working-class neighborhood of Berlin-Wedding lived in tenements of one/two rooms and 81 percent had no electricity; see Bullock, 'First the Kitchen', pp. 188–90.

[129]   Hagemann, 'Of "Old" and "New" Housewives', p. 323.

proportion per hectare of agricultural land than any other German state.[130] While the 22 percent investment in tools most likely to be used by women, such as hand-powered centrifuges and household conveniences, was small, investment in such items was even lower on farms of the same size in Brandenburg and Bavaria.[131] Furthermore, the low investment in conveniences like plumbing and electrification suggests that most farm wives in Saxony could not take advantage of small electric motors and appliances advertised in periodicals such as *Land und Frau*, much less the labor-saving possibilities offered by an electric stove or hot water heater. Not surprisingly, investment in machines of all kinds was higher on family farms with good soil, while farms on poor land invested more in livestock and less in machines.[132]

Some insights into farm women's daily lives in Weimar Germany, and in particular about the (limited) impact of modern conveniences on their work, may be gleaned from the firsthand reminiscences of farm wives born between 1898 and 1908 in southeastern Württemberg.[133] Recorded in the early 1980s, all were asked about their work in the 1920s and early 1930s and how their lives differed from those of their mothers. "Frau B." stated matter-of-factly, "What I would have wished for? Well, there should have been machines. Then I'd still be fit today. Unloading the hay, binding the sheaves. My son was the first to get a tractor. That was about 1960. Yes, I did everything by hand, even when I was pregnant. Often in my ninth month ... But I never lost courage ... there would have been no point."[134] While she went on to insist that she had "probably had it better" than her mother, Frau B. pointed out that she had never had any respite or relaxation: "At most we women sometimes stood around in the yard and chatted." Another, "Frau C.", explained, "I had to do a lot outdoors ... We had nothing extra so that we could get ahead a little. My husband was very cautious about all the new things coming to the countryside."[135]

In Saxony, the agricultural diary kept by Marianne Elsa Lantzsch (b. 1915) in Sora, a village *c.* 15 kilometers west of Dresden, offers a first-hand account of women's farm work on a prosperous family farm there between 1930 and 1932.[136] The diary asked her to document her weekly work, including kitchen and housework, her chores in the dairy, the garden, and stall, as well as field work.

---

[130]   Hans-Ludwig Fensch, *Der Wert des landwirtschaftlichen Inventars*, Heft 5, *Deutscher Landwirtschaftsrat Veröffentlichungen* (Berlin: Deutscher Schriftenverlag, 1926), p. 80.

[131]   Fensch, *Der Wert*, p. 80.

[132]   Fensch, *Der Wert*, p. 69.

[133]   Ursula Schlude (ed.), *"Ich hab's gern gemacht": Die Lebensgeschichte einer Bäuerinnengeneration* (Ravensburg: Verlag "Schwäbischer Bauer," 1989).

[134]   Schlude, *"Ich hab's gern gemacht"*, p. 18.

[135]   Schlude, *"Ich hab's gern gemacht"*, p. 33.

[136]   Marianne Elsa Lantzsch, *Tagebuch für weibliche Landwirtschaftslehrlinge* (Dresden: LKR für den Freistaat Sachsen, 1929). Author's collection. Thanks to M. Blümel.

There was also space for her to record personal events such as celebrations, trips, or special purchases. While she frequently mentioned that she completed a particular task with her sister or mother, there is no mention of her father in the diary except on the first page where she noted that she was the daughter of "Farmer Lantzsch." Marianne's conscientious entries in the diary, the sort used in Saxon agricultural schools for girls and published by the Saxon Agricultural Chamber, suggest that the women in this particular farm household followed many of the prescriptions of rationalization experts.[137] At the same time, she described a work regimen that was continuous, painstaking, and often strenuous, much of it completed without the help of "modern conveniences." Her entries under "personal" reflect the impact of new technology and forms of entertainment, such as a radio or a rare visit to the movies, but as a rule she described her social life in terms of family visits and community activities, especially her involvement in the local girls' club [*Jungmädchenverein*] and agricultural school.

The influence of the rationalization campaign is most striking in the questionnaire located at the end of the diary. Marianne was required to draw the plan of the kitchen in relation to the other farm buildings and their dimensions, and to answer questions about the type and the brand names of the family stove and other machines or equipment.[138] She gave the same information for the laundry.[139] The diary also required her to calculate the costs of an average day's meals, and to answer numerous questions about how the laundry was done, from how it was sorted, to the detergents used, and the washing, bleaching, rinsing, wringing, hanging, starching, and ironing.[140] At the end of the diary, Marianne described the two- to three-day process in detail, noting that while there was a washing machine, she, her mother, and sister also used buckets, basins, a washboard, and hand wringer, and that the laundry was done every month. According to Marianne, the Lantzsch farm had electric lighting and an electric water pump, but the women used a coal- and wood-burning stove for cooking, and only hand-powered machines such as a coffee mill, a meat grinder, and a grater. When asked to name the most important tools for cleaning a room, Marianne answered, "Bucket, water, rags, brushes, soap, dust cloth, and broom."[141] In response to a question about the "Big Cleaning" [*Großreinemachens*], she detailed the arduous process of cleaning before festivals, moving all the furniture out, scrubbing floors, walls, and furniture with soap and water, and blacking and polishing the stove, "which creates a lot of dust."[142]

---

[137] *Tagebuch für weibliche Landwirtschaftslehrlinge*, gestiftet von der Landwirtschaftskammer für den Freistaat Sachsen (Dresden, 1929).

[138] Lantzsch, *Tagebuch*, p. 173. See also Schwarz, *Landfrauenbewegung*, p. 168.

[139] Lantzsch, *Tagebuch*, p. 183.

[140] Lantzsch, *Tagebuch*, p. 176, 184.

[141] Lantzsch, *Tagebuch*, p. 185.

[142] Lantzsch, *Tagebuch*, p. 186.

Marianne also described her productive work on the farm, including cleaning milk containers and the milk separator mornings and evenings, processing the milk into *quark*, and boiling fodder for various livestock, all of which were daily tasks. In November 1930, Marianne noted for the first time that she used an electric milk separator, and how she learned to make it work. She also described how to nurse sick livestock, and how to care for very young calves. Her work in the *Aussenwirtschaft*, together with her sister, included loading manure, hoeing and weeding root crops, mowing hay, corn, and oats, threshing wheat, and digging and sorting potatoes. While housework and stall work entries appeared throughout the year, field and garden work began in early March and lasted through mid-December. During the winter respite from field work, Marianne described household chores in more detail: processing meat into sausage, making feather beds and dusters, baking for holidays, mending clothes, and repairing the barns.

Like her descriptions of household and productive work, Marianne's entries under "personal" sketched a social life that revolved around female family members, including aunts, female cousins, and a sister living away from home, and the community. She documented her active involvement in the local girls' club and the agricultural school, where she had parts in plays and visited local sights and exhibitions, including one on hygiene in July 1930. She also mentioned embroidery, sewing, or darning projects every week. In terms of new forms of recreation and acquiring new items, Marianne recorded receiving a radio in September 1930, and made the first mention of a bicycle, which she used to visit cousins and friends. The only other possession noted was the gift of a winter coat in November, while her entries in December described decorating the house for Christmas, her part in a "theater evening" held at their house, and a two-day trip to Dresden with her sister to see the movie, "Wiener Herzen." For Christmas 1931 Marianne received a puppy, but she does not mention any new purchases or other gifts that year.

While the diary sheds no light on farm women's attitudes toward the rationalization campaign, the very existence of the diary, with its detailed entries and illustrations, suggests that the prescriptions of agricultural home economists did not go unheeded, at least on prosperous family farms like the Lantzsch's. At the very least, girls like Marianne, despite their heavy workloads, made time to record their weekly tasks in an organized fashion, and that in itself was something new. Moreover, her decisions about what to write in terms of her work and social life reflected the campaign's focus on traditionally female tasks, such as cooking, cleaning, milking, and sewing, and suggests that communities of women shared ideas about organizing work, if not about new machines and gadgets.

Conclusion

Despite Weimar scholars' cataloging of the drastic effects of overwork on farm wives, their families, and by extension the nation's economic and social welfare, social scientists like Kempf praised the family farm as the *only* workplace where married women could combine housework and productive work with ease.[143] Buoyed by this ideal, the campaign to rationalize farm women's work did not question established gender divisions of labor. In this respect, the campaign did not depart from the movement to rationalize urban women's housework. Indeed, as Barbara Orland and others have argued in the urban context, the introduction of more efficient tools and techniques transformed the nature, but not the amount, of German women's housework.[144] Moreover, the availability of new gadgets designed to ease women's household labor reveals little about the conditions that dictated when or if such items were acquired.[145] As the evidence suggests, most farm households could not afford many of the new labor-saving machines, much less pay for the electricity to run them.

Farm wives' reactions to the campaign's efforts to persuade them to reorganize their workday, their workplaces, and even their production emphases are much more difficult to gauge. Certainly the explosive growth of courses in all areas of women's farm work and local girls' agricultural schools suggest that the new home economics found eager and enthusiastic participants. Yet there were also numerous complaints from agricultural experts that women rejected or resisted their advice about the proper way of doing things, especially if they belonged to the prewar generation. Karen Hagemann's observation about working-class housewives is just as applicable to farm wives in the Weimar period, namely that, "With their time at a premium, working-class women ... *were compelled to manage their households rationally anyway*."[146]

While the impact of the rationalization campaign on farm women is difficult to measure, the widespread effort to draw them into the broader Weimar rationalization movement is significant. On the one hand, farm wives were now perceived as potentially authoritative managers of productive and reproductive spheres, with a corresponding power to shape Germany's national economy. On the other, the campaign's relatively limited impact on farm households, as evidenced by the continued resistance of young women to agricultural work and the ongoing reports of farm wives' overburdening, had important ramifications for Weimar agrarian politics that are explored in Chapter 5.

---

[143]   Kempf, *Die deutsche Frau nach der Volks-, Berufs-, und Betriebszählung von 1925* (Mannheim: Bennsheimer Verlag, 1931), pp. 57–8.

[144]   Orland, Nolan, Hagemann, and Schmidt-Waldherr all make this point in their discussions of housework. See also Peukert, *The Weimar Republic*, p. 100.

[145]   For a discussion of the ways in which gender relations shaped the timing and decisions about household technology in the twentieth century see Sibylle Meyer and Eva Schulze, 'Fernseher contra Waschmaschine: wie das Geschlechterverhältnis auf Technik wirkt', in Barbara Orland et al. (eds), *Haushalts-Träume: Ein Jahrhundert Technisierung und Rationalisierung im Haushalt* (Königstein im Taunus: Langewiesche, 1990), pp. 103–8.

[146]   Hagemann, 'Of "Old" and "New" Housewives', p. 328. Emphasis mine.

Chapter 5

The Farm Wife as Preserver of the Nation: Gender and Conservative Agrarian Politics in Weimar Germany

By the early 1930s, it was clear that most German farm wives were not the happy household managers depicted in rural rationalization campaigns. Instead, stories of their suffering had persisted throughout the "golden years" of the Weimar Republic between 1924 and 1927, and peaked during the economic crisis that devastated the countryside between 1928 and 1933. A variety of observers in Saxony and across Germany routinely described farm wives as "tormented," "downtrodden," and "bitter."[1] Furthermore, these observers increasingly linked the physical and psychological overburdening of farm wives to the broader agricultural crisis, and to the perceived betrayal of rural interests by the Weimar state. As one member of the Saxon Agricultural Chamber remarked acidly in 1927, "farm wives' situation is irreconcilable with all that is said and written about women's work and women's protection."[2]

This chapter traces the dramatic politicization of farm wives' (over)work and its impact on right-wing politics in the Weimar countryside. In particular, it asks how the varied discourses about wives' overburdening came to dominate contemporary debates over the rural social question in Germany after the mid-1920s. In the Saxon case, it also traces how the figure of the beleaguered farm wife became a central focus of right-wing agrarian splinter parties hostile to the Republic, presaging the Nazi glorification of her after 1931. For although by the late 1920s, the Nazis actively sought to exploit the rural population's distress and repeatedly exhorted Saxon farmers to "wake up!," they made no concerted effort to mobilize farm women. Indeed, as historians Matthew Stibbe and Julia Sneeringer have argued, before 1932 Nazi efforts to mobilize women in general amounted to "no more than a gesture."[3] That did not mean, however, that Saxon farm women were mute

---

[1]   Amtlicher Bericht über die 4. Gesamtsitzung der Landwirtschaftskammer [hereafter Amtlicher Bericht, LKR, 3.1927] am 21. und 22. März 1927 (Dresden: LKR für den Freistaat Sachsen, 1927), p. 330.

[2]   Amtlicher Bericht über die 5. Gesamtsitzung der LKR für den Freistaat Sachsen am 15. November 1927 [hereafter Amtlicher Bericht, LKR, 11.1927] (Dresden: Selbstverlag des LKR, 1928), p. 15.

[3]   Matthew Stibbe, *Women in the Third Reich* (London: Arnold Publishers, 2003), p. 21; Julia Sneeringer, *Winning Women's Votes: Propaganda and Politics in Weimar*

bystanders in the increasingly fraught political climate of the postwar era. Indeed, they took active part in the insurgent rallies, marches, and festivals characteristic of late Weimar politics in the countryside.[4]

Some of the earliest reports of Saxon farm wives' overburdening surfaced in the mainstream conservative and agricultural press, which also railed against the state's decision to make girls' attendance mandatory at rural continuation schools, its refusal to reenact prohibitions on rural youth's freedom of movement, and unemployment benefits that exceeded agricultural wages. Especially after 1925,

„Laft“. Radierung von Rudolf Hendschel in Meißen, nachgezeichnet von Hermann, Droop in Dresden.

Figure 5.1 " 'Burden' Front Page, *Sächsische Landwirtschaftliche Zeitschrift*, January 22, 1928."

Germany (Chapel Hill: University of North Carolina Press, 2002), pp. 158–9, 173–4, 223. On Nazi propaganda in rural Saxony see 'Our Work in Saxony', *Völkischer Beobachter* 84/11 (April 1928), reprinted in Detlef Mühlberger (ed.), *Hitler's Voice: The Völkischer Beobachter, 1920–1933* (Oxford: Peter Lang, 2004), pp. 264–7; Gerhard Donner, 'Die Bedeutung der nationalsozialistischen Propaganda für die Entwicklung der NSDAP im Gau Sachsen' (Dissertation, Universität Leipzig, 1942), p. 93, 98, 111–12, 149; Benjamin Lapp, *Revolution from the Right: Politics, Class, and the Rise of Nazism in Saxony, 1919–1933* (Atlantic Highlands, NJ: Humanities Press, 1997); Claus-Christian Szejnmann, *Nazism in Central Germany: The Brownshirts in 'Red' Saxony* (New York: Berghahn Books, 1999).

[4]   On Saxon farmers' disenchantment with the Republic see Lapp, *Revolution*, pp. 166–70.

the National Rural Housewives Association [RLHV] expressed many of the same grievances in their weekly periodical, *Land und Frau*. Their editorialists voiced growing dismay over the ways that "politics" had distorted "traditional German values" like duty and self-sacrifice, and by the early 1930s they frequently suggested that readers would welcome radical political change: "Parties no longer have a role to play in the question of survival or destruction. The people will follow a leader that thinks and acts German, and who acts decisively."[5]

Between 1928 and 1933, a new generation of rural sociologists also drew attention to the plight of German farm wives, documenting their overburdening across the nation.[6] In addition to repeating older worries about its impact on the food supply, they detailed a frightening array of reproductive and cultural threats posed by farm wives' overwork, including frequent miscarriages, inability to nurse, increased infant mortality, and the destruction of German rural culture.[7] Also new was their engagement in contemporary political debates over the crisis. In particular, many used the *völkisch* language of the far right to emphasize the link between their findings and the broader economic and political upheavals of late Weimar. Gerhard Schützhold's study of Saxon farm wives exemplified the new tone:

> If we ease some of the farm wife's burdens, she can and will devote more of her time to her duties as preserver of the family and the nation's assets ... If the family farm, and especially the farm wife, is destroyed, the entire nation will be endangered! If we want to prevent this, then we must ensure that the she is no longer burdened beyond her strength ... If all goes well for the farm wife, all goes well for the *Volk*![8]

By equating farm wives' welfare with that of the nation, Schützhold and his colleagues both reinforced the *völkisch* construction of the farm wife as a potent symbol of Germanness and cast the Weimar state's failure to rescue her as unequivocal evidence of its illegitimacy.

---

[5]   M. Friese, 'Deutschlands Lage', *Land und Frau* 15/40 (October 3, 1931): 720.

[6]   Luise Fritsch, *Stellung und Tätigkeit der Landhausfrau in der landwirtschaftlichen Produktion des Deutschen Reiches* (Berlin: Deutsche Tageszeitung, 1929); Elisabeth Baldauf, *Die Frauenarbeit in der Landwirtschaft* (Borna-Leipzig: Robert Noske, 1932); Marie Berta von Brand, *Die wirtschaftliche und kulturelle Lage der Bäuerin auf den Fildern* (Stuttgart: Körner, 1933); Gerhard Schützhold, *Die sächsische Landfrau: ihr Aufgaben- und Pflichtenkreis im bäuerlichen Landwirtschaftsbetrieb* (Dresden: Theodor Steinkopff, 1934).

[7]   Fritsch, *Stellung*, p. 9.

[8]   Schützhold, *sächsische Landfrau*, p. 78.

Weimar agrarian romantics also seized on the figure of the embattled farm wife as the embodiment of the struggling postwar German nation.[9] Unsurprisingly, however, they were not interested in the miserable details of farm women's daily lives. Instead, *völkisch* activists used farm wives' overburdening to call for a broader "moral cleansing" campaign. Blending prewar discourses of agrarian nationalism that extolled the countryside as the cultural and biological "wellspring of the nation" with the wartime "discovery" of farm wives as workers and mothers, they asserted that the German farm wife epitomized qualities previously attributed to the farming population as a whole: the love of *Heimat* and hard work, thriftiness, and the embrace of (patriarchal) "family values."[10] Thus, while Weimar agrarian romantics certainly found it opportune to condemn farm wives' overburdening, they never questioned the suitability of agricultural work for women. Instead there was broad consensus that farm wives' productive and reproductive labor was vital for the present and future prosperity of the *Volk*.

In the realm of electoral politics, the new agrarian splinter parties that crystallized in the late 1920s were the first to exploit the opportunities for political mobilization presented by the growing outrage over farm wives' overburdening.[11] In addition to rising taxes, lack of credit, increased debt, low agricultural prices, and threats of foreclosure, parties like the Saxon Rural People's Party [*Sächsisches Landvolk*, or SLV] condemned Weimar officials' mishandling of the labor shortage and their patent disregard for farm wives' physical and psychological well-being. Likewise the SLV appealed directly to farm wives as voters *and* potential demonstrators, rather than merely using the issue to whip up anti-Weimar feeling more generally. And while they never became mass movements, agrarian splinter parties' aggressive pursuit of farm women's support set an important precedent for the National Socialists and their aggressive campaigns to court rural voters after 1930.[12] Indeed, facing huge losses after the 1930 Saxon *Landtag* elections,

---

[9]   Klaus Bergmann, *Agrarromantik und Großstadtfeindschaft* (Meisenheim am Glan: Verlag Anton Hain, 1970); Peter Weingart et al., *Rasse, Blut und Gene: Geschichte der Eugenik und Rassenhygiene in Deutschland* (Frankfurt/Main: Suhrkampf Verlag, 1988).

[10]   Jaschke calls these "radicalized Prussian values" gender-neutral. Hans-Gerd Jaschke, 'Zur politischen Orientierung von Frauen und Frauen-Verbänden in der Weimar Republik', in Detlef Lehnert and Klaus Megerle (eds), *Politische Teilkulturen zwischen Integration und Polarisierung: zur politischen Kultur in der Weimarer Republik* (Opladen: Westdeutscher Verlag, 1990), pp. 143–60, esp. p. 155.

[11]   On agrarian splinter parties see Larry Eugene Jones, 'Crisis and Realignment: Agrarian Splinter Parties in the Late Weimar Republic, 1928–1933', in Robert G. Moeller (ed.), *Peasants and Lords in Modern Germany: Recent Studies in Agricultural History* (Boston: Allen & Unwin, 1986), pp. 198–232; Stephanie Merkenich, *Grüne Front gegen Weimar: Reichs-Landbund und agrarischer Lobbyismus 1918–1933* (Düsseldorf: Droste Verlag, 1998), pp. 247–66.

[12]   Grill stresses that some Nazi activists were focused on the countryside by the mid-1920s, but there is consensus that the party made rural voters a top priority only after the

the SLV, along with other conservative parties and the Rural League, collaborated closely with the Nazis.[13]

But the overburdened farm wife was more than a banality that served either to inflame anti-Republican sentiment or to embody the conservative moral values of the prewar German nation. While it is impossible to generalize about ordinary farm women's reactions to right-wing appeals for drastic political change, many were active in conservative grassroots politics.[14] As early as 1921, for example, many Saxon farm women joined men in signing a "protest petition" against the new law mandating girls' attendance at rural continuation schools, for fear that it would intensify the shortage of *Mägde*.[15] While the effort failed, it suggests that at least some rural officials recognized early that women's support was crucial to bolstering conservative sentiment in the countryside, and more importantly, that labor issues were of vital importance to farm women. After 1925, the provincial press routinely noted women's participation in rallies against the Weimar state.[16] In addition, farm girls across Germany joined *völkisch* groups like the *Junglandbund* and the *Artamanen* and took part in the village festivals and marches they organized.[17]

The historical narrative of right-wing insurgency in the Weimar countryside culminating in a Nazi victory over divided and disorganized rivals is a familiar one.[18] More recently, scholars have argued that parties like the *Landvolk*, the

---

1930 elections. Johnpeter Horst Grill, 'The Nazi Party's Rural Propaganda Before 1928', *Central European History* 15/2 (1982): 149–85.

[13]   Lapp, *Revolution,* pp. 168–70, 184, 189, 203.

[14]   On gender and Nazi voting patterns Jürgen Falter, *Hitlers Wähler* (München: C. H. Beck, 1991), pp. 136–46; Eve Rosenhaft, 'Women, Gender, and the Limits of Political History in the Age of "Mass Politics"', in Larry Eugene Jones and James Retallack (eds), *Elections, Mass Politics, and Social Change in Modern Germany* (Cambridge: Cambridge University Press, 1992), pp. 149–73.

[15]   Sächsicher Bauernbund, Verband Sächsischer Landwirte; Freiberg (Sa.)12.1920, Landtag Nr. 546, 'Eingaben gegen die verbindliche Einführung der Mädchenfortbildungsschule auf dem Lande', SäHStA, p. 116.

[16]   Helene Wenck, 'Die Landfrauen in Berlin', *Land und Frau* 9/9 (February 28, 1925): 98–100. The earliest Saxon example I found is from March 1925. 'Eine machtvolle Kundgebung der vogtländischen Kreislandbundes', *Vogtländischer Anzeiger und Tageblatt* (Plauen), March 14, 1925; Staatskanzlei, Nachrichtenstelle, 'Landwirtschaft', Nr. 961, SäHStA, no page numbers. The story reported that "large numbers of farm women" attended.

[17]   Ludger Elsbroek, *Vom Junglandbund zur Landjugend: Ländliche Jugend-verbandsarbeit zwischen Berufsstand und Jugendkultur* (Frankfurt/Main: Peter Lang, 1996), pp. 85–94.

[18]   Hans-Jürgen Puhle, *Politische Agrarbewegungen in kapitalistischen Industriegesellschaften: Deutschland, USA und Frankreich im 20. Jahrhundert* (Göttingen: Vandenhoek & Ruprecht, 1975), pp. 77–94; J. E. Farquharson, *The Plough and the Swastika: The NSDAP and Agriculture in Germany, 1928–45* (London: Sage Publications,

Christlich-Nationale Bauernpartei, and the SLV served as key "transmission belts" between established conservative parties like the German National People's Party [DNVP] and the Nazis by proclaiming their disillusionment with the Republic in ever more populist terms and taking over public spaces to demand radical political change.[19] Yet women rarely surface in the story, and when they do it is usually as farm dependents who passively supported the increasingly insurgent political opinions and activities of their menfolk.[20] This is all the more surprising given historians' attention to farm wives as political symbols and actors in the years after 1933, whether as quintessential icons of the Nazis' "Blood and Soil" ideology or as reluctant participants in the "Battles for Agricultural Production."[21]

In addition, bourgeois women's role in right-wing politics before, during, and especially after the war, whether as activists or subjects, has been the subject of intense scholarly debate.[22] In particular, historians have traced the careers of leading activists like Käthe Schirmacher to explain how elite women created and defended new political spaces for themselves despite the blatantly anti-feminist rhetoric of their parties. These women's support for the far right, they conclude,

1976); Zdenek Zofka, *Die Ausbreitung des Nationalsozialismus auf dem Lande* (München: Kommissionsverlag R. Wölfle, 1979). More recently, see Shelley Baranowski; *The Sanctity of Rural Life* (New York: Oxford University Press, 1995).

[19]   Lapp, *Revolution*, p. 170; Bernd Weisbrod, 'Die Krise der Mitte oder "Der Bauer stund auf im Lande"', in Lutz Niethammer et al. (eds), *Bürgerliche Gesellschaft in Deutschland: Historische Einblicke, Fragen, Perspektiven* (Frankfurt/Main: Fischer Verlag, 1990), pp. 396–410, esp. p. 410; Reinhold Weber, *Bürgerpartei und Bauernbund in Württemberg: Konservative Parteien im Kaiserreich und in Weimar (1895–1933)* (Düsseldorf: Droste Verlag, 2004), pp. 501–2; Peter Fritzsche, *Germans into Nazis* (Cambridge: Harvard University Press, 1998), pp. 172–84; Peter Fritzsche, 'Weimar Populism and National Socialism in Local Perspective', in Jones and Retallack (eds), *Elections*, pp. 287–306, esp. pp. 301–2.

[20]   Fritzsche, *Germans*, p. 177.

[21]   Helene Albers, *Zwischen Hof, Haushalt und Familie: Bäuerinnen in Westfalen-Lippe (1920–1960)* (Paderborn: F. Schöningh, 2001), pp. 284–374; Daniela Münkel, '"Du, Deutsche Landfrau bist verantwortlich!": Bauer und Bäuerin im Nationalsozialismus', *Archiv für Sozialgeschichte* 38 (1998): 141–64; Daniela Münkel, '"Ein besseres Leben für die Landfrau"? Technik im bäuerlichen Haushalt während der NS-Zeit', *metis* 4/1 (1995): 41–59.

[22]   Weber, *Bürgerpartei*, pp. 163–9; Raffael Scheck, *Mothers of the Nation: Right-Wing Women in Weimar Germany* (Oxford: Berg, 2004); Elizabeth Harvey, 'Visions of the Volk: German Women and the Far Right from Kaiserreich to Third Reich', *Journal of Women's History* 16/3 (2004): 152–67; Ute Planert (ed.), *Nation, Politik und Geschlecht: Frauenbewegungen und Nationalismus in der Moderne* (Frankfurt: Campus Verlag, 2000); Andrea Süchting-Hänger, *Das 'Gewissen der Nation': Nationales Engagement und politisches Handeln konservativer Frauenorganisationen 1900 bis 1937* (Düsseldorf: Droste Verlag, 2002); Johanna Gehmacher, *'Völkische Frauenbewegung': Deutschnationale und nationalsozialistische Geschlechterpolitik in Österreich* (Wien: Döcker Verlag, 1998).

sprang from fears about the upheavals of the 1918–1919 revolution and the belief that women's essential differences from men should be preserved and protected by the new Weimar state, especially in their roles as mothers. With respect to the countryside, several scholars have noted that the longtime president of the RLHV, Elisabet Boehm, was an early Nazi supporter who zealously promoted the organization's integration into the Nazi "Peasant Estate" in 1934.[23] More generally, and echoing the bridge metaphors used to describe the role of agrarian splinter parties, Renate Bridenthal has argued that "The momentum of the countrywomen's associational life ... helped the Nazis come to power as much as electoral politics did."[24]

Undoubtedly Boehm and her colleagues were instrumental in advancing the Rural Housewives' Association's rightward drift. At the same time, it would be too simple to assume that ordinary farm wives responded only to cues from the RLHV leadership with respect to their support for ultra-conservative parties and organizations. While farm wives probably appreciated the traditional conservative celebrations of motherhood that spoke so persuasively to their bourgeois counterparts, appeals that embraced their lives as mothers *and* workers probably carried more weight. Indeed, the rich material and statistical evidence about farm women's daily lives in Weimar suggests that labor grievances may have surpassed all others in motivating women to sign petitions, attend demonstrations, or cast votes that strengthened opponents of the Republic, including the National Socialists.

Agricultural Interest Groups, the Weimar State, and the Politics of Women's Labor in the Countryside

If the 1890s marked the first major political shift in the modern German countryside, when the grievances of small- and medium-sized farmers sparked growing worries about rural unrest among agricultural elites and local officials, the years between 1925 and 1933 witnessed a second watershed in the relations between farmers and those who claimed to represent their professional and political interests. While the earliest historical treatments of German farmers' prewar political mobilization emphasized their susceptibility to manipulation by the Junker-dominated Agrarian

---

[23]   Christoph Hinkelmann, "'Es war ihr Schicksal, vorauszueilen – die anderen konnten nicht so schnell folgen" – Elisabet Boehm, geb. Steppuhn', in Ostpreußisches Landesmuseum, Lüneburg (ed.), *Elisabet Boehm und die Landfrauenbewegung* (Husum: Druck- und Verlagsgesellschaft mbH u. Co. KG, 1998), pp. 15–30, esp. pp. 26–7.

[24]   Renate Bridenthal, 'Organized Rural Women and the Conservative Mobilization of the German Countryside in the Weimar Republic', in Larry Eugene Jones and James Retallack (eds), *Between Reform, Reaction, and Resistance: Studies in the History of German Conservatism from 1789 to 1945* (Oxford: Berg Publishers, 1993), pp. 375–405, here p. 404.

League, more recent work has upended the stereotype of the stoic or deferential family farmer.[25] For example, David Blackbourn has argued strongly that prewar farmers' discontent "manifested itself as a prickly but organizationally invertebrate rejection of outside manipulation." Furthermore, their grievances had the potential to spark "an inchoate revolt in the countryside."[26] Blackbourn details the impact of this "rural alienation" on agrarian party politics, emphasizing the slow and often clumsy reaction of traditional conservative political parties and the Agrarian League to farmers' complaints, and the sprouting up of populist independent Peasant Leagues [*Bauernbünde*] that were often anti-Semitic.[27] More recently, historian Reinhold Weber has emphasized that especially before the war, the political activities of these organizations constituted "almost without exception a male domain."[28] While this work argues that by 1900 the League managed to paper over the conflicting economic and social priorities that divided its members and succeeded in forging a mass political movement, it also underscores the tensions that continued to simmer between the largely Prussian agrarian elite and farmers in the south and southwest.[29]

As historians of Weimar agriculture have emphasized, these same tensions shaped postwar agrarian interest politics even more profoundly.[30] Indeed, farmers' pressure on conservative parties and agricultural associations to communicate

---

[25]   The classic work is Hans-Jürgen Puhle, *Agrarische Interessenpolitik und preußischer Konservatismus im wilhelminischen Reich (1893–1914)* (Hannover: Verlag für Literatur und Zeitgeschehen, 1966). For critiques see Jens Flemming, *Landwirtschaftliche Interessen und Demokratie: Ländliche Gesellschaft, Agrarverbände und Staat 1890–1925* (Bonn: Verlag Neue Gesellschaft, 1978); David Blackbourn, *Class, Religion, and Local Politics in Wilhelmine Germany: The Centre Party in Württemberg before 1914* (New Haven: Yale University Press, 1980); Geoff Eley, 'Anti-Semitism, Agrarian Mobilization, and the Conservative Party: Radicalism and Containment in the Founding of the Agrarian League, 1890–93', in Jones and Retallack, *Between Reform*, pp. 187–227; Ian Farr, '"Tradition" and the Peasantry: On the Modern Historiography of Rural Germany', in Richard Evans and W. R. Lee (eds), *The German Peasantry: Conflict and Community in Rural Society from the Eighteenth to the Twentieth Centuries* (London: Croom Helm, 1986), pp. 1–36; Ian Farr, 'Peasant Protest in the Empire – the Bavarian Example', in Moeller, *Peasants and Lords*, pp. 110–39.

[26]   David Blackbourn, 'Peasants and Politics in Germany, 1871–1914', *European History Quarterly* 14/1 (Jan. 1984): 47–75, esp. p. 51.

[27]   Blackbourn, 'Peasants', pp. 56–8.

[28]   Weber, *Bürgerpartei*, p. 161.

[29]   Blackbourn, 'Peasants', pp. 63–8; Weber, *Bürgerpartei*, pp. 88–96. Moeller argues that the League was able to achieve unity by emphasizing the cultural values shared by all agricultural producers with respect to "the patriarchal family and the sanctity of private property." Robert Moeller, *German Peasants and Agrarian Politics, 1914–1924: The Rhineland and Westphalia* (Chapel Hill: University of North Carolina Press, 1986), p. 22.

[30]   Moeller, *German Peasants*; Flemming, *Landwirtschaftliche Interessen*, pp. 198–228.

their demands to the top levels of government was both more insistent and more intense than in the Kaiserreich. Studies of what Jonathan Osmond has termed the "second agrarian mobilization" in the 1920s have focused above all on the fluid and often bitter internal politics of the Rural Leagues and farmers' grievances about the controlled economy before 1923, and thereafter on farmers' objections to the "unfair" taxes on land, the lack of credit, and low agricultural prices.[31] At the same time, scholars have had almost nothing to say about the labor crisis on family farms, despite the fact that it runs like a red thread throughout local, state, and national reports about the state of Weimar agriculture. In particular, the emphatic refrain that young women continued to resist agricultural work and its devastating impact on small and medium-sized enterprises is unmistakable. Even more striking is contemporaries' new attention to the suffering of farm dependents, especially wives, as a result.

Although German farmers rejoiced at the lifting of the last vestiges of the controlled economy in 1923 and, if they were fortunate, the erasure of their debts by the inflation, they continued to complain bitterly and incessantly about the shortage of female labor. In late 1925, a Silesian farmer sent a caustic memo to the Agricultural Chamber in Breslau entitled "The Labor Shortage in the Countryside."[32] The author explained that contract-breaking among hired hands was having a "catastrophic" impact on family farms in the region. He continued:

> In particular there is no one to do the urgent and necessary work of livestock care. It is not uncommon that when the "young lady" [*das "Fräulein"*] condescends to work for a farmer that she announces flatly that she refuses to enter a stall. Recently I had the chance to spend time with a labor broker. A large group of girls was seeking work, but only in the city. I asked the broker whether they were city girls. Her answer was "all from the countryside" … If farmers are lucky enough to find one, then "the guests" [*die Herrschaften*] stay only four weeks and then move on, after frittering away their wages.

---

[31]   Jonathan Osmond, 'A Second Agrarian Mobilization? Peasant Associations in South and West Germany, 1918–24'," in Moeller, *Peasants and Lords*, pp. 168–97; Jonathan Osmond, *Rural Protest in the Weimar Republic: The Free Peasantry in the Rhineland and Bavaria* (New York: St. Martin's Press, 1993); Martin Schumacher, *Land und Politik: Eine Untersuchung über politische Parteien und agrarische Interessen, 1914–1923* (Düsseldorf: Droste Verlag, 1978); Guido Dressel, *Der Thüringer Landbund – Agrarischer Berufsverband als politische Partei in Thüringen 1919–1933* (Weimar: Wartburg Verlag, 1998); Merkenich, *Grüne Front*; Andreas Müller, *'Fällt der Bauer, stürzt der Staat': Deutschnationale Agrarpolitik 1928–1933* (München: Herbert Utz Verlag, 2003).

[32]   'Arbeiternot auf dem Lande', Landwirtschaftskammer Schlesien an den Herrn Reichskanzler, October 26, 1925, R 43 I (Reichskanzlei)/1292 betr. Landarbeiter, Bundesarchiv Berlin-Lichterfelde [hereafter BAB], pp. 165–7.

The author was equally sarcastic about the state's refusal to force young women to remain in their jobs as *Mägde* or to compel those who were collecting unemployment insurance to accept agricultural work. He added that, "As they say, getting a stamp (on your unemployment card) is easier than working." A few weeks later, the Chamber's secretary forwarded the Silesian memo to the national Labor and Agriculture ministries in Berlin.[33] Both ministries replied that they had received similar complaints from agricultural associations across Germany, but the Labor Minister explained that his consultations about the issue with numerous state representatives had produced no new legislation.[34] He added blandly that despite his best efforts, there were very few new ideas about how to prevent rural flight.

Several years later, in 1928, the national Labor Ministry informed various organizations of industrial employers that the agricultural labor shortage was growing worse in almost every region.[35] But it also sought to reassure them that the government would continue to resist farmers' demands for stronger measures and instead focus on the enforcement of existing laws. In that spirit, labor exchange officials were urged to guarantee that anyone seeking unemployment insurance who refused agricultural work "without grounds" did not receive benefits. The Labor Ministry also recommended that industrial employers avoid hiring former agricultural workers "in the interest of public-spiritedness" and, in the event of lay-offs, to let former agricultural workers go first.[36] The appeal concluded with the familiar platitude: "Only in this way can we ensure that agriculture retains the necessary labor and succeeds in attracting new workers, thereby strengthening its production capacity and guaranteeing the prosperity and well-being of the entire *Volk*."

In Saxony, several members of the DNVP also had grown impatient with the official response to the labor shortage on family farms and introduced an interpellation in the *Landtag* in April 1925 that demanded, "Is the government aware

---

[33]   Der Staatssekretär in der Reichskanzlei an den Herrn Reichsarbeitsminister, den Herrn Reichsminister für Ernährung und Landwirtschaft, Berlin, November 11, 1925, R 43 I/1292, BAB, p. 168.

[34]   Der Reichsminister für Ernährung und Landwirtschaft an den Herrn Staatssekretär der Reichskanzlei, December 23, 1925, der Reichsarbeitsminister an den Herrn Staatssekretär, January 2, 1926, R 43 I/1292, BAB, pp. 170–1. The meeting included representatives from Prussia, Bavaria, Saxony, Württemberg, Baden, Thüringen, Hessen, Mecklenburg-Schwerin, Oldenburg, and Braunschweig.

[35]   Der Reichsarbeitsminister an die Vereinigung der Deutschen Arbeitgeberverbände, den Reichsverband der Deutschen Industrie, den Deutschen Industrie- und Handelstag, den Deutschen Handwerks- und Gewerbekammertag, Berlin, April 3, 1928, R 43 I/1292, BAB; p. 257.

[36]   Abschrift zu IV 3014/28, Staatsministerium für Soziale Fürsorge, für Landwirtschaft und für Handel, Industrie und Gewerbe. Aufruf an die wirtschaftlichen Vereinigungen der Arbeitgeber in Handel, Industrie und Gewerbe, n.d. R 43 I/1292, BAB, p. 258.

of the significant shortage of female labor in agriculture?"[37] In a private discussion that preceded the debate, a representative of the Saxon Economics Ministry, like his counterparts in Berlin and Munich, demurred on the subject of coercion. He noted that the Ministry "could not promise anything in light of the experiences with the 1919 demobilization ordinances," and cautioned that "under today's conditions such laws would be unenforceable."[38] During the *Landtag* debate, the DNVP representative revisited farmers' grievances about young women in numbing detail, but the government countered diffidently that it was "doing all it could," and reiterated that the "only solution to the question lies in the close cooperation" between agricultural employers, the labor exchanges, and industry."[39]

Saxon district officials were also well aware of the problem. In 1927, the monthly economic reports from Dresden district invariably included comments like, "The transfer of older workers into agriculture continued, but a shortage of workers under 18, especially *Mägde*, persists;"[40] "the shortage of female workers is overwhelmingly evident;"[41] or "the shortage of labor is worsening ... Female agricultural workers are looking for jobs in industry, find and take them, even if [these jobs] pay less than what they made previously."[42] Like farmers in Silesia, Saxon farmers also complained vociferously about the impact of the new unemployment benefits on their quest to hire young women. As the Dresden representative observed earnestly, "Farmers do not understand the labor shortage in light of the large number of unemployed and they place most of the blame on the rate of unemployment compensation, which apparently exceeds the wages of agricultural workers."[43] At the same time, Saxon farmers also resolutely refused to hire boys or men in place of young women, and not merely because young women were cheaper.[44] Indeed, to the intense irritation of labor exchange officials, they resisted hiring boys even if they were offered bonuses to do so.[45] Saxon farmers were not unusual in this respect. In a national meeting of agricultural experts from across Germany in 1927, a Pomeranian

---

[37] 'Zur Landtags-Anfrage 1207 der Abgeordneter Schreiber/Pagenstecher', n.d., Ministerium des Innern [hereafter MdI], 'Maßnahmen zur Behebung des Arbeitermangels in der Landwirtschaft 15933, SäHStA, p. 307.

[38] 'Zur Landtags-Anfrage 1207,' MdI 15933, SäHStA, pp. 308–9.

[39] 132. Sitzung des Sächsischen Landtages, MdI 15933, SäHStA, p. 311 folio, S. 4236.

[40] Die Kreishauptmannschaft [hereafter KH] Dresden, 'Wirtschaftliche Nachrichten', Dresden, March 6, 1927, KH Dresden 262, SäHStA, p. 34.

[41] KH Dresden, June 9, 1927, KH Dresden 262, SäHStA, p. 55.

[42] KH Dresden, August 9, 1927, KH Dresden 262, SäHStA, p. 98.

[43] KH Dresden, February 6, 1927, KH Dresden 262, SäHStA, p. 13.

[44] Elizabeth Bright Jones, 'The Gendering of the Postwar Agricultural Labor Shortage in Saxony, 1918–1925', *Central European History* 32/3 (1999): 311–29, esp. pp. 326–7.

[45] 95. Sitzung des Sächsischen Landtages, February 9, 1922, MdI 15933, SäHStA, p. 95 folio, S. 3212.

official singled out *Mägde* for their growing unwillingness to work and for their declining productivity, but later insisted that "male workers cannot replace female. We must be absolutely clear about that."[46] Likewise, in response to a national survey conducted in 1929, one farmer remarked, "It is said, and I can confirm it, that we really only rarely need male workers, or not at all ... I can replace male agricultural workers with machines, but for the most part there is no substitute for girls."[47]

The Saxon Agricultural Chamber also appealed for state intervention into the agricultural labor market, and warned that if the state continued on its present course that "disastrous consequences will follow, more disastrous even than the inflation."[48] In 1927 it conducted its own survey of 350 farm families in order to report on the specific hardships precipitated by the labor shortage. According to the reporters, the survey results as well as "countless individual grievances" sent to its members were amassed and sent to the Saxon government:

> not a systematic, scientific report, but instead a collective impression of the countless desperate cries for help that are reaching all levels of agricultural organizations ... a statement about farmers' thoughts and perceptions of the causes and the impact of the labor shortage, and what conclusions they believe should be drawn [from the crisis].[49]

The report emphasized the sufferings of small and medium-sized farms, and especially lamented the fate of farm wives.[50] The report also complained about the refusal of unemployed workers to give farmers even short-term help with the harvest and the state's lack of social support for farmers, adding harshly, "Let me remind you how the shortage of female hired labor compels farm wives to make sacrifices that are unfit for human beings."[51]

An encyclopedic investigation of German agricultural labor relations submitted by the Sub-Committee for Agriculture in 1929, headed by the former national minister for Food and Agriculture Andreas Hermes, reached many of the same conclusions. The first section, which summarized the committee's findings, noted that rural flight had intensified dramatically between the fall of 1923 and the middle

---

[46]   Representative Ruge, 'Gekürzte Niederschrift der Vernehmung von Sachverständigen (Arbeitgeber- und Arbeitnehmervertretern sowie Landarbeitsforschern) über die Landarbeitsverhältnisse am 28. Oktober 1927', Anlage III, Ausschuß zur Untersuchung der Erzeugungs- und Absatzbedingungen in der deutschen Wirtschaft, *Untersuchungen über Landarbeitsverhältnisse*, Band 7 (Berlin: E. S. Mittler, 1929), pp. 226–87, here pp. 235, 282.

[47]   Cited in Baldauf, *Frauenarbeit* , p. 81.

[48]   Amtlicher Bericht, LKR, 11.1927, p. 15.

[49]   Amtlicher Bericht, LKR, 11.1927, p. 13.

[50]   Amtlicher Bericht, LKR, 11.1927, p. 15.

[51]   Amtlicher Bericht, LKR, 11.1927, p. 31.

of 1925, and continued at a record pace.[52] It also emphasized that in 1928, female youth under 18 were especially likely to be among those collecting unemployment insurance for the first time.[53] As a result, "the position of the farm wife demands unrelenting, strenuous, and often uncomfortable work." While the reporters insisted that they had not detected any "profound, generalized dissatisfaction of farm dependents with their lot," they declared that the survival of the farming sector depended on dependents' willingness to devote their utmost physical effort to work and to forgo many material advantages.[54] In conclusion, they warned that "if too much sacrifice is demanded, if despite all subordination [of desires] and hard work they must still live close to the margins, then we must sooner or later expect the next generation to disappear."

Rural Sociologists, Farm Wives, and the Creation of a Social Question

In the final years of the Weimar Republic, a number of social scientists undertook ambitious studies of farm women's productive and reproductive work. They concluded that despite reformers' best efforts, little had changed, especially for farm wives. Finding remedies to the crisis was presented as vital not only for women themselves, but for their children. Many also emphasized the extraordinary cultural value of motherhood for the nation's recovery and future stability. At the same time, all the authors enthusiastically affirmed farm women's productive and professional identities and maintained that their economic contributions were essential for maintaining national security.

One of these social scientists, Luise Fritsch, placed her 1929 study of farm wives' work in a national context, observing that

> The current agricultural crisis has inspired us to revisit its possible origins and has prompted numerous proposals that explain agriculture's decline ... In this respect the woman question in agriculture has assumed new importance ... It is precisely because the much-discussed products of poultry-raising, gardening, and dairying in large part fall under the special category of women's work that this question needs closer examination.[55]

Fritsch cautioned that "special interests" had thwarted an objective consideration of these matters in recent years, and argued that agricultural associations and rural housewives' associations bore part of the blame. She expressed special concern about the risks of heavy and unrelenting physical work on farm wives' health and their tendency to resume work immediately after giving birth, noting that in this

---

52   Ausschuß zur Untersuchung, *Untersuchungen*, p. 15.

53   Ausschuß zur Untersuchung, *Untersuchungen*, p. 30.

54   Ausschuß zur Untersuchung, *Untersuchungen*, p. 50.

55   Fritsch, *Stellung*, p. 5.

respect female industrial workers were protected while farm wives were not.[56] She added that while farm wives were no longer responsible for manufacturing many household consumer goods, their increased field labor more than made up for the time saved: "This argument about the unburdening of farm wives does not apply to women on small and medium-sized enterprises. It is a statistically-proven fact that today these farm wives are being pushed to the limit of their physical capabilities."[57] Indeed, Fritsch described in detail a 1927 survey conducted by the RLHV and a sub-committee of the national Agricultural Ministry that enumerated all the ways that farm wives were overworked.[58] The results of this overburdening included "the disintegration of rural culture and the disadvantaging of family life, especially child-rearing and education; health damages; decline in fertility rates; and higher infant mortality; despite an increase in rural housewives' work, no increase in production."[59]

A few years later, her colleague Elisabeth Baldauf described the work of wives on family enterprises as:

> frequently the dirtiest and heaviest. For they cannot afford a hired hand ... So we see the farm wife unloading and spreading manure, cleaning out stalls, using pitchforks, driving wagons, harrowing, cutting grass ... It's even worse in mountainous regions ... Here women are bowed over with their burdens. They do not notice the mountains' beauty, they see only the burdens that they create.[60]

Like her colleagues, Baldauf also relied heavily on statistics collected by other scholars, including the work of prominent agricultural economist Adolf Münzinger and others.[61] Among their findings were that farm wives worked on average longer hours than their husbands and that farm daughters increasingly sought to avoid the same pressures by leaving the farm altogether.[62]

---

[56]   Fritsch, *Stellung*, pp. 9, 23. On Weimar maternity legislation see Cornelie Usborne, *The Politics of the Body in Weimar Germany: Women's Reproductive Rights and Duties* (Ann Arbor: University of Michigan Press, 1992), pp. 31–68, esp. pp. 47–9; Schwarz emphasizes the RLHV's intense opposition to the proposed maternity legislation, see Christina Schwarz, *Die Landfrauenbewegung in Deutschland: zur Geschichte einer Frauenorganisation unter besonderer Berücksichtigung der Jahre 1898 bis 1933* (Mainz: Gesellschaft für Volkskunde im Rheinland-Pfalz, e.V., 1990), pp. 226–7.

[57]   Fritsch, *Stellung*, p. 8.

[58]   Fritsch, *Stellung*, p. 22. The sub-committee was the Enquête-Ausschuß zur Erhebung der Erzeugungs- und Absatzbedingungen in der Landwirtschaft.

[59]   Fritsch, *Stellung*, p. 22.

[60]   Baldauf, *Frauenarbeit*, p. 47.

[61]   In this case, she used Adolf Münzinger, *Der Arbeitsertrag der bäuerlichen Familienwirtschaft* (Berlin: Paul Parey, 1929) and Anna Massante, 'Die Bäuerin im landwirtschaftlichen Betriebe', *Land und Frau* 45 (1929): 857.

[62]   Baldauf, *Frauenarbeit*, pp. 52–3.

Finally, Baldauf also devoted an entire section of her study to farm wives' maternal duties and to the declining birthrate in the German countryside. She noted that before the war, there was a steady increase in the proportion of babies born to rural versus urban mothers, "which has also held true for the postwar years, although not so consistently. However 1925 appears to be the turning-point, because since then the difference between urban and rural birthrates has diminished … It is clear that the tempo of the birthrate decline in the countryside is approaching that of the city."[63] Baldauf attributed the decline to farm wives' overwork and to mothers' anxiety that their children might not "get ahead."[64] By this time her verdict had a familiar ring: not only was the crisis attributable to the physically-taxing work and long hours, which were having a negative impact on menstruation and pregnancy, but "to the fact that because they are married, they are constantly torn back and forth between agricultural work, housework, and childcare."[65]

Marie von Brand's 1930 dissertation, completed under the direction of Adolf Münzinger, was a detailed profile of three farm wives in the Swabian countryside southeast of Stuttgart, the so-called *Filder*. In her description of the average day, von Brand commented ruefully that her subjects' days were "so hectic and filled with so much toil" that the farm wife needed "two sets of hands and feet."[66] Von Brand also described farm wives' work from a seasonal perspective, accompanied by detailed charts of their month-to-month activities. Like Fritsch and Baldauf, she too was deeply concerned about the ways in which women's agricultural workload superseded all else, and bemoaned the fact that their responsibilities as mothers and housewives always came last.[67] Von Brand insisted that:

> Farm wives' cultural worth has declined due to the conditions I have described. It is not normal and healthy that the farm wife is only an agricultural worker and that this work drains her so entirely. According to women's nature, she should have not only the time but the physical and psychological energy to be a housewife and mother. But today the farm wife no longer fulfills the function of housewife; and although she is bearing the next generation – although in a more limited way due to the desperation of our times – she is not able to guide and nurture the next generation in the correct way.[68]

Von Brand also expressed deep consternation that because of their workloads, farm wives could no longer appreciate the value of their contributions, or "the worthiness of their existence."[69] And she decried yet another destructive side-effect of farm

[63]   Baldauf, *Frauenarbeit*, p. 55.
[64]   Baldauf, *Frauenarbeit*, p. 56.
[65]   Baldauf, *Frauenarbeit*, p. 69.
[66]   von Brand, *wirtchaftliche und kulturelle Lage,* p. 28.
[67]   von Brand, *wirtschaftliche und kulturelle Lage*, p. 42.
[68]   von Brand, *wirtschaftliche und kulturelle Lage*, pp. 45–6.
[69]   von Brand, *wirtschaftliche und kulturelle Lage*, p. 58.

wives' overwork, namely that they were too busy to keep track of their household expenses. "The origins of this wrongheaded household politics lie in the basic evil of their daily lives: in their extreme burdens as *agricultural workers.*"[70]

Like her colleagues, von Brand's study ended with a plea for greater public attention to the crisis. She also reminded her audience that farm wives' rescue was imperative because they would bear the next generation, whose responsibility would be to "rescue the nation from the damage caused by the urban devouring of humanity."[71] To reinforce the anxiety about the nation's demographic health, von Brand's appendix included local statistics on the declining birthrate in five villages in the *Filder*. According to her calculations, between 1908 and 1928 the number of children borne by farm wives declined by 35 percent, from an average of just over six (6.1) to an average of less than four (3.8); even more ominously, von Brand warned that the decline between 1898 and 1928 was 50 percent.[72] At the same time, she noted that infant mortality had declined over the same period and that life expectancies for farm wives had increased 10–20 percent, which she attributed to improved rural hygiene.[73]

Of all the new research, Gerhard Schützhold's investigation offered the most meticulous documentation of farm wives' work, and it is the only research of its kind for Saxony. His stated purpose, outlined in the introduction, was to evaluate public perceptions of farm wives. He argued that the public could be divided into three camps: those that admired farm wives for their independence and self-reliance; those who pitied them as "overworked, oppressed beings who know nothing of the aforementioned advantages;" and those whose pity for farm wives was mixed with contempt.[74] Although Schützhold did not revisit these issues in the course of his study, he counseled in his conclusion, "To those who might think of becoming a farm wife, my findings are an admonition to use your education to build an armor that will help you fulfill your future duties, and allow you to emerge as victors in the battle to preserve the soil. Let my research also remind those in other professions to pay farm wives the respect they deserve for their achievements!"[75] Schützhold's sources were the daily diary entries of 11 farm wives from different regions of Saxony, eight of whom kept records for one year and three of whom agreed to continue the diaries for a second year. All the farms were medium-sized family farms ranging in size from 10–23 hectares. The "diary" was a form that Schützhold's research subjects were required to fill out daily that recorded each task, how long it took to complete, whether they received any assistance, and their own comments. Although his approach clearly reflected the influence of contemporary time/motion studies, Schützhold made a strong case for

---

[70]   von Brand, *wirtschaftliche und kulturelle Lage*, pp. 115–16. Emphasis in original.

[71]   von Brand, *wirtschaftliche und kulturelle Lage*, p. 59.

[72]   von Brand, *wirtschaftliche und kulturelle Lage*, p. 100.

[73]   von Brand, *wirtschaftliche und kulturelle Lage*, pp. 106–7, 111.

[74]   Schützhold, *sächsische Landfrau*, p. 1.

[75]   Schützhold, *sächsische Landfrau*, p. 76.

the overburdening of farm women that refuted contemporary claims that labor- and time-saving devices eased the heavy workload of farm wives.

According to his findings, the most overburdened wives – defined by the number of minutes worked in the stall, the garden, the fields, and doing housework – were married to farmers who owned the most livestock: "Either more time will be spent on housework if the number of livestock decreases, or caring for livestock will prevent wives from caring adequately for their families."[76] Thus, in this case the farm wife had to choose between generating much-needed income from livestock holding, or neglecting her stall work in favor of family duties. Like Fritsch, he also noted that time saved from one activity was devoted to another: "The farm wife always strives to use the time spared by pasturing to increase her field work, or by allowing the hired labor to work less in the stalls."[77] The same pattern emerged in Schützhold's description of the seasonal changes in wives' field work, where extra time in the weeks between harvests was used for more housework.[78]

On a weekly basis, the author observed a similar phenomenon on Saturdays, which he argued were especially hectic as wives tried to make up for the time not spent in the fields on Sundays.[79] Sundays, he added, were more like less strenuous workdays for wives than days of rest due to the required stall work and the expectation of others in the household that a special meal would be served.[80] In addition to productive and reproductive work, Schützhold also included a category labeled "free time," defined as meals; dressing and undressing; professional, religious, or political obligations (i.e., voting); and illness. In terms of washing, dressing, and undressing, the author noted that although wives spent on average only 15 minutes a day, they repeatedly insisted that they did not take more time, preferring instead to sleep.[81] Although mealtime was defined as free time, Schützhold stressed that wives had an obligation to make sure that harmony reigned so that plans for the next day's work could be discussed.[82]

Farm wives' constant juggling of their multiple burdens according to the day and the season, the crops cultivated and numbers of livestock, and their personal preferences emerged as the central theme of Schützhold's research, and one of the hallmarks of farm wives' work. Time saved was never used as a respite from work, but instead devoted to other tasks in order to decrease the need for hired help, to ease another family member's labor burden, or to make up for previous neglect, especially in the case of housework. Summarizing the diary entry of farm wife no. 8 he concluded that,

---

[76] Schützhold, *sächsische Landfrau*, p. 20.

[77] Schützhold, *sächsische Landfrau*, p. 17.

[78] Schützhold, *sächsische Landfrau*, pp. 24–5.

[79] Schützhold, *sächsische Landfrau*, p. 20.

[80] Schützhold, *sächsische Landfrau*, p. 11, 20.

[81] Schützhold, *sächsische Landfrau*, p. 4.

[82] Schützhold, *sächsische Landfrau*, p. 10.

This farm offers a shocking example of the farm wife's punishing struggle for existence. From spring through fall, her workday demands more of her than might be expected for any woman. Given that in this time she also gave birth, and could not rest either before or afterwards, it is not surprising that for health reasons she cannot work as much as before, despite the fact that the need for extra help is now more urgent than ever.[83]

Taken together, this research confirmed both the failure of the Weimar rationalization campaign to alleviate farm wives' overburdening in any measurable sense and underscored the growing consensus among contemporary observers that farm wives had become the most worrisome casualty of the broader economic, moral, and cultural crisis of the Weimar Republic.

Gendering Agrarian Romanticism: Farm Women and *Völkisch* Discourse, 1918–1933

The fate of farm wives after the war also emerged as a theme in the writings of conservative agricultural, state, and social welfare policymakers, prominent academics, and self-styled *völkisch* activists like Dresden-based Bruno Tanzmann. In speeches, pamphlets, and journal articles they presented farm women's overburdening as just one of the many dire symptoms of Germany's decline due to rural flight. Thus their laments invariably used farm wives' material suffering as a metaphor for the broader moral and cultural disintegration of the nation, and drew on the long tradition of prewar agrarian romanticism to amplify their warnings about the long-term consequences of industrialization, urbanization, and the glorification of "selfish individualism" over the needs of family and community. But while earlier generations of agrarian romantics had argued that the *countryside* provided a much-needed moral and biological counter-balance to the dangers of the big city and leftist political agitation, the postwar discourse placed farm wives at the center of the fight for a return to an agrarian state. Moreover, while they professed deep concern about farm wives' overburdening and its consequences for future generations, they also recognized that the crisis offered rich possibilities for launching attacks on the Republic and its "betrayal" of German agriculture.

Agrarian romantics in Weimar borrowed heavily from the ideas of mid-nineteenth century conservatives like Moritz Arndt and Wilhelm Heinrich Riehl about the countryside as the "wellspring of the German nation," and even more so from Riehl's turn-of-the-century "re-discoverers" like Otto Ammon and Georg Hansen.[84] As early as 1840, for example, Arndt appealed for "The preservation and maintenance of the law-abiding peasantry … so that they may act as a

---

[83]   Schützhold, *sächsische Landfrau*, p. 73.

[84]   For a detailed description of all three, see K. Bergmann, *Agrarromantik*, pp. 33–135, esp. pp. 48–62.

counterweight and antidote to the increasing threat posed by the plebeian rabble, whose turmoil will shatter itself on this rock of the state."[85] Decades later, in 1889, Georg Hansen declared that "The farmer's duty is not only to supply the city with butter and cheese, but above all with people."[86] Of course, such statements ignored the fact that it was farm women who produced the cheese and butter for urban consumers, not to mention their role in maintaining the birth rate. Hansen also preached that, "the question of profitability is secondary. If you want to judge whether latifundia, family farm, or dwarf holding is most advantageous to the nation, then you must look not at which enterprises are the most profitable, but instead at which produce the largest surplus of people."[87] Hansen's "national over rational" thinking resonated strongly among ultra-conservative agricultural policymakers before the war.[88] As agricultural economist Heinrich Dade warned after the results of the 1895 census,

> The presentation of these facts should spur every conscientious economist to grapple with the most important socio-political challenge [we face] until a solution is found. The problem ... is the preservation and increase of the agricultural population. The solution to this problem must and will be found, or the marrow of our social structure and economic life will be devoured.[89]

In contrast, Weimar conservatives framed the biological and moral virtues of the German countryside in explicitly feminized terms. In particular, they seized on the notion that farm wives, by upholding agriculture's work ethic and setting a moral example, would restore Germany's national greatness. Conservative agriculture experts like Georg Stieger, who worked for the German Agricultural Association [*Deutsche Landwirtschafts-Gesellschaft*], and Friedrich Falke, an agricultural economist and Leipzig University rector, were even more explicit about the social and cultural role of farm wives in the conservative battles against rural flight and the perceived deficiencies of the Weimar state. In his 1922 agricultural manual, Georg Stieger borrowed many of the prewar conservative images of farm families, praising them as "the sturdiest supporters of the nation ... because rural inhabitants produce the ever more valuable, often overlooked *byproduct* of agriculture, namely the refreshing of nerves and moral cleansing and steadfast efficiency that the cities and industries need, and which they deplete despite all health-preserving measures."[90] On the overburdening of farm wives, Stieger pontificated that the

---

[85]   K. Bergmann, *Agrarromantik*, p. 47.

[86]   K. Bergmann, *Agrarromantik*, p. 54.

[87]   Cited in K. Bergmann, *Agrarromantik*, p. 54.

[88]   This is Bergmann's term. K. Bergmann, *Agrarromantik*, p. 93.

[89]   Heinrich Dade, *Die landwirtschaftliche Bevölkerung des Deutschen Reiches um die Wende des 19. Jahrhunderts* (Berlin: Paul Parey, 1903), p. 1.

[90]   Georg Stieger, *Der Mensch in der Landwirtschaft. Grundlagen der Landarbeitslehre* (Berlin: Paul Parey, 1922), p. 131.

difficulty and strenuousness of a particular task "depends as much on the subject as the object, and that the 'malice of the object' is less burdensome for those who have found joy in their work."[91] In a long chapter on the farm household and family, Stieger drew on Riehl's comment that the "pure morals of the *Bürger* are nothing more than exalted peasant morals" to argue that the restoration of German morals in the postwar period "must make a detour through the farm household."[92] The author concluded that *all* farm wives were protectors of rural German culture, and that they were more critical than their husbands in the battle against rural flight, for "they know, or certainly should know, whom they can help and advise in their communities, and where the physical and spiritual wounds are that need their caring, nurturing hands."[93]

Echoing the concerns of rural sociologists, *völkisch* activists characterized the overburdening of farm wives in terms of a crisis that threatened the nation by increasing infant mortality and subverting the health and well-being of the next generation of farm families. In 1928, rural social welfare reformer Johann Dieing published an article called simply, "Farm Wives' Suffering!"[94] Dieing faulted the poor working conditions on family farms that increased wives' labor burden, but pointed to the lack of respect accorded them by the general public as the true heart of the problem. He argued that "The fundamental damage ... destroying the village and preventing it from finding new living space [*Lebensraum*] is of a social-ethical nature."[95] If farm families regained the public's lost respect, according to Dieing, then solutions to all the other economic problems "will find fertile soil." He asserted that the new respect for farm wives would prevent their daughters from leaving the countryside, easing the labor burden of women who "have not yet been swept away by the tide."[96]

In a 1929 speech on rural flight at Leipzig University, rector Friedrich Falke opened with a reference to the world agricultural crisis, and blamed "political squabbling" for the failure to recognize the value of farm families to the nation's economy and society.[97] He prefaced his remarks about farm wives with phrases from nineteenth-century agrarian conservatives, referring repeatedly to farm families as the "fountain of life for the nation," as well as from contemporary works like Oswald Spengler's *Decline of the West*. In his discussion of family farms, Falke acknowledged that farm wives were "among the most tormented

---

[91]   Stieger, *Mensch*, p. 240.

[92]   Stieger, *Mensch*, p. 343.

[93]   Stieger, *Mensch*, p. 350.

[94]   J. B. Dieing, *Landfrauennot!* (Freiburg/Br.: Verlag der Arbeitsgemeinschaft für Dorfcaritas, 1928), pp. 1–16.

[95]   Dieing, *Landfrauennot!*, p. 6.

[96]   Dieing, *Landfrauennot!*, p. 7.

[97]   Friedrich Falke, 'Die Landflucht, Ihre Ursachen und Wirkungen', *Rektorwechsel an der Universität Leipzig am 31. Oktober 1929* (Leipzig: Alexander Edelmann, 1929), pp. 27–48.

creatures on earth." In the same breath, however, he complained that farm girls refused to marry farmers not because they disrespected the profession but due to their aversion to the workload, and that they now preferred to marry a teacher or an official than to inherit a farm.[98] Echoing conservative prewar observers like Georg Bindewald, he minimized the disadvantages of farm wives' work by arguing that many studies of rural flight demonstrated that "even if [industrial] work is easier, the rise in social status that perhaps many seek is seldom attained."[99] According to Falke, the primary danger of rural flight was not the suffering of farm families due to overwork and Germany's increased reliance on food imports, although both were discussed, but instead the decline in the birth rate. "Marital fertility is still twice as high in the countryside as in the city, but even there the birth rate has declined one third since 1913; this is not surprising, because its source of strength is being sapped." Falke ended his speech with bleak warnings that Germany's fate would be like that of Babylon, Alexandria, or Rome if rural flight, and its most distressing manifestation, the population decline, persisted.

Leaders of popular *völkisch* movements echoed these warnings about agriculture's impending doom and condemnations of the Weimar state. In their view, the morality of farm wives would act as a glue that would reinforce other conservative efforts to strengthen the rural population and prepare the way for a return to an agrarian state. They exhorted farm wives to revive the "old discarded virtues" of industriousness, selflessness, and cheerfulness toward work and family that would sustain the nation as it underwent this difficult, but necessary, transformation. At the same time, extreme right-wing organizations like the *Artamanen* employed the rhetoric of farm wives' morality to critique the chaotic, misguided, and treacherous Weimar state that had failed to halt Germany's descent into urbanization, industrialization, economic crisis, and endless political squabbling.

Bruno Tanzmann, the founder of the *Artamanen*, presented the most inflated, idealized vision of the farm woman as a moral force in a corrupt world, and draped her in the most aggressively anti-Weimar rhetoric. Born in rural Saxony, Tanzmann was one of the few right-wing agrarian conservatives who actually farmed before the war. In 1919 he founded the Swastika Press and his own self-published newspaper, *The German Farmers' School: Newspaper for German Farmers' Culture and Germanic Farmers' Education*.[100] In Hellerau, the famed garden suburb of Dresden, Tanzmann led workshops on "farmers' education" beginning in 1921, and by 1923 there were six schools in Saxony that followed his curriculum guidelines and were

---

[98] Falke, 'Landflucht', p. 34.

[99] Falke, 'Landflucht', p. 35.

[100] For an excellent discussion of the broader *Bauernhochschulbewegung*, see Dietmar von Reeken, 'Bildung als Krisenbewältigungsinstrument? Die Bauernhochschulbewegung in der Weimarer Republik', in Daniela Münkel (ed.), *Der lange Abschied vom Agrarland: Agrarpolitik, Landwirtschaft und ländliche Gesellschaft zwischen Weimar und Bonn* (Göttingen: Wallstein Verlag, 2000), pp. 157–76.

supported by various private Saxon agricultural organizations as well as by the Saxon Agricultural Chamber.[101] Tanzmann's curriculum ignored agricultural science, and consisted instead of civics (defined as the study of "Germanic heroes"), philosophy, racial science, economics, Germanic arts and literature, farmers' culture, physical training, and settlement/colonization.[102] The larger purpose of the *Artamanen*, as one Frau Schmidt explained to the Saxon Agricultural Chamber, was to mobilize young German men and women to work for farmers, who would provide room and board, as a means of easing youth unemployment and driving out all foreign workers employed in German agriculture.[103]

In a lengthy 1921 editorial on the role of women in his movement, Tanzmann first condemned the New Woman and the social chaos and moral corruption she symbolized: "The Revolution has broken the last boundaries, and has engulfed us in the chaos of the streets. The woman with make-up, cigarette, and almond-shaped eyes has become fashionable." Tanzmann argued that these hallmarks of moral decline could be combated with "pulpit phrases" or "parliamentary slogans," but even better with the "shining, living example of our national life … the farm wife."[104] According to Tanzmann, she was "modest, and maybe even nothing to look at. But from her rough handshake we realize at once that she is queen of the kingdom of highest virtue: work."[105]

Tanzmann celebrated farm wives for battling everything from livestock sickness, flooding, hail, family arguments, and the loss of hired hands, and taunted "unemployed demonstrators in the cities" and "middle-class housewives" to apply for agricultural work, "where the only reply would be excuses and insults." He declared that farm wives could quell the present chaos only if they recognized their own worth as mothers and workers, which would enable them to fight the disadvantages and shortcomings of their present existence and free themselves from the heaviest work. Furthermore, farm wives should reject movies, department store fashions, factory-made furniture, "as well as all other baubles and smut."[106]

The program of the *Artamanen* to reverse rural flight and revive the sense of community in the countryside attracted the attention, and intense admiration, of the Saxon Agricultural Chamber. In a 1925 report on a spring festival sponsored by the *Artamanen*, one of its representatives praised the goals of the movement to establish a mandatory agricultural work-service program and to "restore the respect for

---

[101]   Bruno Tanzmann, 'Die Beispiel-Bauernhochschule in Hellerau', *Die deutsche Bauernhochschule* 3 (December 1921): 1–6. See also K. Bergmann, *Agrarromantik*, p. 226.

[102]   Tanzmann, 'Die Beispiel-Bauernhochschule', pp. 3–4.

[103]   Arbeitsamt der Deutschen Bauernhochschule an die Landwirtschaftskammer des Freistaates Sachsen, Hellerau bei Dresden, 16.12.1925, MdI 15934, 'Artamanen', SäHStA, p. 5.

[104]   Bruno Tanzmann, 'Die Frau der Bauernkultur', *Die deutsche Bauernhochschule* 2 (September, 1921), p. 2.

[105]   Tanzmann, 'Die Frau', p. 3.

[106]   Tanzmann, 'Die Frau', p. 5.

agricultural work through their high spirit," and the recognition of the *Artamanen* that the continued employment of foreigners in German agriculture "constituted a threat to the nation."[107] He described the 25 young men and 10 "girls" as "displaying an ideal engagement with agriculture and with the German *Volk*." The report concluded with a description of the boisterous parade through the village, noting that "The girls in white linen dresses of simple cut, their hair tamed in two braids over their shoulders, and bare feet with sandals, the men in old-fashioned traditional German dress ... showed their strong bodies and faces full of character."

The images of farm women promoted by the *Artamanen* and praised by the Saxon Agricultural Chamber were highly stylized and idealized, but they left no doubt about farm women's roles in the redefinition of German nationalism after the war. While organizations devoted to improving rural social welfare and promoting the interests of farm wives doggedly insisted on their apolitical stance, their agenda for restoring the vitality of rural communities and traditional morals also borrowed the language of the new agrarian romanticism to frame their appeals. In a 1926 speech on farm wives and rural social welfare, a representative of the Association for Rural Social Welfare and *Heimat* Protection, Aenna Gausebeck, asked rhetorically:

> Is this all, this constant hurrying between cow stall and kitchen, between house and field? Are these all of her duties, or does the farm wife take part in a larger world order, does her circumscribed work have a deeper meaning, a larger context? The answer is unequivocally yes! ... The limitations of the farm wife's existence are only illusory, and instead her life is bound in myriad tangible and intangible ways to the whole life of her people.[108]

Gausebeck also described a purported medieval custom in her home region, the Rhineland, where a farmer's wife welcomed a new *Magd* into the household by cutting a small piece of wood out of the doorframe, grinding it up, baking the sawdust into a loaf of bread, and sharing it with the *Magd*:

> a beautiful custom, that symbolized to the *Magd* that she was a firm member of the household, bound up in its duties but also certain of her belonging and her care ... the spirit of such customs should be carried on by our farm wives and daughters, who should make every effort to invent new traditions, because we human beings yearn for outward signs that bolster our inner strength.[109]

---

[107] Ministerialrat von Wenckstern, Bericht über die Frühlingsfeier bei Rittergutspächter Obendorfer-Limbach bei Wilsdruff, 16. Mai 1925, MdI 15934, SäHStA, p. 1.

[108] Aenna Gausebeck, 'Vom Landmädchen zur Landfrau', in *Wohlfahrt und Wirtschaft: Bericht über die 29. Hauptversammlung des deutschen Vereins für ländliche Wohlfahrts- und Heimatpflege am 25. und 26. Februar 1926 in Berlin* (Berlin: Deutscher Verein für ländliche Wohlfahrts- und Heimatpflege, 1926), pp. 19–27, here p. 20.

[109] Gausebeck, 'Vom Landmädchen', p. 22.

In sum, historian Dietmar von Reeken's description of the efforts by Tanzmann and others to "educate" young farm women and men about their duties to the *Volk* also characterized the broader aims of Weimar agrarian romantics like Falke, Stieger, and others. Von Reeken argues that their primary goal was to highlight "the crass urban-rural dichotomy" and the "segmentation of Weimar society ... What motivated them was not so much the real experience of agricultural crisis ... but the construction of a crisis of the peasantry that was simultaneously a crisis of the entire society."[110]

Right-Wing Politics, Gender, and the Agricultural Press

Despite frequent declarations of political neutrality, representatives of the National Rural Housewives' Association often made their conservative sentiments clear. Throughout the 1920s and early 1930s, numerous articles appeared in *Land und Frau* that advised farm wives about how they might use their new voting rights to usher in a government more sympathetic to farm families' needs. At the same time, their contributors frequently invoked the neutrality of the RLHV with regard to party politics and condemned political squabbling as unproductive.[111] Nevertheless, as early as 1920, an editorial entitled "New Responsibilities for Housewives in the Countryside" observed that the better and more efficient the farm wife, the less likely she would be to consider political and economic questions, but "If the rural housewife does not make herself a factor in our economic life and the rebuilding of the nation, then she will end up with a government that pays no attention to her. Because today the only thing that counts is the unified mass."[112] The article ended with an avowal by rural housewives' associations to remain aloof from party politics, but added, "If one wants to view [the farm wife's] work as political, then it is the politics of the economy that drives her activities."[113]

In the spring of 1923, an article on farm wives and a new bank founded by the Rural League opened by disclaiming any opinion about whether farm wives or their husbands were better household financial managers, but urged farm wives to use the new bank as a means of remedying the unfortunate advantages that urban banks and industry maintained over agriculture.[114] The author argued that the bank would help rural inhabitants' struggle for equality with the city and anchor that status for the future, and urged farm wives to deposit any funds or savings they might have in the Bank for Agriculture. Farm wives were reminded that, "The

---

[110]   von Reeken, 'Bauernhochschulbewegung', p. 173.

[111]   On the tensions between women declaring themselves "above" party politics despite their vigorous political activism see Scheck, *Mothers*, p. 6.

[112]   Konstanze vom Berge, 'Neue Aufgaben für die Hausfrauen auf dem Lande', *Land und Frau* 4/18 (May 1, 1920): 141.

[113]   vom Berge, 'Neue Aufgaben', p. 142.

[114]   Anon., 'Die Landfrau und die Bank für Landwirtschaft', *Land und Frau* 7/12 (May 24, 1923): 93.

politics of German farm families must move unanimously and decisively toward success, and it is precisely the farm wife whom we are calling … to benefit the Bank for Agriculture." Notably, the article directed farm wives interested in the bank to seek additional information through their local rural housewives' association.

By the late 1920s, the rhetoric of many *Land und Frau* editorials was overtly conservative, expressing the editors' frustrations with the Weimar state's failure to address the agricultural crisis as well as their disillusionment with the democratic political system. In 1928, articles on rural flight appeared with titles like, "The Nation-Devouring City," "Fighting the Birth Rate Decline," and "The Farm Wife and the Current Agricultural Crisis."[115] All deplored the deteriorating economic, social, and cultural health of the nation due to industry's favored economic position in relation to agriculture, and warned of the dangerous political consequences that would result from the sufferings of farm wives and daughters.

In "The Nation-Devouring City," the author stressed that while the flight of young men from the countryside and the corresponding disrespect for farmers that had begun before the war was regrettable, it was also "natural."[116] Much more dangerous was the "female stream" from the countryside after the war, due to the "loosening of relationships between hired hands and employers … and the utter lack of moral ties carrying young women away to the free life. Short hours of wantonness make them hate the days they must work."[117] The author cited Saxony as a particularly egregious example of women's flight from the countryside, and condemned the "thousands of unemployed young women living off the state," and where "the city is inexorably sucking up new sacrifices from the countryside, who are lured by the shining department store windows and the soft hotel carpets."

A *Land und Frau* editorial several months later, "The Farm Wife as Voting Factor," cited farm wives' overburdening as the reason for their "astounding participation" in farmers' demonstrations and public protests.[118] The author emphasized that farm wives were bearing the brunt of the agricultural crisis, leading to neglect of the household and the children and to their own physical and emotional decline. The article also blamed the state for its generous protection of industrial workers while farm wives continued to suffer. As part of the solution, the author exhorted all farm wives and daughters to take part in the nation's political life by voting for candidates that pledged to protect agricultural interests. At the

---

[115] See the Table of Contents, section 1, 'Soziale Wirtschaft, Volkswirtschaft, Wohlfahrtspflege, Berufsfragen', *Land und Frau* 12 (1928).

[116] K. M. Schöller, 'Die volkssaugende Stadt', *Land und Frau* 12/1 (January 7, 1928): 3.

[117] Like the prewar rhetoric of Pan-Germanists, the postwar language of agrarian conservatives about rural flight frequently used water imagery to describe the crisis. See Roger Chickering, *We Men Who Feel Most German: A Cultural Study of the Pan-German League, 1886–1914* (Boston: Allen & Unwin, 1984), p. 83.

[118] Anon., 'Die Landfrau als Wahlfaktor', *Land und Frau* 12/20 (May 19, 1928): 387.

same time, the *Reichstag* was chided for failing to provide the funds agriculture needed to recover and the author cautioned that any self-help initiatives farming communities undertook could not succeed without farm wives' support.

Finally, an editorial by Elli Heese entitled "Rationalization of our National Strength" asked how the lessons of economic and social rationalization that industry, agriculture, commerce, and housewives had followed so assiduously might transform the nation's fragmented political life into a unified whole.[119] Heese referred to the conflicts between different "tribes" that were the legacy of Germany's rapid industrialization and bemoaned the fact that even individual groups were plagued by internal divisions. She asserted that while sometimes such differences led to progress and innovation, in Germany's case these had caused merely "fruitless bickering." Indeed, Heese continued, "We have long known that we are wasting our strength in these political battles, and that our strength could instead be used to rebuild the nation … The *Stahlhelm* has pointed us in the right direction by urging the *Volk* to reject parliamentarianism." She concluded that the same "tight discipline" that had rationalized economic life must be transferred to the nation's cultural and political life, which desperately needed "the strength provided by women's collective household efficiency."

Moreover, *Land und Frau* reported frequently on the RLHV's close ties with ultra-conservative women's organizations like the Women's Committee for the Struggle Against the War-Guilt Lie, the Queen Luise Alliance, and the Fatherland Association; it also reported on women's involvement in various eastern settlement initiatives.[120] Likewise RLHV founder and president, Elisabet Boehm, often used the pages of *Land und Frau* to signal her own ultra-conservative sentiments. For example, in a report on the RLHV conference in Berlin in early 1925, Boehm warmly recounted the recent demonstrations by farmers against the state and urged her colleagues to support the "battle cries of the Rural League, 'For Land and Grain!' and 'Everything for the Fatherland!'"[121] More tellingly, in September 1931 Boehm formally apologized to readers who were offended by an article she had written for the leading Nazi newspaper, the *Völkischer Beobachter*.[122] She explained that the "misunderstanding" was caused by a fellow RLHV member and contributor to the East Prussian Nazi newspaper *die Landpost*, who had reprinted Boehm's original piece to introduce a larger group of articles entitled "Farm Women under the Swastika," purportedly without her consent. In any case,

[119]   Elli Heese, 'Rationalisierung unserer Volkskraft', *Land und Frau* 12/46 (November 17, 1928): 839–40.

[120]   On conservative women's organizations in general, see Scheck, *Mothers*; 'Aus der Arbeit des RLHV' (hereafter 'Aus der Arbeit') *Land und Frau* 9/3 (January 17, 1925): 30; 'Aus der Arbeit', *Land und Frau* 9/9 (February 28, 1925): 103; S Rogge-Börner, 'Unser Bauernblut gehört dem Deutschtum!', *Land und Frau* 15/8 (February 21, 1931): 131.

[121]   Helene Wenck, 'Die Landfrauen in Berlin', *Land und Frau* 9/9 (February 25, 1925): 98–100, here p. 98.

[122]   'Klarstellung in eigener Sache', *Land und Frau* 15/38 (September 19, 1931): 694.

Boehm amended, the Nazi press' "blunder" would not incriminate the association, since she was no longer its official president, "and although I myself am not a National Socialist, I have worn the swastika for 40 years, as an old Germanic sign of leadership."

In Saxony, the agricultural press, the mainstream conservative press, and the right-wing SLV also sought to publicize the twin crises of rural flight and farm women's overburdening and to inflame popular indignation over the government's inaction. As the farmer in a December 1928 cartoon "The modern Goddess of Fate" implored, "What good do 150 [parliamentary] petitions do if they remain on paper?" Sometimes the goal was to motivate constituents' support for self-help initiatives, like the lottery sponsored by the Saxon Rural League in 1927 to fund the "vacation home" for farm wives in Bad Elster. As the first of many appeals for support declared, "One can state without exaggeration that the wife of a small or medium-sized farmer is the most burdened and busy person of all. She enjoys no peace, no respite. The result of these circumstances is an early and powerful ebbing of her strength that is a misfortune to her, to her family, and to the economy. The need for assistance is urgent."[123] In a January 1929 article, the *Leipziger Neueste Nachrichten* bemoaned the growing impoverishment of farm families, but added that "Farmers' pride does not allow us to see [how terrible things are]. The fate of the farm wife is far more difficult than we surmise ... The *Junglandbund*, which includes both 'Young Farmers' and 'Young Farm Wives' has set itself lofty goals, because one realizes that the only source of healing for our *Volk* must come from the countryside."[124] In the same month, the *Volkszeitung Dresden* ran a story on the agricultural crisis in Bavaria, which began by proclaiming "German agriculture is at the end of its rope and gives the national government until the end of this year's harvest [to act]. If our demands remain unfulfilled, then *agriculture will stop working to provision the cities* and will only work enough to provide for their families and hired hands."[125]

Beginning in 1928 the SLV, with the strong support of the Saxon Rural League, appealed in the pages of the agricultural press directly to farm women to support its radical right-wing platform. The League's support for the new party, which had been organized in the wake of the right-wing *Landvolk* movement in Schleswig-Holstein, was in part a frantic effort to contain farmers' growing disaffection with its representatives in the League and the DNVP.[126] Between 1928 and 1932, the

[123] 'Landwirtschaftliche Wohlfahrtslotterie zur Schaffung eines Erholungsheims für Landwirtsfrauen', *Sächsische Bauernzeitung* [hereafter *SBZ*], February 13, 1927.

[124] Anon., 'Rückblick auf die "Grüne Woche" in Dresden', *Leipziger Neueste Nachrichten*, January 30, 1929, Staatskanzlei, Nachrichtenstelle Nr. 977, 'Landwirtschaft', SäHStA, no page number.

[125] Anon., 'Bayrische Bauernrevolte angedroht', *Volkszeitung Dresden*, January 19, 1929, Staatskanzlei, Nachrichtenstelle Nr. 977, SäHStA, no page number. Emphasis in the original.

[126] Lapp, *Revolution*, p. 168.

SLV relentlessly exhorted farm women to support their candidates in state and local elections. These appeals stressed that farm women were an essential part of the "Community of Suffering and Fate" and celebrated their dual identities as workers and mothers. For example, a May 1928 voting ad in the *Sächsische Bauernzeitung* blared "Farm Women! You too must decide your lives and fates by the ballot! Don't forget this and vote: *Saxon Landvolk*."[127] The lead article in the next issue was entitled "A Word to the Farm Wife."[128] The article's author was the SLV candidate and Meißen Rural League representative, and the headline was embellished with the admonition "Read Immediately!" He began, "In no other profession that we are familiar with is the profession of the wife so closely allied with her husband's ... Possessing equal value, equal responsibility, and equal rights, the farm wife stands beside the farmer in the house, in the yard, and in the field. She is not only a mother and wife to the farmer, but his true helpmeet and comrade in every sort of work." He added that he had heard from many farm wives that their lives were more difficult now than during the war and asked rhetorically, "Can farm women's strength still help us when the crisis in the countryside is so extreme that many are threatened with the loss of their enterprises? What are we to do if the farm wife loses heart and abandons [the cause]? But, thank God, she does not ... Let the farm wife set a good example by voting on election day." In case there were any doubts about how to mark one's ballot, the article included a sample with the SLV and the name of its candidate highlighted in bold, and clearly marked with a large "X."[129]

These were the first of numerous appeals to farm women by the SLV that appeared in the *Sächsische Bauernzeitung* between 1928 and 1932. Furthermore, during this five-year period the tone of their entreaties grew ever shriller. In April 1929, one ad blustered, "Farm women – do you want a Red *Landtag*?"[130] Eighteen months later, in September 1930, a front-page appeal by "Ilse Huhn, farm wife," proclaimed,

> "German Women, German Loyalty"! ... In the difficult years of war, the farm wife unquestioningly assumed her duty of running the enterprise, took up the plow, in order to provide bread for the *Volk*. Is it not the same show of loyalty when in the present crisis the farm wife uses all her energy, enduring every privation at the risk of her health, in order to help steer the economy through this craggy reef? But all is in vain unless every one of us votes for the *Landvolk* in the *Reichstag* elections.[131]

---

127   *SBZ*, May 6, 1928, p. 193.
128   'Ein Wort für die Bäuerin', *SBZ*, May 13, 1928, pp. 197–8.
129   *SBZ*, May 20, 1928, p. 214.
130   *SBZ*, April 21, 1929; p. 156; *SBZ*, May 12, 1929, p. 184.
131   *SBZ*, September 7, 1930, p. 1.

Figure 5.2 "Sächsisches Landvolk Appeal to Farm Women" [Source: *Sächsische Bauernzeitung*, September 7, 1930].

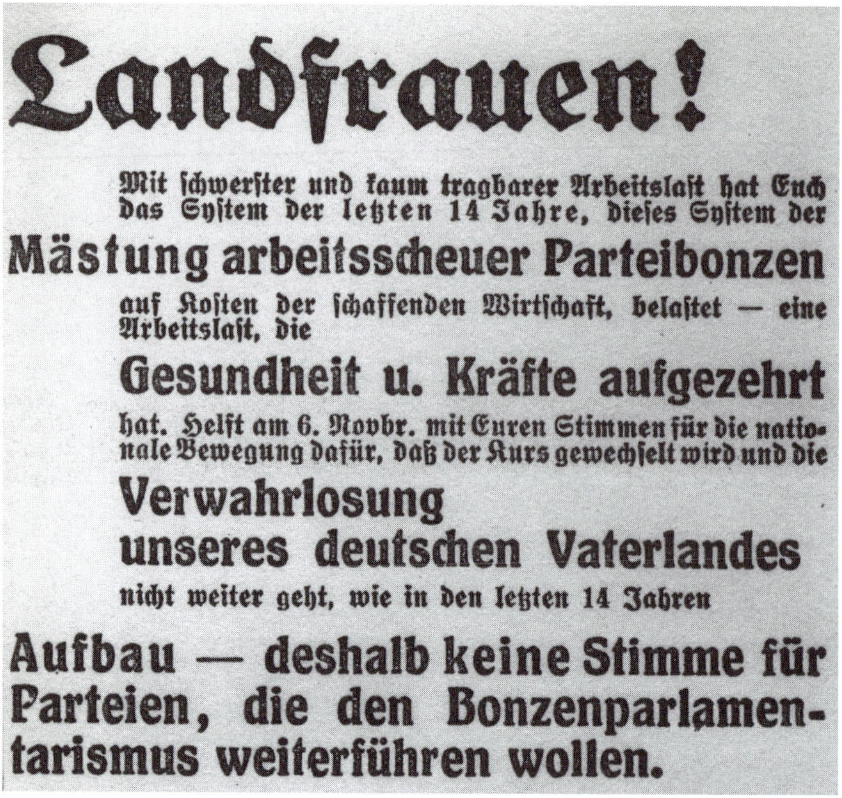

Landfrauen!

Mit schwerster und kaum tragbarer Arbeitslast hat Euch das System der letzten 14 Jahre, dieses System der

Mästung arbeitsscheuer Parteibonzen

auf Kosten der schaffenden Wirtschaft, belastet — eine Arbeitslast, die

Gesundheit u. Kräfte aufgezehrt

hat. Helft am 6. Novbr. mit Euren Stimmen für die nationale Bewegung dafür, daß der Kurs gewechselt wird und die

Verwahrlosung
unseres deutschen Vaterlandes

nicht weiter geht, wie in den letzten 14 Jahren

Aufbau — deshalb keine Stimme für Parteien, die den Bonzenparlamentarismus weiterführen wollen.

Figure 5.3   "Sächsisches Landvolk Appeal to Farm Women" [Source: *Sächsische Bauernzeitung*, October 30, 1932].

The following week, another article with the headline "In the Name of Women" condemned female Social Democrats ["*Sozis*"] for accepting the Versailles Treaty and the Dawes Plan "in women's name" and spat, "Shame on them!"[132] By October 1932, the outraged, condemnatory tone of right-wing appeals to farm women were no different than those aimed at men, and once again emphasized their extraordinary labor burdens as a source of anguish and turmoil.

> *Farm Women!* The system of the last 14 years has overloaded you with the heaviest of labor burdens, this system of *fattening work-shy party bosses* at the cost of the productive economy, a labor burden that *devours your health and strength*. Help us with your votes on the 6th of November to unleash a national movement that will secure a change of course and *prevent the further demoralization of our*

---

[132]   *SBZ*, September 14, 1930, p. 398.

> *German Fatherland ... Reconstruction – therefore do not vote for any party that*
> *supports the continuation of Bigwig-Parliamentarianism.*[133]

Finally, it is worth emphasizing that there were surprisingly few mentions of Hitler and the Nazi party in the pages of either the *Sächsische Bauernzeitung* or the *Sächsische landwirtschaftliche Zeitung* before the spring of 1933, when the *SLZ* published a glowing article by Elisabet Boehm entitled "The New Times and their Demands on Us."[134] In the opening lines, she urged farm women to celebrate the "National Socialist revolution, which has put an end to Marxism, Communism, and Internationalism and instead promised us clear German relationships." She declared,

> Now the demands of the "integration" [*Gleichschaltung*] are upon us ... The pests of the *Volk* will stay out, hopefully they will undertake this separation themselves. But we who love the *Volk* and Fatherland should thank God for sending us such a genial, strong man to lead us out of our degradation ... and should help him transform the German *Volk* into a loyal, clean, and healthy *Volk*.

Farm Women as Political Actors in Weimar: Petitions, Demonstrations, and *Völkisch* Organizations in the Saxon Countryside

While historians disagree somewhat over the timing and significance of the radicalization of Weimar agrarian politics and to what degree the Nazis profited from the fickleness of rural voters, there is broad consensus that the forms of rural political expression became much more raucous, diverse, and unyielding than before the war.[135] Peter Fritzsche's observation that middle-class political activism, including the activities of the *Landvolk* in Schleswig-Holstein, "developed an insistent repertoire of public activism similar to the one that Social Democrats had honed for over thirty years" applies equally well to Saxon rural politics throughout Weimar.[136] But it was not only men who participated in the new politics of the village square. Instead, there is ample evidence that many farm women responded

---

[133]   *SBZ*, October 30, 1932, p. 435. Emphasis in the original.

[134]   Elisabet Boehm, 'Die Landfrau', supplement to the *SLZ,* May 28, 1933, p. 1.

[135]   On the political homelessness or "Heimatlosigkeit" of farmers in Weimar see Jürgen Bergmann and Klaus Megerle, 'Gesellschaftliche Mobilisierung und negative Partizipation. Zur Analyse der politischen Orientierung und Aktivitäten von Arbeitern, Bauern und gewerblichem Mittelstand in der Weimarer Republik', in Peter Steinbach (ed.), *Probleme politischer Partizipation im Modernisierungsprozeß* (Stuttgart: Klett-Cotta, 1982), pp. 376–437, here p. 390.

[136]   Peter Fritzsche, 'Weimar Populism and National Socialism in Local Perspective', in Jones and Retallack, *Elections*, pp. 287–306, here pp. 301–2.

to a variety of right-wing appeals for support, and that their political engagement often extended well beyond the ballot box. Indeed, although women are not the focus of Reinhold Weber's study of conservative politics in Württemberg during the Kaiserreich and Weimar, he briefly mentions a variety of political activities undertaken by farm women and girls there after 1924, including going from house to house on election days to get out the vote, putting up political posters for the local *Bauernbund*, and distributing political fliers.[137]

In Saxony, the "protest petition" organized by the Farmers' League and the Association of Saxon Farmers in Freiberg and sent to the Saxon *Landtag* is an early example of the ways that gender structured rural political grievances and of women's direct involvement in popular political activism in Weimar. The invitation to participate in the petition, organized in late 1920 "in response to numerous complaints" about the plan to make girls' continuing education mandatory, requested that local representatives collect "as many signatures as possible, whether or not they belong to our organization."[138] The petition announced that: "The organization of continuation schools in the countryside is filling farmers with intense anxiety." It continued that while boys' education was disrupting many farming operations and should be restricted to five months a year, that the plan to make girls' education mandatory "has aroused even greater unease among the agricultural population ... To send the girls to school means sending away many enterprises' only hired help."[139] The petition cited an experiment in Grimma where the girls "spent the whole morning cooking ... and the afternoons learning to sew, as well as learning German ethnology and infant care." Not only did rural inhabitants vehemently object to the high cost of providing new cookstoves, sewing machines, and the teacher's salary, the petition continued, but even worse was their certainty that "in this way rural girls will become even more estranged than they already are from agricultural work."[140] In closing, it warned that "The countryside is disintegrating more and more and the result will be less food for the urban population. Therefore we demand that the *Landtag* suspend plans for mandatory girls' continuation schools."

It is difficult to know exactly how many village petitions were sent to the *Landtag* in January 1921, but the number exceeded 450; the total number of signatures on each ranged from as few as 10 or 12 to several that had over 80.[141] Some contained only men's signatures, but many others included those of both women and men;

---

[137]   Weber, *Bürgerpartei*, pp. 320, 325, 347.

[138]   Sächsischer Landbund and Verband Sächsischer Landwirte, 'Protestpetition', Freiberg, December 1920, Landtag Nr. 546, SäHStA, p. 116 (hereafter 'Protestpetition').

[139]   'Protestpetition', p. 2.

[140]   More than ten years later, Marie Berta von Brand made the same argument, criticizing the politics of Weimar farm women for placing too much emphasis on the household, which she argued was impractical for most farm wives and encouraged their resistance to agricultural work. See Albers, *Hof, Haushalt und Familie*, p. 282.

[141]   'Protestpetition', pp. 3, 320, 454.

of those, women's names made up between one-third to one-half of the list.[142] While the majority of the petitions were simply lists of names, some included an indication of the signer's status. Although most women described themselves as "[farm] wife" [*Ehefrau*], others wrote "woman farmer" [*Landwirtin*].[143] Men most often used either farmer [*Landwirt*] or landowner [*Gutsbesitzer*].

The petition ultimately failed, and a national law was enacted in July of 1923 allowing individual states to require young women between the ages of 14 and 18 to attend rural continuation schools unless they were enrolled in other schools.[144] In Saxony, a member of the Agricultural Chamber remarked dryly in 1925 that "It would be a mistake to attribute the increase [in the number of girls' continuation schools] to farmers' desire for improved educational opportunities for their daughters. The impetus has much more to do with the law that requires girls to attend until the end of their 17th year."[145] While the same observer commented that a few rural districts had made great efforts to equip the schools, the issue remained hotly contested.[146] This was the case even though according to the Agricultural Chamber's own statistics, the number of girls who enrolled in such schools and attended at least one class in all five Saxon districts numbered only 2,953 between 1919 and 1925.[147] For example, in an article in the *Sächsische Staatszeitung* in March 1925, a farmer bemoaned the "dreadful state of labor relations in agriculture … that absolutely prevent the farmer from getting ahead. The planned expansion of agricultural continuation schools, especially those for girls, will do great damage to family farms, which rely almost completely on workers of that age."[148] A columnist for the conservative *Volkszeitung Dresden* put it more bluntly, "As far as we're concerned, all the continuation schools can go to the devil!"[149]

A few years later, beginning in 1924, a wave of popular demonstrations against the Weimar government swept the German countryside, especially in Schleswig-Holstein. Historians have frequently portrayed them as a key turning-point in the radicalization of Weimar agrarian politics.[150] The most infamous demonstrations

---

[142] 'Protestpetition', pp. 24, 59, 233, 244, 274, 320, 337, 391, 454.

[143] 'Protestpetition', pp. 24, 391.

[144] Baldauf, *Frauenarbeit*, p. 67.

[145] Bruno Schöne, *Die sächsische Landwirtschaft: Ihre Entwickelung bis zum Jahre 1925* (Dresden: Verlag des Landeskulturrats Sachsen, 1925), pp. 177–8.

[146] Schöne, *sächsische Landwirtschaft*, p. 178.

[147] Schöne, *sächsische Landwirtschaft*, pp. 180–1.

[148] Anon., 'Jubiläumstagung des Landeskulturats', *Sächsische Staatszeitung* 65, March 18, 1925, Staatskanzlei, Nachrichtenstelle Nr. 961, SäHStA, no page number.

[149] Anon., 'Landeskulturrat', *Volkszeitung Dresden*, March 18, 1925, Staatskanzlei, Nachrichtenstelle Nr. 961, SäHStA, no page number.

[150] The two classic studies of the *Landvolkbewegung* in Schleswig-Holstein include Gerhard Stoltenberg, *Politische Strömungen im schleswig-holsteinischen Landvolk 1918–1933: Ein Beitrag zur politischen Meinungsbildung in der Weimarer Republik* (Düsseldorf: Droste Verlag, 1962); Rudolf Heberle, *Landbevölkerung und Nationalsozialismus: Eine*

occurred in early 1928, when crowds as large as 40,000 gathered in market squares in East Friesland to protest against low agricultural prices, the credit squeeze, "unfair" tax burdens, and the rising cost of wages. Unlike those in other parts of Germany, the demonstrations in northwest Germany often ended in violent clashes with the police and several of its leaders were tried in 1929 for a series of bomb attacks. But as Jürgen Bergmann and Klaus Megerle argue in their analysis of the rural "protest wave," there were important regional differences.[151] In particular, they emphasize that the grievances driving rural protests varied according to geographic location and average farm size. While eastern estate owners expressed their frustration in terms of crushing debt and the threat of foreclosure, family farmers that comprised the majority protested the exploitation of dependents that stemmed, at least in part, from the chronic shortage of labor.[152] The authors note that the symptoms of overwork included drastically reduced standards-of-living.

The first protests began in January 1924 in Pomerania over tax increases and quickly spread to the Saxon districts of Bautzen and Dresden. In July, farmers in Schleswig-Holstein, the Saxon district of Pirna, Stendal, the Oberpfalz, and Brandenburg marched under the slogan, "*Landvolk* in Crisis."[153] In late 1925 and early 1926, Saxony was at the center of a second, mostly peaceful, protest wave as farmers in Dresden, Leipzig, Plauen, Rochlitz, Bautzen, and Bischofswerda took to the streets.[154] In the spring of 1928, after more than a year of relative calm, a third group of protests and "calls to action" erupted across much of rural Germany, once again including some 150,000 Saxon farmers in Zwickau, Meißen, Freiberg, Pirna, Döbeln, Zittau, Löbau, Stollberg, and Cottbus, finally ebbing away once and for all in 1929.[155] Bergmann and Megerle argue that the reason for the decline in these popular demonstrations was not that farmers' circumstances had improved or that they were any less embittered. As an example, they cite a warning from the Saxon Rural League in January 1929 that "The weather signals on the political horizon, the events in Kyritz and Schleswig-Holstein [the sites of *Landvolk* trials] are the first warning signs of the desperate mood that could set all of Germany

---

soziologische Untersuchung der politischen Willensbildung in Schleswig-Holstein 1918– 1932 (Stuttgart: Deutsche Verlags-Anstalt, 1963). See also Klaus Schaap, *Die Endphase der Weimarer Republik im Freistaat Oldenburg 1928–1933* (Düsseldorf: Droste Verlag, 1978).

[151]   J. Bergmann and Megerle, 'Protest'; Peter Fritzsche, *Rehearsals for Fascism: Populism and Political Mobilization in Weimar Germany* (New York: Oxford University Press, 1990), pp. 114–18.

[152]   J. Bergmann and Megerle, 'Protest', p. 209.

[153]   J. Bergmann and Megerle, 'Protest', pp. 212–13.

[154]   J. Bergmann and Megerle, 'Protest', pp. 215–16.

[155]   J. Bergmann and Megerle, 'Protest', pp. 225, 229; Lapp, *Revolution*, p. 168. Lapp notes that the Landbund was responsible for the claim of 150,000 in March, but this seems reasonable based on reports in the *SBZ*.

in flames overnight. Woe to the state that alienates its farmers."[156] Instead, they conclude that it was only after the protests failed to improve their situations that farmers threw their support behind radical political solutions.[157]

These accounts give a rich picture of the rhythms, scale, and focus of male farmers' discontent in Weimar. Yet the calls to action that appeared in the Saxon agricultural press and the subsequent reports on rural demonstrations reveal that women as well as men marched through the streets, and that labor issues often topped the list of grievances. Farm women and girls were also present at smaller demonstrations and political meetings. For example, according to a March 1925 article in the *Vogtländischer Anzeiger*, "numerous farm women" attended a "powerful demonstration" of farmers in the Vogtland.[158] Additionally, a variety of local right-wing paramilitary groups was well-represented, including "the *Reichsflagge*, the *Jungdeutsche-Orden,* the *Frontbann Viking,* and the *Landbundjugend Spalier.*" The Berlin-based *Deutsche Tageszeitung* also reported on the meeting, noting that the strong paramilitary presence "accompanied by their many flags, gave the meeting a definite patriotic appearance."[159] In March 1927, an article on the first meeting of the *Junglandbund* [veterans' association] in the Saxon village of Leisnig observed that it was very well attended by "rural youth and *Landbäuerinnen* [the young women's branch of the *Junglandbund*] from near and far."[160] It also included a female speaker, who "addressed the crowd, in particular the *Jungbäuerinnen*, in an especially invigorating and stirring way, urging them to bring courage, idealism, and perseverance to the *Bund*. She closed her speech with the enthusiastic call, 'Save the land! [*Landheil!* Also, 'Save the nation!']" Later that year, a meeting of 800–900 farmers from western Saxony, "among them many women" ended with the elevation of a bust of General Hindenberg accompanied by a "strong and vigorous speech by a young woman."[161]

---

[156] Resolution of the Saxon Landbund, January 25, 1929, cited in J. Bergmann and Megerle, 'Protest', p. 235.

[157] J. Bergmann and Megerle, 'Protest', pp. 235–7.

[158] Anon., 'Eine machtvolle Kundgebung der vogtländischen Landwirtschaft: der Kreistag des vogtländischen Kreislandbundes', *Vogtländischer Anzeiger und Tageblatt* 62 (Plauen) March 14, 1925, Staatskanzlei, Nachrichtenstelle Nr. 961, SäHStA, no page number.

[159] Anon., 'Kreistagung des vogtländischen Landbundes', *Deutsche Tageszeitung*, March 14, 1925, Staatskanzlei, Nachrichtenstelle Nr. 961, SäHStA, no page number.

[160] Anon., '1. Kreistagung des sächsischen Junglandbundes in Leisnig', *Leisniger Tageblatt*, March 7, 1927, Staatskanzlei, Nachrichtenstelle Nr. 970, Teil 1, SäHStA, no page number.

[161] Anon., 'Landbundtreffen in Ponitz der Landbünde Thüringen-Ost, Glauchau und Westsachsen', *Chrimmitzschauer* (sic) *Anzeiger*, May 24, 1927, Staatskanzlei, Nachrichtenstelle Nr. 970, SäHStA, no page number.

The coverage of farmers' demonstrations in Leipzig and Dresden was more substantial. In May 1927, the *Leipziger Neueste Nachrichten* described a meeting in the Leipzig suburb of Knauthein where

> In the early morning farmers and farm women traveled from all directions on foot, by bicycle, and by carriage, so that the meeting room was quickly overcrowded. Through the participation of 700 farmers and farm women the meeting assumed the tone of a rural demonstration that expressed Leipzig farmers' determination … to continue the battle for better living conditions and the recognition of agriculture as central to the state's survival.[162]

In February 1928, the *Sächsische Bauernzeitung* reported that farm men and women "from all corners of Saxony … streamed into the capital city to demand an about-face from the government with respect to its agricultural policies, which are responsible for an existential crisis that has grown from year to year."[163] Women also attended the series of protest speeches held in Dresden's circus grounds, which were "addressed to the farm men and women of Saxony who had come together to make this announcement to the public." The first speaker condemned the "small measures" of the Saxon government and demanded a sweeping solution to the crisis; he declared:

> 1927 was an especially bad year for agriculture in light of the floods, the poor harvest, and above all because of the labor shortage. The government has tried to alleviate the problem by finding enough workers but we blame the government *in Berlin* that has done too little too late … In addition to profitability and debt issues, the *labor shortage* must be solved, both in terms of the number and the quality [of workers]."[164]

The speaker concluded with the warning that "*The new year must bring a decision* … peace, order and discipline still reign … Only by following your *Landbund* representative will we reach our goal: *a healthy agricultural sector and a healthy state and Volk. The farmers' suffering is the suffering of the nation!*" According to the reporter, the speech brought down the house. Others followed that included the familiar condemnations of the Versailles Treaty and the Dawes Plan, as well as the demand to close the country's borders to imports.

---

[162]   Anon., 'Tagung der Leipziger Landwirte', *Leipziger Neueste Nachrichten*, May 10, 1927, Staatskanzlei, Nachrichtenstelle Nr. 970, Teil 2, SäHStA, no page number.

[163]   Anon., 'Die Kundgebung der sächsischen Landwirtschaft in Dresden', *SBZ*, February 5, 1928, p. 54.

[164]   Emphasis in original.

Conclusion

Whether portrayed as the ultimate victims of an uncaring and impotent regime or as authentic symbols of the German *Volk*, German farm wives became the focus of intense political debate during the final years of the Weimar Republic. The mounting evidence of their overburdening and expert warnings about its potentially ruinous effects on both the food supply and the nation's birthrate provoked widespread condemnation. In particular, *völkisch* activists and organizations dedicated to fomenting anti-Weimar sentiment repeatedly cast farm wives' overburdening as a major political failure, adding it to the long list of grievances fueling the right-wing insurgency in the countryside. Indeed as other scholars of Weimar politics have noted, the egalitarian, pluralist political climate so abhorred by conservatives also offered unique opportunities to mobilize new constituencies, including farm women. Moreover, by celebrating farm wives' unique contributions as workers and mothers under the most adverse conditions, parties like the SLV suggested that they were *already* active participants in the battle to remake the German nation according to *völkisch* principles.[165] Thus, by the time the National Socialists turned their full attention to winning over the German countryside they could tap into an array of familiar messages and symbols, including the overburdened farm wife, to persuade both men and women to support their cause.[166]

Women were key participants in the radicalization of grass-roots politics in the Weimar countryside and they were viewed as such by the activists who organized these initiatives and events. Farm women participated in a range of actions that aimed both to undermine the political status quo of the Republic and to celebrate the conservative cultural and moral values that had been "lost" during the revolution. Although these women may not have represented the majority, their presence at raucous, often overtly militarized, political gatherings demonstrates that the farm wife was not merely a symbol or at most a silent observer of right-wing political radicalism, but played an active role in the "crowded arena" of Weimar politics throughout the decade.

---

[165]   This point also has been made for fascist Italy. See Perry Willson, 'Cooking the Patriotic Omelette: Women and the Italian Fascist Ruralization Campaign', *European History Quarterly* 27/4 (1997): 531–47; Silvia Salvatici, 'Die bäuerliche Frau. Ein Frauenbild in der Propaganda des italienischen Faschismus. Zur Lektüre historischer Photographien', *Werkstatt Geschichte* 11 (1995): 19–32.

[166]   R. Walther Darré et al., *Das Bauerntum als Lebensquell der nordischen Rasse* (München: J. F. Lehmanns Verlag, 1929).

Conclusion
Gender History, Rural History, and the Making of Modern Germany

Soon after Hitler's accession to power in 1933, tensions emerged between his vaunted pledge to return Germany to an agrarian state and the harsh realities experienced by farm families, especially wives. While the Nazis staged extravagant celebrations of farm women as "Mothers of the *Volk*" and "Protectors of Tradition and Morals" at events like the annual Harvest Festival in Bückeberg, farm wives continued to bear an unequal share of the labor burden.[1] Above all, the regime's autarky campaign vigorously reinforced the link between women's labor and agricultural intensification.[2] In 1934, one prominent female official declared that farm wives would find the strength to work harder by recalling their sacrifices during "the era of the [Weimar] System, when no one noticed the Cinderella of the nation, the woman who worked 14 hours a day to secure food for the *Volk*."[3] Several years later, Nazi Agricultural Minister R. Walther Darré pontificated: "The 'Battle for Production' is a bitterly earnest necessity for the *Volk* to which we must accede, despite the many sacrifices and deprivations of our hard-working farm wives and farm women."[4]

Nazi propagandists also exhorted rural female youth to assist their mothers in the fields and stalls. For example, at a 1933 "integration" [*Gleichschaltung*] ceremony of the Saxon *Junglandbund* into the Nazi *Landstand* in Dresden, one

---

[1]   See the images of farm women in Bernhard Gelderblom, *Die Reichserntedankfeste auf dem Bückeberg, 1933–1937* (Hameln: Niemeyer Buchverlage, 1998).

[2]   See for example the illustrations of women planting potatoes, weeding, and hoeing in Fritz Reichardt, *Wie schlägt man die Erzeugungsschlacht: Richtige Ratschläge in drastischen Bilderfolgen* (Essen: Bildgut-Verlag, 1935), pp. 40, 57, 77, 81; Gustavo Corni and Horst Gies, *'Blut und Boden': Rassenideologie und Agrarpolitik im Staat Hitlers* (Idstein: Schulz-Kirchner, 1994), p. 19; H. von Rheden, 'Die Aufgabe der Bäuerin im Dritten Reich', in Reichsnährstand, *Der 1. Reichsbauerntag in Weimar am 20. und 21. Januar 1934* (Berlin: Neudeutsche Verlags- und Treuhand-Gesellschaft, 1934), pp. 41–6; Aenne Sprengel, 'Die Bauersfrau als Berufstätige in der Landwirtschaft', and Anne Marie Köppen, 'Die bäuerliche Frau in ihrer kulturellen Aufgabe', in Ellen Semmelroth and Renate von Stieda (eds), *N.S. Frauenbuch* (Munich: J. F. Lehmanns Verlag, 1934), pp. 98–112.

[3]   von Rheden, 'Aufgabe', p. 46.

[4]   Cited in Sigrid Jacobeit, '"… dem Mann Gehilfin und Knecht. Sie ist Magd und Mutter …": Klein- und Mittelbäuerinnen im faschistischen Deutschland', in Johanna Werckmeister (ed.), *Land-Frauen-Alltag: Hundert Jahre Lebens- und Arbeitsbedingungen der Frauen im ländlichen Raum* (Marburg: Jonas Verlag, 1989), pp. 66–90, here p. 66.

speaker warmly praised farm girls for their participation in the movement.[5] But she also intoned: "no one will escape the duties that await us in the new Germany! The more earnest the task, the happier it makes us. But first the work, and then the celebration!" By 1938, however, the tone of these appeals had shifted dramatically. In his address at the final National Peasant Assembly in Goslar, Darré beseeched rural female youth "not to become deserters" and excoriated farm daughters for inciting rural flight.[6] He thundered, *"The total loss of agricultural workers in recent years – as Reich official Behrens noted yesterday, citing the fifty percent decline in girls who perform stall work in his home district – can without exaggeration be estimated at 700,000–800,000."*[7] Besides lamenting the shortage of girls in Hildesheim district, Behrens also had stressed the dire consequences for farm wives: *"The entire additional labor burden, through the entire year, weekdays and Sundays, Sundays and holidays, falls relentlessly on the shoulders of the German farm wife."*[8]

The 1938 oratories in Goslar were the most public admission to date that Nazi officials, like their much-maligned Weimar predecessors, had found no viable solutions to the shortage of women's agricultural labor and the overburdening of farm wives. But they capped five years of internal debate over coercive regulations to prevent rural flight; the meager results of rural public works programs; numerous secret reports about the labor shortage's threat to Nazi agricultural production; and the impact of overburdening on farm wives' reproductive health.[9] Moreover, although Nazi agricultural experts acknowledged that some of farm women's most arduous tasks could be eased by electrification, indoor plumbing, and the like,

---

[5]   Anon., 'Generalappell der Führerschaft am 16. September in Dresden', *Sächsische Landjugend* 11, Dresden, October 15, 1933, pp. 41–3. See also Ludger Elsbroek, *Vom Junglandbund zur Landjugend: Ländliche Jugendverbandsarbeit zwischen Berufsstand und Jugendkultur* (Frankfurt/Main: Peter Lang, 1996), pp. 153–6.

[6]   Reichsnährstand, *Der 6. Reichsbauerntag in Goslar vom 20.–27. November 1938* [hereafter *6. Reichsbauerntag*] (Berlin: Reichsnährstand Verlags-Gesellschaft, 1939), pp. 48–9.

[7]   Emphasis in original.

[8]   *6. Reichsbauerntag*, p. 62. Emphasis in original.

[9]   Daniela Münkel, *Nationalsozialistische Agrarpolitik und Bauernalltag* (Frankfurt/Main Campus Verlag, 1996), pp. 337, 344–8; Corni and Gies, *'Blut und Boden'*, pp. 52–4; Helene Albers, *Zwischen Hof, Haushalt und Familie: Bäuerinnen in Westfalen Lippe (1920–1960)* (Paderborn: F. Schöningh, 2001), pp. 319–28; Falk Wiesemann, 'Arbeitskonflikte in der Landwirtschaft während der NS-Zeit in Bayern 1933–1938', *Vierteljahresschrift für Zeitgeschichte* 25 (1977): 573–90; Beatrix Herlemann, 'Bäuerliche Verhaltensweisen unter dem Nationalsozialismus in niedersächsischen Gebieten', *Niedersächsisches Jahrbuch für Landesgeschichte* 62 (1990): 59–75, esp. pp. 70–1; Matthew Stibbe, *Women in the Third Reich* (London: Arnold Publishers, 2003), pp. 116–20; J. E. Farquharson, *The Plough and the Swastika: The NSDAP and Agriculture in Germany, 1928–1945* (Wayne, IN: Landpost Press, 1976), pp. 183–202.

there was scant improvement in basic farm household conveniences.[10] After the Second World War began, farm wives' burdens increased still further. In 1941, Charlotte von Reichenau's study of farm wives eerily echoed the conclusions of Maria Bidlingmaier a generation earlier: "If overburdening decreases due to one factor, it merely increases due to another … Wherever farm wives are studied today one invariably finds an intolerable workload, accompanied by serious health conditions."[11] More poignant were the recollections of several Swabian farm wives who married between the late 1920s and mid-1930s.[12] Recalled one who bore five children between 1932 and 1948, "I was constantly overwhelmed. There was simply too much that depended on me … The difference between my life and my mother's was very small. It's only since my children are grown that things have really improved in the countryside."[13] Another commented ruefully that, "The men could sit down when they were done … My day ended only when I climbed into bed."[14]

If farm women's everyday lives had changed little between the 1880s and the 1930s, it is also true that younger women were even more likely to reject the expectation that they remain on the farm. As we have seen, over the course of these decades, young farm women participated ever more actively in public and official debates over their labor. Early signs of young women's discontent with agricultural work emerged in the late-nineteenth-century grievance cases of *Mägde*. While exceptional, they hinted that the hallowed prescriptions of the *Gesindeordnungen* masked growing gender and generational tensions on agricultural enterprises. The differing expectations about individual rights that fueled these cases erupted with new intensity during and after the First World War, when new notions of collective national duty augmented familiar incantations about the importance of preserving the rural status quo. Yet despite the outcry over young women's public challenges to bans on their freedom of movement, these encounters pushed expert observers to reconsider the use of force and increased pressure on state officials to suspend the laws. Unfortunately, the optimistic forecasts of Weimar rationalization experts

---

[10]   Jacobeit, "'… dem Mann Gehilfin'", pp. 81–3; Beate Krieg, *Landfrau, so geht's leichter!': Modernisierung durch hauswirtschaftliche Gemeinschaftsanlagen mit Elektrogeräten im deutschen Südwesten von 1930 bis 1970* (Munich: tuduv-Verlagsgesellschaft, 1996), pp. 115–18; Daniela Münkel, "'Ein besseres Leben für die Landfrau?' Technik im bäuerlichen Haushalt während der NS-Zeit', *metis* 4/1 (1995): 41–9.

[11]   Charlotte von Reichenau, 'Die Bäuerin: Ein methodischer Versuch', *Jahrbücher für Nationalökonomie und Statistik* 153 (1941): 678–700, here p. 692.

[12]   Ursula Schlude (ed.), *'Ich hab's gern gemacht': Die Lebensgeschichte einer Bäuerinnengeneration* (Ravensburg: Verlag Schwäbischer Bauer, 1989).

[13]   Frau A., 'Aber fortgehen durfte ich nicht', in Schlude, *'Ich hab's gern gemacht,'* pp. 7–14, here p. 13.

[14]   Frau E., 'Erinnerung an die Allgäuer Heimat', in Schlude, *'Ich hab's gern gemacht'*, pp. 43–52, here p. 50.

that it was only a matter of time before farm daughters' longings for "something better" would be replaced by joyful anticipation at the prospect of becoming a farm wife failed to materialize.

One might have expected the 1934 Nazi ban on agricultural labor's freedom-of-movement, which duplicated earlier Wilhelmine and Weimar efforts, to meet with greater success. Indeed, the Political Police who oversaw its enforcement labeled runaway hired hands "asocial," and those who were especially rebellious were dispatched to concentration camps, or "protective custody."[15] Still, as in earlier decades, the ban was lifted in late 1936 amid admissions of defeat.[16] As the Reich Labor Minister conceded in retrospect, "Coercive legal measures prohibiting the movement of workers will do more harm than good in the long run ... We must at all costs avoid giving the public the impression that agricultural work is equivalent to forced labor."[17] Nonetheless, as Darré's diatribe in Goslar highlighted, official frustration over girls' stubborn resistance to agricultural work continued to flare. One observer griped in 1939, "If [a girl] does enter farm service, then it is with the condition that it will not be recorded in her *Arbeitsbuch*, for fear that she may be tied forever to agricultural work. Often the parents object if the girl is asked to do field work, never mind stall work. These days it is exceptional if a girl deigns to help in the stalls."[18]

As many German historians have stressed, there is no better place than the countryside to study the yawning gap between the Nazis' exalted rhetoric and the regime's actual economic and social policy decisions.[19] At the same time, it is equally important to recognize that the twin crises of young women's rural flight and the overburdening of farm wives had daunted German policymakers across the political spectrum over many decades. In the first instance, the Nazi discourse over agricultural intensification powerfully reinforced the importance of the countryside as a site of women's labor. The late-nineteenth-century conviction that agricultural work was women's work persisted, despite protestations that farm

---

[15]   See especially Wiesemann, 'Arbeitskonflikte', p. 585; Farquharson, *Plough*, p. 186.

[16]   Tim Mason, *Social Policy in the Third Reich: The Working Class and the 'National Community'*, trans. John Broadwin (Oxford: Berg Publishers, 1993), pp. 147–8.

[17]   'Aus der Antwort des Reichsarbeitsministers vom 3. September 1937', cited in Corni and Gies, *'Blut und Boden'*, p. 168. See also Gerhard Albrecht, 'Soziale Probleme und Sozialpolitik in Deutschland während des Weltkrieges', *Jahrbücher für Nationalökonomie und Statistik* 144 (1936): 96–107, 215–32.

[18]   Toni Walter, 'Die Frau in der Landwirtschaft Mitteldeutschlands, dargestellt an der Provinz Sachsen', in Marie von Brand et al. (eds), *Die Frau in der deutschen Landwirtschaft* (Berlin: Franz Vahlen, 1939), pp. 103–30, here p. 117.

[19]   See especially Daniela Münkel, '"Du, Deutsche Landfrau bist verantwortlich!": Bauer und Bäuerin im Nationalsozialismus', *Archiv für Sozialgeschichte* 38 (1998): 141–64; Clifford R. Lovin, 'Farm Women in the Third Reich', *Agricultural History* 60/3 (1986): 105–23.

women were mothers of the *Volk* whose duties were confined to family and hearth. Equally significant were the growing worries about farm wives' overburdening expressed by Nazi officials, agricultural experts, and social welfare reformers. Whether motivated by genuine concern or resigned cynicism, Nazi officials clearly felt compelled to address the crisis publicly, even if it was merely to reiterate empty promises of future improvement. Finally, young women's resistance to agricultural work remained a formidable test of state authority. Although Hitler's decision to pursue full-scale remilitarization certainly complicated efforts to restrict rural labor's mobility, young women's canny exploitation of the loopholes in the 1934 ban and their willingness to object publicly to the expectation that they remain on the farm also contributed to its dismal failure.[20]

The continuities and changes briefly traced here emphasize once more that rural Germans, like their urban counterparts, grappled with the same contradictions that historians have identified as emblematic of German and European modernity. Simply put, rural people could be agents of change as well as defenders of the status quo. They shaped contemporary discourses over individual rights versus collective duties; the limits of state intervention; women's proper role in a rapidly changing political economy; and who or what represented the nation. In particular, exploring these debates over the course of two very different regimes, punctuated by the unprecedented upheavals of the First World War, underscores the resilience of the dilemmas that accompanied Germany's transition from an agrarian to an industrial state and rural inhabitants' wide variety of responses to the modern age.

The sentiment expressed above by one farm wife that it was only following the Second World War that things "really changed" in the countryside is echoed in recent research on mid-twentieth-century rural Germany. Historian Paul Erker, who coined the term "the long farewell" to describe the multitude of changes that transformed the German countryside over the course of the twentieth century, argues persuasively that the 1960s represented a decisive watershed.[21] Although in many respects the concept of a "long farewell" aptly describes the waning economic and political importance of German agriculture between Weimar and Bonn, it also reinforces historians' tendency to overlook or discount the importance of the countryside and rural inhabitants in the making of modern Germany. This is surely unintentional, but it speaks to the challenges of writing history from the margins. That said, there is ample evidence to suggest that a multiplicity of rural modernities flourished in the German countryside throughout the nineteenth and

---

[20] See the cases of runaway *Mägde* discussed in Wiesemann, 'Arbeitskonflikte'.

[21] Paul Erker, 'Der lange Abschied vom Agrarland. Zur Sozialgeschichte der Bauern im Industrialisierungsprozeß', in Matthias Frese and Michael Prinz (eds), *Politische Zäsuren und gesellschaftlicher Wandel im 20. Jahrhundert: Regionale und vergleichende Perspektiven* (Paderborn: F. Schöningh, 1996), pp. 327–60. The title of Erker's essay was revived recently in Daniela Münkel (ed.), *Der lange Abschied vom Agrarland: Agrarpolitik, Landwirtschaft und ländliche Gesellschaft zwischen Weimar und Bonn* (Göttingen: Wallstein Verlag, 2000).

twentieth centuries. The work of women and girls on agricultural enterprises, and their evolving engagement with those burdens during the tumultuous Wilhelmine and Weimar eras, defined one important aspect of that complex and varied history.

Bibliography

I. Archival Sources: Sächsisches Hauptstaatsarchiv Dresden

Amtshauptmannschaft Flöha 2431, "Maßnahmen gegen die Jugendlichen."

Amtshauptmannschaft Flöha 2506, "Über Gesinde-Differenzen."

Amtshauptmannschaft Flöha 2507, "Über Gesinde-Differenzen."

Amtshauptmannschaft Flöha 2509, "Behebung des Arbeitermangels in der Landwirtschaft."

Amtshauptmannschaft Flöha 2510, "Behebung des Arbeitermangels in der Landwirtschaft."

Kreishauptmannschaft Dresden Nr. 262, "Monatsberichte an das Ministerium des Innern über politisch bedeutsame Vorgänge, 1927–1928."

Ministerium des Innern 15497–98, "Allgemeine landwirtschaftliche Angelegenheiten."

Ministerium des Innern 15498/2, "Anfragen auswärtiger Regierungen über hiesige landwirtschaftliche Verhältnisse und Einrichtungen."

Ministerium des Innern 15798/1, "Haus- und landwirtschaftliche Schule Arwedshof/Elbisbach."

Ministerium des Innern 15829, "Ländliche Wohlfahrts- und Heimatpflege (1907–20)."

Ministerium des Innern 15847–50, "Arbeitsverhältnisse bei der Landwirtschaft."

Ministerium des Innern 15876, "Das Gesindewesen."

Ministerium des Innern 15925, "Verbot des Arbeitswechsels der landwirtschaftlichen Arbeiter und Dienstboten."

Ministerium des Innern 15933, "Maßnahmen zur Behebung des Arbeitermangels in der Landwirtschaft."

Ministerium des Innern 15934, "Artamanen."

Ministerium des Innern 16426/1, "Ausstellungen landwirtschaftlicher Gegenstände im Inlande."

Ministerium des Innern 16599, "Arbeiter und Hilfskräfte für die Landwirtschaft."

Ministerium des Innern 16614, "Verpflichtung von Landarbeitern im Krieg: Kriegszustand."

Sächsischer Landtag Nr. 546, "Eingaben gegen die verbindliche Einführung der Mädchenfortbildungsschule auf dem Lande."

Staatskanzlei, Nachrichtenstelle, Nr. 961, "Landwirtschaft."

Staatskanzlei, Nachrichtenstelle, Nr. 970, Teil 1-2, "Landwirtschaft."

Staatskanzlei, Nachrichtenstelle, Nr. 977, "Landwirtschaft."

II. Archival Sources: Staatsarchiv Leipzig

Amtshauptmannschaft Borna 3857, "Allgemeine Landwirtschaftliche Angelegenheiten."
Amtshauptmannschaft Oschatz 1114, "Einzelne Gesindepolizeisachen betreffend."

III. Archival Sources: Bundesarchiv Berlin-Lichterfelde

R 43 I (Reichskanzlei)/1292 "betr Landerbeiter."
R 1501 (Reichsministerium des Innern)/115485 "Arbeiternoth in der Landwirtschaft."

IV. Periodicals and Agricultural Calendars

Land und Frau.
Land und Frau (ed.), Landfrauen Kalender (Berlin: Paul Parey, 1932).
Landwirtschaftlicher Damen-Almanach 1922 (Berlin: G. Kühn, 1922).
Landwirtschaftlicher Kalender für das Vogtland (1929).
Der landwirtschaftliche Kalender für den Freistaat Sachsen (Dresden: Verlag des Landeskulturrats Sachsen, 1929).
Die praktische Landwirtin: Blätter für die Hausfrau des Landwirts. Monatliche Beilage zur Fachzeitung Der praktische Landwirt (Magdeburg)
Sächsischer Bauernkalender, 1920–22 (Dresden: Verlag des Landeskulturrats Sachsen).
Sächsische Bauernzeitung.
Sächsische landwirtschaftliche Zeitschrift.

V. Unpublished Private Collection

Three reference books [*Dienstbücher*].
Diary of Marianne Elsa Lantzsch, under auspices of Landeskulturrat für den Freistaat Sachsen, Dresden, 1929, *Tagebuch für weibliche Landwirtschaftslehrlinge.*

VI. Published Primary Sources

'Abteilung Frauenarbeit', Bericht über die Tätigkeit der Landwirtschaftskammer für den Freistaat Sachsen im Jahre 1927 und amtlicher Bericht über die 6. Gesamtsitzung am 27. März 1928 (Dresden: Selbstverlag der Landwirtschaftskammer für den Freistaat Sachsen, 1928).

Achter, Franz, 'Die Einwirkung des Krieges auf die bäuerliche Wirtschaft in Bayern' (Dissertation, München: 1920).

Aereboe, Friedrich, 'Ursachen und Formen wechselnder Betriebsintensität in der Landwirtschaft', *Thünen-Archiv: Organ für exakte Wirtschaftsforschung* 2/3 (Jena: Gustav Fischer, 1907): 363–94.

Aereboe, Friedrich, *Der Einfluß des Krieges auf die landwirtschaftliche Produktion in Deutschland* (Stuttgart: Deutsche Verlags-Anstalt, 1927).

Albrecht, Gerhard, 'Soziale Probleme und Sozialpolitik in Deutschland während des Weltkrieges', *Jahrbücher für Nationalökonomie und Statistik* 144 (1936): 96–107, 215–32.

'Der Arbeitermangel in der Landwirtschaft', *Volksstimme Chemnitz*, December 27, 1921.

'Die Arbeiternot in der sächsischen Landwirtschaft', *Amtlicher Bericht über die 5. Gesamtsitzung der Landwirtschaftskammer für den Freistaat Sachsen am 15. November 1927*, vol. 5 of *Aus der Tätigkeit der Landwirtschaftskammer für den Freistaat Sachsen* (Dresden: Selbstverlag der Landwirtschaftskammer für den Freistaat Sachsen, 1928), pp. 12–46.

'Aus der Arbeit', *Land und Frau* 9/9 (February 28, 1925): 103.

Baldauf, Elisabeth, *Die Frauenarbeit in der Landwirtschaft* (Leipzig: Universitätsverlag von Robert Noske, 1932).

Beaufreton, Maurice, 'Farm Household Management Travelling Schools', *International Review of Agricultural Economics* 31 (1925): 147–64.

'Die Bedeutung der Frauen im Obst und Gartenbau', *Land und Frau* 4/7 (February 7, 1920): 41–2.

Behme, Theda, 'Ländliche Wohnungseinrichtung der Gegenwart', *Land und Frau* 15/22 (May 30, 1931): 417–18.

Berge, Konstanze vom, 'Neue Aufgaben für die Hausfrauen auf dem Lande', *Land und Frau* 4/18 (May 1, 1920): 141–2.

Bericht über die Tätigkeit der Landwirtschaftskammer für den Freistaat Sachsen (Dresden: Selbstverlag der Landwirtschaftskammer für den Freistaat Sachsen, 1926–1933).

Bidlingmaier, Maria, *Die Bäuerin in zwei Gemeinden Württembergs*, Vol. 17 *Tübinger staatswissenschaftliche Abhandlungen* (Stuttgart: W. Kohlhammer, 1918).

Bielefeldt, Karl, *Das Eindringen des Kapitalismus in die Landwirtschaft unter besonderer Berücksichtigung der Provinz Sachsen und der angrenzenden Gebiete* (Berlin: Gebr. Unger, 1910).

Bindewald, Georg, *Die Wehrfähigkeit der ländlichen und städtischen Bevölkerung* (Halle/Saale: Pierer, 1901).

Bindewald, Georg, *Sesshaftigkeit und Abwanderung der weiblichen Jugend vom Lande* (Berlin: Deutscher Landwirtschaftsrat, 1905).

Böhm, Käthe, 'Volt X Ampère (gleicht) Watt, das 1 x 1 der Elekrotechnik für die Frau. Elektrische Waschmaschinen', *Land und Frau* 15/9 (March 1931): 153.

Brady, Robert A., 'The Status of Rationalization in other Industries: the Case of Agriculture', in Robert A. Brady (ed.), *The Rationalization Movement in German Industry: A Study in the Evolution of Economic Planning* (Berkeley: University of California Press, 1933), pp. 271–81.

Brand, Marie Berta von, *Die wirtschaftliche und kulturelle Lage der Bäuerin auf den Fildern* (Stuttgart: Körner, 1933).

Brinkmann, Theodor, 'Kritische Beobachtungen und Beiträge zur Intensitätslehre', *Frühlings landwirtschaftliche Zeitung* 58/23 (December 1, 1909): 833–50, 873–90.

Brirup-Lindemann, Agnes, *Der Arbeits- und Pflichtenkreis der ländlichen Hausfrau in Westfalen und Lippe* (Warendorf i. Westf.: Heimatverlag der J. Schnellschen Buchhandlung, 1926).

Buchenberger, Adolf, *Agrarwesen und Agrarpolitik. Erster Band* (Leipzig: C. F. Winter'sche Verlag, 1892).

Buchenberger, Adolf, *Grundzüge der deutschen Agrarpolitik* (Berlin: Paul Parey, 1897).

Burckhardt, Dr., 'Die Entwicklung der sächsischen Bevölkerung in den letzten hundert Jahren', *Zeitschrift des sächsischen statistischen Landesamtes* 77 (1931): 1–69.

Cauer, Marie, *Frauendienstpflicht* (Tübingen: J. C. B. Mohr, 1916).

Chemnitz, Walter, *Frauenarbeit im Kriege* (Berlin: Verlag von Emil Ebering, 1926).

Conrad, Frau A., 'Die Elektrizität als Helferin der Landfrau', *Land und Frau* 12/7 (February 18, 1928): 125.

Corvey, Johannes, 'Der Arbeitermangel in der sächsischen Landwirtschaft', *Der Arbeiterfreund* 40 (1902): 395–404.

Dade, Heinrich, *Die landwirtschaftliche Bevölkerung des Deutschen Reiches um die Wende des 19. Jahrhunderts* (Berlin: Paul Parey, 1903).

Darré, R. Walther et al., *Das Bauerntum als Lebensquell der nordischen Rasse* (München: J. F. Lehmanns Verlag, 1929).

David, Eduard, *Sozialismus und Landwirtschaft: Erster Band: Die Betriebsfrage* (Leipzig: Verlag von Quelle & Meyer, 1922).

Delbrück, Clemens von, *Die wirtschaftliche Mobilmachung in Deutschland 1914. Aus dem Nachlaß herausgegebenen, eingeleitet und ergänzt von Joachim von Delbrück* (München: Verlag für Kulturpolitik, 1924).

Derlitzki, Dorothea, *Arbeitsersparnis im Landhaushalt. Eine zusammenfassende Darstellung der 'Arbeitslehre im Landhaushalt' unter Berücksichtigung der haushaltswissenschaftlichen und hauswirtschaftlichen Bestrebungen der Jetztzeit für Landfrauen, wirtschaftliche Frauenschulen, Haushaltungsschulen, usw* (Berlin: Paul Parey, 1926).

Derlitzki, Georg, 'Versuchsanstalt Pommritz', in *Vorträge: Die Neuorganisation der landwirtschaftlichen Versuchsanstalten in Sachsen und ihre Aufgaben* in series *Schriften der Oekonomischen Gesellschaft im Freistaat Sachsen* (Leipzig: Reichenbach'sche Verlagsbuchhandlung, 1920), pp. 12–22.

Derlitzki, Georg, *Berichte über Landarbeit* 1 (Stuttgart: Franckh'sche Verlagshandlung, 1927).

Derlitzki, Georg, 'Die Landarbeitsforschung, dargestellt an den Arbeiten der Versuchsanstalt für Landarbeitslehre Pommritz i. Sa.', in Georg Derlitzki (ed.), *Berichte über Landarbeit* 1 (Stuttgart: Franckh'sche Verlagshandlung, 1927), pp. 9–61.

Derlitzki, Georg, 'Die Forschungsarbeit der hauswirtschaftlichen Abteilung Pommritz unter Berücksichtigung der Hygiene der Landfrauenarbeit', *Land und Frau* 16/34 (August 1932): 571.

Dieing, J. B., *Landfrauennot!* (Freiburg i. Br.: Verlag der Arbeitsgemeinschaft für Dorfcaritas, 1928), pp. 1–16.

Dietze, C. v., 'Die Lage der deutschen Landwirtschaft', *Jahrbücher für Nationalökonomie und Statistik* 130 (dritte Folge, Band 750/1929): 653–80.

Donner, Gerhard, 'Die Bedeutung der nationalsozialistischen Propaganda für die Entwicklung der NSDAP im Gau Sachsen' (Dissertation, Universität Leipzig, 1942).

Druffel, Frau von, 'Weibliche Jugendpflege auf dem Lande', in *Die Landfrauenarbeit* (*2. Kriegslehrgang*): 227–32.

Dyhrenfurth, Gertrud (ed.), *Ergebnisse einer Untersuchung über die Arbeits- und Lebensverhältnisse der Frauen in der Landwirtschaft*, in *Schriften des ständigen Ausschusses zur Förderung der Arbeiterinnen-Interessen*, Heft 7 (Jena: Gustav Fischer, 1916).

'Eine elektrische Küche', *Land und Frau* 4/6 (February 7, 1920): 44.

Eßlen, Joseph Bergfried, *Die Fleischversorgung des deutschen Reiches: Eine Untersuchung der Ursachen und Wirkungen der Fleischteuerung und der Mittel zur Abhilfe* (Stuttgart: Verlag von Ferdinand Enke, 1912).

'Etwas über die Geldnot und ihre Beiseitigung! Es gibt einen Ausweg aus der Geldnot!', *Der landwirtschaftliche Kalender für den Freistaat Sachsen* (Dresden: Verlag des Landeskulturrates Sachsen, 1929), p. 141.

Falke, Friedrich, 'Die Landflucht. Ihre Ursachen und Wirkungen', *Rektorwechsel an der Universität Leipzig am 31. Oktober 1929* (Leipzig: Alexander Edelmann, 1929).

Fensch, Hans-Ludwig, *Der Wert des landwirtschaftlichen Inventars*, Heft 5, *Deutscher Landwirtschaftsrat Veröffentlichungen* (Berlin: Deutscher Schriftenverlag, 1926).

Fensch, H. E., et al., *Zahlen und Bilder aus dem deutschen Landbau bearbeitet auf Grund zehnjähriger Buchführungsunterlagen* (Berlin: Reichsnährstand Verlag, 1936).

'Die Förderung und Ausgestaltung der hauswirtschaftlichen Unterweisung für die gesamte weibliche Jugend. Verhandlungen der 2. Konferenz am 11. und 12. Mai 1908 in Berlin', *Schriften der Zentralstelle für Volkswohlfahrt* 2 (Berlin: Carl Heymanns Verlag, 1909): 1–42.

Förster, Eva, 'Buchführung im Landhaushalt', *Land und Frau* 15/1 (January 8, 1931): 7.

Frankenstein, Kuno von, 'Königreich Sachsen' in *Schriften des Vereins für Sozialpolitik*, vol. 54, reprint 1892 ed. (Vaduz: Topos Verlag, 1989), pp. 193–226.

Frau P. in Polen, 'Nochmals: Wege zur Gewinnung des Marktes für deutsches Obst', *Land und Frau* 12/32 (August 11, 1928): 600.

Friese, M., 'Deutschlands Lage', *Land und Frau* 15/40 (October 3, 1931): 720.

Fritsch, Luise, *Stellung und Tätigkeit der Landhausfrau in der landwirtschaftlichen Produktion des Deutschen Reiches* (Berlin: Deutsche Tageszeitung, 1929).

Fuhrmann, Hans, *Die Versorgung der deutschen Landwirtschaft mit Arbeitskräften im Weltkriege* (Würzburg: Verlag wissenschaftlicher Werke Konrad Triltsch, 1937).

'G. C.', 'Measures Adopted during the War to Maintain the Supply of Agricultural Labour', *International Review of Agricultural Economics*, 13th year, no. 3 (May 1922): 337–66.

Gausebeck, Aenna, 'Vom Landmädchen zur Landfrau', in *Wohlfahrt und Wirtschaft: Bericht über die 29. Hauptversammlung des deutschen Vereins für ländliche Wohlfahrts- und Heimatpflege am 25. und 26. Februar 1926 in Berlin* (Berlin: Deutscher Verein für ländliche Wohlfahrts- und Heimatpflege, 1926), pp. 19–27.

'Generalappell der Führerschaft am 16. September in Dresden', *Sächsische Landjugend* 11, Dresden, October 15, 1933, pp. 41–3.

Giese, Fritz, *Die Idee einer Frauendienstpflicht* (Langensalza: Wendt & Klauwell, 1916).

Gnauck-Kühne, Elisabeth, 'Die allgemeine Bedeutung und Notwendigkeit des Ausbaus der weiblichen Jugendpflege', *Schriften der Zentralstelle für Volkswohlfahrt* 9 (Berlin, 1912): 186–98.

Gogarten, Arete, 'Die hauswirtschaftliche Ausbildung der Töchter der ärmeren Landbevölkerung', in Frida zur Lippe-Oberschönfeld (ed.), *Die Frau auf dem Lande: Ein Wegweiser für Haus-, Guts-, und Gemeindepflege* (Berlin: Deutsche Landbuchhandlung, 1908), pp. 67–74.

Goltz, Theodor von der, *Die ländliche Arbeiterfrage und ihre Lösung* (Danzig: A.W. Kasemann, 1872).

Goltz, Theodor von der, *Die sociale Bedeutung des Gesindewesens. Zwei Vorträge* (Danzig: Verlag von A.W. Kasemann, 1873).

Goltz, Theodor von der, *Die agrarischen Aufgaben der Gegenwart* (Jena: Gustav Fischer, 1894).

Goltz, Theodor von der, *Agrarwesen und Agrarpolitik*, 2nd edn (Jena: Gustav Fischer, 1904).

Goltz, Theodor von der, *Geschichte der deutschen Landwirtschaft, Band 2: das 19. Jahrhundert,* reprint 1903 ed. (Aalen: Scientia Verlag, 1963).

Heese, Elli, 'Rationalisierung unserer Volkskraft', *Land und Frau* 12/46 (November 17, 1928): 839–40.

Hohmann, Leo, and Ernst Reichel, *Die Dienstpflicht der deutschen Frauen* (Berlin: Mathilde-Zimmer-Haus, 1917).

Hübel, Leopold, *Die Gestaltung des landwirtschaftlichen Betriebs mit Rücksicht auf den herrschenden Arbeitermangel* (Dresden: Zahn & Jaensch, 1902).

Hurwicz, E., 'Kriminalität und Prostitution der weiblichen Dienstboten', *Archiv für Kriminalanthropologie* 65 (1916): 185–251.

Huxdorff, Dr., 'Arbeitsphysiologische Aufgaben bei der Untersuchung der Arbeiten von Landfrauen', *Land und Frau* 16/34 (August 20, 1932): 575–6.

Institut für soziale Arbeit München, *Die weibliche Dienstpflicht* (München: Verlag des Aerztlichen Rundschau Otto Gmelin, 1916).

Jahres-Bericht über die Landwirtschaft im Königreich Sachsen für das Jahr 1902 bis 1912 (Leipzig, Dresden: Verlag des Landeskulturrats Sachsen, 1903–1912).

Kähler, Wilhelm, *Gesindewesen und Gesinderecht in Deutschland* (Jena: Gustav Fischer Verlag, 1896).

Kallbrunner, Hermann, 'Measures Taken During the War to Maintain the Supply of Agricultural Labour', *International Review of Agricultural Economics*, XIII/3-4 (March–April 1922): 219–33.

Kaup, Ignaz, *Ernährung und Lebenskraft der ländlichen Bevölkerung: Tatsachen und Vorschläge* (Berlin: Carl Heymanns Verlag, 1910).

Kautsky, Karl, *The Agrarian Question in Two Volumes*, trans. Peter Burgess (London: Zwan Publications, 1988).

Kempf, Rosa, 'Ausbildungsmöglichkeiten für Mädchen und Frauen auf dem Lande', in Gertrud Dyhrenfurth (ed.), *Ergebnisse einer Untersuchung über die Arbeits- und Lebensverhältnisse der Frauen in der Landwirtschaft* (Jena: Gustav Fischer, 1916), pp. 77–94.

Kempf, Rosa, 'Das weibliche Dienstjahr', *Archiv für Sozialwissenschaft und Sozialpolitik* 41 (1916): 422–37.

Kempf, Rosa, 'Schriften vom weiblichen Dienstjahr und Verwandtes', *Archiv für Sozialwissenschaft und Sozialpolitik* 44 (1917/1918): 854–66.

Kempf, Rosa, *Arbeits- und Lebensverhältnisse der Frauen in der Landwirtschaft Bayerns* (Jena: Gustav Fischer, 1918).

Kempf, Rosa, 'Aufgaben und Ziele der ländlichen Pflichtfortbildungsschule', *Vorträge anläßlich der zweiten sächsischen landwirtschaftlichen Woche in Dresden vom 23. bis 27. Januar 1922* (Dresden: Verlag des Landeskulturrats, 1922), pp. 45–57.

Kempf, Rosa, *Die deutsche Frau nach der Volks-, Berufs-, und Betriebszählung von 1925* (Mannheim: Bennsheimer Verlag, 1931).

Kerkerink, Maria, *Was erwarten wir von der ländlichen Fortbildungsschule für Mädchen und welche Anforderungen sind an sie zu stellen?* vol. 7 of *Schriften der Provinzialabteilung Rheinprovinz des Deutschen Vereins für ländliche Wohlfahrts- und Heimatpflege* (Bonn: Verlag der Provinzialabteilung Rheinprovinz des Deutschen Vereins für ländliche Wohlfahrts- und Heimatpflege, 1917).

evangel. Jugendpflege auf dem Lande (Berlin: Evangel. Verband zur Pflege der weiblichen Jugend Deutschlands, 1917).

Rogge-Börner, S., 'Unser Bauernblut gehört dem Deutschtum!', *Land und Frau* 15/8 (February 21, 1931): 131.

Roth, Hugo, *Über den Einfluß des Zuckerrübenbaues auf die Höhe der landwirtschaftlichen Kapitalien besonders im Königreich Sachsen* (Diss. Universität Leipzig, 1892).

Rundstedt, Malita von, *Die Arbeit des Landmädchens* (Berlin-Dahlem: Burckhardthaus-Verlag, 1917).

Sander, Friedrich, 'Die Bedeutung der Arbeitspsychologie für die Landarbeitslehre', in G. Derlitzki (ed.), *Berichte über Landarbeit*, vol. 1 (Stuttgart: Franckh'sche Verlagshandlung, 1927), pp. 99–104.

Scheller, Heinrich, *Das Gesinderecht und seine Aufhebung* (Borna-Leipzig: Robert Noske, 1919).

Schmidt, Georg, 'Einige Arbeitsverfahren bei der Hackfruchternte', in G. Derlitzki (ed.), *Berichte über Landarbeit*, vol. 1 (Stuttgart: Franckh'sche Verlagshandlung, 1927), pp. 161–9.

Schöller, K. M., 'Die volkssaugende Stadt', *Land und Frau* 12/1 (January 7, 1928): 3.

Schöne, Bruno, *Die wirtschaftlichen und sozialen Verhältnisse der Gemeinde Kühren* (Dahlen in Sachsen: R. Irrgang, 1904).

Schöne, Bruno, *Die Sächsische Landwirtschaft: ihre Entwickelung bis zum Jahre 1925* (Dresden: Verlag des Landeskulturrats Sachsen, 1925).

Schuler, M., 'Hauswirtschaftliche Beratungsarbeit', *Land und Frau* 3/4 (April 4, 1931): 261.

Schützhold, Gerhard, *Die sächsische Landfrau: ihr Aufgaben- und Pflichtenkreis im bäuerlichen Landwirtschaftsbetrieb* (Dresden: Verlag von Theodor Steinkopff, 1934).

Schwiening, Georg, *Die Dienstpflicht der Frauen* (Cassel: Ernst Hühn, 1900).

Seufert, Hans, *Arbeits- und Lebensverhältnisse der Frauen in der Landwirtschaft in Württemberg, Baden, Elsaß- Lothringen und Rheinpfalz* (Jena: Gustav Fischer, 1914).

Siemering, Hertha, 'Pflege der schulentlassenen weiblichen Jugend', *Schriften der Zentralstelle für Volkswohlfahrt* 10 (Berlin: Carl Heymanns Verlag, 1914): 1–48.

Skalweit, August, 'The Maintenance of the Agricultural Labour Supply during the War', *International Review of Agricultural Economics* 12/12 (December 1922): 836–90.

Sohnrey, Heinrich, *Kriegsarbeit auf dem Lande. Wegweiser für ländliche Wohlfahrts- und Heimatpflege in Kriegszeit* (Berlin: Deutsche Landbuchhandlung, 1915).

'Soziale Wirtschaft, Volkswirtschaft, Wohlfahrtspflege, Berufsfragen', *Land und Frau* 12 (1928).

Sprengel, Aenne, 'Die Bauersfrau als Berufstätige in der Landwirtschaft', in Ellen Semmelroth and Renate von Stieda (eds), *N.S. Frauenbuch* (Munich: J. F. Lehmanns Verlag, 1934), pp. 98–105.

'Die Stellung der Frau in der Landwirtschaft', *Die Praktische Landwirtin. Blätter für die Hausfrau des Landwirts* 14/7 (Magdeburg, August, 1922): 1.

Stieger, Georg, *Der Mensch in der Landwirtschaft. Grundlagen der Landarbeitslehre* (Berlin: Paul Parey, 1922).

Strantz, Aenne von, 'Bericht über die Arbeiten der hauswirtschaftlichen Abteilung der Versuchsanstalt für Landarbeitslehre Pommritz', *Land und Frau* 16/34 (August 20, 1932): 574.

Strebel, Ernst von, *Der Krieg und die deutsche Landwirtschaft* (Stuttgart: Eugen Ulmer, 1915).

Stumpfe, A., 'Zur Dienstbotenfrage: die soziale Lage der weiblichen Dienstboten', *Soziale Revue: Zeitschrift für die sozialen Fragen der Gegenwart* 7 (Essen, 1907): 428–38.

Tanzmann, Bruno, 'Die Beispiel-Bauernhochschule in Hellerau', *Die deutsche Bauern-Hochschule* 3 (December 1921): 1–6.

Tanzmann, Bruno, 'Die Frau der Bauernkultur', *Die deutsche Bauern-Hochschule* 2 (September 1921): 1–6.

Tasch, 'Die Landfrau und die aktuellen agrarpolitischen Problemen', *Land und Frau* 12/3 (January 21, 1928): 35.

Thering, Irmgard von, 'Wie arbeiten wir durch ländliche Jugendpflege auf den Dörfern gegen die Landflucht?', in *Die Landfrauenarbeit im Kriege. Dreiundzwanzig Vorträge (2. Kriegslehrgang)* (Berlin: Deutsche Landbuchhandlung, 1916), pp. 211–16.

'Übersicht über die Tätigkeit in den Verbänden', *Landfrauen-Kalender 1932*, ed. *Land und Frau* (Berlin: Paul Parey, 1932).

Verein für Sozialpolitik, *Die Verhältnisse der Landarbeiter in Deutschland*, Bd. 53–55 (Leipzig: Duncker & Humblot, 1892).

Wagner, Willi, *Die Schule der Jungbäuerin* (Berlin: Paul Parey, 1926).

Walter, Toni, 'Die Frau in der Landwirtschaft Mitteldeutschlands, dargestellt an der Provinz Sachsen', in Marie von Brand et al. (eds), *Die Frau in der deutschen Landwirtschaft* (Berlin: Franz Vahlen, 1939), pp. 103–30.

Waterstradt, Franz, 'Ein Beitrag zur Methodik der Wirtschaftslehre des Landbaues', *Landwirtschaftliche Jahrbücher* 33 (1904): 477–515.

Weber, Max, 'Die Verhältnisse der Landarbeiter im ostelbischen Deutschland', in *Schriften des Vereins für Sozialpolitik LV: Die Verhältnisse der Landarbeiter in Deutschland 3* (Leipzig, Duncker & Humblot, 1892).

Wenck, Helene, 'Die Landfrauen in Berlin', *Land und Frau* 9/9 (February 28, 1925): 98–100.

Wenck, Helene, 'Landfrauenarbeit "Grüne Woche" 1928', *Land und Frau* 12/7 (February 18, 1928).

Wenckstern, H. v., 'Landfrau und Volkswirtschaft im Spiegel der Statistik', *Land und Frau* 16/34 (August 20, 1932): 569–70.

Witte, Irene, *Die rationelle Haushaltsführung. Betriebswissenschaftliche Studien* (Berlin: Julius Springer, 1920, 1922), translation of Christine Frederick, *The New Housekeeping: Efficiency Studies in Home Management* (Garden City, NY: Doubleday, Page and Co., 1913, 1916).

Witte, Irene, *Taylor, Gilbreth, Ford: Gegenwartsfragen der amerikanischen und europäischen Arbeitswissenschaft*, 2nd edn (Berlin: Verlag von R. Oldenbourg, 1925).

Witte, Irene, *Heim und Technik in Amerika* (Berlin: VDI Verlag, 1928).

Wohlfarth, O., 'Hundert Jahre sächsische Agrarstatistik', *Zeitschrift des sächsischen statistischen Landesamtes* 78/79 (Dresden: Zahn & Jaensch, 1932/1933), pp. 9–44.

Wohlgemuth, Marta, *Die Bäuerin in zwei badischen Gemeinden*, no. 20 of Karl Diehl et al. (eds), *Volkswirtschaftliche Abhandlungen der badischen Hochschulen* (Karlsruhe: G. Braunsche Hofbuchdruckerei und Verlag, 1913).

'Women and Farm Labour', *International Review of Agricultural Economics* 70/10 (October 1916): 115–18.

'Women Workers on the Farm', *International Review of Agricultural Economics,* 8th year, no. 4 (April 1917): 106–8.

Wrisberg, Ernst von, *Heer und Heimat, 1914–1918* (Leipzig: Koehler, 1921).

Wygodzinski, Willi, *Die Hausfrau und die Volkswirtschaft* (Tübingen: J. C. B. Mohr, 1916).

Wygodzinski, Willi, 'Produktionszwang und Produktionsförderung in der Landwirtschaft', in *Beiträge zur Kriegswirtschaft* Heft 5 (Berlin: Volkswirtschaftliche Abteilung des Kriegsernährungsamts, 1917).

Wygodzinski, Willi, *Die Landarbeiterfrage in Deutschland* (Tübingen: J. C. B. Mohr, 1917).

VII. Secondary Sources

Achilles, Walter, *Deutsche Agrargeschichte im Zeitalter der Reformen und der Industrialisierung* (Stuttgart: Verlag Eugen Ulmer, 1993).

Adams, Jane, *The Transformation of Rural Life: Southern Illinois, 1890–1990* (Chapel Hill: University of North Carolina Press, 1994).

Albers, Helene, *Zwischen Hof, Haushalt und Familie: Bäuerinnen in Westfalen-Lippe, 1920–1960* (Paderborn: F. Schöningh, 2001).

Allen, Keith, 'Sharing Scarcity: Bread Rationing in the First World War in Berlin', *Journal of Social History* 32/2 (1998): 371–93.

Allen, Keith, *Hungrige Metropole: Essen, Wohlfahrt und Kommerz in Berlin* (Hamburg: Ergebnisse Verlag, 2002).

Ankum, Katharina von (ed.), *Women in the Metropolis: Gender and Modernity in Weimar Culture* (Berkeley: University of California Press, 1997).

Armitage, Susan, 'Household Work and Childrearing on the Frontier: The Oral History Record', *Sociology and Social Research* 63 (April 1979): 467–74.

Bade, Klaus, '"Billig und willig"– die "ausländischen Wanderarbeiter" im kaiserlichen Deutschland', in Klaus Bade (ed.), *Deutsche im Ausland-Fremde in Deutschland: Migration in Geschichte und Gegenwart* (Munich: C. H. Beck, 1992), pp. 311–24.

Baranowski, Shelley, *The Sanctity of Rural Life: Nobility, Protestantism, and Nazism in Weimar Prussia* (Oxford: Oxford University Press, 1995).

Barclay, David E., and Eric D. Weitz (eds), *Between Reform and Revolution: German Socialism and Communism from 1840 to 1990* (New York: Berghahn Books, 1998).

Barkin, Kenneth D., *The Controversy over German Industrialization, 1890–1902* (Chicago: University of Chicago Press, 1970).

Becker, Peter, 'Randgruppen im Blickfeld der Polizei: Ein Versuch über die Perspektivität des "praktischen Blicks"', *Archiv für Sozialgeschichte* 32 (1992): 283–304.

Becker, Siegfried, 'Der Dienst im fremden Haus: Sozialisation und kollektive Identität ehemaliger landwirtschaftlicher Dienstboten', in Becker and Matter, *Gesindewesen in Hessen*, pp. 241–70.

Becker, Siegfried, *Arbeit und Gerät als Zeichensetzung bäuerlicher Familienstrukturen: Zur Stellung der Kinder im Sozialgefüge landwirtschaftlicher Betriebe des hessischen Hinterlandes zu Beginn des 20. Jahrhunderts* (Inaugural-Dissertation, Philipps-Universität, Marburg/Lahn, 1985).

Becker, Siegfried, and Max Matter (eds), *Gesindewesen in Hessen*, vol. 22 of *Hessische Blätter für Volks- und Kulturforschung* (Marburg: Jonas Verlag, 1987).

Berger, Stefan, 'Historians and Nation-Building in Germany after Reunification', *Past and Present* 148 (August 1995): 187–222.

Berghahn, Volker, *Imperial Germany, 1871–1914: Economy, Society, Culture, and Politics* (New York: Berghahn Books, 1994).

Bergmann, Jürgen, 'Das Land steht rechts! Das agrarische Milieu', in Detlef Lehnert and Klaus Megerle (eds), *Politische Identität und nationale Gedenktage: zur politischen Kultur in der Weimarer Republik* (Wiesbaden: Westdeutscher Verlag, 1989).

Bergmann, Jürgen, and Klaus Megerle, 'Gesellschaftliche Mobilisierung und negative Partizipation. Zur Analyse der politischen Orientierung und Aktivitäten von Arbeitern, Bauern und gewerblichem Mittelstand in der Weimarer Republik', in Peter Steinbach (ed.), *Probleme politischer Partizipation im Modernisierungsprozeß* (Stuttgart: Klett-Cotta, 1982), pp. 376–437.

Bergmann, Jürgen, and Klaus Megerle, 'Protest und Aufruhr der Landwirtschaft in der Weimarer Republik (1924–1933). Formen und Typen der politischen Agrarbewegung im regionalen Vergleich', in J. Bergmann et al. (eds), *Regionen im historischen Vergleich: Studien zu Deutschland im 19. und 20. Jahrhundert* (Wiesbaden: Westdeutscher Verlag, 1989), pp. 200–87.

Bergmann, Klaus, *Agrarromantik und Großstadtfeindschaft* (Meisenheim am Glan: Verlag Anton Hain, 1970).

Berthold, R., 'Bemerkungen zu den Wechselbeziehungen zwischen der industriellen Revolution und der kapitalistischen Intensivierung der Feldwirtschaft in Deutschland im 19. Jahrhundert', *Jahrbuch für Wirtschaftsgechichte I* (1972): 261–7.

Berthold, R., 'Zur Entwicklung der deutschen Agrarproduktion und der Ernährungswirtschaft zwischen 1907 und 1925', *Jahrbuch für Wirtschaftsgeschichte IV* (1974): 87.

Bessel, Richard, '"Eine nicht allzu große Beunruhigung des Arbeitsmarktes": Frauenarbeit und Demobilmachung in Deutschland nach dem ersten Weltkrieg', *Geschichte und Gesellschaft* 9 (1983): 211–29.

Bessel, Richard, 'State and Society in Germany in the Aftermath of the First World War', in W. R. Lee and Eve Rosenhaft (eds), *The State and Social Change in Germany* (Oxford: Berg Publishers, 1990), pp. 206–7.

Bessel, Richard, *Germany After the First World War* (Oxford: Clarendon Press, 1993).

Bessel, Richard, 'Mobilizing German Society for War', in Roger Chickering and Stig Förster (eds), *Great War, Total War: Combat and Mobilization on the Western Front, 1914–1918* (Cambridge: Cambridge University Press, 2000), pp. 437–51.

Blackbourn, David, *Class, Religion, and Local Politics in Wilhelmine Germany: The Centre Party in Württemberg before 1914* (New Haven: Yale University Press, 1980).

Blackbourn, David, 'Peasants and Politics in Germany, 1871–1914', *European History Quarterly* 14 (1984): 47–75.

Blackbourn, David, and Geoff Eley, *The Peculiarities of German History: Bourgeois Society and Politics in Nineteenth-Century Germany* (Oxford: Oxford University Press, 1985).

Boelcke, Willi, 'Wandlungen der deutschen Agrarwirtschaft in der Folge des Ersten Weltkriegs', *Francia* 3 (1975): 498–532.

Bridenthal, Renate, 'Organized Rural Women and the Conservative Mobilization of the German Countryside in the Weimar Republic', in Larry Eugene Jones and James Retallack (eds), *Between Reform, Reaction, and Resistance: Studies in the History of German Conservatism from 1789 to 1945* (Oxford: Berg Publishers, 1993), pp. 375–405.

Brose, Eric Dorn, *German History 1789–1871: From the Holy Roman Empire to the Bismarckian Reich* (New York: Berghahn Books, 1997).

Bullock, Nicholas, 'First the Kitchen: Then the Façade', *Journal of Design History* 1/3–4 (1988): 177–92.

Canning, Kathleen, *Languages of Labor and Gender: Female Factory Work in Germany, 1850–1914* (Ithaca: Cornell University Press, 1996).

Chickering, Roger, *We Men Who Feel Most German: A Cultural Study of the Pan-German League, 1886–1914* (Boston: Allen & Unwin, 1984).

Chickering, Roger, *Imperial Germany and the Great War, 1914–1918* (Cambridge: Cambridge University Press, 1998).

Chickering Roger, and Stig Förster (eds), *Great War, Total War: Combat and Mobilization on the Western Front, 1914–1918* (Cambridge: Cambridge University Press, 2000).

Confino, Alon, *The Nation as a Local Metaphor: Württemberg, Imperial Germany, and National Memory, 1871–1918* (Chapel Hill: University of North Carolina Press, 1997).

Constantine, Simon, 'Migrant Labour in the German Countryside: Agency and Protest, 1890–1923', *Labour History* 47/ 3 (2006): 319–41.

Constantine, Simon, *Social Relations in the Estate Villages of Mecklenburg ca. 1880–1924* (Aldershot: Ashgate Publishing, 2007).

Corni, Gustavo, and Horst Gies, *'Blut und Boden': Rassenideologie und Agrarpolitik im Staat Hitlers* (Idstein: Schulz-Kirchner, 1994).

Corni, Gustavo, and Horst Gies, *Brot – Butter – Kanonen: Die Ernährungswirtschaft in Deutschland und der Diktatur Hitlers* (Berlin: Akademie Verlag, 1997).

Crew, David, *Germans on Welfare: From Weimar to Hitler* (Oxford: Oxford University Press, 1998).

Culleton, Claire A., *Working-Class Culture, Women, and Britain, 1914–1921* (New York: St. Martin's Press, 1999).

Czok, Carl, *Geschichte Sachsens* (Weimar: Hermann Böhlaus Nachfolger, 1989).

Dammer, Susanna, *Mütterlichkeit und Frauendienstpflicht: Versuche der Vergesellschaftung 'weiblicher Fähigkeiten' durch eine Dienstverpflichtung (Deutschland 1890–1918)* (Weinheim: Deutscher Studienverlag, 1998).

Daniel, Ute, 'Fiktionen, Friktionen und Fakten—Frauenlohnarbeit im Ersten Weltkrieg', in Günther Mai (ed.), *Arbeiterschaft in Deutschland 1914–1918. Studien zu Arbeitskampf und Arbeitsmarkt im Ersten Weltkrieg* (Düsseldorf: Droste Verlag, 1985), pp. 277–323.

Daniel, Ute, 'Women's Work in Industry and Family: Germany, 1914–1918', in Richard Wall and Jay Winter (eds), *The Upheaval of War: Family, Work, and Welfare in Europe, 1914–1918* (Cambridge: Cambridge University Press, 1988), pp. 267–96.

Daniel, Ute, 'Der Krieg der Frauen 1914–1918: Zur Innenansicht des Ersten Weltkrieges in Deutschland', in Gerhard Hirschfeld, Gerd Krumeich, and Irina Renz (eds), *Keiner fühlt sich hier als Mensch... Erlebnis und Wirkung des Ersten Weltkrieges* (Essen: Klartext Verlag, 1993), pp. 131–49.

Daniel, Ute, *The War from Within: German Working-Class Women in the First World War*, trans. Margaret Ries (Oxford: Berg Publishers, 1997).

Darrow, Margaret H., *French Women and the First World War: War Stories of the Home Front* (Oxford: Berg Publishers, 2000).

Davidoff, Leonore, 'The Rationalization of Housework', in Leonore Davidoff (ed.), *Worlds Between: Historical Perspectives on Gender and Class* (New York: Routledge, 1995), pp. 73–102.

Davis, Belinda, *Home Fires Burning: Food, Politics, and Everyday Life in World War I Berlin* (Chapel Hill: University of North Carolina Press, 2000).

Devine, T. M., 'Women Workers, 1850–1914', in T. M. Devine (ed.), *Farm Servants and Labour in Lowland Scotland, 1770–1914* (Edinburgh: John Donald Publishers, 1984), pp. 98–123.

Dillwitz, Sigrid, 'Die Struktur der Bauernschaft von 1871–1914', *Jahrbuch für Geschichte 9* (1973): 47–95.

Dobson, Sean, *Authority and Upheaval in Leipzig, 1910–1920: The Story of a Relationship* (New York: Columbia University Press, 2001).

Dressel, Guido, *Der Thüringer Landbund – Agrarischer Berufsverband als politische Partei in Thüringen 1919–1933*, vol. 12 of *Schriften zur Geschichte des Parlamentarismus in Thüringen* (Weimar: Thüringer Landtag/Wartburg Verlag, 1998).

Eley, Geoff, 'Anti-Semitism, Agrarian Mobilization, and the Conservative Party: Radicalism and Containment in the Founding of the Agrarian League, 1890–93', in L. E. Jones and James Retallack (eds), *Between Reform, Reaction and Resistance: Studies in the History of German Conservatism from 1789 to 1945* (Oxford: Berg Publishers, 1993), pp. 187–227.

Elsbroek, Ludger, *Vom Junglandbund zur Landjugend: Ländliche Jugend-verbandsarbeit zwischen Berufsstand und Jugendkultur* (Frankfurt/Main: Peter Lang, 1996).

Erker, Paul, 'Der lange Abschied vom Agrarland. Zur Sozialgeschichte der Bauern im Industrialisierungsprozeß', in Matthias Frese and Michael Prinz (eds), *Politische Zäsuren und gesellschaftlicher Wandel im 20. Jahrhundert: Regionale und vergleichende Perspektiven* (Paderborn: F. Schöningh, 1996), pp. 327–60.

Evans, Richard J., *In Hitler's Shadow: West German Historians and the Attempt to Escape the Nazi Past* (New York: Pantheon Books, 1989).

Falter, Jürgen, *Hitlers Wähler* (Munich: C. H. Beck, 1991).

Farquharson, J. E., *The Plough and the Swastika: The NSDAP and Agriculture in Germany, 1928–1945* (Wayne, IN: Landpost Press, 1976).

Farr, Ian, 'Peasant Protest in the Empire – The Bavarian Example', in Robert Moeller (ed.), *Peasants and Lords in Modern Germany: Recent Studies in Agricultural History* (Boston: Allen & Unwin, 1986), pp. 110–39.

Farr, Ian, '"Tradition" and the Peasantry: On the Modern Historiography of Rural Germany', in Richard J. Evans and W. R. Lee (eds), *The German Peasantry: Conflict and Community in Rural Society from the Eighteenth to the Twentieth Centuries* (London: Croom Helm, 1986), pp. 1–36.

Feldman, Gerald, *Army, Industry and Labor in Germany, 1914–1918*, 2nd edn (Providence, RI: Berg Publishers, 1992).

Feldman, Gerald, *The Great Disorder: Politics, Economics, and Society in the German Inflation, 1914–1924* (Oxford: Oxford University Press, 1997).

Flemming, Jens, *Landwirtschaftliche Interessen und Demokratie: ländliche Gesellschaft, Agrarverbände und Staat, 1890–1925* (Bonn: Verlag Neue Gesellschaft, 1978).

Frauendorfer, Sigmund von, and Heinz Haushofer, *Ideengeschichte der Agrarwirtschaft und Agrarpolitik im deutschen Sprachgebiet* (München: Bayerischer Landwirtschaftsverlag, 1957).

Fritzsche, Peter, *Rehearsals for Fascism: Populism and Political Mobilization in Weimar Germany* (Oxford: Oxford University Press, 1990).

Fritzsche, Peter, 'Weimar Populism and National Socialism in Local Perspective', in Larry Eugene Jones and James Retallack (eds), *Elections, Mass Politics, and Social Change in Modern Germany* (Cambridge: Cambridge University Press, 1992), pp. 287–306.

Fritzsche, Peter, *Germans into Nazis* (Cambridge: Harvard University Press, 1998).

Führer, Karl-Christian, *Arbeitslosigkeit und die Entstehung der Arbeitslosenversicherung in Deutschland, 1902–1927* (Berlin: Kolloqium Verlag, 1990).

Gatrell, Peter, *Russia's First World War: A Social and Economic History* (Harlow: Pearson Longman, 2005).

Gehmacher, Johanna, *'Völkische Frauenbewegung': Deutschnationale und nationalsozialistische Geschlechterpolitik in Österreich* (Wien: Döcker Verlag, 1998).

Gelderblom, Bernhard, *Die Reichserntedankfeste auf dem Bückeberg, 1933–1937* (Hameln: Niemeyer Buchverlage, 1998).

Gersdorff, Ute von, 'Frauen im Kriegsdienst', *Wehrkunde: Organ der Gesellschaft für Wehrkunde* 14 (1965): 576–80.

Gessner, Dieter, 'The Dilemma of German Agriculture during the Weimar Republic', in Richard Bessel and Edgar J. Feuchtwanger (eds), *Social Change and Political Development in Weimar Germany* (London: Croom Helm, 1981), pp. 134–54.

Geyer, Martin H., 'Teuerungsprotest und Teuerungsunruhen 1914–1923: Selbsthilfegesellschaft und Geldentwertung', in Manfred Gailus and Heinrich Volkmann (eds), *Der Kampf um das tägliche Brot: Nahrungsmangel, Versorgungspolitik und Protest 1770–1990* (Opladen: Westdeutscher Verlag, 1994), pp. 319–45.

Gray, Marion, *Productive Men, Reproductive Women: The Agrarian Household and the Emergence of Separate Spheres during the German Enlightenment* (New York: Berghahn Books, 2000).

Gray, Marion, 'Microhistory as Universal History', *Central European History* 34/3 (2001): 419–31.

Grayzel, Susan, *Women's Identities at War: Gender, Motherhood, and Politics in Britain and France during the First World War* (Chapel Hill: University of North Carolina, 1999).

Grill, Johnpeter Horst, 'The Nazi Party's Rural Propaganda Before 1928', *Central European History* 15/2 (1982): 149–85.

Grossmann, Atina, 'The New Woman and the Rationalization of Sexuality in Weimar Germany', in A. Snitow et al. (eds), *Powers of Desire: The Politics of Sexuality* (New York: Monthly Review Press, 1983), pp. 153–76.

Grossmann, Atina, *Reforming Sex: The German Movement for Birth Control and Abortion Reform, 1920–1950* (New York: Oxford University Press, 1995).

Gullace, Nicoletta F., *'The Blood of Our Sons': Men, Women, and the Renegotiation of British Citizenship during the Great War* (New York: Palgrave MacMillan, 2002).

Hagemann, Karen, 'Of "Old" and "New" Housewives: Everyday Housework and the Limits of Household Rationalization in the Urban Working-Class Milieu of the Weimar Republic', *International Review of Social History* 41 (1996): 305–30.

Harvey, Elizabeth, *Youth and the Welfare State in Weimar Germany* (Oxford: Clarendon Press, 1993).

Harvey, Elizabeth, 'Visions of the Volk: German Women and the Far Right from Kaiserreich to Third Reich', *Journal of Women's History* 16/ 3 (2004): 152–67.

Hausen, Karin, 'Unemployment also Hits Women: The New and the Old Woman on the Dark Side of the Golden Twenties in Germany', in Peter Stachura (ed.), *Unemployment and the Great Depression in Weimar Germany* (New York: St. Martin's Press, 1986), pp. 78–120.

Haushofer, Heinz, *Ideengeschichte der Agrarwirtschaft und Agrarpolitik im deutschen Sprachgebiet Band II: Vom Ersten Weltkrieg bis zur Gegenwart* (München: Bayrischer Landwirtschaftsverlag, 1958).

Haushofer, Heinz, *Die deutsche Landwirtschaft im technischen Zeitalter* (Stuttgart: Verlag Eugen Ulmer, 1972).

Heberle, Rudolf, *Landbevölkerung und Nationalsozialismus: Eine soziologische Untersuchung der politischen Willensbildung in Schleswig-Holstein 1918–1932* (Stuttgart: Deutsche Verlags-Anstalt, 1963).

Herbert, Ulrich, *A History of Foreign Labor in Germany: Seasonal Workers, Forced Laborers, Guestworkers*, trans. William Templer (Ann Arbor: University of Michigan Press, 1990).

Herlemann, Beatrix, 'Bäuerliche Verhaltensweisen unter dem Nationalsozialismus in niedersächsischen Gebieten', *Niedersächsisches Jahrbuch für Landesgeschichte* 62 (1990): 59–75.

Hinkelmann, Christoph, '"Es war ihr Schicksal, vorauszueilen – die anderen konnten nicht so schnell folgen" – Elisabet Boehm, geb. Steppuhn', in Ostpreußisches Landesmuseum, Lüneburg (ed.), *Elisabet Boehm und die Landfrauenbewegung* (Husum: Druck- und Verlagsgesellschaft mbH u. Co. KG, 1998), pp. 15–30.

Hoffmann, Walther G., *Das Wachstum der deutschen Wirtschaft seit der Mitte des 19. Jahrhunderts* (Berlin: Springer Verlag, 1965).

Hohorst, Gerd, et al., *Sozialgeschichtliches Arbeitsbuch Band II: Material zur Statistik des Kaiserreichs 1870–1914*, 2nd edn (München: Verlag C. H. Beck, 1978).

Hong, Young-Sun, *Welfare, Modernity, and the Weimar State, 1919–1933* (Princeton: Princeton University Press, 1998).

Horne, John, 'Mobilizing for "Total War", 1914–1918', in John Horne (ed.), *State, Society and Mobilization in Europe during the First World War* (Cambridge: Cambridge University Press, 1997), pp. 1–17.

Hüchtker, Dietlind, 'Die Bäuerin als Trope: Sprache und Politik in der polnischen Frauen- und Bauernbewegung an der Wende vom 19. zum 20. Jahrhundert', *Werkstatt Geschichte* 37 (2004): 49–63.

Huegel, Arnulf, *Kriegsernährungswirtschaft Deutschlands während des Ersten und Zweiten Weltkrieges im Vergleich* (Konstanz: Hartung-Gorre Verlag, 2003).

Hunt, J. C., 'Peasants, Grain Tariffs and Meat Quotas', *Central European History* 7 (1974): 311–31.

Jacobeit, Sigrid, 'Zum Alltag der Bäuerin in Klein- und Mittelbetrieben während der Zeit des deutschen Faschismus 1933 bis 1939', *Jahrbuch für Wirtschaftsgeschichte* (1982/I): 7–29.

Jacobeit, Sigrid, ' "… dem Mann Gehilfin und Knecht. Sie ist Magd und Mutter …": Klein- und Mittelbäuerinnen im faschistischen Deutschland', in Johanna Werckmeister (ed.), *Land-Frauen-Alltag: Hundert Jahre Lebens- und Arbeitsbedingungen der Frauen im ländlichen Raum* (Marburg: Jonas Verlag, 1989).

Jaschke, Hans-Gerd, 'Zur politischen Orientierung von Frauen und Frauenverbänden in der Weimarer Republik', in Detlef Lehnert and Klaus Megerle (eds), *Politische Teilkulturen zwischen Integration und Polarisierung. Zur politischen Kultur in der Weimarer Republik* (Opladen: Westdeutscher Verlag, 1990), pp. 143–60.

Jellison, Katherine, *Entitled to Power: Farm Women and Technology, 1913–1963* (Chapel Hill: University of North Carolina Press, 1993).

Jenkins, Jennifer, *Provincial Modernity: Local Culture and Liberal Politics in Fin-de-Siècle Hamburg* (Ithaca: Cornell University Press, 2003).

Jones, Elizabeth Bright, 'The Gendering of the Postwar Agricultural Labor Shortage in Saxony, 1918–1925', *Central European History* 32/3 (Fall 1999): 311–29.

Jones, Elizabeth Bright, 'A New Stage of Life?: Young Women's Changing Expectations and Aspirations about Work in Weimar Saxony', *German History* 19/4 (2001): 549–70.

Jones, Elizabeth Bright, 'Girls in Court: *Mägde* versus their Employers in Saxony, 1880–1914', in M. J. Maynes and Birgitte Soland (eds), *Secret Gardens, Satanic Mills: Placing Girls in European History, 1750–1960* (Bloomington: Indiana University Press, 2004), pp. 224–38.

Jones, Elizabeth Bright, 'Pre- and Postwar Generations of Rural Female Youth and the Future of the German Nation, 1871–1933', *Continuity and Change* 19/3 (2004): 1–19.

Jones, Elizabeth Bright, 'Landwirtschaftliche Arbeit und weibliche Körper in Deutschland, 1918–1933', in B. Binder, S. Göttsch, W. Kaschuba and K. Vanja (eds), *Ort. Arbeit. Körper.: Ethnographie Europäischer Modernen* (Münster: Waxmann Verlag, 2005), pp. 477–84.

Jones, Larry Eugene, 'Crisis and Reallignment: Agrarian Splinter Parties in the Late Weimar Republic', in Robert Moeller (ed.), *Peasants and Lords in Modern Germany: Recent Studies in Agricultural History* (Boston: Allen & Unwin, 1986), pp. 198–232.

Jones, Larry Eugene, and James Retallack (eds), *Elections, Mass Politics, and Social Change in Modern Germany* (Cambridge: Cambridge University Press, 1992).

Jones, Larry Eugene, and James Retallack (eds), *Between Reform, Reaction, and Resistance: Studies in the History of German Conservatism from 1789 to 1945* (Oxford: Berg Publishers, 1993).

Krieg, Beate, *'Landfrau, so geht's leichter!' Modernisierung durch hauswirtschaftliche Gemeinschaftsanlagen mit Elektrogroßgeräten im deutschen Südwesten von 1930 bis 1970* (Munich: tuduv-Verlagsgesellschaft, 1996).

Krug-Richter, Barbara, 'Agrargeschichte der frühen Neuzeit in geschlechtergeschichtlicher Perspektive: Anmerkungen zu einem Forschungsdesiderat', in Werner Troßbach and Clemens Zimmermann (eds), *Agrargeschichte: Positionen und Perspektiven* (Stuttgart: Lucius & Lucius, 1998), pp. 33–55.

Kühne, Thomas, 'Imagined Regions: The Construction of Traditional, Democratic, and other Identities', in James Retallack (ed.), *Saxony in German History: Culture, Society, Politics, 1830–1933* (Ann Arbor: University of Michigan Press, 2000), pp. 51–62.

Lapp, Benjamin, *Revolution from the Right: Politics, Class, and the Rise of Nazism in Saxony* (Atlantic Highlands, NJ: Humanities Press, 1997).

Lapp, Benjamin, 'Remembering the Year 1923 in Saxon History', in James Retallack (ed.), *Saxony in German History: Culture, Society, and Politics, 1830–1933* (Ann Arbor: University of Michigan Press, 2000), pp. 322–35.

Lässig, Simone, and Karl Heinrich Pohl (eds), *Sachsen im Kaiserreich: Politik, Wirtschaft und Gesellschaft in Umbruch* (Weimar: Böhlau Verlag, 1997).

Lee, W. R., 'Women's Work and the Family: Some Demographic Implications of Gender-Specific Rural Work Patterns in Nineteenth-Century Germany', in Pat Hudson and W. R. Lee (eds), *Women's Work and the Family Economy in Historical Perspective* (Manchester: Manchester University Press, 1990), pp. 50–75.

Lees, Andrew, *Cities, Sin, and Social Reform in Imperial Germany* (Ann Arbor: University of Michigan Press, 2002).

Lekan, Thomas, *Imagining the Nation in Nature: Landscape Preservation and German Identity, 1885–1945* (Cambridge: Harvard University Press, 2004).

Linton, Derek, 'Between School and Marriage, Workshop and Household: Young Working Women as a Social Problem in Late Imperial Germany', *European History Quarterly* 18/4 (1988): 387–408.

Linton, Derek, *'Who has the Youth, Has the Future': The Campaign to Save Young Workers in Imperial Germany* (Cambridge: Cambridge University Press, 1991).

Lovin, Clifford, 'Farm Women in the Third Reich', *Agricultural History* 60/3 (Summer 1986): 105–23.

Mai, Günther (ed.), *Arbeiterschaft in Deutschland 1914–1918: Studien zu Arbeitskampf und Arbeitsmarkt im Ersten Weltkrieg* (Düsseldorf: Droste Verlag, 1985).

Mai, Uwe, *'Rasse und Raum': Agrarpolitik, Sozial- und Raumplanung im NS-Staat* (Paderborn: F. Schöningh, 2002).

Mason, Tim, *Social Policy in the Third Reich: The Working Class and the 'National Community'*, trans. John Broadwin (Oxford: Berg Publishers, 1993).

Matter, Max, '"Ech stohn net ob – ech treck net us – leck mech em Asch – me Johr os us": Gesindeverhältnisse, Gesindeordnungen und Wechseltermine in Hessen und der ehemaligen preußischen Rheinprovinz', in Siegfried Becker and Max Matter (eds), *Gesindewesen in Hessen*, vol. 22 of *Hessische Blätter für Volks- und Kulturforschung* (Marburg: Jonas Verlag, 1987), pp. 12–34.

Matthews, William Carl, 'The Rise and Fall of Red Saxony', in David E. Barclay and Eric D. Weitz (eds), *Between Reform and Revolution: German Socialism and Communism from 1840 to 1990* (New York: Berghahn Books, 1998), pp. 293–313.

Merkenich, Stephanie, *Grüne Front gegen Weimar: Reichs-Landbund und agrarischer Lobbyismus, 1918–1933* (Düsseldorf: Droste Verlag, 1998).

Meyer, Sibylle, and Eva Schulze, 'Fernseher contra Waschmaschine: wie das Geschlechterverhältnis auf Technik wirkt', in Barbara Orland et al. (eds), *Haushalts-Träume: Ein Jahrhundert Technisierung und Rationalisierung im Haushalt* (Königstein im Taunus: Langewiesche, 1990), pp. 103–8.

Mitterauer, Michael, 'Geschlechtsspezifische Arbeitsteilung und Geschlechter-rollen in ländlichen Gesellschaften Mitteleuropas', in Jochen Martin and Renate Zoepffel (eds), *Aufgaben, Rollen und Räume von Frau und Mann, Teilband 2* (München: Verlag Karl Alber Freiburg, 1989), pp. 819–936.

Moeller, Robert 'Peasants and Tariffs in the Kaiserreich: How Backward were the "Bauern"?', *Agricultural History* 55 (1981): 370–84.

Moeller, Robert, 'Dimensions of Social Conflict in the Great War: A View from the Countryside', *Central European History* 14/2 (June 1981): 142–68.

Moeller, Robert, 'Winners as Losers in the German Inflation: Peasant Protest over the Controlled Economy, 1920–23', in Gerald Feldman (ed.), *Die Deutsche Inflation: eine Zwischenbilanz* (Berlin: De Gruyter, 1982), pp. 255–88.

Moeller, Robert, 'The Kaiserreich Recast? Continuity and Change in Modern German Historiography', *Journal of Social History* 17 (1984): 654–83.

Moeller, Robert, *German Peasants and Agrarian Politics, 1914–1924: The Rhineland and Westphalia* (Chapel Hill: University of North Carolina Press, 1986).

Moeller, Robert (ed.), *Peasants and Lords in Modern Germany: Recent Studies in Agricultural History* (Boston: Allen & Unwin, 1986).

Moeller, Robert, 'Economic Dimensions of Peasant Protest in the Transition from Kaiserreich to Weimar', in Robert Moeller (ed.), *Peasants and Lords in Modern Germany: Recent Studies in Agricultural History* (Boston: Allen & Unwin, 1986), pp. 140–67.

Mühlberger, Detlef (ed.), *Hitler's Voice: The Völkischer Beobachter, 1920–1933* (Oxford: Peter Lang, 2004).

Müller, Andreas, *'Fällt der Bauer, stürzt der Staat': Deutschnationale Agrarpolitik 1928–1933* (Munich: Herbert Utz Verlag, 2003).

Müller-Staats, Dagmar, *Klagen über Dienstboten: eine Untersuchung über Dienstboten und ihre Herrschaften* (Frankfurt/Main: Insel Verlag, 1987).

Münkel, Daniela, '"Ein besseres Leben für die Landfrau"? Technik im bäuerlichen Haushalt während der NS-Zeit', *metis* 4/1 (1995): 41–59.

Münkel, Daniela, *Nationalsozialistische Agrarpolitik und Bauernalltag* (Frankfurt/Main: Campus Verlag, 1996).

Münkel, Daniela, '"Du, Deutsche Landfrau bist verantwortlich!": Bauer und Bäuerin im Nationalsozialismus', *Archiv für Sozialgeschichte* 38 (1998): 141–64.

Münkel, Daniela (ed.), *Der lange Abschied vom Agrarland: Agrarpolitik, Landwirtschaft und ländliche Gesellschaft zwischen Weimar und Bonn* (Göttingen: Wallstein Verlag, 2000).

Neth, Mary, *Preserving the Family Farm: Women, Community, and the Foundations of Agribusiness in the Midwest, 1900–1940* (Baltimore: Johns Hopkins University Press, 1995).

Nolan, Mary, '"Housework Made Easy": The Taylorized Housewife in Weimar Germany's Rationalized Economy', *Feminist Studies* 16/3 (Fall 1990): 549–77.

Nolan, Mary, 'Das Deutsche Institut für technische Arbeitsschulung und die Schaffung des neuen Arbeiters', in Dagmar Reese et al. (eds), *Rationale Beziehungen? Geschlechterverhältnisse im Rationalisierungsprozeß* (Frankfurt/Main: Suhrkamp, 1993), pp. 189–221.

Nolan, Mary, *Visions of Modernity: American Business and the Modernization of Germany* (New York: Oxford University Press, 1994).

Nonn, Christoph, *Verbraucherprotest und Parteiensystem im wilhelminischen Deutschland* (Düsseldorf: Droste Verlag, 1996).

O'Donnell, K. Molly, Renate Bridenthal, and Nancy Reagin (eds.), *The Heimat Abroad: The Boundaries of Germanness* (Ann Arbor: University of Michigan Press, 2005).

Offer, Avner, *The First World War: An Agrarian Interpretation* (Oxford: Clarendon Press, 1989).

Oltmer, Jochen, *Bäuerliche Ökonomie und Arbeitskräftepolitik im Ersten Weltkrieg* (Emsland, Bentheim: Verlag der Emsländischen Landschaft e.V., 1995).

Orland, Barbara, 'Effizienz im Heim: die Rationalisierungsdebatte zur Reform der Hausarbeit in der Weimarer Republik', *Kultur und Technik: Zeitschrift des deutschen Museums München* 4/7 (1983): 221–7.

Orland, Barbara (ed.), *Haushalts-Träume: Ein Jahrhundert Technisierung und Rationaliserung im Haushalt, Begleitbuch zur gleichnahmigen Ausstellung* (Königstein im Taunus: Karl Robert Langewiesche Nachfolger, 1990).

Orland, Barbara, 'Emanzipation durch Rationalisierung? Der "rationelle Haushalt" als Konzept institutionalisierter Frauenpolitik in der Weimarer Republik', in Dagmar Reese et al. (eds), *Rationale Beziehungen?: Geschlechterverhältnisse im Rationalisierungsprozeß* (Frankfurt/Main: Suhrkamp, 1993), pp. 222–50.

Osmond, Jonathan, 'A Second Agrarian Mobilization?: Peasant Associations in South and West Germany', in Moeller, *Peasants and Lords in Modern Germany* (Boston: Allen & Unwin, 1986), pp. 168–97.

Osmond, Jonathan, *Rural Protest in the Weimar Republic: The Free Peasantry in the Rhineland and Bavaria* (New York: St. Martin's Press, 1993).

Perkins, J. A., 'The Agricultural Revolution in Germany, 1850–1914', *Journal of European Economic History* 10 (1981): 71–118.

Peters, Jan (ed.), *Gutsherrschaft als soziales Modell: Vergleichende Betrachtungen zur Funktionsweise frühneuzeitlicher Agrargesellschaften* (München: R. Oldenbourg, 1995).

Peukert, Detlev, *The Weimar Republic: The Crisis of Classical Modernity*, trans. Richard Deveson (New York: Hill and Wang, 1989).

Pfalzer, Stephan, 'Der "Butterkrawall" im Oktober 1915. Die erste größere Antikriegsbewegung in Chemnitz', in Helga Grebing et al. (eds), *Demokratie und Emanzipation zwischen Saale und Elbe: Beiträge zur Geschichte der sozialdemokratischen Arbeiterbewegung bis 1933* (Essen: Klartext Verlag, 1993), pp. 196–213

Planert, Ute (ed.), *Nation, Politik und Geschlecht: Frauenbewegungen und Nationalismus in der Moderne* (Frankfurt/Main: Campus Verlag, 2000).

Puhle, Hans-Jürgen, *Agrarische Interessenpolitik und preussischer Konservatismus im wilhelminischen Reich (1893–1914): Ein Beitrag zur Analyse des Nationalismus in Deutschland am Beispiel des Bundes der Landwirte und der Deutschen Konservativen Partei*, 2nd edn (Bonn-Bad Godesberg: Verlag Neue Gesellschaft, 1975).

Puhle, Hans-Jürgen, *Politische Agrarbewegungen in kapitalistischen Industriegesellschaften: Deutschland, USA und Frankreich im 20. Jahrhundert* (Göttingen: Vandenhoek & Ruprecht, 1975).

Reagin, Nancy, 'Comparing Apples and Oranges: Housewives and the Politics of Consumption in Interwar Germany', in Susan Strasser et al. (eds), *Getting and Spending: European and American Consumer Societies in the Twentieth Century* (Washington, DC: German Historical Institute, 1998), pp. 241–62.

Reagin, Nancy, *Sweeping the German Nation: Domesticity and National Identity in Germany, 1870–1945* (Cambridge: Cambridge University Press, 2006).

Reeken, Dietmar von, 'Bildung als Krisenbewältigungsinstrument? Die Bauernhochschulbewegung in der Weimarer Republik', in Daniela Münkel (ed.), *Der lange Abschied vom Agrarland: Agrarpolitik, Landwirtschaft und ländliche Gesellschaft zwischen Weimar und Bonn* (Göttingen: Wallstein Verlag, 2000), pp. 157–76.

Retallack, James, 'Anti-Socialism and Electoral Politics in Regional Perspective: The Kingdom of Saxony', in Larry Eugene Jones and James Retallack (eds), *Elections, Mass Politics and Social Change in Modern Germany: New Perspectives* (Cambridge: Cambridge University Press, 1992), pp. 49–92.

Retallack, James (ed.), *Saxony in German History: Culture, Society, Politics, 1830–1933* (Ann Arbor: University of Michigan Press, 2000).

Roerkohl, Anne, *Hungerblockade und Heimatfront: Die kommunale Lebensmittelversorgung in Westfalen während des Ersten Weltkrieges* (Stuttgart: Franz Steiner Verlag, 1991).

Roller, Kathrin, *Frauenmigration und Ausländerpolitik im Deutschen Kaiserreich: polnische Arbeitsmigrantinnen in Preußen,* 2nd edn (Berlin: Dieter Bertz Verlag, 1994).

Rose, Sonya, '"Gender at Work": Sex, Class and Industrial Capitalism', *History Workshop Journal* 21 (1986): 113–31.

Rosenhaft, Eve, 'Women, Gender, and the Limits of Political History in the Age of "Mass Politics"', in Larry Eugene Jones and James Retallack (eds), *Elections, Mass Politics, and Social Change in Modern Germany* (Cambridge: Cambridge University Press, 1992), pp. 149–73.

Rouette, Susanne, 'Nach dem Krieg: Zurück zur "normalen" Hierarchie der Geschlechter', in Karin Hausen (ed.), *Geschlechterhierarchie und Arbeitsteilung: Zur Geschichte ungleicher Erwerbschancen von Männern und Frauen* (Göttingen: Vandenhoek & Ruprecht, 1993), pp. 167–90.

Rublack, Ulinka, *The Crimes of Women in Early Modern Germany* (Oxford: Clarendon Press, 1999).

Rund, Jürgen, *Ernährungswirtschaft und Zwangsarbeit im Raum Hannover 1914 bis 1923* (Hannover: Hahnsche Buchhandlung, 1992).

Sabean, David, 'Small Peasant Agriculture in Germany at the Beginning of the Nineteenth Century: Changing Work Patterns', *Peasant Studies* 7/4 (Fall 1978): 218–24.

Sabean, David, *Property, Production and Family in Neckarhausen, 1700–1870* (Cambridge: Cambridge University Press, 1990).

Sabean, David Warren, *Kinship in Neckarhausen, 1700–1870* (Cambridge: Cambridge University Press, 1998).

Saldern, Adelheid von, 'Social Rationalization of Living and Housework in Germany and the United States in the 1920s', *The History of the Family* 2/1 (1997): 73–97.

Salvatici, Silvia, 'Die bäuerliche Frau. Ein Frauenbild in der Propaganda des italienischen Faschismus. Zur Lektüre historischer Photographien', *Werkstatt Geschichte* 11 (1995): 19–32.

Schaap, Klaus, *Die Endphase der Weimarer Republik im Freistaat Oldenburg 1928–1933* (Düsseldorf: Droste Verlag, 1978).

Scheck, Raffael, *Mothers of the Nation: Right-Wing Women in Weimar Germany* (Oxford: Berg, 2004).

Schlude, Ursula (ed.), *'Ich hab's gern gemacht': Die Lebensgeschichte einer Bäuerinnengeneration* (Ravensburg: Verlag Schwäbischer Bauer, 1989).

Schmidt-Waldherr, Hiltraud, 'Rationalisierung der Hausarbeit in den zwanziger Jahren', in Gerda Tornieporth (ed.), *Arbeitsplatz Haushalt: Zur Theorie und Ökologie der Hausarbeit* (Berlin: Dietrich Reimer Verlag, 1988), pp. 32–54.

Schmitt, Sabine, *Der Arbeiterinnenschutz im deutschen Kaiserreich: Zur Konstruktion der schutzbedürftigen Arbeiterin* (Stuttgart: Verlag J. B. Metzler, 1995).

Schulte, Regina, *Das Dorf im Verhör. Brandstifter, Kindsmörderinnen und Wilderer vor den Schranken des bürgerlichen Gerichts Oberbayern, 1848–1910* (Hamburg: Rowohlt, 1989).

Schumacher, Martin, *Land und Politik. Eine Untersuchung über politische Parteien und agrarischer Interessen, 1914–1923* (Düsseldorf: Droste Verlag, 1978).

Schumacher, Martin, 'Agrarische Wahlbewerbungen zum Reichstag 1912–1920/22: Ergebnisse einer Auszählung', in Peter Steinbach (ed.), *Probleme politischer Partizipation im Modernisierungsprozeß* (Stuttgart: Klett-Cotta, 1982), pp. 353–75.

Schwarz, Christina, *Die Landfrauenbewegung in Deutschland. Zur Geschichte einer Frauenorganisation unter besonderer Berücksichtigung der Jahre 1898 bis 1933* (Mainz: Gesellschaft für Volkskunde in Rheinland Pfalz, e.V., 1990).

Schwarz, Christina, 'Zur Geschichte der Landfrauenbewegung in Deutschland', *Zeitschrift für Agrargeschichte und Agrarsoziologie* 40/1 (1992): 28–42.

Schwarz, Christina and Friederike v. Natzmer, '"Frauen im Zeichen der Biene" – die Geschichte der deutschen Landfrauenbewegung', in *Elisabet Boehm und die Landfrauenbewegung*, museum catalog ed. Ostpreußisches Landesmuseum, Lüneburg (Husum: Husum Druck- und Verlagsgesellschaft, 1998).

Shearer, J. Ronald, 'Talking About Efficiency: Politics and the Industrial Rationalization Movement in the Weimar Republic', *Central European History* 28/4 (1995): 483–506.

Sneeringer, Julia, *Winning Women's Votes: Propaganda and Politics in Weimar Germany* (Chapel Hill: University of North Carolina Press, 2002).

Steinmetz, George, *Regulating the Social: The Welfare State and Local Politics in Imperial Germany* (Princeton: Princeton University Press, 1993).

Stibbe, Matthew, 'Anti-Feminism, Nationalism and the German Right, 1914–1920: A Reappraisal', *German History* 20/2 (2002): 185–210.

Stibbe, Matthew, *Women in the Third Reich* (London: Arnold Publishers, 2003).

Stoltenberg, Gerhard, *Politische Strömungen im schleswig-holsteinischen Landvolk 1918–1933: Ein Beitrag zur politischen Meinungsbildung in der Weimarer Republik* (Düsseldorf: Droste Verlag, 1962).

Süchting-Hänger, Andrea, *Das 'Gewissen der Nation': Nationales Engagement und politisches Handeln konservativer Frauenorganisationen 1900 bis 1937* (Düsseldorf: Droste Verlag, 2002).

Szejnmann, Claus Christian W., *Nazism in Central Germany: The Brownshirts in 'Red Saxony'* (New York: Berghahn Books, 1999).

Teuteberg, Hans-Jürgen (ed.), *Durchbruch zum Massenkonsum: Lebensmittelmärkte und Lebensmittelqualität im Städtewachstum des Industriezeitalters* (Münster: Coppenrath Verlag, 1987).

Tillmann, Doris, *Der Landfrauenberuf: Bäuerliche Arbeit, Bildungstätten und Berufsorganisation der Landfrauen in Schleswig-Holstein* (Neumünster: Wachholtz Verlag, 1997).

Tillmann, Doris, *Früh aufstehen, arbeiten und sparen: Landfrauenleben zwischen 1900 und 1933* (Heide: Boyens & Co., 1997).

Troßbach, Werner, 'Beharrung und Wandel "als Argument": Bauern in der Agrargesellschaft des 18. Jahrhunderts', in Werner Troßbach and Clemens Zimmermann (eds), *Agrargeschichte: Positionen und Perspektive* (Stuttgart: Lucius & Lucius, 1998), pp. 123–30.

Ulbrich, Claudia, 'Überlegungen zur Erforschung von Geschlechterrollen in der ländlichen Gesellschaft', in Jan Peters (ed.), *Gutsherrschaft als soziales Modell: Vergleichende Betrachtungen zur Funktionsweise frühneuzeitlicher Agrargesellschaften* (München: R. Oldenbourg, 1995), pp. 359–64.

Usborne, Cornelie, *The Politics of the Body in Weimar Germany: Women's Reproductive Rights and Duties* (Ann Arbor: University of Michigan Press, 1992).

Vanja, Christina, 'Zwischen Verdrängung und Expansion, Kontrolle und Befreiung: Frauenarbeit im 18. Jahrhundert im deutschsprachigen Raum', *Vierteljahresheft für Sozial- und Wirtschaftsgeschichte* 79 (1992): 457–82.

Verdun, Nicola, *Rural Women Workers in 19th-Century England: Gender, Work and Wages* (Woodbridge, Suffolk: Boydell Press, 2002).

Vormbaum, Thomas, *Politik und Gesinderecht im 19. Jahrhundert (vornehmlich in Preußen 1810–1918)* (Berlin: Duncker & Humblot, 1980).

Wall, Richard, and Jay Winter (eds), *The Upheaval of War: Family, Work and Welfare in Europe, 1914–1918* (Cambridge: Cambridge University Press, 1988).

Webb, Steven B., 'Tariff Protection for the Iron Industry, Cotton Textiles and Agriculture in Germany, 1879–1914', *Jahrbücher für Nationalökonomie und Statistik* 192 (1977): 336–57.

Weber, Reinhold, *Bürgerpartei und Bauernbund in Württemberg: Konservative Parteien im Kaiserreich und in Weimar (1895–1933)* (Düsseldorf: Droste Verlag, 2004).

Weber-Kellermann, Ingeborg, *Landleben im 19. Jahrhundert* (Munich: C.H. Beck, 1988).

Weber-Kellermann, Ingeborg, 'Land-Stadt-Bewegungen als Kontext für das Gesindewesen im 19. Jahrhundert', in S. Becker (ed.), *Gesindewesen in Hessen* (Marburg: Jonas Verlag, 1987), pp. 65–84.

Weingart. Peter et al., *Rasse, Blut und Gene: Geschichte der Eugenik und Rassenhygiene in Deutschland* (Frankfurt/Main: Suhrkampf Verlag, 1988).

Weitz, Eric D., *Weimar Germany: Promise and Tragedy* (Princeton: Princeton University Press, 2007).

Werckmeister, Johanna (ed.), *Land-Frauen-Alltag. Hundert Jahre Lebens- und Arbeitsbedingungen im ländlichen Raum* (Marburg: Jonas Verlag, 1989).

Wierling, Dorothee, *Mädchen für alles: Arbeitsalltag und Lebensgeschichte städtischer Dienstmädchen um die Jahrhundertwende* (Berlin: Dietz Verlag, 1987)

Wiesemann, Falk, 'Arbeitskonflikte in der Landwirtschaft während der NS-Zeit in Bayern 1933–1938', *Vierteljahresschrift für Zeitgeschichte* 25 (1977): 573–90.

Woitsche, Maria, *Gesindewesen in Tirol im 19. Jahrhundert: Dienstbotenlieder, Dienstbotenrecht – mit einem Versuchen über das Verhältnis zwischen Dienstboten und Gemeinde* (unpublished M.A. thesis, University of Innsbruck, 1989).

Wunderlich, Frieda, *German Labor Courts* (Chapel Hill: University of North Carolina, 1946).

Wunderlich, Frieda, *Farm Labor in Germany 1810–1945: Its Historical Development within the Framework of Agricultural and Social Policy* (Princeton: Princeton University Press, 1961).

Zimmermann, Clemens, 'Bäuerlicher Traditionalismus und agrarischer Fortschritt in der frühen Neuzeit', in Jan Peters (ed.), *Gutsherrschaft als soziales Modell: Vergleichende Betrachtungen zur Funktionsweise frühneuzeitlicher Agrargesellschaften* (München: R. Oldenbourg, 1995), pp. 219–38.

Zimmermann, Clemens, 'Ländliche Gesellschaft und Agrarwirtschaft im 19. und 20. Jahrhundert. Transformationsprozesse als Thema der Agrargeschichte', in Werner Troßbach and Clemens Zimmermann (eds), *Agrargeschichte: Positionen und Perspektiven* (Stuttgart: Lucius & Lucius, 1998), pp. 137–63.

Zofka, Zdenek, *Die Ausbreitung des Nationalsozialismus aut dem Lande* (München: Kommissionsverlang, R. Wolfe, 1979).

Zofka, Zdenek, 'Between Bauernbund and National Socialism. The Political Reorientation of the Peasants in the Final Phase of the Weimar Republic', in Thomas Childers (ed.), *The Formation of the Nazi Constituency, 1919–1933* (Totowa, New Jersey: Barnes and Noble, 1986), pp. 37–63.

Index